Canes
in the
United States

Dust-jacket illustrations

From top left:

Folk Art cane
Tiffany cane handle
Fair cane
Erotica handle
American ivory
Remington gun cane
Gorham handle
Bone handle
Tiffany round knob
Cherrot gun
Silver handle
Scrimshaw cane
Fair cane
American silver
Ivory handle
Handle signed Lyon
Celebrating the end of prohibition
McKinley bust
Cane of the Odd Fellows
College cane of Dartmouth
Ivory handle
Tiffany eagle
Folk Art
Mermaid (folk art)
G.A.R. cane
Constitution wood
Silver Art Nouveau
Civil War
Deringer gun cane
Spitton (gadget)
Tiffany handle
Ivory head
Statue of Liberty
Indian stick
Walrus ivory
Silver handle
Scrimshaw cane
Political cane for FDR
Tiffany handle
World War I stick

Courtesy, collection Catherine Dike.

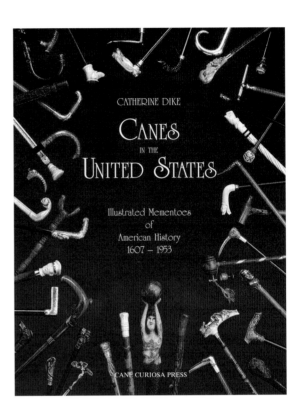

By the same author:

**Les Cannes à Système,
un Monde Fabuleux et Méconnu**
Les Editions de l'Amateur, Paris & Catherine
Dike, Genève. 1982, 1985
ISBN 2-85917-023-5

Cane Curiosa, from Gun to Gadget
Les Editions de l'Amateur, Paris & Catherine
Dike, Geneva. 1983
ISBN 2 85917-027-8

La Canne Objet d'Art
with Guy Bezzaz
Les Editions de l'Amateur, Paris & Catherine
Dike, Genève, 1988
ISBN 2 85917-074-1

Walking Sticks
Shire Publications Ltd
Princes Risborough, G.B.. 1990, 1993
ISBN 0 74780-079-0

CATHERINE DIKE

Canes
IN THE
United States

Illustrated Mementoes
of
American History
1607 – 1953

CANE CURIOSA PRESS

Published by Cane Curiosa Press
250 Dielman Road, Ladue Mo. 63124

ISBN 0-9642249-0-9

Library of Congress Catalog Card
Number: 94-68262

Graphism: Catherine Dike.
Dust-jacket: Catherine Dike.
Photography: museums & Catherine Dike.
Production: Martin Gueissaz & Marie-Claude
Hefti, Geneva.
File imaging: Flashage Service, Geneva.

Printed in Switzerland by
Imprimeries Réunies Lausanne S.A.
Bound by Nouvelle Reliure Industrielle,
Auxerre, France.

Contents

Foreword

It is a pleasure and satisfaction to encounter this scholarly, comprehensive and beautiful book about American canes that now takes its place beside this author's previous works in the field, the equally concise and beautiful *Cane Curiosa - From Gun to Gadget* and *La Canne Objet d'Art.*

Herself a great collector, Catherine Dike has given us a serious book that is also entertaining, with its profusion of detailed illustrations that are so pleasing and useful to students and collectors. The author's photographic skill and taste have been enormous assets, not to speak of the boundless energy necessary for this labor of love, with its need to travel thousands of miles to visit museums and collectors to locate examples of interest, obtain collateral information and, where necessary, secure permission to publish.

Perhaps it is because of my own particular interest in American history and certain fields of American collecting that I invite attention to the fact that a significant portion of canes on this side of the Atlantic transcends merely being evidence of style, materials and usefulness, but presents a unique panorama of American events, famous people, places, buildings, national symbols, political elections and campaigns, wars, and more, in practically unending variety.

Here, one is stuck by a quote from the philosopher and historian David Hume (1711 - 1776): *Trivial circumstances, which show the manners of the age are often more instructive as well as entertaining, that the great transactions of wars and negotiations, which are nearly similar in all periods and in all countries of the world.*

This, indeed, speaks to those of us who have thought of canes, if at all, as simply old-fashioned adjuncts of dress or utility. For the canes in this book are truly those *trivial circumstances* which show not only our ways, but are the souvenirs of American history and of what moved, pleased and interested Americans, and they do *instruct and entertain* us.

It is difficult to imagine how an American collector would remain uninterested in the cane bequeathed by Benjamin Franklin to George Washington with the words *My fine crag tree walking stick with a gold head curiously wrought in the form of the cap of liberty I give to my friend and the friend of mankind, George Washington. If it were a scepter he would merit it and it would become him,* and how it attests to the admiration for Washington and recalls to us Washington's renunciation of monarchical ideas and, not the least, Franklin's whimsical reference to the cane's *cap of liberty* which is, in fact, a tiny replica of Franklin's own fur cap.

This, in its way, sets the tone of this book, while its Table of Contents reveals the breadth and the profusion of these mementos of America's past.

Excepting the carved sticks produced for centuries by native Americans, we learn of the first identifiable American canes, the silver topped Spanish *Vara,* the official gifts of Spain's King Phillip III to Western Indian chiefs, brought in 1620 by Coronado's troops as symbols of royal Spanish rule. For the remainder of the seventeenth century, it is no surprise that those hard early years were not conducive to the production of purely decorative objects, notwithstanding that some artifacts of great beauty has survived, and canes, too, were for the most part rather chase and sober.

By the beginning of the eighteenth century, however, some prosperous colonists were apt to import fancy clothes and furnishings from Europe, a practice that increased until the period of the American Revolution, and again during the growth of the new republic. These members of America's own *landed aristocracy* were sometimes shown with their canes in painted portraits - a welcome source of information on style and colors.

It is in this general period that one begins to note a uniquely American approach to the subjects of this book - the appearance of presentation canes - at first mainly gifts of friendship and respect, but closer to the middle third of the nineteenth century, also to mark an important event or celebrate a distinguished citizen, even commemorating a defunct or restored historic structure of famous ship by using wood from their replaced or salvaged timbers - a custom rarely, if ever, observed in Europe.

The Civil War, America's defining event, after which *the United States ARE* became *the United States IS,* is remembered in countless canes, made of the wood of embattled bridges, ships, battlefield trees, in sticks of veterans marked with their names, their units, their victories, their hard fights.

By this time, mass production methods facilitated the manufacture of canes not only for sale in retail stores, but as implements in presidential campaigns and other election contests, decorated with the names of candidates and their slogans. Similar canes were appropriate for presentations at university graduations, anniversaries, retirements, of the opening of large fairs or buildings, or anything a worth celebrating, not to mention canes for members of societies and other organizations such as Masonic and fraternal groups.

In addition, one can only marvel at canes that contain guns or swords, mechanical, optical and musical devices, games and lights, as well as surprises of all sorts. One may allow for a small twinge of frustation at the relatively modest quantity included here - a result not of the author's omission, but rather of the very real scarcity of gadget canes that exist in truly American examples.

Still more are remarkable for the elegant use of precious metals or glass, while others are examples of American folk art or scrimshaw, and the use of interesting materials.

They are all represented in this book and I cannot think of anything the author has omitted. They form an American synopsis of a very special kind.

Kurt Stein

Springfield, Pennsylvania
August 1994

Kurt Stein is the author of the first
American book on canes:
Canes & Walking Sticks, 1974

Preface

What makes a collector of walking sticks? There are a multitude of reasons. Perhaps you are fascinated by the range of objects which can be hidden in gadget canes, or attracted by the historic associations of canes which belonged to leading citizens. Others are drawn to the subtle shine of ivory handles, the diversity of silver handles, or the variety of materials used to form canes. Still others confine their collecting to particular representations, sometimes as narrowly as searching out only those handles featuring dogs or cats. For me, it all began with two radiators!

Twenty-five years ago, an architect modernized the heating system in my home near Geneva, replacing flat radiators with ugly, bulky ones. I possessed about 15 canes which had belonged to my father and father-in-law, and thought perhaps that they might make an interesting decorative camouflage. I placed 13 sticks in a fan-like shape in front of one radiator, and then needed to acquire more in order to do the same for the second.

I looked first in the direction of gadget canes, being attracted by their dual purpose aspect. I already possessed a rare example, which I had inherited from my father, Alfred Pochon, a founding member of the Flonzaley Quartet. Knowing that he was interested in objects hidden inside one another, Fritz Kreisler had given him a walking stick which contained a violin. After a little time I had collected about 15 gadget sticks, and with a neophyte's pride in a budding collection, thought it was comprehensive!

Twenty years ago one searched in vain for any written material devoted to canes. In order to find references to objects which could be found inside walking sticks, one had to wade through collections and books on dozens, even hundreds, of topics. This dearth of material on the subject led me to write *Cane Curiosa, from Gun to Gadget*, (Translated from the French, 1983). Despite limiting myself to the world of gadget sticks, there was no difficulty in filling 400 pages. In the meantime, A. E. Boothroyd of

England had written *Fascinating Walking Sticks* (1970), and in the United States Kurt Stein came forth with *Canes and Walking Sticks* (1974).

Having dealt with, so to speak, the world of gadget canes, my attention turned to what collectors call decorative canes . This field encompasses an artistic appreciation of cane handles made in a great variety of materials. The result was the publication in 1988 of *La Canne Objet d'Art*, another volume of 400 pages. Published only in French, the title translates as *The Cane as Art*.

The size of the present volume, devoted to walking sticks in America, may surprise the reader. It certainly surprises the author! On my many visits to the United States I naturally came into contact with American enthusiasts, and took snapshots of their collections of American canes. Thinking a small book might be of interest to fellow collectors, I embarked on this enterprise, finishing, to my astonishment, with 400 pages and over 1,000 pictures.

Projects that initially seem simple, that one thinks might take twelve months or so to complete, can lead to a winding road of inescapable drudgery. Undoubtedly the greatest task was contacting the many museums and historical societies which have interesting cane collections. Not being associated with any European museum, my inquiries on walking sticks, which were inevitably deeply buried in storage, provoked a variety of reactions from curators, rather luke warm at least at the outset. Two years, and the exchange of countless letters, were to pass before this volume began to assume a coherent shape.

Once contact had been established, most historical societies were willing to allow me to bring along my equipment and photograph their most interesting canes, although they did not hesitate to impose considerable, sometimes prohibitive, fees. Typically, I was given a limited time in which to take pictures, usually in some cellar or dark corner of an office in the company of an official. Due to these conditions, this book has few color pictures. It usually proved impossible even to change the backdrop when switching to black-and-white film.

The same conditions prevailed even in the homes of friends. A professional photographer might take an entire day to shoot ten to fifteen canes, but I was expected to toss the job off in an hour or two!

This book details only a small portion of the number of American canes which once existed. The enthusiast would break his heart contemplating the number of canes which must have been simply thrown away in the years between the two World Wars. When the day arrives that the tie no longer forms an essential part of men's dress, ties will suddenly become collectibles. So it is with canes. Once the elegant finishing touch of a man's - or woman's - attire, today canes are used, rather than worn, solely by the lame and halt. Fortunately, collectors have preserved an astonishing variety of sticks, as this volume bears witness.

Due to the number of museums and historical societies contacted, it is impossible for me to acknowledge everyone who contributed a share towards making this book possible. My grateful thanks go to each curator and assistant who aided me along the long road. I thank also the collectors who allowed me to photograph their collections and who generously offered their help in providing me with innumerable supporting documentation. My friends Dorothy Mog and Lou Gilula helped me with my *Franglais*, and Diane de Coppet brought a fine finishing touch to the text. Kurt Stein was of invaluable help in writing the chapter pertaining to wars, George H. Meyer, author of the book *American Folk Art Canes,* read the chapters on Folk Art and Shirlee and Larry Kalstone were always ready to call and seek out information I could not obtain from abroad. Martin Gueizzas labored to try to teach me the XPress program, and scanned the many pictures. Michel Gutknecht helped with the graphics, Virginia Pepper corrected the text. Truly, this is a book which many friends helped to bring forth.

Geneva, September 22, 1994

Note. Unlike other authorities, I do not think it important to give the height of the owner of a cane, from which is determined the length of the stick. Measurments are only given when they deviate from normal proportions.

I Historical Canes

1 **Leading Citizens**

2 **Canes worn by United States Presidents**

3 **Political Canes**

4 **Canes worn by College Students**

5 **Patriotic Canes**

6 **Canes Relating to Secret Societies**

7 **Canes Commemorating Fairs and National Events**

▲ 1/1   The first settlers building the *Onrust.* Taken from the book *Old Times in the Colonies,* by Charles Carleton Coffin, New York, Harper & Brothers, 1881.

Leading Citizens

The Spanish "Vara"

When Coronado first encountered the Pueblo Indians in 1540, he found a peaceful people with a well-established hierarchial government of their own. Eighty years later, in 1620, King Phillip III of Spain issued a Royal Decree commanding each Pueblo tribe to choose a governor by popular vote, without any interference of Crown or Church. This governor would be elected in the first week of the new year and would serve a single term lasting the remainder of the year. A silver headed *Vara* or cane was given to each governor upon his election and passed on to his successor at the end of his term of office. The *Vara* served as a symbol of his authority and was used in all the Indian ceremonies and festivities.

In 1680 the Pueblo Indians rebelled against Spanish domination. Such was the slaughter that the Spanish did not return until 1696, when de Varga recognized the supremacy of the *Vara* and the annual elections were resumed.

The word *Vara* literally meant a Spanish measurement of the time, thirty-two and 5/8 inches (83,5 cm). The sticks themselves were used by the *Alcades* (mayors) to measure the boundries of land grants.

Many 19th century travellers observed these canes, which accompanied the Governors on any type of official occasion. In 1807, Lt. Zebulon Pike wrote that he had met a Pueblo Governor who was holding *a cane with a silver head and a black tassel.* When General Lew Wallace was appointed Governor of the Territory after the Civil War, his wife Susan A. Wallace, wrote of these canes.

Chester E. Faris served more than 40 years with the U.S. Indian Bureau. When Mexico won independence from Spain in 1821, he wrote: *Sovereignty was successfully established and new staffs, silver thimbled were presented to the several Pueblos and they were again authorized and commissioned to function in line with their long custom, having two canes each in symbolic support.*

In 1863, following the tradition of Phillip III of Spain, President Abraham Lincoln gave each Pueblo Chief a silver-topped cane engraved with the name of the Pueblo and a fascimile of Lincoln's signature.

In recent times, in 1981, Governor Bruce King presented each Pueblo Chief with a white bronze topped cane. King Juan Carlos of Spain in 1987 presented the Pueblo Governors with a turtoise-shell covered shaft topped with an elegant gold knob, and in 1992, Cristobal Colon, descendant of Christopher Columbus making a personal visit to the United States in the year of the Quincentennial celebrations, presented a cane to the Pueblo Chiefs. Some reportedly elected to refuse the gift.

The Spanish Pueblo *Vara* may be said to be the first canes brought to the New Continent.

▲ 1/2 Indian Tesuque Pueblo Governor holding at right the silver headed "Cane of Authority" presented by the Spanish Government in the early 17th century and at left, the silver knob presented by Lincoln in 1863.
Courtesy, Museum of New Mexico.

17th Century

The popular conception of early settlers in America is of the group of Pilgrims who journeyed across the Atlantic on the Mayflower. Subsequent arrivals, however, certainly included groups of settlers with backgrounds of wealth and refinement. The few portraits which survive readily illustrate this social difference, and the listings of succession of 1633 tell us how people of the time were dressed. These men and women preferred bright colors to Puritan gray and black, and their canes accompanied them to the New World as a part of their fashionable wardrobes. The Chicago Historical Society owns the early 17th century English walking stick worn by Governor William Bradford (1588-1657), and the Massachusetts Historical Society has the cane worn by John Norton (1651-1716). Norton was the second minister at Hingham. His direct descendant presented the cane to the Society. The austere Puritans, feeling fashion had become altogether too rich and immodest, passed laws prohibiting the wearing of silver, gold, silk and lace, girdles, hatbands, and other supposed luxuries. Sombre homemade dress was the rule, although not all citizens complied. Governor Winthrop was one who did not adopt these sober costumes.

▲ 1/4 Portrait of Captain George Corwin (1610-1684) by an unknown artist. The cane he holds, as well as the cravat he wears, have survived to the present day. His son, Jonathan Corwin, was a witchcraft judge.
Courtesy, Essex Institute, Salem, Massachusetts

◀ 1/3   Sword cane with an ivory head owned in turn by:

Edward Gove	1686-1691
his son John Gove	1691-1737
his son Edward Gove	1737-1802
his son Edward Gove	1802-1861
his nephew Edward S. Gove	1861-1917
his son Frank Drew Gove	1917-1921

This sword cane lacks a release button or knob which can be turned to expose the blade, an important distinction in recognizing early sword canes. It was given to the Essex Institute by the last member of the Gove family. The knob bears the inscription *E.G.*
Courtesy, Essex Institute, Salem, Massachusetts.

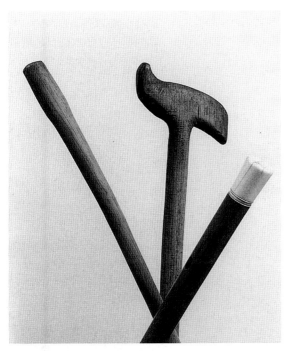

▲ 1/5 Three canes associated with witchcraft. The two simple ones were reputedly used by George Jacobs who was hanged as a witch in 1692. The third, with an ivory top, belonged to Philip English who was sentenced to death but managed to escape from the Salem jail and flee to New York. Another cane belonging to the Essex Institute could be associated with witchcraft; its shaft is made of wood taken from the Witch House.
Courtesy, Essex Institute, Salem, Massachusetts.

▲ 1/6 Governor Benning Wentworth in official dress holding a cane that is today the property of the New Hampshire Historical Society. A silver band is engraved *Benning Wentworth 1730*.
Courtesy, New Hampshire Historical Society.

18th Century

Eighteenth-century canes are to be found in many Historical Societies. The Boston Society has a cane formerly owned by the Reverend Mather Byles (1706-1788); the Massachusetts Historical Society has - among others - a cane which belonged to Henry Bromfield (1727-1820) and another worn by Jabez Huntington between 1760 and 1770; the Rhode Island Historical Society has a cane marked B.B. for Beriah Brown, Sheriff of King's County 1740-1782.

Gentlemen depicted in 18th and early 19th century portraits are more likely to be shown holding walking sticks.

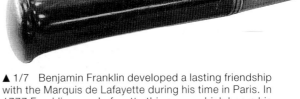

▲ 1/7 Benjamin Franklin developed a lasting friendship with the Marquis de Lafayette during his time in Paris. In 1777 Franklin gave Lafayette this cane, which bears his initials. It was acquired in 1907 from Lafayette's descendant, the then Marquis, and presented to the Pennsylvania University Library. It is without doubt French.
    When Franklin left Paris in 1785 he left many parting presents for his friends, including *his magic cane with its hidden compartments*.
Courtesy, University of Pennsylvania.

▲ 1/8 A portrait of the Marquis de Lafayette by Charles Willson Peale. The position of the hand is similar to the Peale portrait of Washington in the Brooklyn Museum.
Courtesy, Virginia Historical Society.

▼ 1/9 Antlers were often used as cane tops at the turn of 18th century.
Courtesy, collection Kurt Stein.

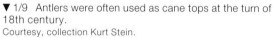

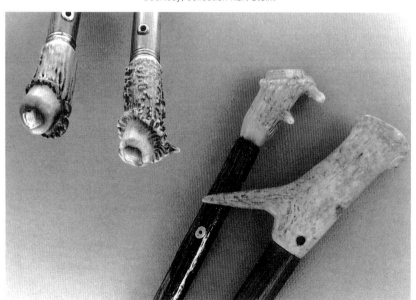

▲ 1/10 Statue of Benjamin Thompson, Count of Rumford, erected on the main street of Munich, Germany. Thompson was born in 1753 in Massachusetts where his ancestors had settled in 1642. He studied medecine, algebra, geometry, astronomy and mathematics with the Rev. Thomas Barnard of Salem, and also conducted experiments with gunpowder. He sided with the British during the Revolution and eventually returned to England in 1783 with the rank of colonel of the King's American Dragoons. He then travelled to the Continent and reorganized the Bavarian army, for which service the Elector of Bavaria created him a Count. Elected to several European acadamies for his continuing research and experiments in scientific fields, he died in Paris in 1814.

▲ 1/11 Along with silver-topped and ivory-handled canes are found some simple and modest examples. The "T" model seems to have been made by a carpenter, the dowels and tenons being so neatly fashioned. The ferrule is painted black.

Other models imitate the ridge of the malacca, or are painted black to resemble mahogany. One stick has two holes driven through it, but lacks the finishing eyelets.
Courtesy, collection Kurt Stein.

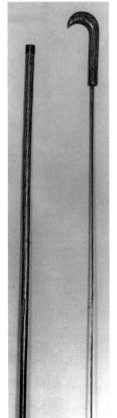

◄ 1/12   A sword cane worn by Thomas Norman of Caldwell and New York (1751-1834). He was the son-in-law of Colonel Crean Brush, Loyalist and member of the New York British Provincial Assembly (1773-1775).
Courtesy, New York Historical Society.

▲ 1/13   Portrait by Charles Willson Peale of William Whetcroft, an Annapolis, Maryland, silversmith who died in 1789.
Courtesy, Yale University Art Gallery.

► 1/14   Dagger cane said to have belonged to Patrick Henry (1736-1799). It has a simple ivory knob with gold bands.
Courtesy, Missouri Historical Society.

19th Century

This chapter examines a selection of canes which belonged to prominent men, but no attempt has been made to give a comprehensive list of notable citizens who wore canes, given that a stick was an indispensable part of fashionable dress in the nineteenth century.

A cane from the early part of the century makes an interesting beginning. This stick, with a leaded top and a large silver cap dated 1812, is today the property of the Massachusetts Historical Society. It belonged to Nathaniel Bowditch (1773-1838), a well-known mathematician and astronomer famous for his treatises on navigation. His son Henry added the following inscription: *This was given to my father by his father as a defense if need be against political opponents, spurious Democrats, worthy ancestors of modern copperheads. H.I.B.* Obviously political arguments of the last century waxed as hot as do those of our era - and nineteenth century politicians did not confine their battles to oratory!

Sam Houston is known to have whittled many canes, often using a large ivory-handle clasp knife given him by the Creek Chief, Opoth-ley-ahola. On his way to Washington in December 1831, he stopped in Houston where he cut himself a thick branch of hickory. This he transformed into a walking stick, and on arrival in Washington, he gave this stick to a friend.

Some time later Houston learned of insulting remarks made about him by William Stanbery, Congressman from Ohio. Enraged, he visited his friend to reclaim the stick. One dark evening he caught up with the Congressman and gave him a good "caning". It was the first time a Congressman had suffered this indignity, and we can imagine the ensuing uproar.

Another caning, even more dramatic, took place on May 22, 1856. Senator Charles Sumner of Massachusetts delivered a bitter anti-slavery speech in which his main targets were the State of South Carolina and its senior Senator, A. P. Butler, who was not present at the time. Preston S. Brooks, a 37 year old Congressman from

▲ 1/15   The Sam Houston Memorial Museum has two canes worn by Sam Houston. Pictured is a gold headed top inscribed with his name and the word *Texas*. The other was a gift from the English diplomat Sir Alex Frazer. The Museum also owns a crutch Houston used after the battle of San Jacinto.
Courtesy, Sam Houston Memorial Museum.

▲ 1/16   The gold handle which topped a gutta-percha shaft used by Congressman Preston Brooks in his caning of Senator Sumner. At the time it was said that Brooks received many other canes with *Hit him again* inscribed on them!
Courtesy, The Boston Society.

South Carolina, attacked Senator Sumner at his desk after adjournment of the Senate and struck him with his cane, leaving Sumner bleeding and helpless. Brooks who was expelled from the House made political capital from the incident, resigned and was triumphantly re-elected.

The House Committee conducted an investigation of the incident and made a report on June 2. The gutta-percha cane used measured an inch in diameter at the top and half an inch at the bottom. The physician who attended testified five days after the assault that Sumner could have returned to the Senate the day following the attack. Perhaps making some political capital of his own, it was in fact three years before Sumner returned.

The House Report was widely ignored, the Press having presented a far more exciting and inflammatory version. It was reported, needless to say by a journalist who had not been present at the time, that Brooks had bought the cane on his way to the Senate and that it was broken on Sumner's back rather than on his desk or chair. Six speeches on the topic were made at the Citizens Meeting in Cambridge on June 2 1856. Published under the title *The Sumner Outrage*, the text ran to 33 pages.

Many 19th century canes which belonged to political figures have survived. Canes made popular gifts of appreciation or commemorations of historical events, and were often presented to Senators, Congressmen, State Legislators, Judges and Sheriffs.

▼ 1/17   The attack as illustrated by local newspapers.
Courtesy, The Massachusetts Historical Society.

◀1/18 Cane presented to Joseph Powell of South Carolina in 1860. The gold knob is inscribed *If slavery or Union be the issue, I go the Union.* The sides are engraved *Presented to Joseph Powell of South Carolina in 1860 by his admirers for opposing secession.*
Courtesy, collection Smithsonian Institution.

The Massachusetts Historical Society has a cane with a carnelian head and gold band, inscribed: *Presented Jan. 23rd 1852 in behalf of the Junior members of the Senate by Anson Burlingame to Myron Lawrence the Senior Senator.*

The Ohio Historical Society has a cane which was Presented by the 104 members of the 35th Congress to Joshua R. Giddings as a token of their respect for his moral worth and personal intergrity. The date is not given, but it must fall between 1835 and 1860. Lincoln was a student of Giddings. Another cane was given to Nelson Timothy Stephens, a Kansas Judge during the period 1875-1884. The Colorado State Historical Society has a cane presented to the Honorable Alfred H. Butters, Speaker of the House of Representatives, 11th Session of the Legislature of Colorado, by his Democratic friends in the House.

On a less political note, the Rhode Island Historical Society has a cane inscribed on its silver mount: *Staff of Honl. Henry W. Greene, Farmer & Grd. Sagamore of Shores Buttonwoods, Nusauket, Warwick, R.I. Presented by his friends the Gov. of Sachems of the State Forest Tribes. In testimony of Hospitalities rec'. at his doors, A.D. 1840-1896.*

▲ 1/19 A cane presented to *J.F. Cook* from *New Brunswick, N.J. by H. Clay, June" 1849.*
Courtesy, collection Francis H. Monek.

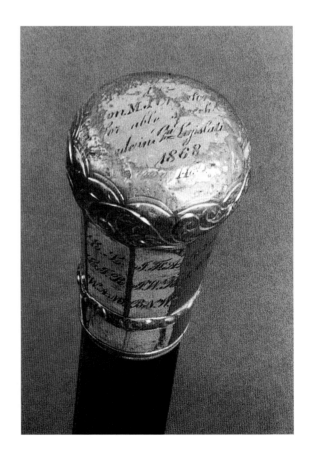

▶ 1/20 Silver knob with the inscription *Presented to Hon. M.G. Crawford for able speech made in Gv. Legislation 1868 ...14th...* On each of the eight sides of the knob, one finds three signatures representing the members who gave the cane.
Courtesy, collection Smithsonian Institution.

▲ 1/21 American gold cane which originally belonged to the Marquis de Lafayette. It was most likely given to him on his triumphal visit to the United States in 1824. Subsequently, as we read by the inscription on top, it was *Presented to General U.S. Grant by the Ladies of Baltimore Forlibus Honor*. Two of the four panels are inscribed *Genl. Lafayette* and *Genl. Grant*, and the other two bear carved eagles.
Courtesy, collection Smithsonian Institution.

▶ 1/24 A cane carved by Duncan Phyfe, the American cabinet maker, circa 1820.
Courtesy, collection Francis H. Monek.

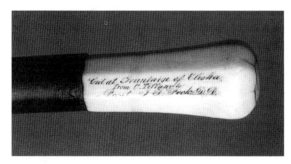

▲ 1/22 A Presentation cane given to I. J. *Peck, D.D.*, made of wood cut at the Fountain of *Eliska* by Comfort Tiffany. He was the father of Charles Louis, founder of Tiffany.
Courtesy, collection Francis H. Monek.

▲ 1/23 A horn knob with a plaque inscribed *J. Brown* 1830. The Rhode Island Historical Society has an ivory head inscribed *John Brown* with the date 1803.
Courtesy, collection Francis H. Monek.

▲ 1/25 A hand carved stick with the initials *J.J.* for John Jellyff, cabinet maker in Newark between 1840 and 1890.
Courtesy, The Newark Museum.

▲ 1/26   Gold topped malacca cane inscribed atop the knob
Warren Delano, October 28th, 1849. Warren Delano
spent many years as a merchant in China. His youngest
daughter, Sara, married James Roosevelt in 1890. She was
the mother of F.D.R.
Courtesy, Peabody Museum of Salem, Mass.

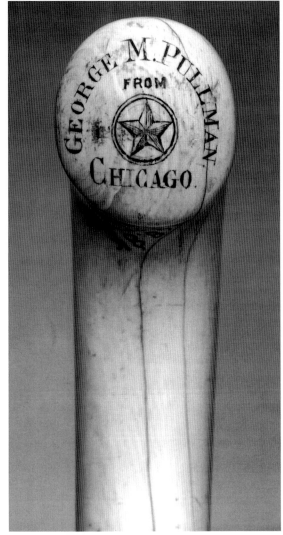

▲ 1/27   J.P. Morgan *caning* away journalists.
Courtesy, collection L.G.

▲ 1/28   A piece of ivory given to George Pullman by a group
of people represented by the star in the middle. The
meaning of this sign remains a mystery. Born in Brocton,
N.J. in 1831, Pullman patented a railway carriage with sleep-
ers in the upper part of the compartment. To this day this
type of sleeping car bears his name.
Courtesy, The Chicago Historical Museum.

▲ 1/29 A highly engraved cane illustrating highlights in the life of Buffalo Bill. Born in Iowa in1846, he took part in the gold rush in 1859, the Civil War, and the military expeditions against the Cheyenne and the Sioux. His last years were given to dramatic presentations.
Courtesy, Buffalo Bill Historical Center, Cody, WY.

▲ 1/30 Portrait of Leland Stanford, painted in 1881 by French painter Jean-Louis Meissonier (1815-1891). Stanford was the founder of the famous University.
Courtesy, Stanford University Archives.

▲ 1/32 Narwhal tusk with a gold knob engraved From Buffalo Bill to Col G. W. Torrence.
Courtesy, Butterfield & Butterfield, San Francisco.

▲ 1/31 A selection of familiar ivory knobs of the 19th century, they are engraved, from left to right:
– *W.H. Morris, from the old courthouse,*
  Philadelphia1836,Joseph Sharples,
– *W.M. Newbold, 1810, Philadelphia.*
  On the silver band we read *D.W.Brown to his friend*
  W. Newbold. The wood is from the liner

Pennsylvania, the largest ship of its time and which never saw action,
– *J. Thomason, 1883,*
– *George Franklin,*
– *Malcom McLeod,*
– *Frans. Gurney, May 9th, 1785.*
Courtesy, collection Kurt Stein.

▲ 2/1   A French engraving showing Washington and General de Rochambeau giving their last orders before the attack on Yorktown. Both wear canes. General de Rochambeau was the French General who, in 1780, was sent to the New Continent and helped take Yorktown in 1781. Courtesy, Lafayette Library.

Canes worn by United States Presidents

Introduction

In this chapter, the focus is on the prominent bearer or owner of a cane. Some sticks were carved by admirers, or commissioned by a group of friends or supporters for presentation to a candidate or newly-elected President. Other canes were issued in commemoration or celbration of an event related to the President.

All the Presidents of the United States wore canes, and these walking sticks can be found in historical societies and museums across the country. Seldom ornate, or made from rare or precious materials, they generally represent their historical periods and reflect the dignity of the office.

With the 18th century Presidents, it is often difficult to know whether their canes were made in Europe or by early American silversmiths. We know that George Washington ordered his clothing in Europe, and he certainly imported some of his canes as well.

Effigies of numerous President

Some canes given to honor a President were carved with the images of each of his predecessors. Due to restricted space, the faces are roughly carved.

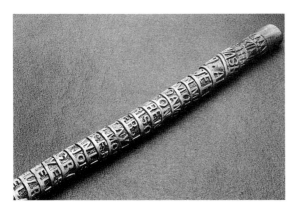

▲ 2/2 Straight staff presented to F.D.R. with the names of each President carved around the shaft.
Courtesy, Franklin D. Roosevelt Library.

▲ 2/3 On this cane, the handle represents an animal. Here the heads are carved on a level on opposite sides. It is believed that a tramp carved it for President Harrison, the last figure at the base.
Courtesy, Nebraska State Historical Society.

▶ 2/4 This cane is carved with the heads of all U.S. Presidents, including Benjamin Harrison. It is believed that President Harrison first wore this cane at the celebration of the 1889 Centennial rather than having received it for his inauguration. Others say that it was presented to him during his 1888 campaign, with his portrait included to influence destiny that he be elected!
Courtesy, President B. Harrison Foundation, Inc.

▲ 2/5   The names of 26 Presidents are carved in a kind of cartouche. Above each, in much smaller letters, are carved the dates of birth (B) and death (D), followed by either *Dem.* (Democrat) or *Rep.* (Republican). The American eagle tops the cane with the dates 1789 to 1912, the year of the Taft / Wilson campaign.
Courtesy, collection Smithsonian Institution.

◄ 2/6   This cane is a combination of carving and pictures.
Courtesy, Little White House, Warm Springs, Ga.

George Washington
1732 - 1799

President, 1789 - 1797

The Houdon statue in the State Capitol in Richmond, Virginia, the portrait by Peal, and numerous other representations of George Washington show how often he wore canes.

His walking sticks are scattered among various museums or historical societies. Generally the canes can be traced back to him or his family.

Washington's most famous cane is the one bequeathed to him in Benjamin Franklin's will dated April 17, 1788 :

My fine crab-tree walking stick with a gold head curiously wrought in the form of the cap of liberty, I give to my friend and the friend of mankind, George Washington. If it were a scepter he has merited it, and would become it. (Color picture).

The American Liberty Cap, as seen on the first American coins, was a close-fitting conical cap tapering to a point which fell forwards. It ressembles the French model in its style. The cap on the Franklin cane, however, is of a completely different design - round in shape and with a bobble or button centered on top.

Washington also gave numerous canes to his loyal friends and supporters. In his will, Washington bequeathed to his brother Charles, the cane he had received from Benjamin Franklin. In his will, Washington added: *To the acquaintances and friends of my juvenile years, Lawrence Washington and Robert Washington of Chotanck, I give my other two gold headed canes, having my arms engraved on them.*

▲ 2/7 A painted wax portrait of Benjamin Franklin made in Paris in 1777 by Jean Baptist Nini. Franklin's headgear is similar to that found on the cane he gave Washington. Why did he call it a Liberty Cap?
    The author's opinion is that the cane in the Smithsonian did belong to Franklin, but was not of European manufacture. During the late 18th century, elegant shafts were made of malacca or mahogany, not the knotty wood of the crab tree. Possibly it was remounted at a later date.
    It also seems somewhat unlikely that Marianne Camasse, who was known as the Countess de Forbach and became at an early age the morganatic wife of the Duc des Deux Ponts, would give Franklin a cane with a Liberty Cap as handle. Before the French Revolution of 1789, it would have been an odd gift from a member of the aristocracy. If she blithely choose such a symbol, it was presumably without a premonition of what the ideal of liberty held in store for her country and its nobility.
    In 1926, Louis Kubler gave a seminar on Marianne de Forbach in Forbach in which he mentioned: *Franklin received from the Countess the valuable gold-topped cane together with verses that Franklin in turn bequeathed to Washington along with the cane.*
Courtesy, collection Kurt Stein.

The Society of Cincinnati claims to have a cane given by Washington to his Paymaster Nathan Beers, but as often happens with these early canes, no proof exists as to the provenance.

Numerous *memorabilia* canes were cut on the grounds of Mount Vernon, particularly from the sites near Washington's tomb. The most famous of these was cut by Abraham Lincoln, while on a visit there in 1847. He had just taken his seat as a member of the U.S. Congress. (Kansas Historical Society).

Joseph Emerson, who fought at Bunker Hill, cut a branch of an evergreen tree near Washington's tomb and made himself a simple cane with a walnut knob. The source of the wood gave it great sentimental value. As with so many canes, there is no direct proof of its romantic origin. The above provenance was given to the DAR Museum in Washington.

The Boston Society has a cane marked: *Wood of the bier taken from the tomb of Gen. Geo. Washington.*

▲ 2/8 The life-size marble statue of George Washington, has stood in the central portion of the Virginia State Capitol since 1796. It is signed by Jean Antoine Houdon, who was taken to Mount Vernon by Benjamin Franklin. There Houdon made a plaster bust of the head of Washington and back in Paris Governor Morris sat for Houdon as a model for the body.
Courtesy, Virginia State Capitol.

The cane given to Lawrence was returned to Mount Vernon. (Color Picture). That given to Robert is today in a private collection.

James Bowdoin, Governor of Massachusetts gave Washington a gold headed cane. (Color picture). Washington gave an ivory horn cane to General John Brooks, who later became Governor of Massachusetts. (Color picture).

A follower of Washington, Joshua Morse, had a cane with a silver band marked *Joshua Morse, Hopkinton, N.H., presented by Gen. Geo. Washington on the White Plains, Nov. 1776.*

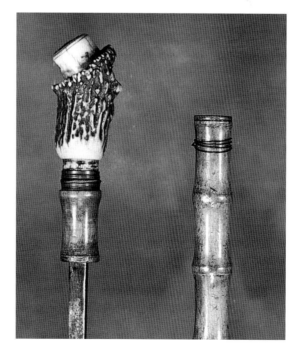

▲ 2/9 Sword stick with the inscription *Gen. Washington to Gen. Wayne, Paoli 1786.* The inscription was most likely a later addition, explaining why the name of the donor precedes that of the recipient.
Courtesy, Valley Forge Historical Society.

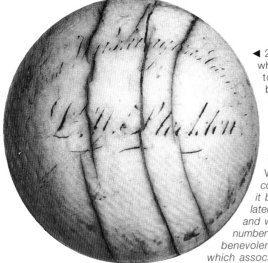

◄ 2/10   Cane made from the wheel spokes of Washington's carriage. The knob bears the name of the owner *L.W. Staelden* and the words *From Washington's carriage.*

Reverend William Mead, who obtained the carriage 15 years after the death of Washington, writes: *In the course of time, from disuse, it being too heavy for these later days, it began to decay and was given away among a number of female associations for benevolent, and religious objects, which associations, at their fairs and other occasions, made a large profit by converting the fragments into walking sticks, picture frames, and snuff boxes.*

Courtesy, collection Francis H. Monek.

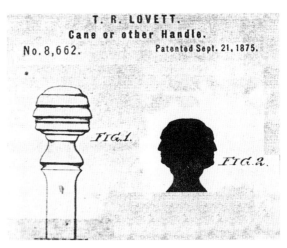

▲ 2/12   In 1875 a Mr. Thomas R. Lovett patented a design for the knob of a stick that projects a recognizable silhouette on a wall when a light is placed before the knob. In this example the silhouette is that of Washington.
Courtesy, U.S. Patent Office.

John Adams
1797 - 1826

President, 1797 - 1801

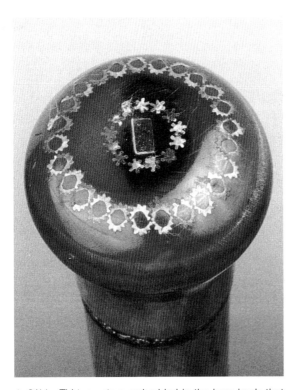

▲ 2/11   Thirteen stars embedded in the horn knob that Washington gave Jerome Bonaparte, the youngest brother of Napoleon. Born in 1784, he visited Norfolk in 1802, also calling at Washington, Mount Vernon and Boston. He married an American and resided in the United States until 1805. He gave the cane to Admiral Charles Bergeret who fought in various sea battles of the Empire. The cane was owned in turn by Sir John Deveton and Charles Russell. Later the U.S. Ambassador to the Court of St. James obtained the cane and presented it to Franklin Delano Roosevelt. Some of the stars are missing.
Courtesy, Franklin D. Roosevelt Library.

▲ 2/13   A portrait of John Adams, showing his hand resting on the cane that can be seen today in the Adams' home, together with the walking sticks of Quincy Adams and other members of the family.
Courtesy, U.S. Department of the Interior, Quincy.

Thomas Jefferson
1743 - 1826

President, 1801 - 1809

As was the fashion at the Court of Louis XVI, Thomas Jefferson undoubtedly wore canes during his mission in Paris between 1785 and 1789. However, today only two canes survive which are definitely indentified as his.

In the chapter on Patriotic Canes, are found dozens of canes connected with his life, but these sticks were never the property of Jefferson.

▲ 2/14   This gold headed cane was presented to President Jefferson in 1805, by John F. Oliveira Fernandes, a Norfolk, Virginia, physician. Jefferson mentions in his letter to Fernandes, dated Feb. 28, 1806, that he considered the stick: *The most elegant thing of the kind I have ever seen; and worthy of place, as a curiosity, in any Cabinet whatever. I perceive that it is of the horn of some animal, but cannot conjecture of what.*

Jefferson bequeathed the walking stick to his friend James Madison, who in turn at his death, gave it to Jefferson's grandson, Thomas Jefferson Randolph. His descendents are the present owners of the cane and have loaned it to the Thomas Jefferson Memorial Foundation. The measurements of the cane (forty two and a half inches, 108 cm) and the style of the handle suggest a mid-18th century cane. Rhino horn could have been used to make the shaft.

The other cane was presented in 1809 to Jefferson by a young Virginian Congressman, Joseph Cabell, who supported Jefferson's plan for education. They worked together for years to found the University of Virginia. Cabell was twice Rector of the newly created University. The cane is in whale bone with a knob in sea-lion ivory. A round gold plate is set into the head of the cane, inscribed with the letters *T.J.* together with *Joseph C. Cabell to His Friends / Christmas 1809* written around them.

Courtesy, collection Monticello, Thomas Jefferson Memorial Foundation, Inc.

James Madison

1751 - 1836

President, 1809 - 1817

James Madison is known to have had two canes that are mentioned in his will: *I bequeath to my stepson, John Payne Todd .... and the walking staff made from a timber of the frigate "Constitution" and presented me by Commodore Elliot, her present Commander.*

I desire the gold mounted walking staff bequeathed to me by my late friend, Thomas Jefferson, be delivered to Thomas J. Randolph, as well in testimony of the esteem I have for him, as for the knowledge I have of the place he held in the affections of his grand-father.

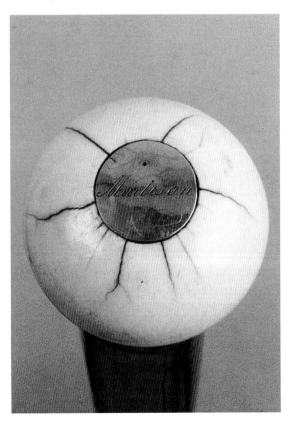

▲ 2/15 An ivory knob tops the cane Madison received from Commodore J.D. Elliot. The shaft is made from timber of the *"Constitution"* and will be seen in the chapter on the canes Carved by Soldiers.
Courtesy, collection Smithsonian Institution.

James Monroe

1758 - 1831

President, 1817 - 1825

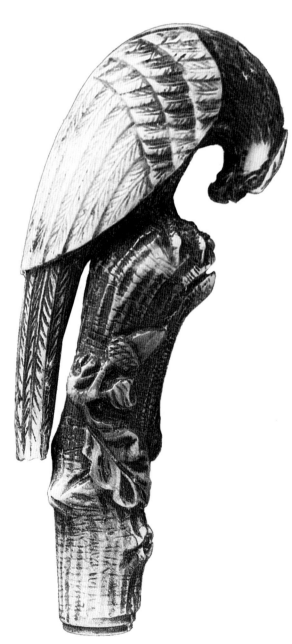

▲ 2/16 An ivory handle shows an eagle protecting its nest. It is carved in the same manner as the ivory handle which is mentioned in the Patriotic Canes chapter.
Courtesy, James Monroe Museum.

John Quincy Adams
1767 - 1848

President, 1825 - 1829

A summary of the canes belonging to John Quincy Adams is given in his will: *I give and bequeath to the people of the United States of America an ivory cane presented to me by Julius Pratt of Meriden in Connecticut and by me deposited in the custody of the Commissioner of Patents at Washington to remain in his custody until called by me. The said cane bears on it an inscription in honor of the repeal of the House of Representatives prohibiting the reception of petitions on the subject of Slavery, 3d December 1844 being inserted therein as the date upon which the said rule was rescinded, according to the request of the donor - which said cane it is my desire should be kept in the Patent Office of the United States in future as it has been heretofore.*

I give and bequeath to my grandson John Quincy Adams son of my son Charles Francis Adams, a gold headed cane cut from the timbers of the frigate "Constitution" and presented to me by Minot Thayer, Samuel A. Turner, Ebenezer T. Fogg, Solomon Richards & Harvey Field, Committee April 1st 1837 on the head of which is engraved the members of the House of Representatives of Massachusetts from the several towns of my District in the year 1837, in token of their sense of my public services in defending in the Congress of the United States the right of petition of the people of the United States in that body.

I give and bequeath to my grandson Charles Francis Adams second son of my son aforesaid a cane also cut from the timbers of the frigate "Constitution", and given to me by its Commander Commodore Isaac Hull in the year 1836, which is marked upon a silver ring immediately under the head of said cane.

I give to my grandson Henry Brooks Adams, third son of my son aforesaid a cane made of olive from Mount Olive in Jerusalem, given to me by my nephew Joseph Harrod Adams by whom it was caused to be cut on the spot, he being personally there as an Officer of the United States.

▶ 2/17   Ivory cane given to John Quincy Adams by Julius Pratt of Meriden in Connecticut.
Courtesy, collection Smithsonian Institution.

▲ 2/18   A group of canes in the Adam's house, among which the ivory top cane belonging to his grand-father, President John Adams, can be recognized.
Courtesy, U.S. Department of the Interior, Quincy.

Andrew Jackson

1767 - 1845

President, 1829 - 1837

It is difficult to trace the canes of Andrew Jackson. In his will he left: *To my beloved son all my walking canes, and other relics, to be distributed amongst my young relatives - namesakes - first, to my much esteemed namesake, Andrew J. Donelson, son of my esteemed nephew, A.J. Donelson, his first choice, and then to be distributed as A. Jackson Jnr. may think proper.*

Today sixteen canes can be seen at the *Hermitage*. Not all belonged to Jackson; some were gifts he presented to others. One of Jackson's canes features in an assassination attempt in 1835. Jackson was descending the Capitol steps when he was attacked by Richard Lawrence. Jackson rushed upon his assailant, his rosewood cane raised to strike, exclaiming: *Let me get to him, gentlemen, I am not afraid.*

Martin Van Buren

1782 - 1862

President, 1837 - 1841

A reference to a cane belonging to President Van Buren appears in a letter dated 1836 and signed by C. Van Buskirk: *As a testimonial of my high regard, not only for your political character, but your private worth, I herewith send you a gold mounted cane, which I trust may assist in supporting you, in ripe Old Age after filling the highest office of your Country's gifts for which I deem you entirely qualified.*

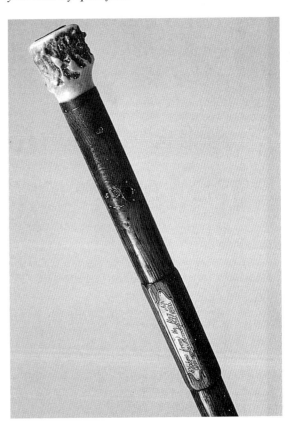

▲ 2/20 Tapered oak cane with three silver plates having the following inscriptions: *Taken from the flagship "Lawrence". March 5th 1836 / We have met the enemy and they are ours / Com. O.H. Perry's victory Lake Erie, Sept. 10th AD 1813.* It was presented to Martin Van Buren in 1836.
Courtesy, Martin Van Buren National Historic Site.

◀ 2/19 Andrew Jackson's cane photographed against the original silhouette drawn by William Brown.
Courtesy, collection The Hermitage, Te.

William Henry Harrison
1773 - 1841

President, 1841

▲ 2/21 Ivory topped cane which belonged to the Benjamin Harrison who was a signatory of the Declaration of Independence. Here it is pictured on a Currier & Ives lithograph portrait of his son, William Henry Harrison. The tassel seems to be original. The cane was presented to his grandson Benjamin Harrison.
Courtesy, The Benjamin Harrison Memorial Home.

John Tyler
1790 - 1862

Vice - President, March - April 1841
President, 1841 - 1845

▲ 2/22 A branch-like cane made of cherry wood with two silver caps. One is marked *From J.W.T. to John Tyler* and in Latin the words *Pul Pulior ut Poliar* ("I become pale to become polished," implying long hours of indoor study) and the other is inscribed with the words *Head Them or Die.* This cane could have been given to President Tyler upon the annexation of Texas into the Union in 1845.
Courtesy, Sherwood Forest Plantation, Va..

James K. Polk
1795 – 1849

President, 1845 - 1849

An estate inventory, made after his death, lists one bundle of walking canes. Today none of his canes can be found in the James K. Polk Memorial Association. The chapter on Political Canes, mentions one of Polk's canes.

Zachary Taylor
1784 - 1850

President, 1849 - 1850

Zachary Taylor, hero of the Mexican war, won two military battles; one in Monterrey, the other in Buena Vista. Without doubt, canes were produced from wood found on those battlefields.

Millard Fillmore
1800 - 1874

President, 1850 - 1853

▲ 2/23 President Fillmore must have worn canes, as he gave a silver topped one to his brother which is marked *M.F. to C. Fillmore.*
Courtesy, Beeman collection.

Franklin Pierce
1804 - 1857

President, 1853 - 1857

In his will, Franklin Pierce gives a good description of his canes:

To Colo. Thomas H. Seymour of Ct. a cane made from the flag staff of the "Castle of Chepultepec" which was cut down by his own sword.

I also give to Colo. George the neatly mounted hickory cane cut at Jamestown Va., my name in Roman letters on the Knots of the stick.

To Hon. Clement March the hickory cane now in his possession.

To Hon. J.G. Abbott of Boston a cane presented by his relative William Fletcher of Chelmsford .... to my father.

To Thomas W. Pierce of Topsfield a cane, now in his possession made from a plank of old "Ironside".

To James Lagdon of Plymouth I give a cane with the inscription "Presented to Franklin Pierce Jany. 1, 1855".

The New Hampshire Historical Society today owns several of his canes, including the one given in his will to James Langdon. A gold band with the inscription *Bequeathed by Franklin Pierce to James F. Langdon, Jan. 1868* has been added to his stick. Such inscriptions should be regarded with care, unless a document - in this case Pierce's will - establshes their authenticity. The same Historical Society has a cane which was presented to his nephew and namesake, Frank H. Pierce, in 1876.

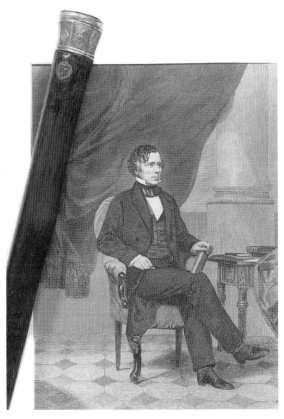

▲ 2/24 Cane with chased gold head engraved *Old Virginia to New Hampshire*. The latter was Pierce's native state. It was presented by the State of Virginia during the presidency of Franklin Pierce. The shaft has 14 knots on which 14 gold letters spell out his name.
Courtesy, New Hampshire Historical Society.

James Buchanan
1791 - 1868

President, 1857 - 1861

▲ 2/25   Gold handle with eight-sided knob. The top is carved with the Federal Eagle, and below it is the name *James Buchanan.* Two of the eight sides are engraved with *From George S. Fogelman, Holly Grove, Crittenden County, Arkansas.* The donor was an important citizen, and it is likely this cane was a present to the President.
Courtesy, collection Mickey Groff.

Abraham Lincoln
1809 - 1865

President, 1861 - 1865

Had Lincoln not been assassinated at the age of only 52, his papers and memorabilia would have been gathered by historical societies for viewing by interested citizens in the same low-key manner that preserved mementos of his predecessors. His Presidency lasted just over four years, from early 1861 to his death in the Spring of 1865. Certainly these were tumultuous years, and his reputation as the Great Emancipator and Chief Executive of the Civil War period would have assured his place in history. But it was the manner of his death which brought forth the flood of objects which show some connection to his Presidency. There are actually not many objects to be found

which are established as dating from his lifetime, in contrast to thousands produced after his death.

A stick made from wood found at Lookout Mountain was supposedly given Lincoln for his 1864 Presidential campaign. It is made in two pieces, the shaft in hickory and the head in burl maple representing an eagle with a shield across its body and a branch with the words *Peace* clutched in the claws of its right foot. Over the eagle's head is a banner with the words *E pluribus Unum,* the United States motto meaning From Many, One. The cane shows the date 1864 and the initials *J.T.H.,* probably for fighting Joe Hooker, the General who led the Union forces in the battle of Lookout Mountain. The cane is forty two and one half inches long (108 cm).

Spelling out names on knots in the wood seems to have been in fashion during the mid-19th century. Presidents Andrew Jackson and Franklin Pierce had such canes. In 1860 President Lincoln received a black cane with a buckhorn handle. The shaft is studded with fourteen knots covered by silver caps upon which each letter of the name Abraham Lincoln is engraved. A metal band bears the inscription that the cane was presented to Lincoln by his old chum, S. Strong in 1860. Lincoln's widow gave it to Frank B. Carpenter, a celebrated artist and friend who had his name engraved on the plate on top of the handle.

After Lincoln's death his grieving widow presented his secretary Noah Brooks, with *Castine,* a favorite cane carried by the President upon his restless night wanderings. Fashioned carefully from an oak timber taken from a vessel sunk at the battle of Hampton Roads, the cane had belonged to a naval officer. The ferrule was an iron bolt from the Confederate Ironclad ship *Merrimac,* and the head was formed by an other bolt from the *Monitor,* the counterpart Union Ironclad.

▶ 2/26   A cane that bears on each of its 14 knots, a letter that together form the name *Abraham Lincoln.* It was auctioned for $ 145.00 at an unknown date. It is referenced in the above paragraph.
Courtesy, private collection.

▲ 2/27 Two pictures of John Wilkes Booth holding a cane
whose brass handle represents a horse's hoof. Such handles are made from casts, and therefore hundreds of models
may be struck over a period of years. The cane in the foreground is similar to Booth's cane, but there is no proof that
it was really his.
Courtesy, collection Francis H. Monek.

▲ 2/28 Four different handles representing Lincoln. The brown one on the right, is made of bakelite, which means that it must
be one of many produced from the same mold. These canes are not campaign canes. They would have been produced for a
centennial or other ceremonial event, or simply as souvenirs to be sold for the benefit of charity.
Courtesy, Museum of American Political Life, Hartford.

▲ 2/29 The War Memorial Museum in Philadelphia has a cane which was claimed to have been found in the presidential box. It is very short, thirty four and one-quarter inches (87 cm). It is shown here against the reward poster issued by the War Department in which Booth is represented holding his brass-handled cane.
Courtesy, The Civil War Museum, Philadelphia.

▶ 2/30 Another cane associated with Lincoln, was called the *Winchester* cane, after the name of the carver. It was made during the Civil War from a branch on which the letters of *Lookout* are carved on each knot. The top carries a gold plaque with the words *To Abraham Lincoln, President of the United States, from B. Frank Winchester, Maryland, Capt.,V.C.S. Vols from the field of Battle, Lookout Mt., Nov. 24, 1863.* The carving represents an eagle crushing the head of a Copperhead snake.
Courtesy, Lincoln Memorial University.

The Chicago Historical Society has a cane with a shaft made from a rib of the Confederate ship *Merrimac.* It was reportedly presented to Lincoln by a New York Regiment in January, 1864. This is a likely instance of a romantic tale woven around a cane. It is hard to believe that anyone would have presented Lincoln a stick thirty four and one half inches long (88 cm). The same Historical Society has a very simple hickory stick with a rough end to serve as handle. It is forty inches high (102 cm), and therefore more likely to have been worn by Lincoln than the *Merrimac* cane.

Of the canes presented to others by Lincoln, the most interesting are those given to the Pueblo Chiefs in 1863. During the Civil War, Navajo and Apaches Indians entered the conflict, while the Pueblo tribes remained neutral.

To mark his appreciation, and to follow in the footsteps of Phillip III of Spain who had presented the chiefs with the *Vara*, Lincoln ordered 19 ebony canes, made to order by John Dold of Philadelphia. Each cane bore an engraving with the name of the Pueblo, the date of *1863*, and a facsimile of the signature *A. Lincoln Pres. U.S..* The cost of the canes was $ 5.50. Each cane was distributed to a Pueblo chief who kept it for a year, before passing it on to his successor. To this day the Lincoln cane and the *Vara* are always in evidence at any ceremony or gathering of each Pueblo. The Indians respect both canes as the Congressmen have respect for the mace in the House of Representatives.

A very similar knob is found on a cane in the Museum of the Lincoln Memorial University in Harrogate, Tennessee. Engraved *A. Lincoln* in script, on the side, it has the same carving as the Pueblo canes but on a longer knob. The story goes that it was also found in the box of the Ford theatre after the assassination and was taken as a memento by an actor named Phelps, who later sold it to a Stephen Mayhew as payment of a debt. It is curious that the ebony cane measures only thirty five and a half inches (95 cm), hardly long enough for the tall President to wear. Mayhew's descendant gave it to the University.

▲ 2/31   Victorian Sisneros, Governor of Santa Clara Pueblo, ca. 1935, holding the cane that Lincoln had given to his Pueblo tribe years before.
Courtesy, Museum of New Mexico.

▲ 2/32   One of the few illustrations of the presentation of a cane to Lincoln. It portrays Mr. Silvester Strong presenting the Honorable A. Lincoln a cane on July 4, 1859. The painting, made by Lloyd Ostendorf, belonged to John Hoblit. In appreciation of their friendship, Lincoln presented John A. Hoblit a cane of which the gold top bears: *This stick cut from a tree grown by A. Lincoln, presented to J.A. Hoblit, Atlanta, Ill.*
Courtesy, Lincoln Memorial University.

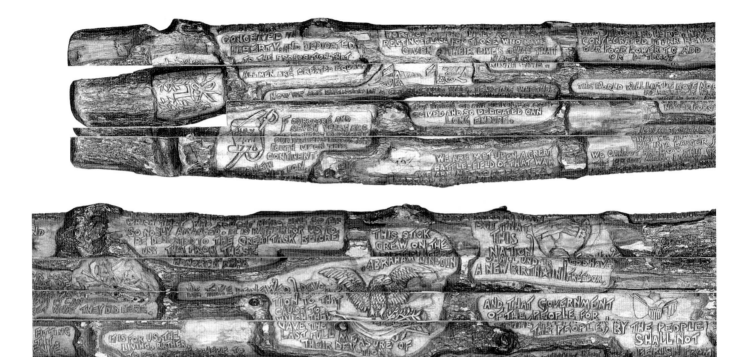

▲ 2/33   John E. Gregory cut the wood of this cane on Lincoln's farm in Hodgenville, Kentucky in 1909. He carved it with the Gettysburg address which reads:

This stick grew on the birthplace of Abraham Lincoln.

Fourscore and seven years ago, our fathers brought forth upon this continent a new nation, conceived in Liberty, and dedicated to the proposition that all men are created equal.

Now we are engaged in a great civil war, testing whether that nation or any nation, so conceived and so dedicated can long endure.

We are met upon a great battle-field of that war, we are met to dedicate a portion of that field as a last resting-place for those who have given their lives that that nation might live.

It is altogether fitting that we should do this. But in a larger sense, we cannot hallow this ground. The brave men, living or dead, who struggled here, have consecrated it far beyond our poor power to add or detract.

The world will little note nor long remember what we say here, but it can never forget what they did here.

It is for us, the living, rather, to be dedicated here to the unfinished work which they who fought here have so far so nobly advanced. It is rather for us to be dedicated to the great task before us: that from these honored dead.

We take renewed devotion to that cause to which they gave the last full measure of their devotion:

That these dead shall not have died in vain but that this nation shall under God have a new birth in freedom and that Government of the people, by the people, for the people shall not perish from the earth.

Courtesy, Chicago Historical Society.

In 1905 Lincoln's birthplace was designated a national monument. A building was erected to shelter the original log cabin to preserve it from the elements, but the structure when built proved too small. Four feet of the cabin were therefore sawn off! The resulting wood was made into canes to be sold by the Hodgenville Lincoln Ladies' League as a souvenir for visitors.

Other canes were made from the benches in the small wooden courthouse where Lincoln first practiced law at Lincoln, Illinois.

Still others came from Lincoln's home in Springfield, Illinois. Souvenir hungers scraped shavings from the window sill. One cane was even made from a tree growing on the ruins of the building in which Lincoln had lived. Many canes appeared allegedly having been cut from the split-rail fences chopped by Lincoln as a youth in the 1830's. They were said to be carried as campaign canes by his supporters during the Presidential campaign of 1860.

A few canes were made several years after his death. One was carved from the wood of a tree under which Lincoln and Douglas held their second debate. One was made from the timber of a log cabin north of Hamilton where Lincoln spent one night before the Douglas debates.

These canes present a perfect example of how careful one must be when faced with a cane - or any object - where no real proof can be given as to its origin. After Lincoln's assassination demand surged for any articles connected with him and thousands of fakes were made, including many canes. It is simple to take any shaft and add a band engraved to represent a cane that Lincoln wore. In fact a picture of Lincoln with a cane in his hand would be a prize item for any cane collector as so few examples are known to exist.

Andrew Johnson
1808 - 1875

Vice-President, March - April 1865
President, 1865 - 1869

▲ 2/34   A gold-handled cane marked *Andrew Johnson, Defender and Protector of the Constitution and of the United States, from friends of the Church of the Immaculate Conception, Washington, D.C., December 8, 1867.*
Courtesy, collection Smithsonian Institution.

Ulysses S. Grant
1822 - 1885

President, 1869 - 1877

▶ 2/35   Cane belonging to Grant's Vice-President marked *Friends in California to Hon. Henry Wilson.*
Courtesy, Richard A. Bourne Co., Inc.

One seldom sees pictures of General Grant wearing a cane; nevertheless, he owned several that can be seen today in various museums.

In the chapter on Leading Citizens, there is illustrated a cane which belonged to the Marquis de Lafayette and which was given to General Grant. The Smithsonian Institution has a simple stick of oak inscribed *U.S.G.* One more elaborate cane has a gold-headed knob with the following inscription: *Wood from Shiloh Church, Pittsburgh Landing Battlefield which was destroyed by cannonball during the engagement April 6, 1862,* and further, *Presented to Gen. U.S. Grant as a tribute of regard of his human treatment of the soldiers and kind consideration of those who ministered to the sick and wounded. By Mrs A.W. of Iowa, 1869.*

▲ 2/36   A cane made at the Norfolk Navy Yard with wood taken from the *U.S. Frigate Cumberland* and the metal part in the shape of a cannon taken from the *Confederate Ram "Merrimac"* This battle took place off Newport News on March 8, 1862.
Courtesy, collection Smithsonian Institution.

Rutherford B. Hayes
1822 - 1893

President, 1877 - 1881

◀ 2/37   A wooden cane, with a large American eagle's head. The cane belonged to Rutherford B. Hayes, but it is not known who presented it to him.
Courtesy, Rutherford B. Hayes Presidential Center.

The Hayes Presidential Center has a collection of canes which belonged to the President. They were presented mainly by admiring citizens and veterans of the Civil War. This last group of sticks represents numerous battlefields: *Lookout Mountain; Gettysburg, July 1,2,3, 1863; Highwater Mark; Winchester 19 Sept. 1864; Red Bud Slough.* It is in this last battle that General Hayes distinguished himself. It is therefore believed that he might have cut the branch himself when visiting the battlefield years later.

James A. Garfield
1831 - 1881

President, March - September 1881

▲ 2/39 A fine selection of Presentation canes that President Garfield must have received before and after his nomination. Each is typical of the gold-headed canes of the era.
Courtesy, President James A. Garfield National Historical Site.

▲ 2/38   Cane carved by Alanson P. Dean, South Adams, Massachusetts who presented it to Rutherford B. Hayes as a Thanksgiving present to celebrate the Centennial of 1876. The cane, carved only with a jack-knife, is of American box-wood. The cap is the root of the tree. On one side there is a Newfoundland dog lying down with a little girl on its back; on the other there is a tiger jumping over a child and the words *Centennial 1776 - 1876*. Sequentially below these words are the face of Rutherford Hayes taken from a photograph, the U.S. Coat of Arms, and the words *Rutherford B. Hayes, Governor of Ohio, born October 4, 1882*. On the opposite side of this cane is an anchor of hope, followed by the passage from the Gospel according to Matthew X, 16, the animals taking the place of words *Behold I send you forth as* sheep *in the midst of* wolves; *Be ye therefore wise as* serpents *and harmless as* doves.
    Alanson Porter Dean (1812 - 1888) carved several identical sticks for people he admired. He carved one for President Garfield, P.T. Barnum, Francis Murphy (a Temperance Movement leader) and for James Francis in Pittsfield, Massachusetts.
Courtesy, Rutherford B. Hayes Presidential Center.

Chester A. Arthur
1830 - 1886

Vice-President, March - September 1881
President, 1881 - 1885

According to your cloth you 've cut your coat,
O Dude of all the White House residents;
We trust that it will help you with the vote,
When next we go to nominating Presidents.

▲ 2/40   President Chester A. Arthur was considered a fop by his opponents. He had a passion for fashionable clothes, and installed the first tiled bathroom in the White House. The limerick explains the cartoon.
Courtesy,The New York Public Library.

Grover Cleveland
1837 - 1908

President,   1885 - 1889
             1893 - 1897

It is interesting to quote an article which appeared on the eve of the re-election of President Cleveland, November 1, 1892: *Grover Cleveland has a fine collection of walking sticks, which he keeps in his gun-room. One of the canes which Mr Cleveland takes a particular pride in was presented to Andrew Jackson in 1881 by a number of citizens. The cane was made from a branch of an oak that grew on the grave of Thomas Jefferson.*

The second in the collection was sent to Mr Cleveland by a gentleman from San Antonio, Texas, and is a beautiful mosaic, made of irregular shaped pieces of horns representing the frontal adornment of all the horned animals of the West. A large piece of Agate forms the knob.

The description of the cane, formed by segment of the horns found in the West, is mentioned in the French book "Les 100.000 curiosités d'hier et d'aujourd'hui", by H. Cordonnier, 1909.

▶ 2/42   Etched cane with the faces and names of Grover Cleveland's second cabinet: *Cleveland, Gresham, Carlisle, Lamont, Herbert, Bissell.* Not shown in this picture are Hoke, Smith, Olney and Morton.
This cane forms part of the great variety of etched canes, numerous models of which are found in the chapter on Patriotic Canes. The Harry S. Truman Library has a second, nearly identical, cane.
Courtesy, Harry S. Truman Library.

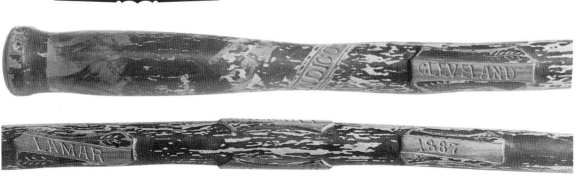

▲ 2/41   A cane which belonged to William C. Endictott, (1826 - 1900), Secretary of State under President Cleveland. Inscribed on top *Sec. Endicott*, with crudely incised crossed cannons and on raised sections of bark, *Cleveland, Hendricks, Manning, Bayard, Garland, Lamar, Whitney*, *Endicott, Vilas, 1887,* all members of Cleveland's first cabinet.
Courtesy, Essex Institute, Salem, Mass.

Benjamin Harrison
1833 - 1901

President, 1889 - 1893

◀ 2/43 Two canes received by President Harrison on some of his trips and which remain today in his Memorial Home.
Courtesy, President Benjamin Harrison Foundation Inc.

At the end of the 19th century it was a popular pastime to whittle sticks in celebration of an event, either for oneself or to present to a friend or leading citizen. President Harrison toured the country in 1891, addressing one hundred forty audiences, and many of his listeners were proud and happy to present their Chief Executive with one of their homemade works of art. Thus President Harrison received a large and singular collection of canes, of which 20 remain today in his Memorial Home.

Several of these canes he passed on to friends. In his will he bequeathed canes to be selected by his wife to his two brothers, Carter and John. Captain David Braden, a fishing and hunting companion, received a rather heavy stick that the President cherished. It was later returned to the Memorial Home. This same Home has the elegant and historical cane which belonged to Benjamin Harrison, one of the signatories of the Declaration of Independence, who passed it to his son, William (9th President), who in turn, gave it to his grandson, Benjamin. The President gave it to his friend and law partner, William Henry Harrison Miller. Miller's heir, in turn, gave it to the Memorial Home in 1939.

William McKinley
1843 - 1901

President, 1897 - 1901

◀ 2/44 An elegant cane carved with roses and shamrocks which belonged to President McKinley. The initials of the President are engraved on the top of the knob and the words *Christmas 1899* on the band.
Courtesy, collection Smithsonian Institution.

Theodore Roosevelt
1858 - 1919

Vice-President, March-September 1901
President, 1901 - 1909

President Theodore Roosevelt did not wear canes, but his words remain important to cane collectors:
Speak softly and carry a big stick, you will go far.

A military man, he saw the stick as an object demanding respect, if not repression. His famous quotation was made at a speech at the Minnesota State Fair, on September 2nd, 1901.

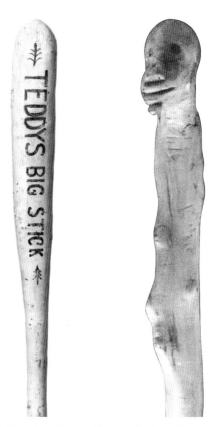

▲ 2/45 Theodore Roosevelt's *Big Stick is* well illustrated by this heavy cane which he had in mind when he mentioned carrying a *big stick.*
Courtesy, Little White House, Warm Springs, Ga.

▶▲ 2/46 A typical African cane that Roosevelt brought back from one of his trips.
Courtesy, Sagamore Hill National Historic Site.

Though we have no pictures of President Roosevelt wearing a cane, the Sagamore Hill Historic Site in Oyster Bay possesses two canes which were given to him. One was presented by citizens of the Seventh Congressional District of Georgia, on September 7, 1902. A silver band is inscribed *General Bragg, General Longstreet, General Wheeler, General Rosecraus, General Thomas, General Boyuton.*

The other cane is a wooden stick with the Lord's Prayer carved upon it.

Adolf Simon, founder of the New York cane and umbrella shop, "Uncle Sam's", claimed he had worked on canes made out of the hide of a rhino shot by Roosevelt. It is well known how much the President liked big game hunting in Africa, this claim is plausible.

William Howard Taft
1857 - 1930

President, 1909 - 1913

▲ 2/48   The first crook handle encountered among Presidents' canes. This form did not appear before the turn of the 19th-20th century.
Courtesy, William H. Taft National Historic Site.

Woodrow Wilson
1856 - 1924

President, 1913 - 1921

▶ 2/49   Although the head of William Jennings Bryan is pictured on the handle of this cane, it was carved and presented to Woodrow Wilson shortly after his election in 1912. At the top of the cane there is a horseshoe engraved with the words *Good Luck.* Then appears the face of Bryan, who was to become Secretary of State. His initials, and the words *Peoples Champion* appear below his face. *My country tis of thee* appears over the profile of Wilson, followed by a horse and the words *The Winner.* Then follows the Latin phrase *Sic Semper Tyrannis* and the limerick, which amused Wilson and which he was fond of quoting:

▲ 2/47   On this political cartoon, is the message of the *big stick.* The Bull Moose Party was the third party Roosevelt formed.
Courtesy, New York Public Library.

*As a beauty, I am not a star
There are others more handsome by far,
But my face - I don't mind it,
For I am behind it,
The people in front get the jar.*

Behind Bryan's head we find a bird, possibly a dove, with the word *Peace* flowing from its beak. Below is a rooster followed by the words *Woodrow Wilson. 28th President Elected Nov. 5, 1912.*

At the very bottom is carved *Mrs A.E. Wiseman / 2458 Summit St. / Columbus, Ohio.* It is unknown whether she was the artist, or whether the cane was made for her.
◄ Courtesy, Woodrow Wilson Birthplace Foundation.

Warren G. Harding
1865 - 1923

President, 1921 - 1923

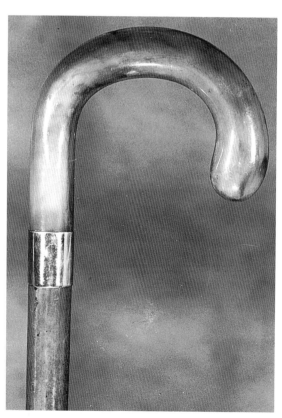

▲ 2/50   Another crook-handle cane which belonged to President Harding. It had a matching umbrella, a pairing often found in the works of Tiffany and Gorham. The shaft is of malacca. On the gold band below is engraved *W.G.H.,* and the horn is of a light colored amber.
Courtesy, collection Smithsonian Institution.

Calvin Coolidge
1872 - 1933

President, 1923 - 1929

Dr. S.G. Watkins, a dentist from Montclair, New Jersey, and a great collector of walking sticks, knew President Coolidge personally. On May 1, 1925, Coolidge presented Watkins with a cane in the White House. Colonel John C. Coolidge, father of the President, sent Watkins several pieces associated with the President including wood from a picket of the broken-down fence of his boyhood home at Plymouth, Vermont. Coolidge's father sent Watkins a stick made out of the mop handle used by the President's stepmother. The Colonel thought it had also been used by his first wife, the President's mother!

▲ 2/51   Two of President Coolidge's canes. The one with the crook has his signature on it; the other, with an ivory knob, has two inscribed bands. The top one refers to the fact that the wood was taken from the *U.S. Frigate "Constitution"* in *June 1833,* and the second reads *Dr. G.E. Whitten. July 4, 1926. To Calvin Coolidge, President U.S.A.*
Courtesy, The Calvin Coolidge Memorial Foundation Inc.

▲ a) Coat of arms of George Washington atop the gold handle.
Courtesy, the Mount Vernon Ladies' Association.

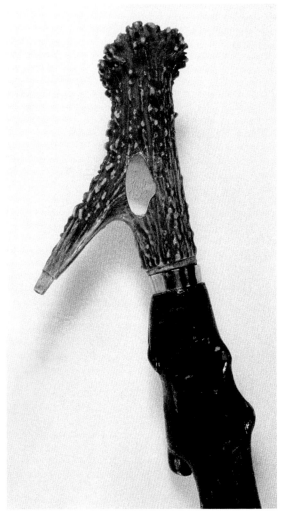

▲ c) Cane given by George Washington to General John Brooks (1752-1825) who was one of the most trusted confidants of the President. Between spells of active service, he practiced medicine and was very active in local politics. He was Governor of Massachusetts between 1817 and 1822.
Courtesy, Massachusetts Historical Society.

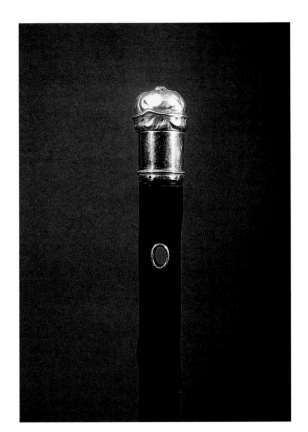

▲ b) Gold headed cane bequeathed to George Washington by Benjamin Franklin in his will dated April 17, 1788. Franklin mentions that the shaft is made of crabtree wood.
Courtesy, collection Smithsonian Institution.

▶ d) A carved cane showing American Presidents from George Washington to Grover Cleveland, made between 1887 and 1897. It resembles the cane made for President Harrison (Photo 2/3).
Courtesy, collection George H. Meyer.

◄ a) All Presidents from George Washington to F.D.R. are carved and painted on this cane. These canes were often made to endorse a political candidate, associating him with exalted company. A similar cane is found at the *Little White House,* in Warm Springs, Ga.
Courtesy, Blue Ridge Institute, Ferrum, Va.

► b) Cane worn by John Norton (1651-1716), second minister at Hingham from 1678 to his sudden death in 1716. He was educated at Ipswich Grammar School and Harvard, he was ordained by Reverend Peter Hobart. The silver collar is engraved *J.Norton 1678,* the year that he was ordained.
Courtesy, Massachusetts Historical Society.

▼► c) Cane once belonging to Thomas Hancock (1703 - 1764), self-made man who became one of the wealthiest and most successful businessmen in Boston. The back of the ivory handle is engraved *Tho. Hancock.* He left his estate and the cane to his nephew, John Hancock.
Courtesy, Massachusetts Historical Society.

▲ d) Cane made of live oak from the *U.S.Frigate Constitution* and given to John Quincy Adams by Commodore Isaac Hull in 1836. John Quincy Adams (1767 - 1848) served as American Minister in various European capitals, and was President of the United States between 1825 and 1829. He bequeathed this cane to his grandson, Charles Francis Adams.
Courtesy, Massachusetts Historical Society.

◄ e) Cane given to George Washington in 1788 by his good friend, James Bowdoin II (1726 -1790). Son of a leading American merchant, he devoted his life to politics. Elected governor of Massachusetts, he was also interested in science and literature.
Courtesy, Massachusetts Historical Society.

Herbert Hoover
1874 - 1964

President, 1929 - 1933

▲ 2/52   Two canes that belonged to President Hoover. The handle of the square cane is a special form to give it more strength. Both are marked with his initials.
Courtesy, private collection.

Franklin Delano Roosevelt
1882 - 1945

President, 1933 - 1945

Franklin Delano Roosevelt presents a different situation. The President needed a support. It was still an era when a fashionable man wore a cane, and presenting a disabled person with a walking stick was not considered in any way a faux-pas. By contrast, in today's "politically correct" climate, such a useful gift would be considered in very bad taste!

Like all fashionable dandies, Roosevelt wore a cane when he was young. After he was stricken by polio his political opponents tried to use his infirmity against him. Hundred of citizens showed their admiration by whittling, carving and writing words of love and devotion on canes: *FDR, The Patriot / FDR, The man who saved the nation / Hon. Franklin D. Roosevelt, Our Hero President / To our beloved President Franklin D. Roosevelt,* and many others.

In the collections of the Hyde Park Library and the Little White House in Warm Springs, Georgia are nearly 250 canes which were presented to FDR by donors who have been identified. It is most improbable that he used any of these canes.

Half these canes are very simply carved and bear initials and/or dates. Sometimes an animal is crudely represented. Another forty or so are more elaborately carved and represent real Folk Art, that of the non-professional carver using his heart and talent to carve a cane for the Chief of State.

▲ 2/53   This cane has initials of the all various administrative agencies engraved along the shaft. A metal handle with the date 1932, commemorating F.D.R's first campaign, was added later.
Courtesy, Franklin D. Roosevelt Library.

52 | Chapter Two Canes worn by United States Presidents

More interesting canes are those linked to the New Deal policies which FDR initiated. Some are engraved with the letters *N.R.A.* (National Recovery Administration, 1933) or *C.C.C.* (Civilian Conservation Corps, 1933). One is carved with the initials of the worker on *C.W.A.* (Civil Works Administration, 1933), *Project MR 14, Mull Valley, California.* One bears the message *Iowa fights,* and another from Mexico is studded with 28 crystal stones taken from the Pecos Valley diamonds, representing the 28 administrative measures inaugurated by President Roosevelt. Canes were made from the planks of the platform on which FDR stood for his inauguration on March 4, 1933, or from wood from the platform of London's Guildhall where Roosevelt made an important speech.

With three exceptions, none of these canes could be called elegant, or the type to be worn with a double breasted suit. Roosevelt certainly owned more formal examples, which have probably remained within the family.

▲ 2/54 Franklin Delano Roosevelt wearing a cane on a transatlantic trip, well before he was struck with polio.
Courtesy, Franklin D. Roosevelt Library.

▲ 2/55 An inlaid cane marked under the handle: *From Phillip M. Schield, V.W.W. No 1 Filipino.* Vertically: *F.D.R. P.U.S.A. 4 T.*
Courtesy, Franklin D. Roosevelt Library.

▲ 2/56 A supporter gave FDR a Big Stick, which had been used so well by Theodore Roosevelt.
Courtesy, Little White House, Warm Springs, GA.

Harry S. Truman
1884 - 1972

Vice-President, January - April 1945

President, 1945 - 1953

With Harry Truman and the end of World War II, we come not only to the last President to have worn a cane, but also to the end of centuries during which a cane, staff or stick represented an important function in society. The stick had been the symbol of discipline, order, leadership, respect, and even repression. Today all this has disappeared along with the walking stick. We may hope for its return, because one cannot imagine what object or instrument could replace the function of a stick.

▶ 2/57 Truman received numerous canes as gifts from foreign countries. Most are more decorative than those presented to his predecessor. In this picture, assembled for a 1977 exhibition at the Truman Library, we see a variety of his canes. Some of them are featured in other chapters.
Courtesy, Harry S. Truman Library.

▲ 2/58 Truman was never seen without a cane that had a simple crook handle. In this picture, he marches with his brother and the Mayor of St. Louis. The other gentlemen carry their canes awkwardly, probably having been told to wear a cane for the parade.
Courtesy, Harry S. Truman Library.

▶ 2/59 A cane made for a President. It is doubtful whether Truman ever wore it, but it is a typical presentation stick.
Courtesy, Harry S. Truman Library.

▲ 3/1 Spring Day,1904, taken by Robertson Matthews at Cornell University, Ithaca, New York.
Several political canes are pictured, with shafts covered in red, white and blue. These canes usu-
ally carried firecrackers at the tip.
Photography, courtesy The Region of Peel Archives.

Political Canes

Introduction

As well as the canes directly associated with U.S. Presidents, a wide variety of canes with political associations can be found. Many of these were issued as souvenirs of the campaign efforts of candidates running for office.

The custom of issuing campaign memorabilia by which supporters could show their allegiance to the candidate of their choice began with the 1828 and 1832 elections. Flasks, plates and pitchers endorsing Andrew Jackson appeared in family parlors, and Jackson followers could adorn themselves with clothing, buttons and ribbons extolling their candidate. No canes dating from this campaign are known to exist, but for the election of William Henry Harrison in 1840, a large amount of paraphernalia was produced. Collectors of campaign memorabilia consider that the serious production of these items began with this campaign. No mass-produced canes were manufactured, but several carved and inscribed canes exist. These were obviously personal walking sticks which the supporter had carved before attending political meetings or conventions.

Similar canes are found for the 1844 Polk-Dallas campaign, but for General Zachary Taylor, hero of the Mexican War who was elected President in 1848, his name is found only on soldiers' canes. His successors, Millard Fillmore (1850) and Franklin Pierce (1852), had few campaign trinkets to glorify them, and if James Buchanan (1856) wore canes, none representing his supporters are found. Abraham Lincoln (1860) occasionally wore canes himself, and numerous others are associated with him. (See chapter on Presidents).

By 1868 the issue of campaign memorabilia had greatly increased. The first "parade" cane was issued for Ulysses S. Grant. These canes were hollow-cast in tin, pewter, lead, or some similar alloy, and feature a good likeness of the candidate. Only meant to endure for the duration of the convention, the heads are often dented or generally show signs of wear and tear. The wood used for the shafts is nondescript. These canes exist in various sizes, with a name, signature, or slogan often found at the base of the image.

Numerous canes exist for Rutherford B. Hayes, elected in 1876, and James Garfield, elected in 1880, but none for Chester A. Arthur who became President in 1881 following Garfield's death in office. In 1884 Grover Cleveland ran against the Republican James G. Blaine. 1888 saw the campaign of Benjamin Harrison, grandson of ninth President William H. Harrison, using the slogan of the log cabin.

William C. McKinley defeated William J. Bryan in 1896 and again in 1900 (in total, Bryan ran three losing Presidential races). By this time the political souvenir industry was in full swing, with many objects created for both candidates. Vice-President Theodore Roosevelt succeeded to the Presidency in 1901 upon McKinley's assassination and won the election of 1904. He was an immensely popular President, and cane handles are found among the many souvenirs issued with his image. William Howard Taft succeeded Roosevelt in 1908. This 32-year period, 1876-1908, is a particularly rich era for the collector of campaign memorabilia, with a huge diversity of fascinating objects.

No canes are known to have been manufactured for the convention of 1912 (Woodrow Wilson), or 1924 (Calvin Coolidge).

With the election of Franklin Delano Roosevelt (1933), canes reappear, not only because he was compelled to *use* one, but because it was still the fashion to *wear* a cane. The hundreds of canes carved by admirers and presented to him were not given with the idea of assisting an invalid, but as what we would today call a fashion statement. Canes were still the emblem of the chief. There were few campaign canes as such. Roosevelt's opponents used his handicap against him, so it was hardly likely that, in 1936 and 1940, his supporters would choose as political symbol a cane as a token of their admiration.

Harry Truman constantly wore canes, but no Truman convention canes have been discovered. By the time John F. Kennedy was in office (1960), canes were no longer in fashion. With his back injuries, Kennedy could well have used a cane, but dared not display what was now an accessory of lameness. Effigies of Kennedy upon canes do exist, but as they bear no political slogans, they appear to have been issued as souvenirs after his assassination.

Henry Clay
1824, 1832, 1842

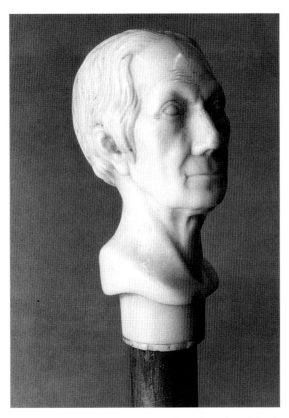

▲ 3/2 Several identical ivory canes have been found, leading to the belief that they were used at conventions. Henry Clay ran against John Quincy Adams, Andrew Jackson and James K. Polk. Molded baleen effigies of Jackson and Clay have been cited.
Courtesy, Missouri Historical Society.

William Henry Harrison
1840

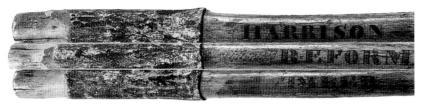

▲ 3/3 A *Reform cane* for the election of Harrison & Tyler. Portions of the bark have been removed to allow drawings in pen of a house with Harrison on top of the door, next to Tom Coran, 21,000. One can read *goarb (?) for Old Tip by in....Frat. 30,000 Ohio.* Horizontally the picture reads *Harrison / Reform / Tyler.*
Courtesy, collection Smithsonian Institution.

▲ 3/4 Part of a cane with a pen drawing on which can be read: *Highlander to the Rescue / HARD CIDER / Highland band / Harrison Tyler and Corwin / Harrison & Tyler / Our country first / Our county last / Our country forever ! / With the gallant old Tip, we'll give them a rip ! / The people must do their own fighting, and their own voting ! 12,123,07 (?) / 1,229,7050 (?) / To London 10 Mil's / Presented to the Hon. Tho's Corwin by John M. Keyes, Hillsboro O. 1840 J.M.*
Courtesy, Ohio Historical Society.

▲▶ 3/5 Here the pen drawing mentions *Tip / Tyler /and Tom.*
Courtesy, Ohio Historical Society.

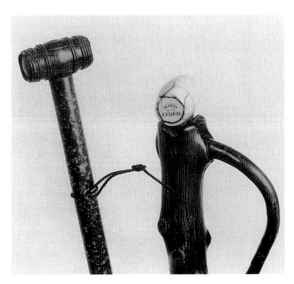

▲ 3/6 Two knobs of canes in the shape of a barrel. The ivory one bears the words *Hard cider* and *Tippecanoe.* The simpler wooden one could have been produced in quantity for the election of Harrison's grandson, Benjamin.
Courtesy, collection Smithsonian Institution.

▲ 3/7   A dark octagonal cane with its knob in the shape of a barrel. The sides of the shaft bear the various slogans of Harrison's campaign: *One Term / Liberty & Union / No Sub Treasury / A Sound Currency / Tippecanoe Club / Lo ! the Star in the East Tyler, V.P. 1841 / Hurrah for Old Tip / Hero of the Thames/ Harrison & Reform.* Under the handle, we find the names of the States: *New York / Ohio / Vermont / Old Bay State / Kentucky / Penn.*
Courtesy, New Hampshire Historical Society.

▲ 3/8   A trimmed tree branch, with an American flag on top of the silver handle and depictions of items connected with Harrison. One knob has a silver cap in shape of a barrel with the word *Hard Cider*. All the other knobs are covered by a silver stud, each engraved with the ten letters: *W.M. H.A.R.R.I.S.O.N.*

A pro-Martin Van Buren newspaper suggested that *on condition of his receiving a pension of $ 2,000 and a barrel of cider, General Harrison would no doubt consent to withdraw his pretensions, and spend his days in a log cabin on the banks of the Ohio.* Whigs developed what became known as the *Log Cabin and Hard Cider* campaign, using these symbols to portray Benjamin Henry Harrison as a sturdy man of the frontier.

An identical cane can be found in the Harry Truman Library.   Courtesy, Kentucky Historical Society.

Rhode Island Election
1843

▲ 3/9   A heavy gnarled wood with the names engraved in gold of *J.L. Boylston 1844 / John Quincy Adams Honest / John Davis / Gov. Paine / Vt. Gov. King 1842 Burgess / Mayor, Gov. Fenner OK 1843 / Gov. Briggs, Mass / Henry Clay.* On other lines are the words: *Washington father of his country / Law & Order.*

The *Law and Order* political party of Rhode Island did not last long. Samuel Ward King was elected over Thomas Door. The Rhode Island Historical Society has two canes which belonged to Door. 1842 was the date of Door's Rebellion.

In this picture, the cane is shown on the letter J. L. Boylston wrote to the Rhode Island Historical Society in 1844 asking them to take care of his *Law and Order Cane.*
Courtesy, Rhode Island Historical Society.

James K. Polk
1845

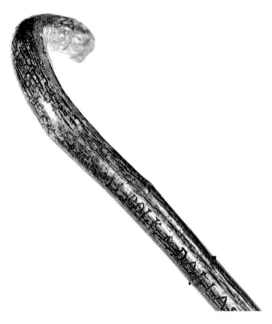

▲ 3/10 Simple crook cane with the names of *Polk - Dallas* carved in the wood. It bears also the initials *L.G.H.*, a member of the New York delegation who attended the Democratic Convention in Baltimore, Maryland on May 27 - 30, 1844.
Courtesy, James K. Polk Memorial Association.

▲ 3/11 *J.K. Polk* is carved on the handle of this cane. Its shaft has been carved with *Vox Populi* and *Veto of 1832* together with *Old Hickory,* the nickname of Andrew Jackson, who had vetoed a bill for rechartering of the National Bank. Polk was Jackson's protege, and took the name of *Young Hickory.*
Courtesy, New York State Historical Association, Cooperstown, N.Y.

Ulysses Grant
1868, 1872

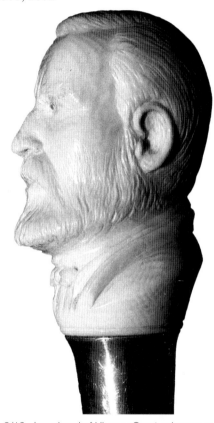

▲ 3/12 Ivory head of Ulysses Grant, whose name is carved on the back of the bust.
Courtesy, collection Jim Gifford.

Horace Greeley
1872

▲ 3/13 Cane offered to Horace Greeley, opponent of Ulysses S. Grant in 1872, by the Exiled Priest of Guatemala.
Courtesy, collection Smithsonian Institution.

Rutherford B. Hayes
1876

James A. Garfield
1880

▶ 3/14   A cane inscribed *Our choice R.B. Hayes* with the handle formed by his image, wearing a black tradesman's cap. On the shaft are numerous tradesmen's tools, undoubtedly representing his various supporters. The hand of this carver reappears in the chapter on Folk Art Canes.
Courtesy, Rutherford B. Hayes Presidential Center.

▲ 3/16   Effigy of James A. Garfield for the 1880 convention.
Courtesy, collection L.G.

Winfield S. Hancock
1880

▲ 3/15   The image of Rutherford B. Hayes for the 1876 convention.
Courtesy, collection L.G.

▲ 3/17   Winfield S. Hancock was the Democratic candidate who opposed James A. Garfield. A gilded presentation cane marked on three sides *Donated by Hon. D.A. MacDonald Oct. 1880 / Won for Major Gen. W.S. Hancock / Of an election for most popular Presidential Candidate.*
Courtesy, collection Smithsonian Institution.

▲ 3/18 Cane presented to Winfield S. Hancock by *several of his Democratic friends in Oregon*, 1880. These words are written on top of the shield of the United States Flag.
Courtesy, collection Smithsonian Institution.

Grover Cleveland
1884, 1888, 1892

Grover Cleveland was elected in 1884 and 1892, and was also a candidate in the election of 1888. Much memorabilia connected with Cleveland has survived, including many canes. One particular stick, made *In the Hickory flag pole erected at the corner of Locust and Market streets in the city of Allegheny, State of Pennsylvania, in the year of A.D. 1892, in the interest of the Election of Grover Cleveland* was years later presented to Franklin D. Roosevelt.

▲ 3/20 Two different effigies of Cleveland from different campaigns.
Courtesy, collection Walter Scholz.

▲ 3/19 A double faced handle representing Cleveland and his Vice-President, Thomas Hendricks.
Courtesy, collection Henry Ford Museum & Greenfield Village.

▲ 3/21 Cleveland as a Roman emperor and the effigy of an older Cleveland, no doubt for his 1892 election.
Courtesy, collection Jim Gifford.

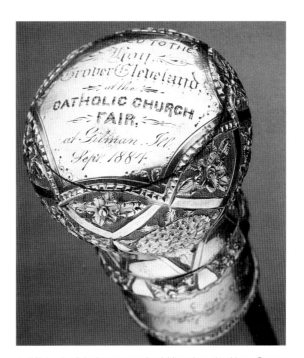

▲ 3/22   This picture of Cleveland is covered with clear celluloid.
Courtesy, collection Smithsonian Institution.

▲ 3/24   A gilded cane marked *Voted to the Hon. Grover
Cleveland at the Catholic Church Fair at Gilman, Ill. Sept.
1884*. A flask can be found inside.
Courtesy, Chicago Historical Society.

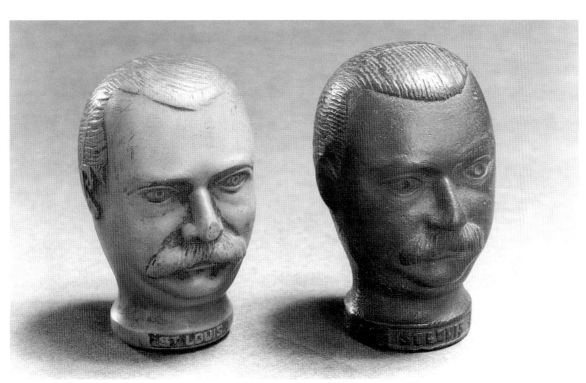

▲ 3/23   Two effigies of Cleveland, marked in front St. Louis, in the rear 1888. Of particular interest is the head to the right,
made in hard rubber.   Courtesy, Ohio Historical Society.

▲ 3/25   During the 1888 Convention, Cleveland's Vice-
Presidential candidate was Allen Thurman. Both are repre-
sented on this double-face handle.
Courtesy, collection Jim Gifford.

▲ 3/27   The same pair adorns the top of the handle. It was
produced by the same firm who made the Cleveland
Hendricks handle.
Courtesy, collection Jim Gifford.

James G. Blaine
1884

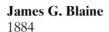

▲3/26   A design patent registered in August 1884 representing Blaine on one side and John A. Logan on the other.
Courtesy, U.S. Patent Office.

▲ 3/28   The Plumed Knight, nickname of James G. Blaine,
who was defeated by Cleveland in 1884. The design patent
was registered in 1884.
Courtesy, Museum of American Political Life, Hartford.

▲ 3/29 The picture of Blaine is held under a clear celluloid top.
Courtesy, collection Stuart H. White.

Benjamin Harrison
1888, 1892

In the chapter on Presidents note was made of how many canes Harrison received during his campaigns. Certain of these have a presentation aspect, such as the one in the Chicago Historical Society, which reads on its gold head: *Presented to / The Hon. C.H. Harrison / by the Popular Vote/ at / St. Patrick's / Bazaar / Oct. 5th / 1872*. Others are linked to the conventions, as is the one at the Benjamin Harrison Memorial Home, which has inscribed on its gilded head *Gen. Ben. Harrison by the Irish Protectionists of Highland, Wisconsin, July 4, 1888*. (The day Benjamin Harrison accepted the nomination). The same Benjamin Harrison Memorial Home has a cane with a rough drawing of a log cabin. The words *Benjamin Harrison, Indianapolis, Indiana* appear on the top, and *Nevada, Ohio, October 19th, 1888* on the side. Thus it can be said that the image of the barrel and the log cabin, always associated with his grandfather, was also used by Benjamin Harrison.

▲ 3/30 Effigy of James G. Blaine.
Courtesy, collection L.G.

▲ 3/31 Two effigies of Benjamin Harrison. The one on the left is in the same alloy with his name on the back. The other is heavy gilded and bears no name.
Courtesy, Museum of American Political Life, Hartford.

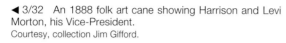

◀ 3/32   An 1888 folk art cane showing Harrison and Levi Morton, his Vice-President.
Courtesy, collection Jim Gifford.

▲ 3/33   Benjamin Harrison's picture is placed under a clear celluloid top.
Courtesy, collection Paul Weisberg.

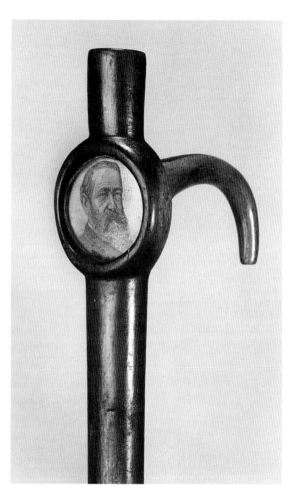

▲ 3/35   Here the picture is placed vertically on the front of the handle, so it is constantly in view. This cane was carved and worn by Joseph Brown McNay.
Courtesy, Nebraska Historical Society.

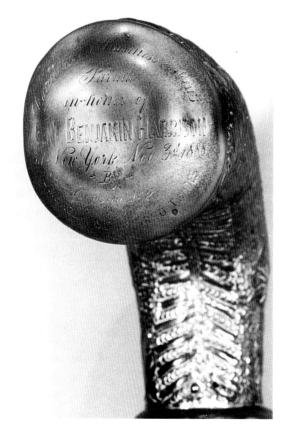

◀ 3/34   A very large cane, measuring forty-two and three-quarter inches in length (108 cm). The width of the handle is fifteen and three-quarter inches (40 cm), and the diameter three and one three sixteenth inches (8 cm). It was carried by Fox & Co. (Emil Fox was a a cane manufacturer at 133 Crosby St. in New-York) at the New York parade in honor of General Harrison. (Color picture).
On the front of the handle are the words *Compliments of the manufacturer / Emil Fox / Carried in the business men / Parade / in honor of / Gen.Benjamin Harrison / at New York, Nov. 3rd 1888 / by / Division No.28/ Umbrella and kindred trades.*
Courtesy, collection Madeleine Gely.

▲ 3/36 An 1892 convention cane marked Harrison and Whitelaw Reid, who both lost to McKinley. A similar cane exists for the 1888 winning team of Harrison and Levi P. Morton.
Courtesy, collection Paul Weisberg.

William McKinley
1896, 1900

▲ 3/38 A flat cane top, completely in tin, representing McKinley. This cane is by the same manufacturer as the one of Harrison and Reid.
Courtesy, collection Smitsonian Institution.

▶ 3/39 Top of a cane with the effigy of McKinley.
Courtesy, collection Jim Gifford.

▲ 3/37 The Benjamin Harrison Memorial Home has this cane with a silver band near the ferrule marked *For the Walkover.* On a silver shield below the handle are the words *Campaign B. H. 1892.*
Courtesy, President Benjamin Harrison Foundation, Inc.

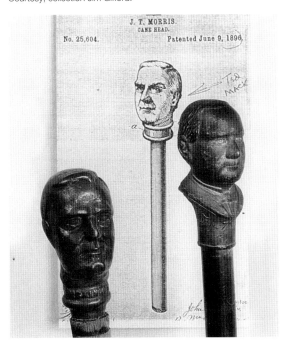

▲ 3/40 Two effigies, one signed on the side *Prosperity and Protection* and the other with McKinley's name embossed in front.
Courtesy, Museum of American Political Life, Hartford.

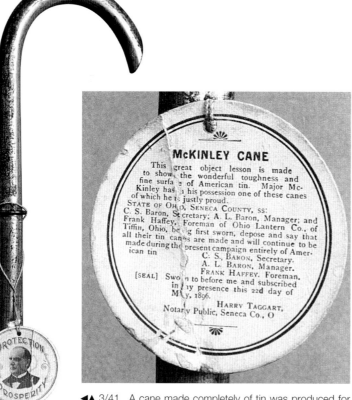

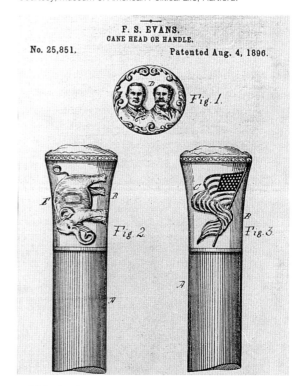

◀▲ 3/41 A cane made completely of tin was produced for the 1896 convention. It boasts that Major McKinley has the *same cane of which he is justly proud.* The reverse side has the slogan *Prosperity, Protection* with a portrait of McKinley in the center. A double advertisement for the Ohio Lantern Co. of Tiffin *Who swears in front of a notary to show the wonderful toughness and fine surface of American tin.*
Courtesy, collection Smithsonian Institution.

▲ 3/43 A metal effigy of McKinley. This was made most likely for his 1900 election.
Courtesy, Museum of American Political Life, Hartford.

▲ 3/42 A flag which pulls out shows McKinley and Hobart.
Courtesy, collection Jim Gifford.

▲ 3/44 Another design showing McKinley and Hobart.
Courtesy, U.S. Patent Office.

▶ d) An 1892 election cane for Grover Cleveland. *Friendship's hand extended:* captions a finely carved hand, and below an American Eagle are the words *Proud bird of the crag thy plume is untorn.* By a buckle, we find *Democratic Platform,* and further down the shaft is the date: *June 92.* and *Cleveland & Good Government / Protection is a Farce, Taxation a Reality.* The signature *A.W. Scott, Morris X Roads. Pa.* follows, perhaps identifying the carver, and then finally the inscription: *To J.C.W. Shibler, Pittsburgh. Pa.* and the letters: *L.A. 300.*
Courtesy, collection Catherine Dike.

▲ a) A Folk Art cane in two pieces: President Cleveland surmounts the American Eagle and the shield of the United States. On the shaft is a rabbit, a lizard, and a snake which twines up from the bottom.
Courtesy, collection Stuart H. White.

▲ b) Canes are often linked to the campaigns of Benjamin Harrison, who frequently associated himself with his grandfather for political capital. This small hat (1" 1/8 / 3 cm) is inscribed *1773 W.H. Harrison / 1811 Benj. Harrison / 1892.* Harrison lost the election of 1892 to Grover Cleveland.
Courtesy, collection L.G.

▲ e) The large parade cane carried by the *Umbrella and Kindred Trades* in a procession in honor of General Benjamin Harrison in New York on November 3, 1888. To give an better idea of its dimensions, it is pictured beside a cane of normal size.
Courtesy, collection Madeleine Gely.

▲ c) A simple straight stick (diameter 1" 1/2 / 44 mm) on which letters from a newspaper have been glued and varnished. One can barely read *Polk / Dallas.* Around the shaft the words: *Our President.*
Courtesy, collection L.G.

▲ a) Allen Thurman was Cleveland's Vice-Presidential candidate in the election of 1888. He used a red bandanna handkerchief when he took snuff, and this became his trademark. When he was nominated, the delegates waved a forest of red bandannas in approval. One delegate is supposed to have said: *We have nominated a pocket handkerchief*. Thurman had unsuccessfully run for President several times.
Courtesy, collection Catherine Dike.

▲ c) An ivory barrel bearing the the words *Hard Cider* and *Tippecanoe*. These were mottoes of William Henry Harrison, but his grandson Benjamin Harrison was much inclined to trade upon his grandfather's reputation by copying his taglines, so definitive dating is impossible.
Courtesy, collection Smithsonian Institution.

▲ b) A series of parade canes showing, from left to right, the crook handle for Jimmy Carter, the bust of McKinley, the crook handle for F.D.R., the busts of B. Harrison and Cleveland and the crook handle for Gerald R. Ford.
Courtesy, collection Catherine Dike.

▲ 3/45 *The McKinley Cane and Torch* is printed on the paper covering the metal cane, as well as the name of the manufacturer, *The Pittibon Bros. Mfg. Co. Campaign Supplies of every Demonstration, Flags, Banners, Buttons, Catalogue Free, 630 Main Street.* The second portrait is that of Garrett Hobart, the Vice-President nominee.
Courtesy, Museum of American Political Life, Hartford.

▲ 3/47 This design patent was registered in 1896 with two faces, one of McKinley and the other of Hobart on the side of the handle. The top shows the head of Liberty.
Courtesy, collection Jim Gifford.

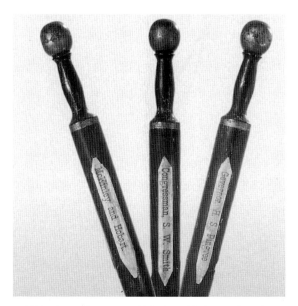

▲ 3/46 A round cane on which three labels are placed, one reading *McKinley and Hobart;* the second, *Congressman, S.W. Smith,* and the third, *Governor, H.S. Pingree.*
Courtesy, Henry Ford Museum & Greenfield Village.

▲ 3/48 A flag showing McKinley.
Courtesy, collection Jim Gifford.

◄3/49 A cane bearing an ink inscription which reads: *State and dates entering Union / Population 75,605,727 / 1900 / Historic wood from every State and Territory in the Union / Plugs of all the States wood / Original Thirteen / Historic cane 1900 / Protection to American Industry / Internal Vigilance is the price of Liberty / Gold Standard Prosperity / Talk about expansion / Electorial vote 1900 / McKinley 292 / Bryan 155 / Total 447 / Millions for Defence, not a cent for tribute.* The inscription is not visible in the photograph, but the plugs of wood are evident.
Courtesy, Ohio Historical Society.

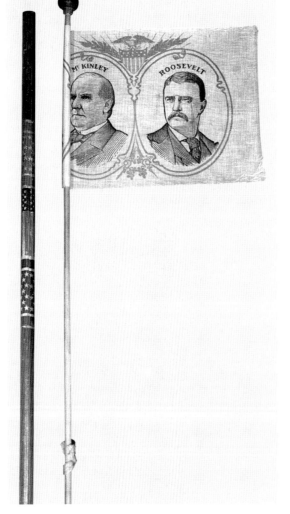

3/50 Here a flag pulls out showing McKinley and Theodore Roosevelt, his Vice-President. The shaft is wrapped in the national colors.
Courtesy, collection Kurt Stein.

◄3/51 The American flag is wrapped around the shaft, which shows small pictures of McKinley and Roosevelt at the time of the 1900 election.
Courtesy, collection Catherine Dike.

▲ 3/52 An etched cane representing McKinley, Roosevelt, Harrison, an unknown politician and Hayes. The small black and white squares which form the background are commonly found on etched canes.
Courtesy, collection Paul Weisberg.

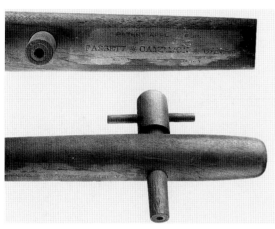

▲ 3/53 Fassett was the original Vice-Presidential designate, later replaced by Theodore Roosevelt. On this handle, which was issued for his nomination as Governor of New York, the spigots make an amusing visual pun on the candidate's name. The handle was made by *Kilmer & Reynolds, Elmira*.
Courtesy, collection Donald J. Grunder.

William J. Bryan
1896, 1900, 1908

William J. Bryan ran for President three times, twice against McKinley (1896 and 1900) and once against W. H. Taft (1908). Canes make up a good part of the multitude of Bryan campaign mementoes. Two effigies, 12 years apart, illustrate the tenacity of this politician. In 1896, his Vice-President nominee was Arthur Sewall; in 1900, Stevenson; and in 1908, Kern. In the 1896 election, Bryan opposed the gold standard with his 16/1 silver position.

▲ 3/54 A flag held in the shaft of the cane. It is uncertain which election produced this specimen.
Courtesy, Nebraska State Historical Society.

▲ 3/55 Three hand-carved canes, two representing Bryan and the third his wife, Mary Baird. The first has *W. J. Bryan Hero for free silver / Democratic President Champion 1896 / The Solon of the 19th Century*, carved in deep block letters. His wife's cane has the same carving with the inscription: *Wife of W. J. Bryan / Hero for free silver / Democratic President Rules / The Solon of the 19th Century*. Another stick by the same sculptor can be found in the chapter on Patriotic Canes.
Courtesy, collection George H. Meyer.

▲ 3/56 *16/1* etched on the band, meaning support for Bryan's pro-silver position in the 1896 campaign. McKinley was for maintaining the gold standard.
Courtesy, Museum of American Political Life, Hartford.

▶ 3/57 Relic of the 1900 campaign. Small pictures of Bryan and Stevenson appear on the shaft, the remainder of which is covered by the American flag.
Courtesy, collection Catherine Dike.

▲ 3/58 *The Presidential Campaign, Torch and Cane combined* written on this torch cane above the portraits of Bryan and Stevenson. The manufacturer is *The Brown Oil Co. Toledo, Ohio.*
Courtesy, Museum of American Political Life, Hartford.

▲ 3/59 Silver effigy, marked *M. R. U. Sterling.* One side reads *Free Coinage,* the other *Prosperity 16/1.*
Courtesy, collection Donald J. Grunder.

▲ 3/60 Here the picture of W.J. Bryan is always visible, being below the knob. The shaft is painted in red, white and blue.
Courtesy, Museum of American Political Life, Hartford.

Theodore Roosevelt
1900, 1904

▶ 3/63   For the campaign of 1904. Theodore Roosevelt with his Vice-Presidential candidate, Charles Warren Fairbanks, and the American flag as background.
Courtesy, collection Francis H. Monek.

Alton Parker
1904

▲ 3/61   The usual effigy of Roosevelt, which was made in varying sizes.
Courtesy, collection L. G.

▲ 3/62   Effigy representing Roosevelt for the 1912 election in which he lost to Woodrow Wilson.
Courtesy, collection Jim Gifford.

▲ 3/64   A cane representing Alton Parker and Henry Davis, losers to Theodore Roosevelt and Charles Fairbanks.
Courtesy, Henry Ford Museum & Greenfield Village.

William Howard Taft
1908

▲ 3/65 This effigy of Taft appears to be the only cane made linked with his campaign.
Courtesy, collection L. G.

▲ 3/66 A 1907 design for a campaign cane in which the transparent head of the candidate can be illuminated by a battery held in the shaft. A similar cane was patented in 1933.
Courtesy, U.S. Patent Office.

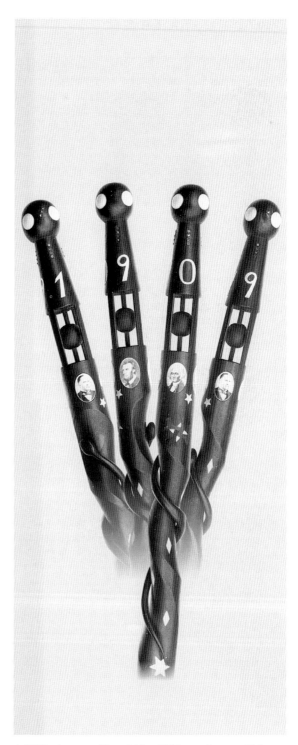

▲ 3/67 A cane with a riddle. 1909 was the year Taft was elected President, but the face below the handle is that of Bryan, wearing a bow tie and without a mustache. Perhaps the carver anticipated a Bryan victory. The other lithograph pictures represent Washington and Lincoln.
Courtesy, Collection George H. Meyer.

Warren C. Harding
1920

Herbert Hoover
1928

▲ 3/69 Three dice covered by clear celluloid with the inscription *Hoover Will Win*.
Courtesy, collection Jim Gifford.

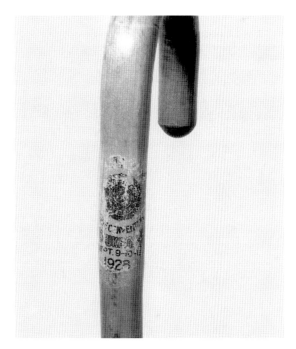

▲ 3/68 Can this be considered a campaign cane? Illustrated from the top to the bottom: President Benjamin Harrison, President Chester Arthur, President Rutherford Hayes, President Millard G. Fillmore, and finally Warren Harding. The portraits are lightly painted.
Courtesy, collection Smithsonian Institution.

▲ 3/70 On the faded paper is written: *State Convention, Sept. 9 - 10 - 11 1929 Wawkyan, Illinois*. As shown here, canes were also made for State Conventions.
Courtesy, collection Catherine Dike.

Franklin Delano Roosevelt
1932, 1936, 1940, 1944

As discussed in the Introduction, campaign canes linked with FDR are a rarity, supporters choosing not to focus on Roosevelt's handicap. (See the chapters on Presidents and on Modern Folk Art, however, for a discussion of the many hundreds of canes presented to Roosevelt by his legion of admirers.) No record has surfaced of a Roosevelt-Cox cane picturing both candidates in the manner of the McKinley-Roosevelt stick. Such a cane would be a fascinating find. There was a cane issued for the 1934 Chicago Fair, bearing the words *A Century of Progress,* with a bust of Roosevelt made from the same alloy as other 19th Century political canes.

▶ 3/71 The cane issued in 1932 bears the name of *Roosevelt* on one side and *For President* on the other, with the date *32*. Apparently it was not reissued for the 1936 and 1940 conventions. This model was also used for later Presidents.
Courtesy, collection Catherine Dike.

▲ 3/72 A six-sided cane bears the inscriptions *Pencil to be used to balance 4 years of Hoover Prosperity,and Elect Roosevelt and Garner. Let's have a New Deal.*
Courtesy, collection Jim Gifford.

▼ 3/73 A stenciled square cane with the inscriptions *Roosevelt and Garner / Vote the Entire Democratic Ticket Nov. 8.* The name of *Clark* appears on the third side. *Stark for Governor* appears on a similar cane.
Courtesy, Museum of American Political Life, Hartord.

▲ 3/74 A hand-carved inscription mentions *Pres. U.S.A. Serving Third Term.*
Courtesy, Franklin D. Roosevelt Library

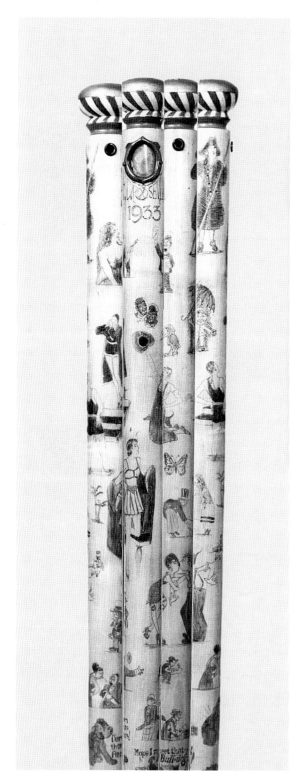

▲ 3/76   A Re-election pendant attached to a cane.
Courtesy, Museum of American Political Life, Hartford.

Alfred M. Landon
1936

▲ 3/75   An odd combination of many different people, with
the portrait of Roosevelt, his name with the year *1933*.
Courtesy, Little White House, Warm Springs, Georgia.

▲ 3/77   The American flag was attached to canes for the
1936 campaign of Landon and Knox who lost to F.D.R.
Courtesy, collection Jim Gifford.

Dwight D. Eisenhower
1952

The Uncle Sam Shop in New York City states that they issued an umbrella with *I like Ike* printed on the fabric.

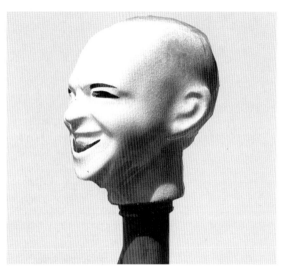

▲ 3/78 An amusing ceramic head represents President Eisenhower.
Courtesy, collection Jim Gifford.

Lyndon B. Johnson
1964

▲ 3/79 The often-seen crook handle with the inscription *Lyndon B. Johnson for President* and the year *64*.
Courtesy, collection Catherine Dike.

▼ 3/80 A Democratic campaign cane with *Walk Away With L.B.J.* on one side and on the other *Texas Yellow Pine, Temple White Co.*
Courtesy, collection Jim Gifford.

Barry M. Goldwater
1964

▲ 3/81 Two canes issued for Goldwater's campaign. He was defeated by Lyndon Johnson in 1964. The top cane is in metal, the lower one has a hollow plastic handle filled with water and floating gold flakes. The letters *H_2O* appear to assist those slow in reading the rebus.
Courtesy, collections Smithsonian Institution and Jim Gifford.

Jimmy Carter
1976

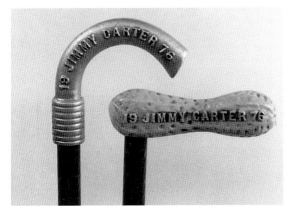

▲ 3/82   A square cane with the candidate's address: *Plains, Georgia — Home of — Jimmy Carter.*
Courtesy, collection Jim Gifford.

Unknown Candidates

▲ 3/83   Two canes bearing the name of *Jimmy Carter* and the date *1976*. Both are in metal. A similar but larger peanut was produced in plastic.
Courtesy, Museum of American Political Life, Hartford.

Gerald Ford
1976

▲ 3/84   Gerald Ford lost to Jimmy Carter in 1976. He too had his crook-handled stick, but with a small inscription below the word for *President*: *C.S.B. Outlaw 76.*
Courtesy, collection Catherine Dike.

▲ 3/85   Three unknown candidates, plainly obscure losers. Harrison has been suggested for two of the images, but there is no real resemblance between the figures.
Courtesy, collections Kurt Stein, L.G. and Jim Gifford.

Other Canes

Along with the effigy, or portrait, canes, other political motifs appear on canes. The Democratic Donkey and the Republican Elephant are common, cast in the same alloy as the effigy canes. Many canes were used to draw attention in parades. American flags in the shaft could be unrolled and waved with patriotic fervor. Mention has been made in other chapters of the torch canes, and some sticks had a trumpet as a handle. Firecrackers inserted at the ferrule allowed the marcher to make even more noise. These canes were not confined to political campaigns; they could be brought forth as well at fairs and patriotic celebrations such as the Fourth of July.

◄► 3/86 On top left and on top rigth two elephant heads. The Republican mascot is found more often than de Democratic donkey.
Courtesy, Museum of American Political Life, Hartford.

▲ 3/88 Two flags, one furled to show how the inner flag pole is attached to the knob. The Chicago Historical Society has a cane with 38 stars, which dates it from 1877. These flags were also used for "Battle Flag Day".
Courtesy, collection Francis H. Monek.

▲ 3/87 A series of crackers. The two on the right have the patriotic colors wrapped around the shaft.
Courtesy, collection Richard W.Carlson.

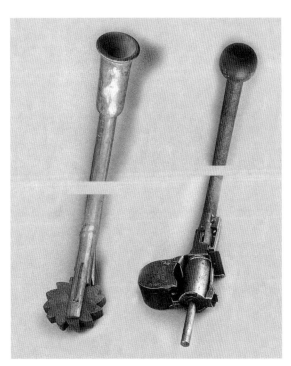

▲ 3/89 Two canes, one with a horn on top and a clacker on the bottom, the other with a cracker at the bottom. These could be used for any kind of noise-making demonstration.
Courtesy, collection Paul Weisberg.

▲ 3/90 Two tin torches. The top one would have the paper wrappings on which the pictures of both candidates would be put. The bottom one would be used just as a torch.
Courtesy, collection Francis H. Monek.

▲ 3/92 A noise-making handle which has a horn, marked on the top with *Patriotism / Protection / Prosperity* and on the side *Pat. Apld. for The Winfield Mfg. Co. Warren, Ohio.*
Courtesy, collection Francis H. Monek.

▲ 3/91 Another trumpet with the same markings as Nu. 92. These canes were made in tin.
Courtesy, collection Francis H. Monek.

▲ 3/93 Modern pewter handles made in England. Beneath the elephant one can read the words *The Grand Old Party*, and beneath the donkey, *The Party of the People.*
Courtesy, collection Francis H. Monek.

▲ 4/1 A cane rush which took place towards the end of the century at Dartmouth College.
Courtesy, Dartmouth College Library.

Canes worn in Colleges

Introduction

In Europe during the 19th century German speaking students wore canes decorated with the emblems of their student association in the same manner as they sported caps and scarves wih such designs. (Color picture). By contrast, students at the Sorbonne in Paris or at Oxford or Cambridge wore canes as the fashion dictated, but without any particular symbols or customs attached. American students adopted the German practice, and also copied the custom of incising upon their canes the names of fellow students. In certain colleges, such as Dartmouth, each student carved his own name or nickname, which produced a unique and original cane but one with an untidy jumble of styles! Sometimes the names were chiselled by professional carvers, which certainly gave a more homogenous result. The carving might be tinted with the color of the owner's Hall, and some of the canes were decorated with colored ribbons.

A purely American custom practiced in most colleges, was the "Cane Rush" or the "Cane Spree". Sophomores wore tall hats and bamboo canes, and considered such dress a privilege of upper-classmen. Students generally came from rural areas, and Freshmen often wished to copy their sophisticated campus elders and gain status by wearing a stick. Upper-classmen would try to grab the bamboo canes from the younger boys, and real battles could result. As the years passed, more students came from urban areas where they and their fathers were accustomed to wearing elegant hats and sticks at home. There was thus no longer a reason to battle over possession of canes at college. Canes continued to be worn as the dictates of fashion demanded, but the "Cane Spree" was transformed into a symbolical battle of two students tussling over a large cane. The tradition died out gradually, either at the end of the 19th century (Rutgers) or between the two World Wars (Bucknell, Michigan, and Princeton). Dartmouth's senior cane tradition ebbed out as late as the 1960s. Other colleges (Massachusetts, Virginia, and Gettysburg) have no records of such student battles over sticks, but their undergraduates certainly wore canes.

Published in an English newspaper of the time, was an article concerning the United States: *A decided novelty, understood to be controlled entirely by Folmer, Clogg & Co., of New York, is the football cane.*

Fastened to the stick is a balloon-like apparatus which, when expanded by means of umbrella ribs, assumes the shape of a regulation football. It may be closed in the same manner as an umbrella. The footballs are made in the colors of Harvard, Yale, Princeton and the University of Pennsylvania, either with or without the initials of the college. It is expected that there will be very large demand for them among the youth of sporting proclivities; particularly as they are cheap enough to be broken in the exuberance of enthusiasm following the victory of one's favorite team.

FRESHMEN!

STOP! READ! OBEY!

You Must NOT

Wear monograms or numerals upon your caps

Smoke on the campus

Carry canes upon the campus

Walk upon the "Res." after 9 P.M

You MUST give preference to upper-class men

Signed

SOPHOMORES

▲ 4/2 A poster that was displayed for the Freshmen on campus.
Courtesy, Tufts University Library.

▲ 4/3 A high school cane marked with various names.
Courtesy, collection Richard W. Carlson.

◄ 4/4 An unknown fraternity symbol. The triangular shaft
has the letters *P. I. O.* set below the handle.
Courtesy, collection L.G

▲ 4/7 The head of a bull adorns this college cane, the shaft
being covered with names. The fraternity is *Sigma Phi
Epsilon.* The carving resembles the "Indian" canes of
Dartmouth.
Courtesy, collection Henri and Nancy Taron.

▲ 4/5 Two college canes: one marked *Hannemann Medical
College 1877* with personalized signatures; the other having
many marks including Hebrew letters. The intertwined initials
B / C, and *S* could be either the name of a college or the ini-
tials of the owner.
Courtesy, collection Lewis A. Nassikas.

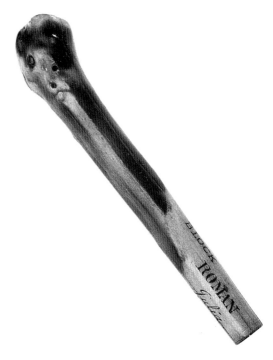

◄ 4/6 A medical cane with names incised and dated 1883
to 1886. The illustration is of a typical doctor with his bag.
Courtesy, Tradewinds Auctions, H. Taron, Manager.

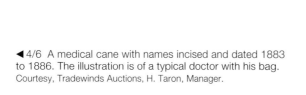

▲ 4/8 This handle shows how a dealer would illustrate the
variety of character styles offered for proposed carving on a
cane.
Courtesy, collection John H. Sterne.

Brown University,
Providence, Rhode Island

An example of how Cane Sprees could degenerate, a passage in "Memories of Brown" by Edward S. Marsh reads: *A cane rush between the Freshmen and Sophomores was then an established institution. One Saturday evening, late in the fall of 1876, the class of 1880 appeared on the back campus stripped for the fray with a cane. Since few of the Sophomores were on hand that evening, no attempt was made to deprive the Freshmen of their precious stick. After parading the campus for a time, they departed unmolested with derisive yells and groans for the Sophomores, and triumphant cheers for themselves. They had the cane sawed into small transverse sections, and appeared Monday morning at chapel wearing these as pins, in token of the bloodless victory. The Sophomores reacted to this sight as the traditional red flag acts upon an inflamed bull. After leaving the chapel, a Freshman adorned with one of the obnoxious pins was seized by a Sophomore. Reinforcements rallied to the aid of each. Soon practically the entire strength of both classes was enlisted, and the melee became general. By all the gods of misrule, that was a battle royal. Clothing was ripped, torn, and demolished.*

▲ 4/10 A handle with letters reading *Class of 1861*.
Courtesy, Brown University Library.

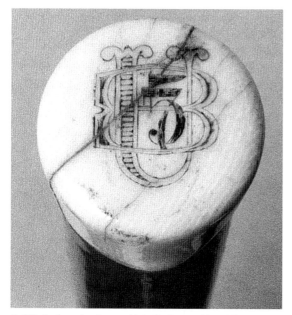

▲ 4/9 An ivory knob on which the letters *U* and *B* are intertwined with numbers.
Courtesy, Brown University Library.

▲ 4/11 Three Brown students each wearing a cane. Norman S. Dike Sr. stands on the right.
Courtesy, collection Anthony R. Dike.

Bucknell University,

Lewisburg, Pennsylvania

The Freshman-Sophomore Class Scrap began in the 1870's and the ritual lasted until about 1949 when it was reorganized into a tug-of-war. In an 1897 "History of the University," is written: *We lined up ... to salute the arrival of the "Innocents Abroad"; but the Freshmen ... made a rush for the canes we were carelessly holding in our hands. A short, though intense, scrap ensued.*

Columbia University,

New York, New York

The Brooklyn Museum possesses a cane bearing the date '78 which was donated by the daughter of a Columbia University graduate.

Cornell University,

Ithaca, New York

▼ 4/12 Besides the usual canes carved with student names, the University Archives has one with 28 names, each with its respective year from 1871 to 1899. We can read *Blood 88,* the sobriquet of *Charles Hazen,* and *Shaler 84*, of *Ira Alexander,* who was a bachelor of Civil Engineering. One wonders whether these names referred to the particular BMOC (Big Man on Campus) of his year, who in turn passed the cane on to his successor. (See Yale University).
Courtesy, Cornell University Library.

Dartmouth College,

Hanover, New Hampshire

The spirit of "Cane Rush" is well illustrated by the text found in the "Dartmouth Sketches of the *class* of 1863*: When we were Freshmen the contest for carrying canes was very sharp and lasted for quite a while, and some of our canes were saved for future use, but it was a hard-fought battle. When we were Sophomores the class of '64 tried to carry canes and a tremendous contest ensued. Our scouts saw four or five Freshmen strutting up the walk with canes and tall hats; as they drew near, our scouts shouted at the top of their voice "Cane rush! '63 to the front"! It was a grand battle, and did not end till every cane was captured or broken and the tall hats were pulverized.*

The Cane Rush of 1882 inspired the following doggerel:
A tear was in the Freshman's eye,
His little heart was filled with pain,
In vain he sued the cruel Soph
To please let him carry a cane.

Dartmouth is one of the few colleges which issued a cane with a distinctive handle, in this case the shape of an Indian head, the college symbol. For the students of the medical school, there was an accurate representation of a human skull.

Charles Dudley, a local merchant and a member of the Class of '02, sold the Indian head cane in his store after patenting the design in 1896. In 1930 Dean Neiglinger designed a more modern head, with the Indian sporting a Mohawk haircut. This cane was sold until 1950, when Dudley's original design was restored. These canes were made at a cane and umbrella factory, "Fulmer, Clogg & Co.", in Lancaster, Pennsylvania.

In recent years sensitivity towards Native Americans resulted in a new design for a "senior" cane. In 1976 a model was offered featuring a hand-carved bust of Rev. Eleazar Wheelock (1711- 1779). Founder and first President of Dartmouth College, he did much to educate the Indians.

▲ 4/13 A pre-Indian cane, in simple briar, with the name of the College and '94, signed by all the students.
Courtesy, collection Neils MacKenna.

▲ 4/15 In a "Class Souvenir of 1885" we find seven "gladiators" taken in *Rush Costume,* bodies and arms greased, hands resined.
Courtesy, Dartmouth College Library.

▲ 4/14 Four hand-carved heads: two Indians with different expressions, a bust of Wheelock, and an Indian with a Mohawk haircut. Courtesy, Dartmouth College Library.

Gettysburg College,
Gettysburg, Pennsylvania

▲ 4/16 Although student battles were known, nothing in the archives indicates whether these were cane fights. Here the tip of a silver ornament is engraved with the name of the College and *99*.
Courtesy, Gettysburg College Library.

Harvard University,
Cambridge, Massaschusetts

Although we have already noted references to "football" canes decorated with the colors of Harvard, the college archives have no records of Harvard University canes, which seems odd.

▲ 4/17 A cane marked on a silver band *Groce Blanchard, Harvard, Ma., 8 Mo. 25, 1849.*
Courtesy, Ohio Historical Society.

M.I.T.,
Boston, Massachusetts

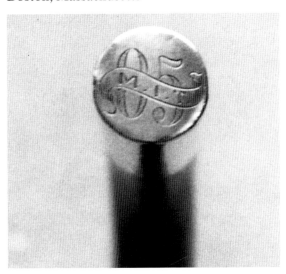

▲ 4/18 A silver tip with the letters *M.I.T.* engraved on the front, together with the year *05*.
Courtesy, collection Henry and Nancy Taron.

Lafayette College,
Easton, Pennsylvania

▲ 4/19 The end of the silver tip bears the words *Lafayette* and *1900*. Lafayette was founded in 1826 as a college for Presbyterian men.
Courtesy, collection L.G.

▲ 4/20 A *Cane Rush,* the fighters surrounded by all the students.
Courtesy, Lafayette College Library.

University of Maine,
Orono, Maine

▲ 4/21 A simple crook handle with the band bearing the letter *M* and the date, *26*.
Courtesy, collection Francis H. Monek.

University of Massachusetts,
Amherst, Massachusetts

Professor Joseph L. Hills wrote an unpublished history of Vermont University in the 1940's: *The annual cane rush between the two lower classes has been held for many decades and still is in operation but in a very different form than in its earlier days. How far back into the past its observance goes the writer cannot say. It was the custom in his own undergraduate days at both colleges in Amherst in the late 1870's. It was not a single affair held early in the fall, but ran through the year, Freshmen attempting to carry canes and Sophomores tearing them from Freshmen's hands whenever and wherever found. He had, for many years, a watch chain constructed of segments of a dozen stout canes wrested by his sturdier classmates from Freshmen, the canes being sawed into tiny fragments and distributed.*

The Archives of the University have pictures of all the late 19th century graduation classes. In every one, the students wear canes.

▲ 4/22 The '97 group at Amherst, each student wearing a cane. What is interesting in this picture is that each cane bears a bow-ribbon, no doubt representing the fraternities. In other universities, long ribbons would hang from below the handle.
Courtesy, Library of the University of Massachusetts.

▲ 4/23 A silver knob engraved with the words *Amherst College, class of 1858.* On both sides are representations of the College buildings. Amherst College (and today a University) is in Amherst, but was separated from the Massachusetts University.
Courtesy, private collection, Boston.

University of Michigan,

Ann Arbor, Michigan

At the University of Michigan in the early 1850's, a senior group attended a speech given by an abolitionist. When protests arose, they restrained the crowd by raising their canes. This may have been the origin of Senior Cane Day, one of Ann Arbor's traditions, but no one can say so with certainty.

A decade later *the Civil War had torn a nation in two, and Michigan's seniors were drilling on the campus grass. Divided into two corps, the Class of '61 marched and countermarched. There were no arms for the drilling Seniors, so each one carried a cane at his shoulder.*

Senior canes go back into the shade of forgotten days. Once or twice the custom has lapsed but as long ago as anyone remembers, one special spring Sunday has seen the graduating class prom-enading in the sunshine with their new sticks and their best girls.

In the 1870's and 1880's class caps were all the rage. A blue university cap was adopted with a silver band featuring the numeral of the class year. Later, each class had its own headgear, with black silk hats for the senior medical students and straw derbies for senior law students. A very popular accessory was the carved "autographed" cane worn in that same era. It had a large *M* and the name of the owner carved on it. Later, other classes had silver bands on which the names of friends were added.

The Senior cane tradition, first mentioned in 1858, continued until the custom began to go out of fashion at the end of the sophisticated 1920's. Nevertheless, in 1935, *The Cane Sunday* was still celebrated. A senior attending said: *A senior cane is a mark of distinction, a privilege, and the foundation of a ripe old memory. I would not be without one.*

▲ 4/24 The '79 class of Michigan University with each student wearing a cane and a tall silk hat.
Courtesy, Library of the University of Michigan.

University of New Hampshire,
Durham, New Hampshire

College of Ohio,
Athens, Ohio

▲ 4/27 A souvenir cane made in wood from a building which had been erected in 1819 and torn down in 1897. The College of Ohio was to become the Ohio University.
Courtesy, collection L.G.

The University of Oklahoma,
Stillwater, Oklahoma

▲ 4/25 The double profile of "The Old Man of the Mountain," which is the New Hampshire State symbol. The shaft is engraved with students' names, indicating it could have come either from the University or New Hampshire College. The head was carved by the same hand who made the Dartmouth "Indian" canes.
Courtesy, collection Henry and Nancy Taron.

The University of North Carolina,
Chapel Hill, North Carolina

▲ 4/26 A shaft covered with the twenty-two names of the students of the *U.N.C. Class.1887* which is marked in the middle of the cane.
Courtesy, Library of the University of North Carolina.

▲ 4/28 Another cane from a college which later became a University. Besides the name of the owner, it is marked *O.A.M.C.* (Oklahoma Agricultural and Mechanical College) and / *B.S. - 1929.* Apparently the cane was presented to graduates by a fraternity.
Courtesy, Oklahoma Historical Society.

The University of Pennsylvania,
Philadelphia, Pennsylvania

Beginning in 1865, a spoon was presented annually to the most popular member of a class, and a (very large) bowl to the second most popular. The runner-up would be put in the bowl, and carried ceremonially around campus. About 1890, a cane and a spade were added to the objects given on Class Day to honor the Senior students, being given to the third and fourth most popular students respectively. The cane was a relic of the *Cane Fights* of earlier days, and the spade was used to plant the *Class Ivy* on *Class Hey Day.* On the same day the Junior *Cane March* was held. Wearing straw hats and canes, the Juniors marched though the campus, met the Seniors, and exchanged class colors. The canes were of cheap bamboo. The tradition continues today.

UNIVERSITY of PENNSYLVANIA   **PLEASE POST**

HEY DAY-1967

THURSDAY, APRIL 20th

CALENDAR

3:30 P. M.

JUNIOR CANE MARCH: Wearing straw skimmer hats and carrying canes, the members of the Men's Junior Class meet at the junior balcony atop McClelland Hall in the men's dormitories and joined by the Dean's march to Irvine Auditorium where Men's HEY DAY ceremonies take place.

4:00 P. M.

MEN'S HEY DAY CEREMONIES: All undergraduate men meet at Irvine Auditorium where the traditional assembly takes place. Here elections to the honorary societies are made public. Senior Class honor men are presented with their awards: the spoon, bowl, cane, and spade. The retiring Senior Class president then transfers to the incoming president a silk academic gown which has been worn since 1887.

▲ 4/30 Part of the program for the *Hey Day*, held in 1967.
Courtesy, Archives of the University of Pennsylvania.

▲ 4/29 A senior cane with the emblems of the University, surrounding the various subjects in which the students could major.
Courtesy, collection L.G.

▲ 4/31 On the *Class Hey Day*, the 1939 Senior Honor Awards.
Courtesy, Archives of the University of Pennsylvania.

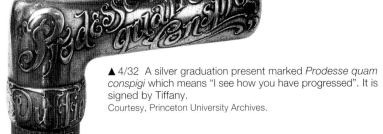

▲ 4/32 A silver graduation present marked *Prodesse quam conspigi* which means "I see how you have progressed". It is signed by Tiffany.
Courtesy, Princeton University Archives.

Princeton University,
Princeton, New Jersey

Classroom disturbances were known as sprees, and in the "Princeton Alumni Weekly" of March 8, 1911 we read the *History of the Cane Spree*: *This was an institution whose roots reach backward almost fifty years into the period when a cane was as much the emblem of a collegian as a scepter is the insignia of a king. So fond were the Princetonians of their sticks in the bellicose days of the '60's, that they laboriously carved into them the autographs of their classmates, tinting each name with the color of the owner's Hall.*

The article also tells how the Sophomores issued a proclamation formally forbidding the class of 1873 to carry canes. Battles raged, and Cane Spreeing became a sport practiced each winter, with its own technical terms. In 1878, it was suggested that Cane Spreeing should become an orderly, man-to-man contest, and by 1881 it had become the custom for each group to select a champion to represent it in the fight over one heavy stick. The melee was always exciting and the outcome unpredictable, bringing fame to the Princeton Cane Spree.

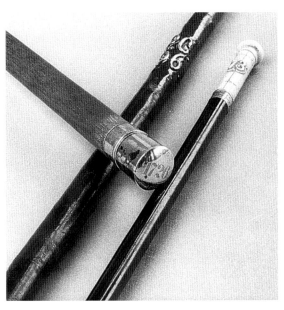

▲ 4/34 Three elegant senior canes. One has a long ivory knob marked '78; another has silver letters and numbers applied to the dark shaft. The silver knob cane bears the date of *1726*, a commemoration of the *Log College*, the predecessor of Princeton.
Courtesy, Princeton University Archives.

▲ 4/33 Central part of a cane used for the *69th Annual Cane Spree* which took part in 1935. There were three classes of fighters, this cane being fought for by the Middleweight.
Courtesy, Princeton University Archives.

▲ 4/35 This cane is marked *Princeton College of N.J.* (before becoming a University)
Courtesy, Princeton University Archives.

▲ 4/36 Princeton's Cane Spree in which everyone is a participant!
Courtesy, Princeton University Archives.

▲ 4/38 Princeton, like many other Universities, had pendants hanging from small canes. The pendants were usually used at football games.
Courtesy, Princeton University Archives.

The University of Rutgers,
New Brunswick, New Jersey

In Richard McCormick's "A Bicentennial History", he states: *The Sophomores assumed the role of instilling in the Freshmen a due sense of their utter worthlessness, and class rushes of all sorts, but most especially the Cane Rush, proved excuses for organized mayhem. The Sophomores exhibition produced such wild disorders that it was discontinued as a public exercise by the faculty in 1882.*

▲ 4/37 A Cane Spree in which students watch the two fighters.
Courtesy, Princeton University Archives.

▲ 4/39 A silver knob marked *Rutgers, class of 90*.
Courtesy, collection Mark Neider.

Stanford University,
Palo Alto, California

The "Daily Palo Alto" of May 6, 1895, prints: *It is suggested that the two classes inaugurate the custom of an annual Cane Presentation. The cane itself, the emblem of Sophomore dignity, could be a very large and handsome stick with a plate of some kind telling what it is. The date and the names of the Presidents should be carved on the stick each year, so that in time the stick would carry a long list of names.* This custom seems not to have lasted after the year 1907.

▲ 4/40 Two Stanford canes, one bears the letters *STA....* and the year *1903*. The other has only the letter *S* linking the date *2*.
Courtesy, Stanford University Museum of Art.

The University of Tennessee,
Knoxville, Tennessee

In this University, canes were worn, but no inscriptions were marked on them. Hazing had been strictly forbidden. "The University of Tennessee Magazine" mentions: *While hazing might be a relatively mild type of exercise, the bone-jarring Cane Rush was altogether different. A broken arm or two and countless black eyes usually accompanied each year's event. A representative from the Freshmen class and one from the Sophomore class met in the center of the parade field and gripped a cane between them - usually a hickory hoe handle since a broom stick could not take the strain. Each class lined up behind its representative, and at a signal all rushed forward to win possession of the cane. In order to win, one side had to get the cane inside the entrance of Humes Hall. The rush divided into two parts. Phase one was decided when one side had gotten full possession of the cane. After this occurred, both groups retired to the entrance of the Humes Hall for a last-ditch stand to prevent or aid the delivery of the cane into the Hall. After the 1909 event, the faculty decided that the contest was too rough to be continued.*

The Tufts University,
Medford, Massachusetts

"The Tuftonian" V.8, No.2, dated November 1881, mentions: Three Freshmen appeared in chapel one morning with canes, and it seemed to have the same effect on the upper-classmen that a red rag has on a bull. After chapel, members of '82 and '83 made the onset, and a short and sharp conflict ensued. No blood was spilt and the canes were speedily demolished.... We doubt if any college in the land can match this rush, in which Sophomores fought with Freshmen to vindicate the divine right of a Freshman to carry a cane.

We can see, under the picture 4/2, what the Freshmen could read on campus!

University of Vermont,
Burlington, Vermont

▲ 4/41 Probably a cane from the University of Vermont, representing Ira Allen, early Vermont statesman and founder of the University. It bears the figure *04*. The wood carving looks like the "Indian" canes of Dartmouth.
Courtesy, collection L.G.

▲ 4/42 Head of Lafayette carved for the 1901 class. Lafayette had laid the cornerstone of the University's oldest existing building in 1825.
Courtesy, University of Vermont Library.

Professor Joseph L. Hills wrote an unpublished history of the University in the 1940s in which we read: *As conducted at UVM in the 1880's the scrap was held over a single stout cane or cudgel. In 1888 ... shirts were ripped, suspenders stretched, hair torn, dirt and grass spat out.* The Professor further mentions that there was always a physician in attendance. At a faculty meeting in 1891, a statement was issued: *The cane rush which usually takes place between the Sophomore and Freshman classes is herewith prohibited. By order of the faculty.* By 1892 commercialism entered the scene. A local haberdashery, convinced that it paid to advertise, promised to furnish canes gratis to the student body, and did so for many years.

University of Virginia,
Charlottesville, Virginia

Though no pictures exist of canes having been worn by the students, in "Student Life at UVA" (1825-1861), there is the description of their Cane Spree: *Fighting, not playful wrestling or rowdy encounters between massed college classes, but serious fighting between students using guns, knives, canes, rocks and fists was a common and regular occurrence throughout the antebellum period.*

United States Military Academy,
West Point, New York

▼ 4/43   West Point Cadet cane, worn by Cadet Albert S. Cummins, Class of 1873. This date is found on one of the tassels.
Courtesy, Museum United State Military Academy.

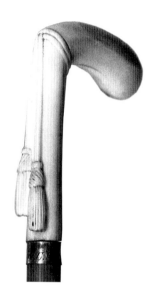

United States Naval Academy,
Annapolis, Maryland

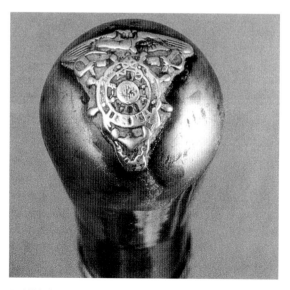

▲ 4/44 A cane that was a class favor in 1938 at a Ring Dance.
Courtesy, Museum United States Naval Academy.

Wisconsin University,
Madison City, Wisconsin

The State Historical Society of Wisconsin has two canes marked *U.W.*, the insignia of their University. Photographs were unobtainable.

Yale University,
New Haven, Connecticut

Yale University took a different approach to the matter of "Cane Rush". In the privately printed booklet "Out of Yale's Past" by Louis Havemeyer, (1960) it can be read: *At the end of the 18th century the ill feeling between the college men and the "townies" seems to have been traditional. The custom of "bullyism" arose from this feud. The leader of the oystermen and sailors used a big club made from an oak limb with a gnarled excrescence on the end. The college men took this from him and bore it off as a trophy to be called, from then on, the "Bully Club".*

To protect themselves against the drunken rowdies who attacked them whenever possible, the students organized a defense committee in each class. They chose as their leader their largest and most muscular man who was called "The Bully". Each class gave their "Bully" a goldheaded cane. But the senior Major "Bully" was THE college "Bully" and had the job of keeping THE "Bully Club". Before the end of the college year he transferred the Club to his successor in the junior class. In 1840, the faculty passed a vote that there should be no class officers and Bullyism was dead.

In the "Four Years at Yale" by a Graduate of '69, published by Charles C. Chatfield & Co., New Haven, Connecticut, 1871, it states: *That at Yale, they mention "bangers" for canes or clubs. Freshmen and Sophomores struggle and twist together, roll each other in the mud and slush, to lose and regain the all important banger. Banger Rushes are of rather intermittent character, happening off and on for the rest of the term. When a solitary Fresh, carelessly swinging his banger, is pounced upon by several Sophs, and cannot escape by flight, he clings to the sacred cane and shouts with all his might the numeral of his class.*

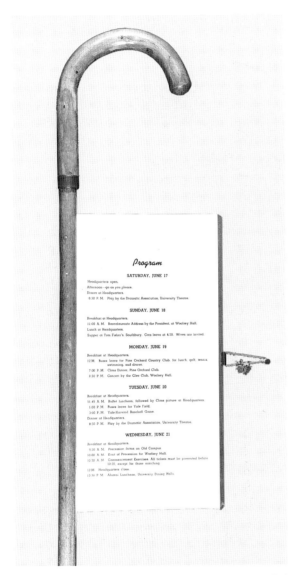

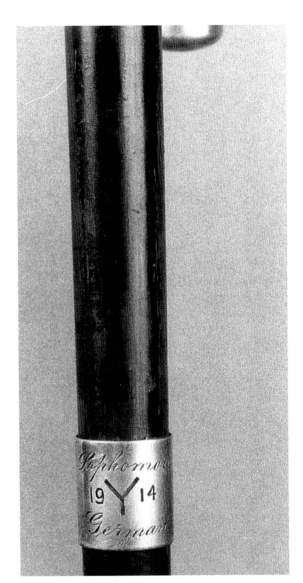

▲ 4/45 The program for the 1899 reunion, which is pulled out of the shaft and on which the various celebrations can be read. Yale University also possesses an ivory knob cane marked *G. & S.* with *Yale* and the name of the owner on the metal band. *F.Bacon 1838, L.F.*
Courtesy, Yale University Library.

▲ 4/46 A simple crook handle which bears on its metal band the words *Sophomores 1914* and the letter *Y,* and *German.*
Courtesy, collection Catherine Dike.

▶ 4/47 A Yale "Bully Club" passed on to the top student year after year.
Courtesy, Yale University Library.

As evidenced by these pictures, Cane Rushes and collegiate canes in general were primarily found in the Northern states. This may possibly be ascribed to a greater German influence in that part of the nation.

In the Southern and Western states, virtually no canes were found at the University of Alabama, Tuscaloosa; the Louisiania State University, Baton Rouge; the University of California, Los Angeles; Duke University, Durham, North Carolina; the University of Florida, Gainesville and the University of North Texas, Denton.

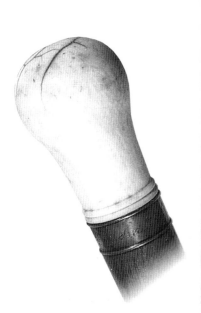

▲ 5/1 The advertisement offering canes and boxes made in the pine under which Jane McCrea was killed in 1777. The tree died in 1849 and the cane to the left was made in it's wood. Samuel Y. Edgerton, Jr., who wrote *The Murder of Jane McCrea,* mentions *It had been computed that enough canes and boxes were sold to have consumed a whole forest of pine trees!*
Courtesy, Fort Edward Historical Association.

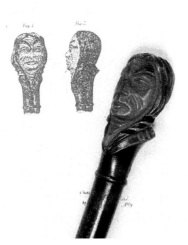

▲ a) Dartmouth's "Indian" cane, its shaft carved by the hands of many different students, each with his own style. It is pictured alongside the patent registered in 1912.
Courtesy, collection Catherine Dike.

▼ b) A group of Princeton student canes, which were all created by professional carvers.
Courtesy, Princeton University Archives.

▲ c) A group of German student's canes, some with an ivory top showing the Fraternity to which the student belonged, the others, in wood, carved with the names of fellow students.
Courtesy, Zofingue Museum, Aarau, Switzerland.

▶ d) A fraternity cane which insignia bears the letter *U.P.* and an up side down *V,* on a silver tip of the handle.
Courtesy, collection L.G.

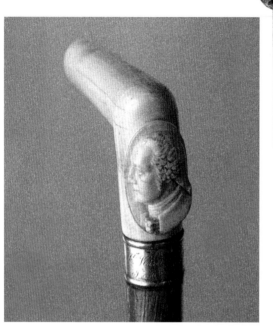

▲ a) The profile of George Washington adorns the front of this ivory handle. The ring is marked *Cut at Mt. Vernon, Oct. 8th, 1858. J.A.B.*
Courtesy, collection Norman Flayderman.

◀ b) A handle made of ivory or ivory composition. The American eagle uses the Flag to protect its young in the nest from a snake which is twining up the shaft. The Federal shield completes this patriotic theme. The back bears the inscription *Patented 1862*. Similar canes are found in other materials.
Courtesy, collection Smithsonian Institution.

▲ d) Uncle Sam carved into wood from a beam taken from the White House, burned by the British in 1812.
Courtesy, Massachusetts Historical Society.

◀ e) A shaft woven in horse hair which has been tinted with the patriotic colors of the American flag.
Courtesy, private collection, Boston.

▼ c)   Shaft made from the original timber of Independence Hall in Philadelphia, salvaged at the time of the 1855 renovation work.
Courtesy, collection Anthony R. Dike.

Patriotic Canes

Introduction

It is difficult to choose which canes should be assigned to this chapter. Some are undoubtedly patriotic, but others could belong to the chapter on Presidents, and still others might more readily be classified as being linked to sporting events, or to folk art!

In the chapter on American wars, we will see examples of shafts made from wood taken from military buildings or ships. Under the general heading of Patriotic canes are those made from wood equally historical but with a less belligerent association. Hundreds of canes spring from the Constitution Hall in Philadelphia, many of which survive today and can be found in museums and historical societies. They were made from wood taken from the building each time the Hall underwent repair. One such cane was given by the Publisher of the "Public Ledger" in Philadelphia to Prince Otto von Bismark who replied with thanks: *Dear Sir, You have had the goodness to send me, as support of my old days, a cane made from the tower from whose heights, ninety-nine years ago, the bell was rung for the first time in honor of that great Commonwealth, whose ship bells now sound their full and welcome tongues in all harbors of the world.*

Many canes were made from materials taken from early buildings. The Peabody and Essex Museum in Salem, Massachusetts, has one made of timber from the *Indian House* in Deerfield, Massachusetts, which escaped the destruction of the remainder of the town by the French and Indians in February 1704. On the band is an inscription and an illustration of the house, which was later destroyed.

Another Historical Society has a cane stamped *Old Middle Dutch Church, New York, 1726*, and the Bostonian Historical Society has one stamped *The Second Church, in Hannover Street, Boston.* The Second Church was built in 1729 and torn down in 1844. The Chicago Historical Society has a cane made from wood of the *First Methodist Church* built in the United States in 1764. These are just a few examples of the many canes which were made from 18th century buildings which were demolished during the following two centuries.

Many other buildings can be cited which became a source of canes. One handle was made from the bell of the City Hall of Chicago which tolled the alarm on October 9, 1871, when the town was ravaged by fire. A cane with a gold knob is marked: *From log found during excavations for lower lock, 64 feet underground. C.Z. (for Canal zone), 1910.* Thirty-six canes were made from the timber of the Wabash - Erie Canal, which was built in 1850 and demolished in 1939.

A white oak tree in Hartford, Connecticut, was nearly 1,000 years old and had a trunk nearly seven feet (2 metres) in diameter. It bore the name *Charter Oak,* as the Connecticut colonial charter was said to have been hidden in the trunk in 1687. When it fell in 1856, numerous objects, including canes, were made from its wood.

▶ 5/3 A gold-gloved hand holding a shaft on which is found the inscriptions: *Presented to A.V. Dike Esq. of Providence R.I. by a friend in Philadelphia. This cane is a portion of the original Independence Hall in the city of Phila. Proclaim Liberty throughout all the Land and unto all the Inhabitants thereof.* A medallion imbedded in the shaft is carved with a representation of the Liberty Bell and the date *1776*. Two other inscriptions read *Camden* and *From Father*. Judging by the dates, the cane was made at the time of the 1855 repairs.
Courtesy, collection Anthony R. Dike.

▲ 5/2 Porcelain base, covered by silver decoration.
Courtesy, collection Esbola.

▲ 5/4 A group of American eagle heads.
Courtesy, collection Paul Weisberg.

Certainly canes were linked with George Washington. Many were made from wood grown at Mount Vernon. The Boston Society has a cane marked *Wood of the Bier taken from the Tomb of Gen. Geo. Washington.* But the canes associated with Washington are nothing compared to the ones devoted to Abraham Lincoln. Of these, some were of wood growing by his birthplace; others from the log cabin in which he was born; several from a tree which grew on the spot where he had lived; from the furnishings of his home in Springfield, Illinois; from the benches where he first practiced law; from his farm in Hodgenville, Kentucky; from part of the log cabin north of Hamilton, Illinois where he spent a night during the Lincoln - Douglas debates; from a tree under which the Lincoln - Douglas debates took place; and from the floor beneath the tables used by President Lincoln and his cabinet. This list does not include the dozens, perhaps hundreds, of canes purportedly made from the rails he split in his youth!

▲ 5/5 One of the numerous canes related to President Lincoln. The knob bears the inscription: *From the log cabin built by A. Lincoln in Macon Co. Illinois. 1830*. On the top is inscribed *Presented James F. Henderson by his sons Charles and Wilbur, 1865*.
Courtesy,collection Francis H. Monek.

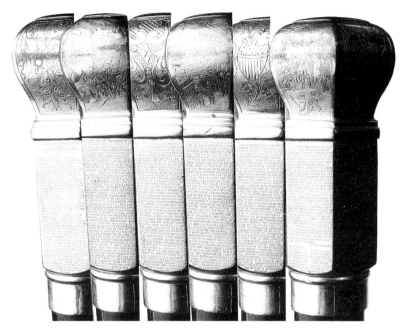

▲ 5/7 At a period when miniaturization was in vogue, this gilded handle had the Declaration of Independence written out completely. The top part of the six sections is decorated with scenes of the Landing of Christopher Columbus, his encounter with the Indians, the Boston Tea Party and the American shield.

    The Essex Insitute in Salem has a cane with a micro image of the Signing of the Declaration of Independence.
Courtesy, collection Paul Weisberg.

▲ 5/6 The details of this cane are carved on the shaft. Lincoln is standing on top, with a kneeling man saluting him. Below the latter one can read *Lincoln*. Further down the shaft a horseman stands on a shield which reads *Gen. Grant, Richmond*.
Courtesy, collection George H. Meyer.

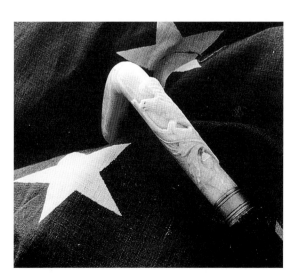

▲ 5/8 The American eagle is often represented on the foreground of an ivory handle.
Courtesy, collection Kurt Stein.

▲ 5/9 Made by the same artist, three handles were carved from the wood of the Charter Oak, with two Indians on each side and the Tree in the middle. On one of the bands can be read *Charter granted May 11,1662. Tree felled August 21st, 1856.*

The Connecticut Historical Society has nearly 20 canes made from the Charter Oak.

Courtesy, Connecticut Historical Society.

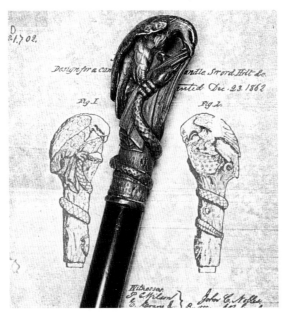

▲ 5/10 Metal handle showing an American eagle covering its young with the American flag to protect them from a snake which encircles the shaft. In the background the hand-drawn design is dated 1862. This handle was made in various sizes, some bearing on the collar the words *Death to the Traitors.* The model in the Smithsonian Institution is made of ivory and painted. It is also engraved with the date of the patent. (Color picture).

Courtesy, collection Catherine Dike.

▲ 5/11 A root carved with Revolutionary images: soldiers, snakes, animals and Masonic symbols. George Washington stands before the inscription *General George Washington the cause of Liberty.* It is believed to have been carved at the time of the Revolution.

Courtesy, collection Thomas Wilson.

▶ 5/12 A cane made from wood of the United States Man of War *Minnesota*. It bears 60 numbers, each corresponding to a piece of wood embedded in the shaft (histories below). It was made by R. L. Reed, assisted by various patriotic and historical Associations who sent him the wood or stone, and was presented to the Grand Army of the Republic of Minnesota in 1904.

1 Rock from Plymouth Ledge.

2 Elm under which Governor Winthrop convened court in 1630, at Charlestown, Massachusetts.

3 Witch elm standing on Boston Common.

4 Wood from tower built in Lexington in 1700, which held the bell rung on April 19,1775.

5 Wood from the home of Thomas Fletcher, a soldier in the French War.

6 Wood from the old Hancock House, Boston, Massachusetts.

7 Wood from the pear tree which was planted in 1635 by Simon and Gregory Stone.

8 Wood from the Wayside Inn, Sudbury, Massachusetts.

9 Wood from the Walker Garrison, Sudbury, Massachusetts, at the time of King Philip's War in 1675.

10 Wood from tree standing in Lexington, Massachusetts where the first blood was shed in the Revolution on April 19,1775.

11 Wood from the home of Captain James Barrett, in Concord, Massachusetts. 1775.

12 Wood from the old Provincial Church at Concord, where the Provincial Congress was held October, 1774. The church burned down in 1900.

13 Wood from the home of Reverend William Emerson, Concord, Massachusetts.

14 Wood from the Clarke House, Lexington, where Hancock and Adams were hiding on April 19, 1775.

15 Wood from Old North Bridge, Concord, Massachusetts, where Captain Isaac Davis of Acton was killed April 19, 1775.

16 Wood from The Old South Church, Boston, where participants in the Boston Tea Party met.

17 Wood from The Old North Church, Boston, where the lantern was hung to warn the approach of the English on the Charlestown shore on April 18, 1775.

18 Wood from The Old Tea House, Boston, Massachusetts.

19 Wood from the Old Pew, Townsend, Massachusetts.

20 Wood from the house of John Stark, hero of the battles of Bunker Hill and Bennington.

21 Wood from the home of Colonel William Prescott of Pepperell. He was a hero of Bunker Hill.

22 Wood from the home of Asa Pollard, Billerica, Massachusetts. Pollard was the first man killed in the battle of Bunker Hill.

23 Wood from Washington Elm, Cambridge, Massachusetts, under which Washington stood when he reviewed the American Army, July 3, 1775.

24 Wood from the tree under which General Joseph Warren fell at Bunker Hill.

25 Piece of the tomb of George Washington,

26 Wood from Eliott's Oak, Natick, Massachusetts under which Eliott is supposed to have preached to the Indians in 1651.

27 Wood from the apple tree which grew on the spot where Captain Davis was killed in 1775.

28 Wood from the National Exhibition, Atlanta, Georgia.

29 Wood from the Old Wright Tavern, Concord, Massachusetts.

30 Wood of the flagstaff bearing one of the flags used by the Sons of the American Revolution in marking the soldier's grave in 1893.

31 Wood from the Old Tremont House, Boston, where the officers of the Sixth Regiment were entertained on their return from Baltimore, August 18, 1861.

32 Wood from the White House.

33 Wood from the Massachusetts State House.

34 Wood from Dismal Swamp, Virginia.

35 Wood from Libby Prison.

36 Wood from Suffolk, Virginia.

37 Wood from the battlefield, at Winchester, Virginia.

38 Wood from the battlefield at Gettysburg, Pennsylvania.

39 Wood from the battlefield at Petersburg, Virginia.

40 Wood from the battlefield at Look Out Mountain.

41 An acorn growing near the grave of 2,200 unknown soldiers at Arlington Soldiers National Cemetery, Washington, D.C.

42 Wood from the platform built at the inauguration of President Harrison.

43 Wood from a tree under which General Sedgwick died, Spotsylvania.

44 Wood from a tree shading the soldiers' monument at Central Park, Manchester, New Hampshire.

45 Wood from a tree planted by General Grant when visiting Lexington, Massachusetts in 1875.

46 Wood from the old French ship sunk by the British in 1759 at Louisburg.

47 Wood from *Old Somerset* which burnt in Charlestown, June 17, 1775.

48 Wood from the old *Kearsarge*.

49 Wood from the old ship *Jamestown*.

50 Wood from the United States Gunboat *Leigh*, used in the Civil War.

51 Wood from the Cruiser *Bancraft*, U.S.N.

52 Wood from the *Vermont*.

53 Wood from the *Hartford,* Farragut's flagship.

54 Wood from the *Wabash*, Dupont's flagship.

55 Wood from the *Merrimac*.

56 Wood from the Gunboat *Ampheite*, U.S.N.

57 Wood from the *Marblehead* which lifted the wires at Santiago.

58 Wood from the *Maine*.

59 Wood from the *Pedro*.

60 Wood from the *Olympia*, Dewey's flagship.

Courtesy, Minnesota Historical Society.

Etched Canes

A fascinating group of patriotic canes is comprised of sticks with shafts completly covered with mottoes and figures. Only a few are mentioned here, though many others must exist. All these canes would seem to have been made in the same factory, or by several artists working under the same guidelines. The wood is always the same, with the etching either directly on the shaft, or on part of the shaft raised to receive it. The knobs show a consistant similarity. As we know that two of these canes were made by jail inmates, we may speculate that this work may have been undertaken in prisons.

At least sixteen various subjects have been observed: ( )
Admiral Dewey and his officers (14).
In memory of Governor Goebel, given by
a prisoner (1).
To our martyred Presidents (1).
Supreme Court (1).
President Harrison (1).
McKinley's cabinet (1).
Cleveland's cabinet (2).
Theodore Roosevelt and his cabinet (1).
Captains of finance and industry (2).
Do unto others .....(1).
Famous actresses (2).
Famous boxers (3).
Famous trotters (2).
Firemen (2).
Fraternal Order of Eagles (1).
Junior Order United American
Mechanics (2).

◄▲ 5/13 Another patriotic cane, by an unknown artist, shows Theodore Roosevelt in uniform. Behind him is carved *Our President.* Between the natural willow diamond forms are found relief busts portraying, from top to bottom, *Lawton, McKinley, Sampson and Dewey.*
Courtesy, collection George. H. Meyer.

▶ 5/14 The most frequently found cane represents Admiral Dewey and his officers. On this cane is found *Admiral George Dewey, Admiral M.T. Sampson, Admiral W.S. Schley, Lieut. R.P. Holson hero of the Merrimac, Capt. C.E. Clark, of the Oregon, Capt. R. Devans, of the Iowa, and Capt. H.C. Taylor, of the Indiana.*
On other canes, the names of officers are found after the three admirals. Their well drawn faces are surrounded by various subjects: ships, sailors or soldiers, guns, Liberty, the US shield, flowers, etc. Some have patriotic or sentimental mottoes, such as *Remember the Maine* or *In Memory of my Shipmates.* Among the many canes observed, several have a background of black and white squares.
Courtesy, collection Catherine Dike.

▶ 5/15 A "Dewey" cane given to the Polish President Ignace
Paderewski on his official visit to the United States in 1915.
The top part bears the inscription *Heroes of the U.S. Navy*.
Courtesy Muzeum Okregowe, Bydgoszcz, Poland.

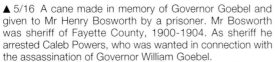

▲ 5/16 A cane made in memory of Governor Goebel and given to Mr Henry Bosworth by a prisoner. Mr Bosworth was sheriff of Fayette County, 1900-1904. As sheriff he arrested Caleb Powers, who was wanted in connection with the assassination of Governor William Goebel.

On the top of the handle there is the seal of Kentucky and two men with the words *United we stand Divided we fall*. The face of Governor Goebel tops the cane, below Mrs Goebel, then Governor Beckman, General Gastleman and finally Mr Henry Bosworth.

Here again is the knob typical of most of these canes.
Courtesy, Kentucky Historical Society.

▲ 5/17 The top of the knob has a flag shield. Below are the words *Our Martyred Presidents* with stars. A raised medallion shows the Capitol and a winged angel, then a flag and a wreath and the words *April 15, 1865, Abraham Lincoln*, followed by *Sep.19,1881, James Garfield,* and finally *September 14, 1901, William McKinley.* It has the same knob as several other canes.
Courtesy, collection Richard W. Opfer Jr.

▲ 5/18 *Captains of finance and industry* are marked on these two canes. The faces are exactly the same but in various positions, and the decorations around them are different. Three identical silhouette medallions appear under the usual knob, then a carved eagle with the words *Pax Vobiscum*. On raised wood, are the figures of J. P. Morgan, J. R. Keene, Wm. Rockefeller, and J. J. Hill. The cane at left has a figure of G. A. Treadwell, and the one at right that of General T. L. Watson. In the background are the usual black and white square decorations.

Courtesy, private collection, Boston.

Courtesy, collection Richard W. Opfer Jr.

▲ 5/19 A cane honoring firemen, picturing the men with their names: *G.H. Thompson, Fames Farrell, Andrew O'Day, H.C. Anderson, J.B. Listman,* and *N.S.Bauer*. Each face is connected to the one below by carved fire ladders. The Minnesota Historical Society has a similar cane with the inscription *St. Paul* below an identical knob.
Courtesy, collection George H. Meyer.

◀ 5/20 On a cane by the same artist as Fig. 5/18 are found the figures of Edwin Markham, Nathan Strauss, Dr. Washington, Samuel M. Jones and Ernest H. Crosby and the words *Peace hast its Victories* on the top. Further down one reads *As ye would that men should do you do even so unto them* .
Courtesy, collection Richard. W. Opfer Jr.

▲ 5/21 Another cane made at the time of McKinley, with crude faces merely scratched into the wood without decoration. It represents the President, Roosevelt, Schley and Dewey.
Courtesy Nebraska State Historical Society.

The Jefferson Canes

So-called by collectors, these numerous canes were all made by the same hand. Over eighty various models have been observed, each one a little different but always bearing the words *Thos. Jefferson of Va. Born Apr. 13, 1743 / Wrote Declaration of Independence 1773 / was President of US 1801 to 1809 / founder of University VA 1819 / Died July 4, 1826 / This cane was cut near Jefferson's tomb.*

Certain canes have added *Jefferson's dying words I resign my spirit to God, my daughter to my country* , while others mention *University of Virginia / Burnt Sunday Oct. 1895, Monticello.*

The canes were made to order by the carver. Some bear the name and address of the owner, while others also carry the name of the donor.

▼ 5/22 One of the numerous Jefferson canes. The carving is easily recognizable. The picture is split in four parts, to show the carving of the letters.
Courtesy, collection Paul Weisberg.

▲ 5/23 Picture of Thomas Jefferson Craddock, the carver of these many canes. Some think that another hand made some of the shafts.
Courtesy, Blue Ridge Institute, Ferrum, Va.

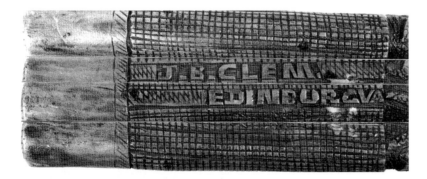

When canes are made in large quantities, such as the Jefferson canes, they can hardly be classified as Folk Art. Many carvers made canes for a living, handling diverse elements in a variety of ways. They are most often recognizable by the subject treated. Some of these canes are signed, the signature most commonly encountered being: *Trade Mark / R.M.Foster / Sparta, Mo.*

Another carver signed his canes, *C.Teale, maker, Bath, N.Y.* He lived in the New York State Soldiers' Home where he must have carved many sticks. (See chapter on Secret Societies.)

◄5/24 The same hand carved this cane which is inscribed *John B. Cary / Chm Com on Schools / This cane was cut from the English walnut tree in the yard of the Jefferson Davis Mansion, Richmond, May 1894 / Jefferson Davis President 1861-1865. Died Dec. 1889.*
Courtesy The Museum of the Confederacy.

Another carver is identified by a distinctive style, although his name is unknown. The carving is rough, with raised letters which are often painted.

▼5/25 Five canes made by the same hand. The small one at bottom is a child's cane, carved with the letters of the alphabet. Some letters are reversed in the manner in which a child might write them. Was the signature WE.Donahue / NY that of the carver or that of the owner? Above it is a cane handle representing a human leg clad in a boot. A man in civilian clothes stands beneath the tall figure of a soldier. The inscription reads *President, U.S. / In God and You / We Trust 1896.*
   The three canes underneath represent *Clayton C. Adams.*Then *Our Heroes,* with the name of *Dewey* carved around the top of the cane. The next shaft is carved with *Patriotic Order Jr.Mc of America / Remember the Maine 1898. Our Heros Dewey, Schley and Hobson.*
Courtesy, collection G. H. Meyer.

▲ 5/26 The entrance to some monumental burial ground, where a vendor is selling carved canes to the visitors.
Courtesy, collection Kurt Stein.

▼ 5/27 Three canes carved and signed by *R. M. Foster*. The top one describes the *Evils of Drink,* and depicts the many temptations of liquor. The two other canes have the usual ribbon-bound fagot which encircles the shaft.
Courtesy, collection George H. Meyer.

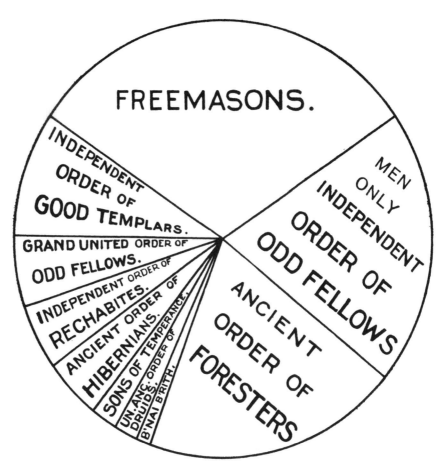

6/1 Chart showing relative size of various secret societies.
Courtesy, Albert C. Stevens, *Cyclopedia of Fraternities*, 1907

Introduction

William J. Whalen in the First Part of his "Handbook of Secret Organizations", mentions: *In almost every culture from the Chinese to the Eskimo and from the South Seas to the African village, men have banded together in secret societies.*

In total numbers of such societies and in total membership, no nation has surpassed the United States .... It is estimated that at least 15,000,000 American men and women belong to one or more secret organizations, and it would be difficult or impossible to understand many aspects of American life without considering the role played by these societies.

During the early 19th century, few secret societies existed in the United States. There were, of course, the Freemasons, from which 600 new societies would break away taking with them many symbols and rites. Therefore on canes we find many Masonic symbols: the all-seeing eye, tools of various professions, the anchor, star, compass, cross and altar etc.

Many churches, including the Protestant, Catholic and Mormon faiths did not approve of these societies and forbade their members to join them.

At the turn of the century, there were 13 Military Orders, 68 Patriotic and Political Orders, 30 Benevolent Societies, 115 Mutual Assessment Fraternities, 17 Mystical Societies, 17 Labor Organizations, six Cooperative and Educational Societies, five Socialistic Associations, nine Social and Recreational Societies, 13 Revolutionary Societies, and six "Others" among which we include the Camorra and the Mafia.

The author has found close to 40 canes bearing the markings of a society or fraternal order; many more must exist.

▶ 6/3 Two badges, one for the 1933 Chicago Convention, the other for the Boston Connection with a drawing of *Paul Revere Rides Again.*
Courtesy, collection Francis H. Monek.

A.A.H.M.E.S.

Ancient Arabic Order of Nobles of the Mystic Shrine.

Some people believe that this society is part of the highest Masonic degree, but this is incorrect. Shriner rituals are modelled upon, without being in any way a part of, the Moslem religion. President Warren G. Harding wore the red Fez which denotes membership, as did F.D.R. and Truman.

Since Blacks were not eligible for membership, they established the "Ancient Egyptian Arabic Order of the Nobles of the Mystic Shrine for North America and South America."

▶ 6/2 This cane was given to President Truman by the honorable Robert H. Fouke, Potentate, AAHMES, Oakland, California.
Courtesy, Harry S. Truman Library.

American Legion

The American Legion was formed at the end of World War I. It held many conventions, and canes often carry badges indicating individual meetings. A collection formed of these insignia would be an interesting sideline

▲◄ 6/4 Two more badges, one for the St. Louis Convention, (1935), and one for the reunion which took place in Paris in 1927.
Courtesy, collection L.G. and Harry S. Truman Library.

B.P.O.E.
Benevolent Protective Order of Elks

▲ 6/6 This order began in New York in 1866, when saloons closed on Sundays. First called "Jolly Corks", the members later took a more serious name.
Courtesy, collection Bruce I. Thalberg.

A.O.F.
Ancient Order of Foresters

▲ 6/5 Developed from one of the schisms which racked the original Forest Order, the *Ancient Order of Forester* also employs the tools of woodmen.
Courtesy, collection Francis H. Monek.

The Society of California Pioneers of New England

▲ 6/7 First named *The La Grange and Pioneer Association.* This name was taken from the bark *La Grange* which sailed from Salem, Massachusetts on March 17, 1849 to arrive in California 6 months later. The members were all "forty-niners" who organized the Society in 1883. It had purely a social aspect. The names of the members are glued below the head which resembles a deer head.
Courtesy, Essex Institute, Salem, Mass.

▶ e) A gilded handle featuring three inter-woven rings surrounding the letters *F.L.T.* (Friendship - Love - Truth). Also represent-ed are the sun and a beehive.
Courtesy, collection Catherine Dike.

▲ a) A folk art cane representing the *Ku Klux Klan* marked on the side with the American flag.
Courtesy, the Barbara Johnson Folk Art collection.

▶ b) *T.O.T.E* (Totem of the Eagle) is inscribed on the top of this cane, with a bow and arrow featured below. An Indian head of shell is inset into the wood.
Courtesy, George H. Meyer, *American Folk Art Canes,* 1992.

▶ c) *United American Mechanics.* Carved on the shaft is *C.F. Snyder Alburtis Pa. 1900 / Dax E. Lax / Sprine No. 398 / O.R.M.* (Tox-E-Lox Tribe No. 398, Improved Order of Red Men). In 1885 the Junior Order of United American Mechanics split from its parent organization, known as United American Mechanism, and went on to become a powerful Order.
Courtesy, George H. Meyer, *American Folk Art Canes,* 1992.

▶ d) The Improved Order of Red Men showing, on the shaft, two Indians, the words *Navajo. Tribe* and *Sam Crew* (maker or owner?) and the letters *No. 105 / Im. P.O.R.M.*
Courtesy, George H. Meyer, *American Folk Art Canes,* 1992.

▲ a) The barrel and wooden chalice commemorate the end of the prohibition and the Chicago World Fair of 1933.
Courtesy, collection Catherine Dike.

▲ c) A handle representing a beer mug and pretzel with the German motto (misspelled) *I vas Dere.* The handle has the word *Chicago Ill.,* but on the reverse side there is *Chas H. Fash* and on the mug: *Ein Beer und Pretzle.* Possibly an early advertising cane, but a souvenir of Chicago seems a more natural supposition.
Courtesy, collection L.G.

▼ b) A map of Chicago for the 1933 World Fair showing the plan of the fairgrounds. The reverse side details the nearby hotels.
Courtesy, collection Francis H. Monek.

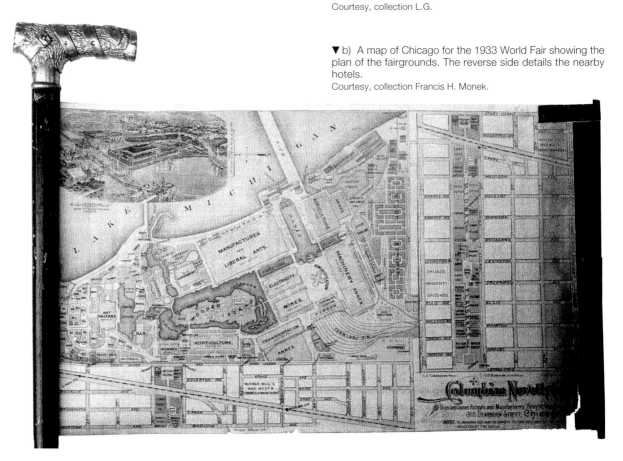

The Society of Cincinnati

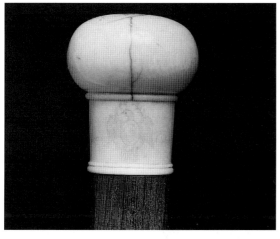

▲ 6/8 This is not a secret society, but a hereditary one, open to descendents of officers who served under Washington during the Revolution. It is said that this cane was given by Washington to General Anthony Wayne. The ivory handle is engraved with the seal of the *Society of Cincinnati*.
Courtesy, Fort Tigonderoga Museum.

Dentist Association

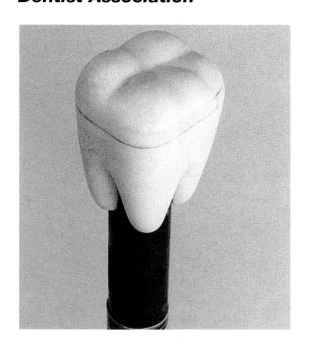

▲ 6/9 This association had a plastic tooth as handle.
Courtesy, collection Francis H. Monek.

F.L.T.
Friendship, Love and Truth

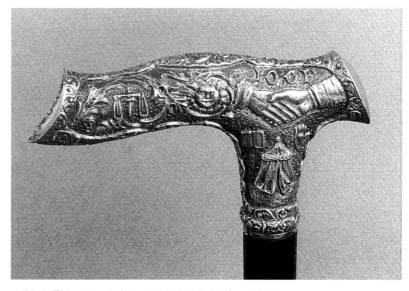

▲ 6/10 This cane belongs to the sub-society of the "Independent Order of Odd Fellows", and is gilded with all the symbols of the organization. (Color picture).
Courtesy, collection Catherine Dike.

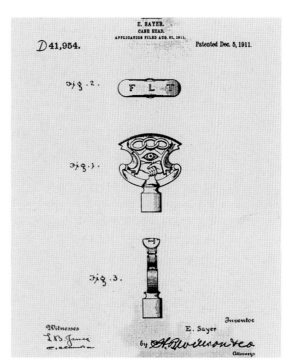

▲ 6/11 A 1911 design patent for a cane handle with the letters *F.L.T.*
Courtesy, United States Patent Office.

F.O.E.
Fraternal Order of Eagles

Founded in 1898 in Seattle, Washington. It was originally an organization focused upon the entertainment of its members, who took the eagle as their mascot. Theodore Roosevelt, Warren Harding, F.D.R., Harry Truman, J.F.K, and other leading politicians were members. In later years it turned towards service and did much to promote social legislation.

Freemasons

It is very difficult to distinguish a genuine Freemason cane, as so many other societies used the same symbols as the Freemasons.

Masons form the largest international society. The organization in the U.S. is not as strict as its English counterpart. Many offshoots were formed, resulting in completely distinct societies. Working class members organized the "Odd Fellows," while others, for religious reasons, formed the "Knights of Columbus." In 1866, it could be said that every white Protestant in the South and Middle West was a Freemason.

Benjamin Franklin was the first Grand Master in 1730, followed by George Washington. Twelve American Presidents were Freemasons: Washington, Jackson, Monroe, Polk, Johnson, Garfield, McKinley, Theodore Roosevelt, Taft, Harding, F.D.R. and Truman.

▲ 6/12 This cane is one of the "etched" canes, (see page 110) dated 1901 with the names of several citizens of Tacoma, Washington.
Courtesy, collection Catherine Dike.

▲ 6/13 The Freemason signs are inscribed on the inside of this ball. It could be English, but In the United States, one sold similar but smaller (8 5/8"diameter), watch charms.
Courtesy, collection Catherine Dike.

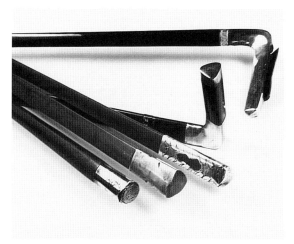

▲ 6/14 The shafts of the five canes are all shaped in a tri-angle, based on the triangle found in Fremasonry. The top one, a match box, was made by Gorham.
Courtesy, collection L.G.

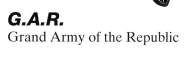

G.A.R.
Grand Army of the Republic

Organized in 1866, *The Grand Army of the Republic* grew to be the nation's largest and most politically active Civil War veter-an's organization. It had a local post in every Northern State, and was politically very active, playing on anti-Confederate feelings. It pro-moted allegiance to the Federal Government and gave support to disabled veterans, their widows and children. Patriotism, good citizenship and a strict moral code were all hallmarks of the G.A.R. It reached its zenith in 1890 when the member-ship neared the 400,000 mark.

▲▶ 6/16 Two G.A.R. canes, the one on the right bearing commonly seen figures, the one on the left featuring the various Corps Badges of the Union Army.
Courtesy, private collection, Boston.

▲ 6/15 An unusual G.A.R. cane representing a cannon along with the customary decorations.
Courtesy, collection Henry & Nancy Taron.

▲ 6/17 Typical G.A.R. canes with representations of the soldier, the sailor, and the cat playing the fiddle.
Courtesy, collection Catherine Dike.

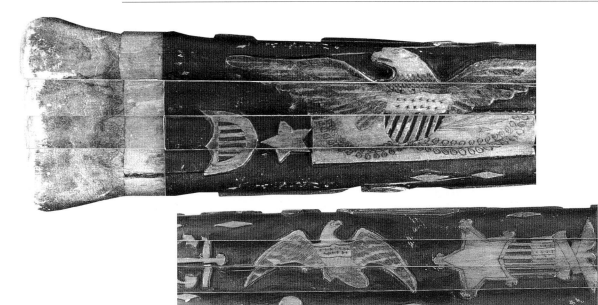

▲ 6/18 Another G.A.R. cane which is very frequently found in collections. They are always signed *C.Tfall, Maker, Bath, N.Y.*. All display the same carvings: the large eagle on top, the coat of arms of the G.A.R., a smaller eagle, a fiddle, an open penknife and numerous other items.
Courtesy, private collection, Boston.

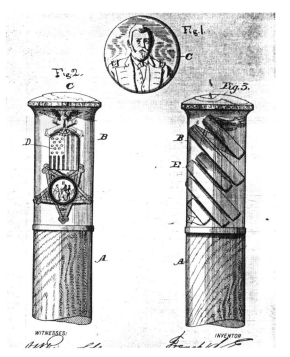

▲ 6/20 Two G.A.R. canes (the top two examples show a different angle) which were sold or given to veterans attending the reunions. The top one has the inscription: *26th Annual Encampment G.A.R. September 20, 1892, Washington, D.C.*
Courtesy, collection Francis H. Monek.

▲ 6/19 General Grant is on top of this patent design which was used for the canes on the right.
Courtesy, United States Patent Office.

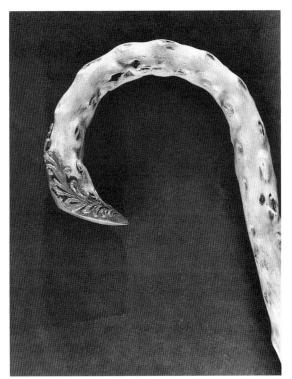

▲ 6/21 Cane given to veterans on the seventy-fifth Anniversary of the Battle of Gettysburg in 1938. Among the articles furnished to "individual veterans for their comfort and use, 250 canes were provided".
Courtesy, Gettysburg College Library.

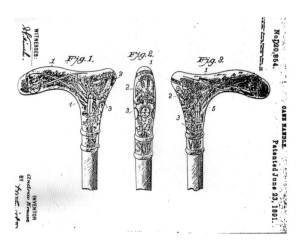

▲ 6/22 A design patented in 1891 showing soldiers and marines surrounded by various weapons.
Courtesy, United States Patent Office.

▲ 6/23 Another dark tinted cane marked *U.V.L.* and *S.O.V.*, showing members of both Army and Navy and corps badges scattered around the shaft.
Courtesy, collection Paul Weisberg.

▶ 6/24 A G.A.R. cane from the *32 O.V.V.I Post Bellum Regimental Organization*. Each silver engraved ring has the name of the president of the organization up to 1922.
Courtesy, Ohio Historical Society.

Harugari Saengerbund

▲ 6/25 This was a nation-wide German fraternal order with at least two chapters in Albany between 1870 and 1900. The Saengerbund was it's singing society. This cane was presented to *K. Koch, on March 5, '84*. It is stamped by the silver company *R.F.G. & Co.*
Courtesy, Albany Institute of History & Art.

I.O.O.F.
Independent Order of Odd Fellows

Many canes are found connected with this secret society. Most types were carved by professional carvers, who would make them in large quantities. This Order started during the 18th century in England, was brought to the United States in 1817, and was officially founded in Baltimore in 1819. The "Rebekah" was formed to allow the ladies to join. The society was open to white men with the exception of gamblers and dealers in liquor. The "Grand United Order of Odd Fellows in America" was later formed to allow blacks to join. It was not recognized by the I.O.O.F.

▶▲ 6/26 This cane represents the tools used by carpenters. The eight-tentacled octopus, along with other lizards and beetles, are on the lower part. Similar canes have been found in other collections.
Courtesy, collection Paul Weisberg.

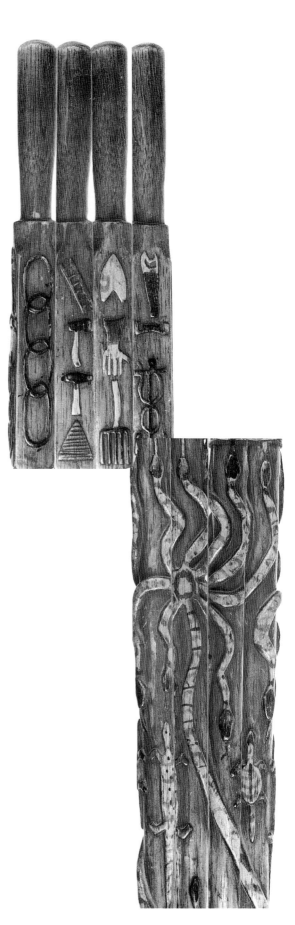

▲ 6/28 This handle represents the three interwoven circles with the words *Indianapolis, 1911,* undoubtedly for a convention held in that city. The reverse side bears the letters *S.C.L.*.
Courtesy, collection L.G.

▲ 6/29 Part of a shaft of a cane often seen in cane collections. It bears the three interwoven circles.
Courtesy, private collection, Boston.

▶ 6/30 The cane knob mentions the *Pennsylvania Centenial, Philadelphia. (1921)*.
Courtesy, collection Catherine Dike.

▲ 6/27 Another black cane carved with various symbols pertaining to this large society. The handle of the cane represents the face of a man, and the bottom has a large snake curling up the shaft.
Courtesy, collection Paul Weisberg.

J.O.U.A.M.
Junior Order United America Mechanics

▲ 6/31 The head of Dewey represents the knob of this cane on which is carved in large block letters *Patriotic Order Jr. Mc. of America. / Remember the Maine 1898 / Our Heroes Dewey, Schley and Hobson.* The carver's hand is cited in the chapter on Patriotic Canes.
Courtesy, Herbert Waide Hemphill Jr.

KERBELA

This group split from their parent organization, the "United American Mechanics", in 1853 and later took over the original society.

The origin of these two orders was the "Union of Workers", formed in Philadelphia in 1845 for and by white Protestant workmen opposing the immigration of Irish, Germans and Catholics. It changed its name in 1853. Only those white men actually trading in liquor were excluded, but its endorsement of abstinence from alcohol kept many men from joining!

▶ 6/32 A souvenir cane of an *Imperial Session* held in *June 1948 in Atlantic City.*
Courtesy, Harry S. Truman Library.

K.K.K.
Ku Klux Klan

Known to all, the KKK was one of the largest Secret Societies. It numbered 5,000,000 members in 1920. The first gathering took place in 1865, and the organization was banned by the Federal Government in 1873. The second wave of members were possibly even more anti-Catholic than anti-Black. The third wave of Klan membership came after the Depression, swelled by the anti-segregation measures of 1954.

K. of C.
Knights of Columbus

Founded in New Haven in 1882. Catholic based, it provided insurance protection for its members.

▲ 6/34 This cane has the signs *K of C* embedded in the shaft.
Courtesy, collection Francis H. Monek.

L.O.O.M.
Loyal Order of Moose

Founded in 1888, with its greatest membership in 1893. Its purpose was charitable, and homes were established for for its aged members.

▲ 6/35 This cane, with a corn-cob handle painted yellow, has on its side the letters of *LOOM, Iowa City*. It was presented to President Truman.
Courtesy, Harry S. Truman Library.

▲ 6/33 This true Folk Art cane has also the symbols of the *K.K.K.* on the top part of its shaft. (Color picture).
Courtesy, Barbara Johnson Folk Art collection.

Mystic Shrine

▲ 6/36 Cane carved and presented to Franklin D. Roosevelt. The emblems are evident under the handle.
Courtesy, Little White House, Warm Springs, Ga.

O.S.C.
Old Settler's Friends

▲ 6/38 On this cane, the name of the association *Old Settler's Friends* is on the side of the handle together with the date *1881*.
Courtesy, Iowa State Historical Department.

N.H.D.V.S
National Home for Disabled Veterans Soldiers

▲ 6/37 The top of the cane bears the intitials of this Association.
Courtesy, collection Paul Weisberg.

Orange Lodge

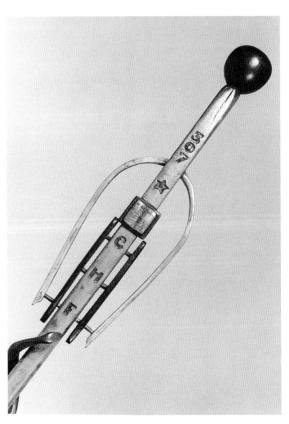

▲ 6/39 An Iroquois cane. Little is known about this Lodge.
Courtesy, Woodland Cultural Centre, Brantford.

Mohammed Temple

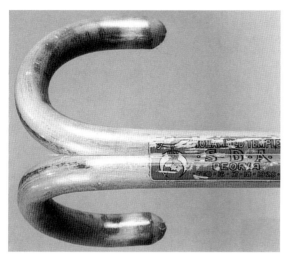

▲ 6//40 The Mohammed Temple is marked *S.D.A. Peoria, Feb. 16. 17. 18. 1928.*
Courtesy, collection H.S.

▲ 6/41 Palestine Temple appears with the name of *Prov. R.I. June 1898* and below, *Buffalo*,
Courtesy, collection L.G.

P.O.R.M.
Improved Order of Red Men

A society which was to perpetuate legends and traditions of a vanishing race ... but no Indians could apply! It was founded in Baltimore in 1834. (Color picture).

T.O.T.E.
Totem of the Eagle

▲ 6/42 This hand carved stick has written on its top *C.H. Waite. P.G.S. / Binghampton. N.Y. / G.E. Green. P.G.S. / From 1n P.O. or R.M.* Further down one finds the letters *TOTE* and an arrow.
Courtesy, collection Herbert Waide Hemphill Jr.

The Western Shrine

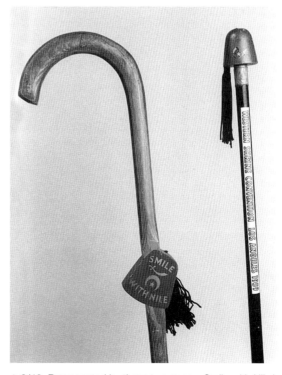

▲ 6/43 Represented by these two canes. *Smile with Nile* is written on one side, the right one held its *Convention in Los Angeles in 1956.*
Courtesy, collection Francis H. Monek.

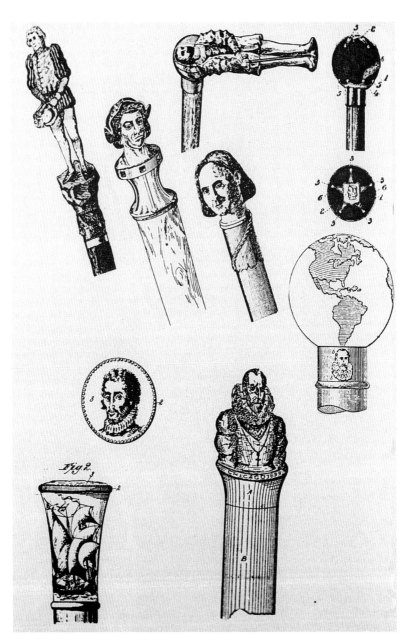

▲ 7/1 Some of the designs, all patented in 1892, to celebrate the discovery of America by Christopher Columbus. A cane of Columbus exists with a beard and no hat.
Courtesy, United States Patent Office.

World Fairs and National Events

Introduction

The first World Fair took place in London in 1851. Its main attraction was the Crystal Palace, a prefabricated glass building which covered 20 acres. It was the first and last world fair to make money! Numerous European canes were exhibited.

By 1930, around 200 companies in the United States were devoted to manufacturing pinback buttons as part of a line of souvenirs. As with the political canes, these buttons adorn cane handles commemorating World Fairs or national exhibition events.

All World Fairs and most National Exhibitions are listed. For ease of reference and identification of specific canes, the most important events are marked with an asterisk *.

1853

New York Crystal Palace.*

Officially designated as the *Exhibition of the Industry of All Nations,* the exhibition was built as a replica of the London Crystal Palace. It provided the first occasion for Americans to view products from all industries. Exhibits included the Colt revolver and a repeating rifle, Daguerreotypes far superior to those from Europe, and the Otis elevator which drew much attention. Samuel F.B. Morse presented his "Morse" code, and a main attraction was Singer's sewing machine.

1876

Philadelphia Centennial. *
U.S. International Centennial Exhibition.

This was a grand affair laced with a great deal of patriotism. Stanhope views (small peep-holes through which was viewed a tiny black-and-white transparency) were in great demand. One cane had a Stanhope view picturing the Horticulture Hall, while another featured several views of various exhibitions halls.

▲ 7/2 A rough stick on which a shield has been nailed. Courtesy, collection Eleanor Zellin, Mantiques Ltd.

▶ 7/3 A simple stick on which there is an ink inscription *Centennial 1876.*
Courtesy, collection Paul Weisberg.

1883
Boston Exhibition.
   The official designation was *Foreign Exhibition.*

1883
Louisville Southern Exhibition.

1884-85
New Orleans Centennial
   World's Industrial & Cotton Centennial Exposition.

1886
Statue of Liberty.

   In 1886 the Statue of Liberty was erected in New York Harbor. A gift of France, it was designed by Frédéric A. Bartholdi.

1893
World Columbian Exposition. *

   In Chicago, forty-seven nations took part in a celebration of the 400th anniversary of the discovery of America by Columbus. Presided over by Thomas Edison, electricity made a debut, with over 5,000 colored bulbs on the "Pillar of Lights". George Westinghouse showed his alternating-current generator. It was the first World Exhibition to feature pure amusement attractions, centered around the giant wheel, two hundred sixty-four feet (76 m) in diameter, built by George Ferris. The same wheel was later featured at the 1904 St. Louis World Fair.

   A Stanhope view made by B.W. Kilborn Bros. of Littleton, N.H., had 15 views of the Columbia buildings. The Cincinnati Art Museum has a map rolled in the shaft of a cane made for the Columbian Exhibition in Chicago in 1893. Libbey Glass Co. made a glass "necktie" cane to commemorate the event. (The Fairfield Historical Society).

▲ 7/4 Cane handle representing the figure of Liberty with a real Liberty cap. It bears a patent dated *Jan.3, 86, Solid Silver.* The patent was actually taken out for the method in which the silver was to be applied to ivory.
Courtesy, collection Catherine Dike.

▲ 7/5 Two busts of Columbus.
Courtesy, collection Francis H. Monek.

1894

San Francisco Mid-Winter Exposition.
    Known as the *California Mid-Winter International Exposition.*

1895

Atlanta Exposition.
    Cotton States & International Expostion.

1898

Trans-Mississippi Exposition.

This exposition was held in Omaha to open the Expansion of the West. Thirty five tribes of Native Americans were invited. During this Exposition Geronimo carved several sticks.
    A cane exists marked *The Great Court* taken from the roof of the Agriculture Building, Omaha, 1898.

▲ 7/6 A pipe to celebrate the Pan-American Exposition of 1901, marked on the top, *Niagara.*
Courtesy, collection Francis H. Monek.

1900

New York Gold Parade.

The New York Historical Society has a cane which was issued for the *Gold Parade* which took place in New York with 85,000 persons, including Governor Roosevelt, attending in spite of rain and mud. Six columns were given to the event on the back page of the "New York Times".

1901

Pan - American Exposition.

This exposition took place in Buffalo, N.Y., which was known as the *Electric City.* The exposition's official symbol was two women representing North and South America clasping hands over Central America. A cane with that image would be a true find.

Albertype Co. Brooklyn is set on a cane with thirty-six black-and-white scenes from the Pan-American Exposition. Another cane is embossed with Pan-American Exposition, 1901.

1904

Saint Louis World Fair. *

This fair also bore the name *Louisiana Purchase Exposition.* It commemorated the 100th Anniversary of the Louisiana Purchase from Napoleon in 1804. The Ferris wheel was again an attraction, and it is said that this exhibition also saw the launch of the hot dog, the ice cream cone, iced tea and the T-shirt. The most enduring image of this fair for most Americans is of Judy Garland's invitation to "Meet me in St Louie, Louie, Meet me at the Fair".

1905

Portland Louis & Clark Centennial Exposition.

1907

Jamestown Ter-Centennial Expostion.

A Stanhope view, by "Keystone View Co.", exists on a cane marked *Opening Day, April 26, 1907. Great Warships at Hampton Roads, Va.*

1907
The Clermont Centennial.

1908
Buffalo Bill Wild West Show.

▲ 7/7 Two pendants hanging from a cane The top one commemorating *Buffalo Bill's Wild West Show*, the lower one celebrating the *Clermont Centennial* on the Hudson. The third cane to the left was one of those light metal canes sold at fairs and at such celebrations.
Courtesy, collection Paul Weisberg..

1909
New York Hudson-Fulton Celebration.

1909
Alaska-Yukon Exposition.

1915
Pan-Pacific Exposition.

A 1915 San Francisco celebration of the opening of the Panama Canal.

A cane made by the *Albertype Co. of Brooklyn, N.Y.* showed thirty-six black-and-white views of the fair.

1915
San Diego Exposition.

1926
Philadelphia Sesqui-Centennial.

1933-1934
Chicago World Fair. *

Also called the *Century of Progress International Expostion*, celebrating Chicago's becoming a city in 1833. New car models made their appearance at this Fair, as did neon lights. The *Hall of Science* was the premier building, and representations are found on canes.

A souvenir cane made in Austria exists which separates into 5 pieces. One holds a pencil which is marked "D. Leonard & Co. Beamtenfeder mit Kugelspitze", others a phial and glass. The top of the cane reads *Chicago / 1833 / Century of Progress / 1933*. These Prohibition canes were manufactured by the thousand in Austria and Germany. (Strong Museum, Rochester, N.Y.).

▲ 7/8 Two simple souvenir sticks.
Courtesy, collection Francis H. Monek.

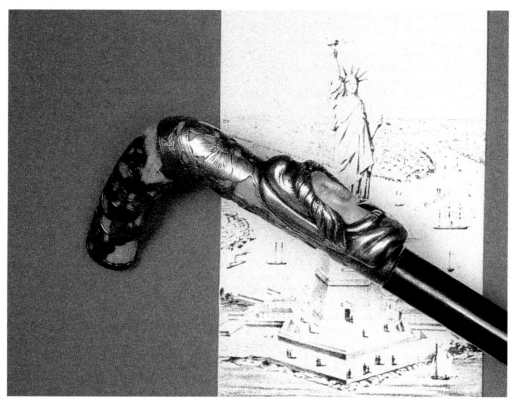

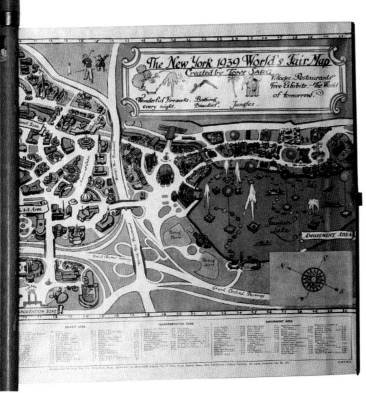

▲ a) A cane made to commemorate the occasion of the presentation of the Statue of Liberty to the United States by the French nation. Marianne, symbol of France, adorns the front of the cane in her Liberty Cap. It is marked: *Pat. Jan. 3, 86, solid silver* (in fact, the method whereby the silver was to be applied to ivory.)
Courtesy, collection Catherine Dike.

◀ b) A map of New York issued for the 1939 World Fair. The reverse side is blank.
Courtesy, collection Catherine Dike.

▲ a) An African head.
Courtesy, collection Catherine Dike.

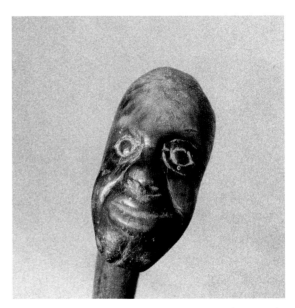

▲ c) An Afro-American head simply carved on the root of a sapling.
Courtesy, collection Catherine Dike.

▼► b) Hands and snakes were a popular motif for European handles and shafts. This ivory group shows a wide array of fists, many grasping assorted objects. Right, the European snake group dates from the turn of the 19th century. They were also carved by the trench soldiers during the 1914-1918 War. Perhaps some carried a symbolic meaning, but in most cases the sinuous winding body was the simplest way to adorn a shaft.
Courtesy, collection Catherine Dike.

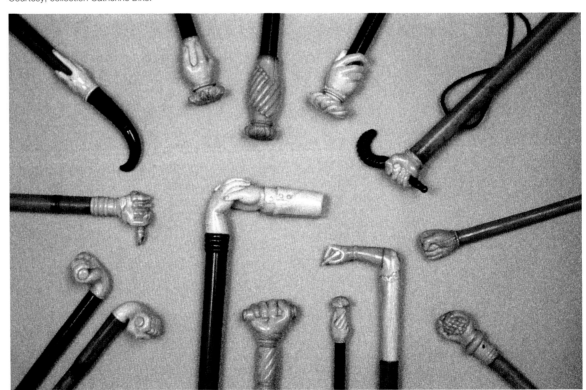

▲ a) An Indian hunkers atop a shaft. The climbing snake could identify it as a World War I souvenir, perhaps carved by a Native-American member of the United States Army. Courtesy, collection Laurence Jantzen.

▲ c) One of the very few polychrome German cane handles where the colors are still visible. The date is undoubtedly late 18th century. Courtesy, Bayerisches Nationalmuseum, Munich.

▶ d) Like Africans, American Indians beaded their shafts in a variety of colors. These sticks made popular exchanges with early colonial settlers during the 19th century. Courtesy, private collection, Boston.

▼ b) Selection of canes representing snakes.

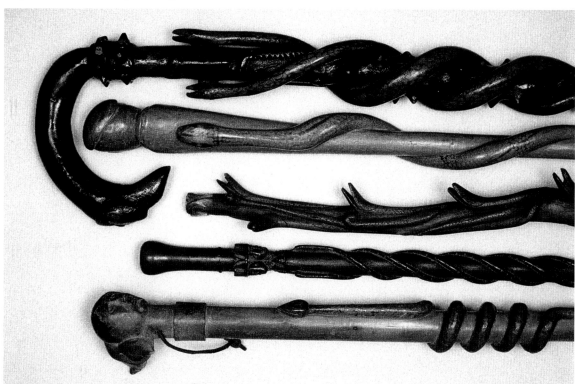

◄ a) Lacking only a high hat, a well-dressed man sits on a stool, with an animal climbing up the shaft.
Courtesy, collection Mark Neider.

▼ c) A mermaid holds up the globe atop a cane of light wood and polychrome. Near the tip are the words *F. Pecton ! Arrowe Park / II S....mlrs* and in different lettering, *Meknes.* Dating from the American-Algerian war? . . . certainly a possibility.
Courtesy, collection Catherine Dike.

▲ b) Two canes from among the many made by Michael Cribbins (1839-1917). A native of Michigan, he invariably signed his canes with the words *Mike* and *Orion.* Like many folk artists, the carver's real identity was unknown for years, until he was finally identified by the collector. The cane at left shows a hand with black nails opposite an eagle and the date *1900.* The stick at right, also of diamond willow, features figures of a man and several animals carved in the recesses of the wood.
Courtesy, George H. Meyer, *American Folk Art Canes.* 1992.

▶ d) A carved cane representing a boy hefting an outsized bottle of Coca-Cola.
Courtesy, collection Catherine Dike.

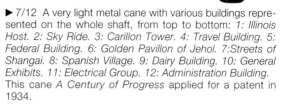

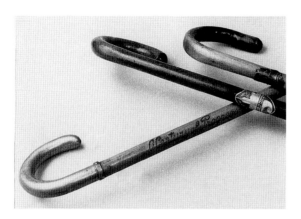

▲ 7/9 Three canes with souvenir emblems.
Courtesy, collection Paul Thalberg.

▶ 7/12 A very light metal cane with various buildings represented on the whole shaft, from top to bottom: *1: Illinois Host. 2: Sky Ride. 3: Carillon Tower. 4: Travel Building. 5: Federal Building. 6: Golden Pavillon of Jehol. 7:Streets of Shangai. 8: Spanish Village. 9: Dairy Building. 10: General Exhibits. 11: Electrical Group. 12: Administration Building.* This cane *A Century of Progress* applied for a patent in 1934.
Courtesy, collection Catherine Dike.

▲ 7/10 A souvenir cane for any German who had attended the Chicago World Fair. This side of the beer mug is marked *Ein Beer / Und Pretzle*. On the handle there is *Chas. H. Fash* and on the reverse side *I Vas Dere*. (Color picture).
Courtesy, collection L.G.

▲ 7/13 A very typical Art Deco handle.
Courtesy, collection Francis H. Monek.

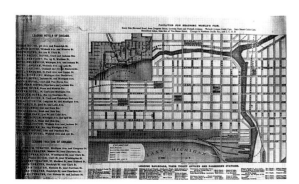

▲ 7/11 A Map held in the shaft, showing on one side the layout of the Fair grounds and on the other nearby streets with hotels. (Color picture).
Courtesy, collection Francis H. Monek.

▲ 7/14 The bust of F.D.R. with the motto *Century of Progress*.
Courtesy, collection Richard W. Carlson.

◄ 7/15 The same idea is repeated on this cane as that in photo 7/12 but using metal shields nailed onto the shaft. It shows the same building adding the *Hall of Science, the Agricultural Buildings, Fort Dearborn, The Observatory Towers, Republic of China, Egyptian Pavillon, Hollywood, Belgian Village* and the *American Legion.*
Courtesy, collection Dorothy Moog.

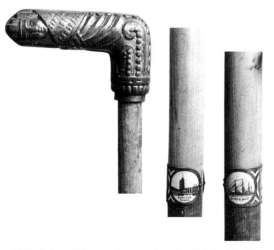

▲ 7/16 A few of the most encountered metal shields. There is also the *Carillon Tower* and *Bird's Ship.* An Art Déco handle with the embossed words *Chicago Ill.* on the reverse side: *A Century of Progress.*
Courtesy, collection Francis H. Monek.

1935
San Diego Exposition.
  Officially the *California-Pacific International Exposition.*

1936 - 1937
Cleveland, Great Lakes Exposition.

1936 - 1937
Texas Centennial.
  Texas Centennial Central Exposition.

▲ 7/17 Two canes celebrating the Texas Centennial and the Cleveland Great Lakes Exposition.
Courtesy, collection Catherine Dike.

1939 - 1940
San Francisco World Fair.
  Golden Gate International Exposition.

  Inaugurated the Golden Gate and the Oakland Bay Bridges. The presence of a Pan-American China Clipper in the harbor was a great event.

  The memorabilia of this exposition took a back seat to those of the New York World Fair.

1939 - 1940
New York World Fair.

Also known as *For Peace and Freedom*, as war was raging in Europe. Futuristic motorways were planned, a model of a giant space rocket was shown, and nylon and Kodak photo slides made their first appearances. Stereophonic sound reproduction was also launched. The New York World Fair produced the largest amount of memorabilia of all the fairs, as seen in the following pictures.

▶ 7/20 A souvenir stick where the names have been stenciled.
Courtesy, collection Mark Neider.

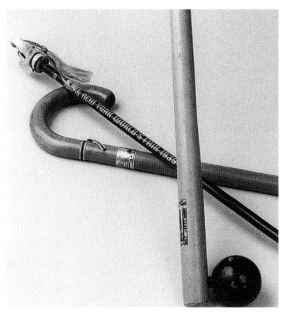

▲ 7/18 Three canes, the front one representing the Trylon and the Perisphere.
Courtesy, collection Bruce I. Thalberg.

▲ 7/21 A cane and a seat issued for the Fair.
Courtesy, collection Richard W. Carlson.

▲ 7/19 A metal seat on which one can recognize the emblems of the Fair.
Courtesy, collection Eleanor Zellin, Mantiques Ltd.

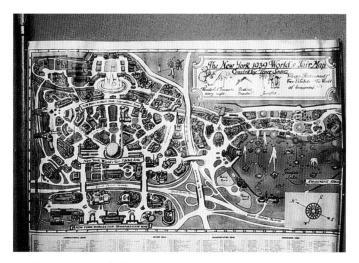

▲ 7/22 A map which rolls into the shaft.
Courtesy, collection Catherine Dike.

II   Folk Art Canes

▲ 8/1 Taken at a veterans' home, this postcard shows a soldier among numerous carvings, done no doubt by himself.
Courtesy, archives James Rutkowski.

Folk Art Canes

Multiple Influences
before the 20th century.

The first point to make in any discussion of the American Folk Art Cane is the virtual impossibility of assigning a date to any individual item, unless by lucky chance it has been dated by the maker. Even canes commemorating a particular event were very often carved afterwards, sometimes years later. Defining the country or region of origin is rarely helpful, particularly in the United States, where people moved around so frequently. The shape and type of ferrule can be a great help in indicating the era of a silver or ivory cane, and obviously a patent can pinpoint a date, but with genuine Folk Art, we often find ourselves very much in the dark in this area.

Indian Influence

For centuries Native American used canes in their most important rituals and celebrations – as an invitation to members of another tribe, for recording noteworthy events, to mark out a calendar upon the shaft, as an accompaniment to dances, etc. A cane was also a symbol of leadership, and numerous photos of the late 19th century show Indian Chiefs holding a walking stick.

▲ 8/3 A cane with many incised symbols and people. It is 45" (114,5 cm) and has segments of bark left between the decorated elements.
Courtesy, collection Catherine Dike.

▲ 8/2 A very stylised head of a horse.
Courtesy, Institute of the Great Plains, Lawton.

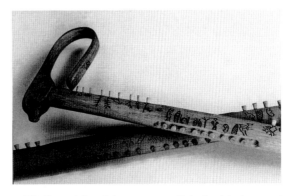

▲ 8/4 Carved *Condolence* canes with incised designs and wooden peg counters.
Courtesy, private collection.

▲ 8/5 Three canes made by Indians in the late 19th centu-
ry. The one on the left is made of cedar and was owned by
Green McCurtain (1848-1910), last elected chief of the
Choctaws. The beaded cane was used by Geronimo, who
also carved the cane with a snake.
Courtesy, State Museum of History, Oklahoma City.

◄ 8/6 During the War of 1812 an Indian gave this cane to
Reuban Waits, whose descendants gave it to the Kentucky
Historical Society.
Courtesy, Kentucky Historical Society.

▲ 8/7 Six Pueblo Governors, each holding a cane.
Courtesy, Museum of New Mexico.

▲ 8/8 A "Coup Stick" which measures fifty-four and a half
inches (140 cm) and which records the exploits of the
owner: the enemies killed, the horses stolen, his battles and
his escapes from capture. It belongs to the Blackfoot Tribe.
Courtesy, National Museum of American Indian, Smithsonian
Institution.

▲ 8/9 A cane attributed to Chief James Beaver, (born 1846) of the Cayuga tribe, part of the Iroquois Confederacy
Courtesy, Woodland Indian Cultural Educational Centre, Brantford.

▲ 8/10 A heavy South Eastern European cane, where the massive head gives a general impression of what is carved below it. The head of the bird measures 6 1/4" (16 cm)
Courtesy, collection Catherine Dike.

European Influence

The first settlers in the United States arrived in small groups, usually by the boatload, and upon arrival tended to remain in communities, often rural, made up of their own ethnic and national fellows. Settled in a new land, their carvings, which naturally included canes, were originally made to a familiar national pattern; only over time did an American style evolve. European Folk Art canes featured more religious, allegorical and fantastical themes than their American counterparts. They are made from hard wood, and are very rarely painted. Animal carvings feature frogs, insects, turtles, and reptiles, particularly snakes, the simplest form to carve. The alligator, indigenous to the New World, is not found on European canes.

European Folk Art canes can be generally grouped by region: the Northern countries with their runic symbols and writings; German and Austrian canes; Eastern and Balkan sticks; Mediterranean walking sticks and the French and English canes. This does not mean that any specific cane can be instantly pinpointed as to region of origin, but the general stylistic trends are there.

▲ 8/11 A French cane, signed and dated, with numerous animals carved on the shaft. Pictured is a snake and the protruding head of an animal.
Courtesy, collection Catherine Dike.

▲ 8/12 An English gentleman standing atop the handle
wearing a stovepipe.
Courtesy, private collection, Boston.

African Influence

European settlers in America brought with
them solid family and social structures which
enabled immigrants to retain their culture, their religion, their art or music, and even their language.
It usually required a generation before English
became the dominant tongue.

Blacks arrived in America in involuntary cap-
tivity, and groups shipped together were scattered
upon arrival to plantations all over the South.
Numerous West African tribes with a multitude of
languages, rituals and religions were represented.
Only memories accompanied these slaves, and
there was small likelihood of finding someone
from the same village with whom to share these memories once across the Atlantic. Thus, what we call
today the Afro-American influence, and the wide
variety expressed in Afro-American folk art canes
represent a culture which evolved from the Black
experience in America as opposed to their origins
on the African continent.

▲ 8/13 A German cane with the motif carved below the
handle.
Courtesy, collection Catherine Dike.

▲ 8/14 Top of a chief's cane. Angola.
Courtesy, Musée Barbier-Mueller, Geneva.

▲ 8/15 Two African canes from the late 19th century, early 20th century.
Courtesy, Musée Barbier-Mueller, Geneva.

▲ 8/17 A South Pacific cane showing the multitude of people put one on top of the other.
Courtesy, Musée Barbier-Mueller, Geneva

▶ 8/18 A Masai cane with snakes curving up the shaft. Snakes are very rarely found on old African sticks.
Courtesy, collection Catherine Dike.

◀ 8/16 A skull, undoubtedly carved from human bone, adorns this stick with a chain decorated with Christian saints and crosses.
Courtesy, collection Catherine Dike.

▲ 8/19 These canes (except possibly the third from the left – the one with the mirrored eyes) have been clearly identified as Indian, although only one has a specific written collection history. Some of these canes may have been made for sale to whites (tourists).
Courtesy, collection George H. Meyer.

◄ 8/20 The racial features of the person who's head is pictured on the cane does not necessarily tell the race of the carver, since blacks were portrayed by white carvers and sometimes vice versa. However, it is believed that all but three of these canes were probably carved by whites.
Courtesy, collection George H. Meyer.

▲ 8/21 Although not signed, all of these canes (except maybe the third from the left) are Afro-American, based on their style and history, and verified by specialists in Afro-American art. The maker of the second cane from the right was known to be a black (the erect abstracted cane).
Courtesy, collection George H. Meyer.

▶ 8/22 Heads of Afro-Americans were carved during the first part of the 20th century.
Courtesy, collection Jan Thalberg.

Signed Canes

Before begining the subject on signed Folk Art Canes, one must speak of the Gudgell cane that every book on Folk Art mentions as being a very good example of a mid 19th century Afro-American cane, made by Henry Gudgell for John Bryan in 1867. The latter was injured in the knee during the Civil War and limped all his life. The cane looks slender, the tip measuring 9/16" (1,5cm) and the straight handle that Gudgell carved would injure the hand which would rest upon it. Perhaps John Bryan was not that severely wounded.

In the 1840s, *Zachariah S. Robinson* carved canes. He was a tavern keeper in what is now Roanoke, Virginia. Little is known about this sculptor whose sticks featured carved animals. He carved his signature in relief letters, unlike Purkins, who used ink. Three of his canes are known to exist. (Color picture).

▶ 8/23 This cane is marked on its rear with the relief letters: *This staff made in the year of our Lord 1838 by Zachariah S. Robinson, Roanoke County, VA.* The animals are low relief. Courtesy, Abby Rockefeller Folk Art Center.

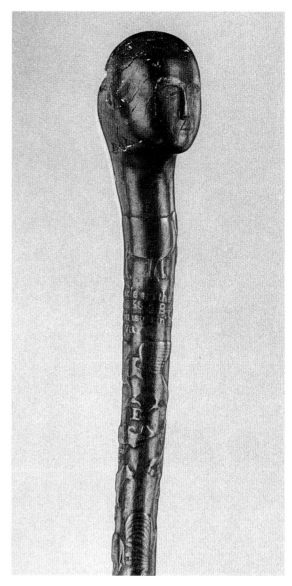

▼ 8/24 Cane bearing the name of the owner (and most probably the carver also) - *John Sheppard, March 4th, 1828, Steal not this cain / or fear of shame / for here you see the owner's name.* His name also circles the bottom of the cane. At the very bottom is found, in a different hand, *Jackson* - no doubt the fellow who stole the cane! Courtesy, Franklin D. Roosevelt Library.

Thomas Purkins (1791-1855) carved at least-fifteen canes which survive today, the property of his descendants or displayed in museums. They form a sequence, virtually one a year, missing only 1849 and 1850. The Abby Rockefeller Folk Art Center has the two which are dated 1846 and 1847, the latter having a handle made in the shape of a snake holding the shaft.

▶ 8/26 The top of the cane represents the heads of an Indian and a Negro, followed by the heads of a horse, a bull, a pig, etc. Geese, hens and swans adorn the rest of the shaft. It is dated 1854. This cane has a lion in the middle of the shaft, a feature of most of Purkins' canes. (Color picture).
Courtesy, private collection.

(Front)

(Back)

▲ 8/25 Two canes carved by Purkins, the left one being the only one to feature a pair of breasts. Rather daring for the period!
Courtesy, private collection.

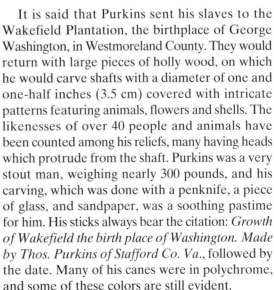

It is said that Purkins sent his slaves to the Wakefield Plantation, the birthplace of George Washington, in Westmoreland County. They would return with large pieces of holly wood, on which he would carve shafts with a diameter of one and one-half inches (3.5 cm) covered with intricate patterns featuring animals, flowers and shells. The likenesses of over 40 people and animals have been counted among his reliefs, many having heads which protrude from the shaft. Purkins was a very stout man, weighing nearly 300 pounds, and his carving, which was done with a penknife, a piece of glass, and sandpaper, was a soothing pastime for him. His sticks always bear the citation: *Growth of Wakefield the birth place of Washington. Made by Thos. Purkins of Stafford Co. Va.*, followed by the date. Many of his canes were in polychrome, and some of these colors are still evident.

▼ 8/27 A stag horn carved with the inscription: *From Tho. Purkins of Va. to the Hon. Henry Clay of Ky. A little token of the high estimation in w. the donor among thousands holds the Orator, the Statesman, the Man ! In these evil times, we feel our need of the Great Pacificator. 1847 Cut from Wakefield, birth place of Washington.*

Above the lion there is an eagle, not very ferocious, holding the national shield to its breast. Below the lion is a log cabin and a horseman. Towards the bottom are various animals and an Afro-American head.

Among the color pictures is shown an identically carved stag horn with a long poem. It is said that Purkins carved a cane for John Adams who lived nearby. It seems that the canes he made for those outside his own family circle had carved stag horns as handles.
Courtesy, Missouri Historical Society.

▲ 8/28 Near the top of the stick one can read Purkins' signature and the date 1853. The head of a lion adorns the middle of the cane, and a polychrome carving shows a hunting scene.
Courtesy, private collection.

▼ 8/29 A group picture of five canes still in the possession of Purkins' descendants.
Courtesy, private collections.

(Back)

(Side)

◄ a) Samuel Slater of the Slater Mill in Pawtucket was given this cane by his employees as a protection on his long journey home on dark nights. The figure is Moses Brown (founder of Brown University), who had been particularly kind to Mr. Slater. It is a heavy stick, 2 1/2 " (6,5 cm) below the head.
Courtesy, Slater Mill Historical Site, Pawtucket, R.I.

▶ b) A sheep forms the handle of a shaft on which a well-dressed man is standing atop a woman who resembles *Liberty*.
Courtesy, collection Norman Flayderman.

▼ c) The figure of a goat, swathed in a curious form of wrapping, forms the handle. There is a definite German influence.
Courtesy, collection Catherine Dike.

◄ a) In two canes Purkins used antlers as a raw material for carving his handles. This cane has written in ink: *See Israel's gentle shepherd stand / with all en——ames / Hark how he calls ——-lands / And folds them in his ——- / Permit them to approach he cries / Nor scorn their humble names / For ——- / The love of glory ——— / Ye tithe flock with pleasure hear / Ye children seek his face / And fly with transport to receive / The blessings of his grace / Watch and pray / My soul be on thy guard / ——-thousand foes arise / And hosts of sins are pressing hard / It draweth from the skies. / I watch and pray / The battle ne'er give o'er; / R ———it bold by every day; / And help divine implore / Never think the won / Nor once at ease sit down / Thy arduous work will not be / done / Till thou' has got the crown.*
Courtesy, Museum of Early Decorative Arts, Winston-Salem, NC.

▶ b) Thomas Purkins carved approximately fifteen walking sticks, all immediately recognizable. A distinctive feature is a lion somewhere along the shaft.
Courtesy, private collection.

▲ a) Carved in 1840 by Zachariah S. Robinson. Block letters read: *This staff carved by Zachariah S. Robinson of Big Lick County, Virginia, in the year of our Lord 1840.* Beneath carvings of domestic and exotic animals and reptiles are the following verses, also carved: *I sigh not for Beauty / Nor languish for Wealth / But grant me kind Fortune / Virtue and Health / Then richer than kings / And happier than they / My days shall pass sweetly / And Swiftly away.* Robinson's signature is in script.
Courtesy, Roanoke Museum of Fine Arts.

▲ b) Two carved figures, an Indian and a white man, top this stick. The entire shaft is carved with a variety of animals and a saddle, and there is a raised band on which the carver could ink his name or that of the person he gave or sold it to. The National Museum of American History has a cane which is virtually identical, except that the white man is carved upside down and entwined by a snake.
Courtesy, collection Catherine Dike.

▲ c) A bear, carved horizontally, forms the handle. An elegantly dressed man adorns the shaft, along with the usual climbing snake.
Courtesy, collection Herbert Waide Hemphill Jr.

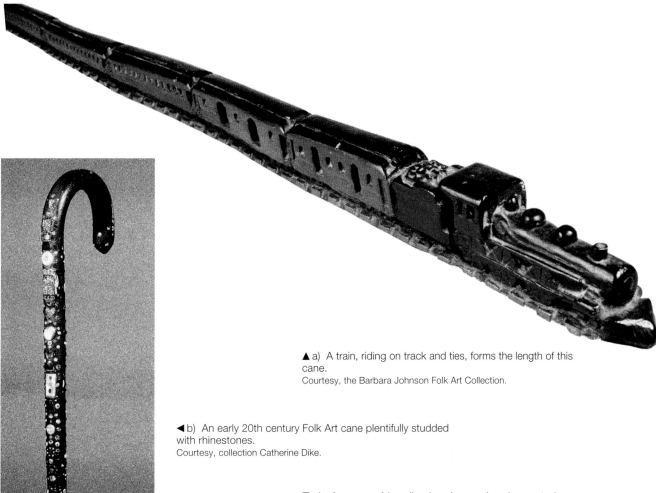

▲ a) A train, riding on track and ties, forms the length of this cane.
Courtesy, the Barbara Johnson Folk Art Collection.

◄ b) An early 20th century Folk Art cane plentifully studded with rhinestones.
Courtesy, collection Catherine Dike.

▼ c) A group of handles hand-carved and mounted on shafts by Williard M. Chandler of the Soldiers Home in Togus, Maine. Chandler carved 299 heads, comprised of 78 dogs, 58 eagles, 44 alligators, 12 frogs, 15 snakes, 5 ducks, 9 parrots, 2 horses, 2 deer hooves, 1 monkey, 1 boat, 2 human hands, 2 seals and 52 miscellaneous.
Courtesy, collection Francis H. Monek.

▲ a) A *Maypole* cane in which the four chains and the cane
are all carved out of one piece of wood. It is 43 1/2 " high
(110 cm).
Courtesy, collection George H. Meyer.

◄ b) Elijah Pierce carved this cane in 1950 as a *Preaching
Stick*. Completely covered with carving, its style is closer to
"old" Folk Art than it is to twentieth century pieces. Pierce
took six years to carve it. Very closely detailed, each figure
or object inspired a story. Pierce was an Afro-American who
died in 1984. Other examples of his work can be found.
Courtesy, Columbus Museum of Art, Columbus, Ohio, collection
Alexis G. Pierce.

► c) Four balls in a cage. The lower one bears the year
1888 on each of the four sides of the handle made with
small nails. In the middle, the decorations are painted and
marked *Meyer*; while the top sphere features colored mar-
bles and was *Presented to J.F. Koonce, Fayetteville, Tenn.
2.4.97 - 2.10.35*.   Courtesy, collection L.G.

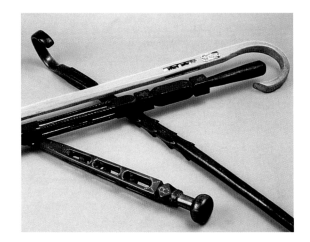

Alanson P. Dean of Western Massachusetts carved very intricate canes for people he admired. For the 1876 Centennial, he gave a cane to Rutherford Hayes, then Governor of Ohio. (See Canes worn by U.S. Presidents). Others were carved for President Garfield, P.T. Barnum, Francis Murphy (a Temperance Movement leader), and James Francis of Pittsfield, Massachusetts.

In the chapter on Patriotic canes, are many sticks commemorating the Civil War which were signed by artists, or, perhaps more appropriately, "manufacturers".

Doctor Watkins was a notable cane collector at the end of the 19th century. He carved sticks as well, specializing in picking up wood from historic sites or from houses due to be demolished. His friends also gave him pieces of wood they came across. Consulting his inventory is an amazing experience. He donated his collection to the Jersey City Museum, who sold the major portion of it in the 1970s. All that remains in the museum today are a few forlorn pieces, often missing their labels. A sad spectacle for the enthusiast!

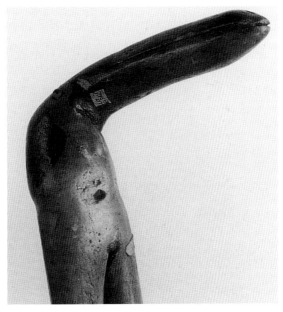

▲ 8/31 A rather erotic cane combining a protuding "object" and a double legged cane which takes the form of a woman's torso. As Watkins possessed numerous canes carved by other artists, it is impossible to say whether or not he was the maker.
Courtesy, Jersey City Museum.

▲ 8/30 Four sticks carved by Dr Watkins, the left one with a tag marked *Blackthorn stick picked up on Broadway at midnight after a dental meeting in 1879.*
     The cane to the left is a carved dog's head with glass eyes. The second cane has a face carved on the inside of the extension, the ends of which are carved with both a canine and a human face. The two examples at right are simply carved by Dr. Watkins.
Courtesy, Jersey City Museum.

▶ 8/32 Towards the end of the 19th century, sitting by his fireside, Reverend Chauncey Hobart, D.D. carved approximately 50 canes. This one has a geometric design going down the whole shaft.
Courtesy, Minnesota Historical Society.

Thomas Otis Jenkins was another carver in the 1900s. He collected canes which he would then carve with a small sharp knife, covering the shaft with a menagerie of animals, including pigs, donkeys, butterflies, ducks and many others. One of his shafts was encrusted with a multitude of buttons of various shapes, and another bore an Indian arrow embedded in the handle

Carved shafts have always been a common characteristic of Folk Art canes, and numerous examples can be found in every country. In the United States, they usually convey a message, expressed in writing, images, or both.

▶▲ 8/33 Two canes carved by Thomas Otis Jenkins, who carved on his sticks the alligators he raised as a hobby. The newspaper clipping dates from 1937.
Courtesy, private collection, Boston.

▼ 8/34 A heavily carved stick on which it is hard to find a square inch without a message. It was carved by G. T. Barbee, who most likely spent four years at the task, judging by the inscription at the bottom (July 31, 1901, 87 years old this day) and at the top (July 31, 1905, 91 years old). He offered it to *Dr. C. T. Lindsey* with the words: *God be praised / I live long / As a Mark of Esteem /The Lord is a Sun and A Gift of Friendship.*
Courtesy,collection George H. Meyer.
Acquired from Bonnie Grossman.

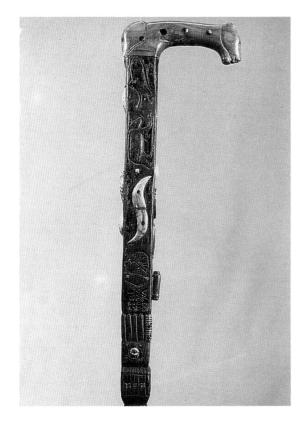

◄ 8/35 The top part is carved with a fish, bear, eagle, moose and human head. The stick is inlaid with shell, ivory and bone. Four of the ivory pieces are Inuit scrimshaw animal carvings. The shaft bears a representation of the Chapel at Fort Ross, California and a cannon. The inscription reads *Polotofsky, at Fort Ross, Russia Alaska in Calif 1805,* and *W.P. Wood 1929.* These two canes are obviously from the Northwest region of the United States, as is apparent by the Inuit faces and the similarity to totem pole design.
Courtesy, San Diego Museum of Man.

► 8/37 Another cane by the same maker. Hand carved hardwood in the manner of a totem pole, with animals and human figures one on top of the other. From the bottom up, we can see a man with a pack on his back straddling a pig, two cat-like creatures, a seated bear and a rattlesnake twining below the handle which bears the signature *W.P.Wood to J.W. Wood, 1906.*
Courtesy, San Diego Museum of Man.

▼ 8/36 William Howard who carved this stick had much on his mind, and he poured it out in 12 lines, concluding with the addresses of various banks, should anyone wish to rob them!
1. What the banks cost the people during the time the National Banking system has been in operation, the people have paid to the banks eighteen hundred
2. millions of dollars for the use of the notes there institution received gratis from the government. These eighteen hundred millions of dollars
3. paid to national Banks for the use of Money which cost them nothing have been so much tax upon the industries of the people. A tax first
4. paid by manufacturers, merchants, traders, planters, farmer & C. and ultimately charged to industrial classes in the shape of reduced
5. wages and increased cost of the necessairies of life after deducting the cost of running the banks the balance left of the 18

6. hundred millions received from the people, was divided among two hundred and fifty thousands stock holders. Had the government loaned the
7. money on the same terms, the 18 hundred millions would have been redistributed among the people from whom it came. The end.
8. This is William Howard's statement about banks, there is seven hundred and eighty two letters in this statement, put here September 1888.
9. Some of the National banks of Philadelphia were located: First national bank No. 315 Chesnut St. Second national bank Frankford Avenue at Frankford. Third
10. National bank South West Corner Broad & Market St. (several inches erased)
11. Sixth National Bank corner Second & Pine Street, Seventh National Bank northwest corner Fourth & Market st. Eigth National bank North 2nd st. corner Girard Ave.
12. Ninth Nat, Bk, corner Norris & Front Street, Tenth N.B. corner Columbia Av. & Camacs.
Courtesy, collection Smithsonian Institution.

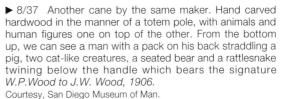

▲ 8/40 Walking stick with a bone handle, carved with the names of *M. Stover / Tanner & Currier / Bot Ct. VA 1822* (standing for Botetourt County, Virginia). Under the name is the masonic sun and compass and the American shield. (Color picture).
Courtesy, Museum of Early Southern Decorative Arts, Winston-Salem, N.C.

◀ 8/38 A carved cane, painted white, showing a variety of faces and animals. It is signed *Gustnabe, N.J. 1924.*
Courtesy, collection Theodore T. Newbold.

▲ 8/39 Half carved, half scrimshawed cane with the portrait of Washington and an Indian. We see a log cabin and what appears to be a barrel in front This piece could have been made for the 1888 election of Benjamin Harrison. It is signed *S. Ashley.*
Courtesy, collection Paul Weisberg.

▲ 8/41 A cartoon cane. The figures are carved and have details drawn in ink. They represent Uncle Sam with an eagle on his hat, the face of a woman, another woman sitting in a rocking chair, "Happy Hoolligan" in a plaid jacket, and his brother "Gloomy Gus." The bottom of the cane has numerous details which obviously refer to these cartoon characters.
Courtesy, collection George H. Meyer.

▲ 8/42 Two canes with barber's tools. The top one is carved and elegantly slim, the bottom one more crude. The instruments have pegs holding them on the shaft.
Courtesy, collection George H. Meyer.

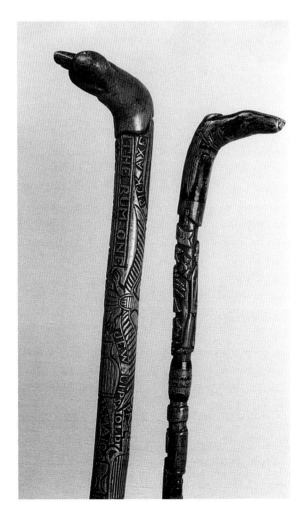

Other Canes

▶ 8/43 A school master's cane with the letters of the alphabet on one side and the numbers 1 to 20 on the other. The handle is made to allow the cane to be used as a pointer, and there is a small recess to hold chalk.
Courtesy, Tradewinds Auctions, H. Taron, Manager.

◀ 8/44 In his book the collector calls this cane *The Joys of Drink.* It is carved with the words *Rosey,* (Could it mean the French "rosé" wine?) *The Rum One, Pick Ice, Jew Lips* (juleps), *Grub Hoe, E Pluribus Unum* inscribed above the wings of an eagle, *Brandy, Old Jamaica, Pandemonium, Gin, Cocktail, Brandy.* Further down is the inscription *Lieut. Gen Cuffrage* together with *Martha's Vineyard* and *Nantucket.* These words are surrounded by a variety of glasses, flasks, decanters, and bottles, all carved in an Art Déco style

The other could be named *The Evils of Drink.* The handle is a black boot from which toes are protruding. A man is carved with a goblet in his hand, while a sheaf of wheat and a vine with grapes adorn the other side. There are various inked names of drinks and containers: *Tickle, Water Cooler, Apple Brandy, Old Little Brown Jug, Rum, Sherry Wine, Brandy, Pocket Flask, Poz Worse, Cherry Herring in Sure Death.*

Further down the shaft, the same man is carved, this time in his coffin with the devil holding the lid, with an inscription *T'was sparkling wine / but led me to an endless hell.* The signature is inked at the very bottom: *Trade Mark / R. M. Foster,* a name found on several Civil War canes.
Courtesy, collection George H. Meyer.

▲ 8/45 A Gold Rush era walking stick depicting the adventures of a miner. We see his house, his mule, the miner meeting Indians, fighting with his partner, buffalo hunting and finally returning home from a deer hunt blowing a hunting-horn.
Courtesy, collection Catherine Dike.

▲ 8/46 A very crudely carved cane with faces and animals carved around the necks of the branches. When turned upside down one little peg has a drawing of a man showing his proudest attribute, a visual pun illustrating why the protuberance has not been cut off.
Courtesy, collection Paul Weisberg.

▲ 8/47 Shaft carved: *1898* and the words *Knavery is the Worst Trade / In God we trust / Boasters are cousins of liars / Birds of a feather will flock together / United we stand, divided we fall.* A great variety of tools and instruments are carved in between the tests.
Courtesy, collection Paul Weisberg.

▲ 8/48 A six-sided cane carved in two directions. Horizontally are the words *Equality / Columbia,* below / *Genesee* and the numbers *1 2 8 5 6 4 0 7.* and *1 7. 0 6 9 5 4 3.* What these numbers refer to is unknown. Vertically, one can read: *Freedom U.S. / Liberty July 4 / Independence / Union 1776 / Harmony. G.W. / Strength / Justice. N.H. / Power & Truth.* The top of the handle has an incised eagle with a shield and the date *1817.*
Courtesy, collection George H. Meyer.

◄ 8/49 An interesting and intricate piece, possibly *Tramp Art,* according to the collector. It is not readily apparent whether the vertical pieces were made first and slotted into the horizontal blocks, or vice versa.
Courtesy, collection Herbert Waide Hemphill Jr.

Carved Natural Wood

Some carved shafts were obviously made taking advantage of a natural formation of the wood.

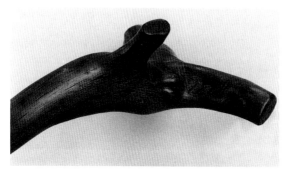

▲ 8/50 A root on which the date 1804 is written in ink.
Courtesy, collection Francis H. Monek.

▲ 8/52 A carved head of a man adorns the end of this root.
Courtesy, collection Richard W. Carlson.

▲ 8/51 An eagle's head carved in the end piece of a root. A snake climbs up the shaft.
Courtesy, collection Francis H. Monek.

▲ 8/53 A fierce lion's head carved from a knot. Adorned with an ivory top, it was presented to Lieutenant Josiah Sturgis in 1838.
Courtesy, Essex Institute, Salem, Mass.

▲ 8/54 A 19th century man's effigy carved in a root.
Courtesy, collection Paul Weisberg.

▲ 8/56 Three shoes, two carved in a sapling root, the one
at left to be added to a shaft.
Courtesy, collection A. Brown.

▲ 8/55 Although a modern eye will see George Washington,
this handle portrays some 19th century notable, not necessarily the Founding Father
Courtesy, collection Kurt Stein.

▶ 8/57 The face has been carved in the root of a sapling
which forms the shaft. It was presented in 1852 to Dr.
Andrew Randall, first president of the California Academy of
Natural Sciences. Randall was a doctor and very active in
San Francisco. He was also Postmaster in Monterrey. The
shield, on the back of the face, and the end of the cap are in
gold.
Courtesy, collection Alder Randall.

◄ 8/58 Cane with a bear at the top which seems to be hugging a beer cask.
Courtesy, Richard W. Carlson.

► 8/60 This body with the head of a bird surely held a meaning which is a mystery to us today.
Courtesy, collection George H. Meyer.

▲ 8/59 Two gentlemen standing on the knob.
Courtesy, collection Franklin D. Roosevelt Library and from the Barbara Johnson Folk Art collection.

▲ 8/61 One of the only canes to be found in Europe showing the hollowed out top. The cane is in hardwood and dates from the late 18th century.
Courtesy, collection Laurence Jantzen.

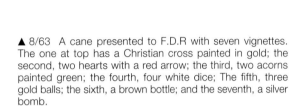

Ball-in-Cage

A typical American design is the ball-in-cage motif, featuring several spheres carved into the shaft and left nestled neatly inside a four-sided frame. Many collectors believe that this is a masonic emblem, but a letter from the Grand Lodge in Washington D.C. states: *The canes shown on your picture where the small balls are floating in a cage are not Masonic. Nowhere is this symbol shown in Masonic literature.*

This design is very rarely found in African sticks and Pinto does not mention it in his book *Treens* which covers all work done in wood. The author has seen two examples in European collections.

▲ 8/63 A cane presented to F.D.R with seven vignettes. The one at top has a Christian cross painted in gold; the second, two hearts with a red arrow; the third, two acorns painted green; the fourth, four white dice; The fifth, three gold balls; the sixth, a brown bottle; and the seventh, a silver bomb.
Courtesy, Franklin D. Roosevelt Library.

▲ 8/62 A very intricate handle in which the spheres are carved from one piece of wood which remains in another cage with six openings.
Courtesy, collection Stuart H. White.

▲ 8/64 In this cane the balls have been replaced by a man and a woman.
Courtesy, collection Francis H. Monek.

▶ 8/65 Two spheres carved at the top of the cane, showing below, four pictures of children in late 19th century clothes.
Courtesy, collection George H. Meyer.

Franklin D. Roosevelt

About 250 canes exhibited at the F.D.R. Library at Hyde Park and at the Little White House in Georgia provide a good idea about what real American Folk Art was like at the beginning of this century. Many canes are extremely simple, embellished only with a name, but others are more intricate. The donor is always received a thank-you letter from the Administration for his or her gift.

▲ 8/66 Washington is carved in the knob and along the shaft one can read *Franklin D. Roosevelt 1933 / President, born 1873 New York /Dem. New Deal.*
Courtesy, Little White House, Warms Springs, Ga.

▲ 8/67 The bark has been stripped away, leaving the profile of F.D.R. and the words *God bless*.
Courtesy, Franklin D. Roosevelt Library.

▲ 8/68 A cane on which the bark has been carved around the letters. It reads on four lines: *The Blue Eagle is flying all over the nation / Scaring the hunger away / We had enough ot this depression / Cheer up the blue eagle is in partnership* with the N.R.A. New York City, 1933. Each side is painted alternately blue, red, blue and red. It also has green and yellow decorative spots. (The Blue Eagle is the symbol of the N.R.A.).
Courtesy, collection Herbert Waide Hemphill Jr.

▶ 8/70 A cane presented to FDR by a Boy Scout group. At top is the Seal of the State of New York, then "Be Prepared", the words *Navy Department United States of America, Senate State of New York*, seals representing marriage, the professions of banker and lawyer, the Seals of Columbia University and Harvard University and a shield with the words *Qui Plantavit Cyr*n. All pertain to the earlier years of F.D.R.
Courtesy, Franklin D. Roosevelt Library.

▼ 8/69 Four hand-carved canes. The two on the left could be by the same hand.
Courtesy, Franklin D. Roosevelt Library.

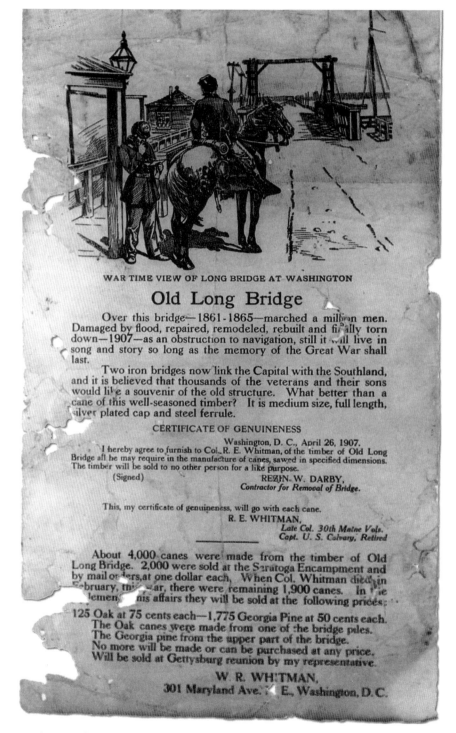

WAR TIME VIEW OF LONG BRIDGE AT WASHINGTON

Old Long Bridge

Over this bridge—1861-1865—marched a million men. Damaged by flood, repaired, remodeled, rebuilt and finally torn down—1907—as an obstruction to navigation, still it will live in song and story so long as the memory of the Great War shall last.

Two iron bridges now link the Capital with the Southland, and it is believed that thousands of the veterans and their sons would like a souvenir of the old structure.   What better than a cane of this well-seasoned timber?   It is medium size, full length, silver plated cap and steel ferrule.

CERTIFICATE OF GENUINENESS

Washington, D. C., April 26, 1907.

I hereby agree to furnish to Col. R. E. Whitman, of the timber of Old Long Bridge all he may require in the manufacture of canes, sawed in specified dimensions. The timber will be sold to no other person for a like purpose.

(Signed)   REZIN. W. DARBY,
Contractor for Removal of Bridge.

This, my certificate of genuineness, will go with each cane.

R. E. WHITMAN,
Late Col. 30th Maine Vols.
Capt. U. S. Calvary, Retired

About 4,000 canes were made from the timber of Old Long Bridge.   2,000 were sold at the Saratoga Encampment and by mail orders, at one dollar each.   When Col. Whitman died in February, this year, there were remaining 1,900 canes.   In the settlement of his affairs they will be sold at the following prices:

125 Oak at 75 cents each—1,775 Georgia Pine at 50 cents each. The Oak canes were made from one of the bridge piles. The Georgia pine from the upper part of the bridge. No more will be made or can be purchased at any price. Will be sold at Gettysburg reunion by my representative.

W. R. WHITMAN,
301 Maryland Ave. N. E., Washington, D. C.

▲ 9/1 4,000 *Old Long Bridge* canes were made when the bridge was torn down in 1907. 2,000 were sold at the Saratoga Encampment and others at the Gettysburg reunions. The price was 75 cents if in oak, 50 cents if in Georgia Pine. The Wisconsin Historical Society and the Vermont Historical Society each possess one of these canes, but none have been seen by the author in private collections.

Courtesy, Gettysburg National Military Park.

Canes Carved by Soldiers

The American Revolution, or War of Independence
1775-1783

The creation of canes allied to the sites of historical battles is a uniquely American idea. These canes may be created on the spot, carved by infantry soldiers, or, more commonly, made many years afterwards by soldiers who sought out wood from the battle site. The same principle applies to canes made from the timber of warships, sunk during battle and dredged up several years later.

Many of these canes can be found today in museums, historical societies and private collections. They are usually marked on a collar or on top of the knob, and are rarely carved, the material itself being the point of interest.

The Carnegie Museum in Pittsburgh has three canes of this type. One is inscribed *Fort Pitt 1958*, and commemorates the erection of the Fort in 1758 by the English. The other two are made with wood from *Fort Duquesne*, which was destroyed by the French in 1758.

The Annapolis Museum has a cane shaft made from the *U.S.S. Concord*, which sank in 1776. The United States National Museum has a cane made from a piece of the British frigate, *Merlin,* which was sunk in an attack on Red Bank, New Jersey, on October 23, 1777. It spent 102 years under water!

The Daughters of the American Revolution in Washington, D.C., have a cane marked *Paul Jones Ship Alliance*. She was the 32-gun Frigate which accompanied Jones's flagship *Bon Homme Richard* to England seeking to sink British ships in their home waters. This 1779 battle was a memorable victory for John Paul Jones.

The following canes have been listed chronologically by date of the battle commemorated, not the date of the cane's manufacture.

The Henry Francis Du Pont Winterthur Museum has an ivory cane handle marked *John Burrows, Sept. 1760*. Burrows was a soldier in the Revolutionary War.

▲ 9/2 Wood from a British War Vessel sunk by the French in Lake George, New York, in 1757. The ship was raised by Mr. Ollie Smith, a local boat builder, and the cane presented by him to Wm. L. Breyfogle.
Courtesy, Chicago Historical Society.

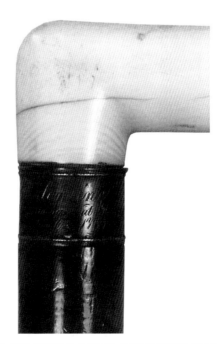

▲ 9/3 Part of *H.M.S. Augusta*, sunk during the Revolution in October 1777.
Collection, Bob Nittolo.

▲ 9/4 A cane bearing the name *Andrew Oliver's Staff* and the date *1778*. Oliver resigned from the post of Stamp Officer before the threats of an angry mob which stormed his house. It is painted black, and one wonders whether it was made by Oliver or taken from a part of his house.
Courtesy, collection Smithsonian Institution.

▲ 9/6 An oak shaft made from Benedict Arnold's flagship *Congress* which sank in Lake Champlain on October 11, 1776. Arnold's delaying action is considered to have saved the day.
Courtesy, Museum, Department of the Navy, Annapolis.

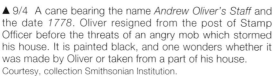

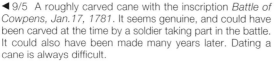

◀ 9/5 A roughly carved cane with the inscription *Battle of Cowpens, Jan.17, 1781*. It seems genuine, and could have been carved at the time by a soldier taking part in the battle. It could also have been made many years later. Dating a cane is always difficult.
Courtesy, Valley Forge Historical Society.

▼ 9/7 A large silver handle, with the R. F. S. & Co. sterling stamp, marked on top: *Piece of the Keel of the American Privateer George captured by H.R.M. Ship Pluto July 15, 1781 and sunk by order of Vice Admiral John Campbell, Governor at St John, New Foundland. Dredged up Nov. 1885*. A large silver band on the shaft has the inscription of two owners: *Col. Julian James* and below that, *Lieut T.B. Mason*.
Courtesy, collection Smithsonian Institution.

a) A Folk Art cane with the face of a soldier, undoubtedly recognizable by his contemporaries. The end of the handle is in the form of a dog's head.
Courtesy, collection Paul Weisberg.

▶ c) A cane painted in dark colors carved with the figures of numerous animals and the following inscriptions: *Andrew Oliver's Staff* and the date *1778*.
Courtesy, collection Smithsonian Institution.

▲ b) A head of a Civil War soldier on a stick which could have been made contemporaneously. Two woods were used, and the collar is roughly made in a metal typically found in an encampment.
Courtesy, George H. Meyer, *American Folk Art Canes.* 1992.

▲ d) Two hand-carved cats flank the shield of the Grand Army of the Republic.
Courtesy, collection George H. Meyer.

◄ a) A heavy polychrome cane made from two pieces of wood. The eagle grasps in its claws an officer with shield and epaulets. Numerous animals are carved descending the shaft, among them a scorpion-like creature with five tentacles and the words *Serpent of Rebel* written on its back. Both animal and human figures represent no doubt leading secessionists in the Confederate States.
Courtesy, George H. Meyer, *American Folk Art Canes.* 1992.

▲ b) A metal handle representing a Confederate soldier and a carpetbagger.
Courtesy, collection Catherine Dike.

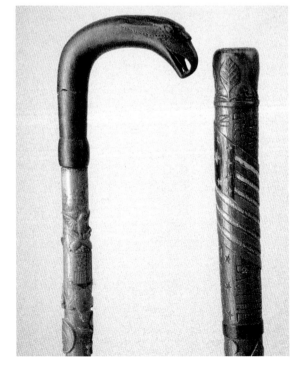

► c) Two "badges" canes made after the War. The eagle head bears the G.A.R. shield, and the other is polychrome. It is marked *In God we Trust / Liberty / We will stand by the Flag /* A black belt with a U. S. shield divides the cane in two parts. It was presented to: *Edwin H. Smith Co.F. 15th Regt. / Heavy Artillery / New York Vols.*

        In the Meyer collection two similar canes are marked: *To Capt.P.R. Schuyler / Post. No. 51 G.A.R. / By / Comrade / J. McClaren / Sept. 4th 1888.* and *To Richard / Edwards / Co. H. 148 Regit N.Y. Vol INFIT / From Sam Garner, Dec. 25, 1891.* Canes of this type were produced in large quantities for presentation at meetings and reunions after the war.
Courtesy, private collection, Boston.

The Kentucky Historical Society has a cane cut by *Judge Thompson in 1882,* which is marked: *Battle of Blue Licks, August 9, 1782.*

During the Revolution, the British used the Liberty Street Sugar House in New York as a prison. For the overcrowded prisoners, one of the few things to do was to carve their name and initials in the wooden beams of the structure. When the building was torn down in 1840, the carved beams were made into canes and other objects.

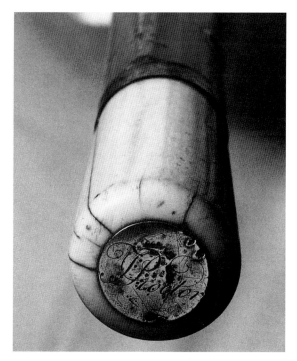

▲ 9/8 An ivory handle with a silver top bearing the inscription: *T. Proctor.* Colonel Proctor was the commanding officer of "Proctor's Artillery" of Philadelphia during the American Revolution.
Courtesy, collection Kurt Stein.

▶ 9/9 *U.S. Frigate Constitution*, with two canes made from its timber. This ship probably had more canes made from its wood than any other. These sticks can be found in many museums and historical societies. Repairs were carried out in 1835, 1876 and 1905, each occasion providing wood for material. In 1925, when Congress authorized her restoration, numerous canes with oak or silver handles were made from her oak stanchions, along with many other mementoes. The cane on the right has its knob made from one of the bolts that fastened her timbers. The bolts in this ship were originally made by Paul Revere.
Courtesy, Museum, Department of the Navy, Annapolis.

The American - Algerian War
1801-1804

Congress had strengthened and increased the Navy and the Marine Corps in 1797 and launched the *United States,* the *Constellation* and the *Constitution.* By 1801 the United States had paid the Barbary Coast (Morocco, Algiers, Tunis and Tripoli) $2 million in ransom for captured seamen, and in May 1801, the Pasha of Tripoli declared war on America. As the army of Napoleon was kept penned in Egypt by the British, this conflict did not involve France, that fearsome foe of this period. In 1804, Jefferson sent Commodore Edward Preble to the waters off Tripoli with a fleet under the Flagship *Constitution.* This ship was also known as *Old Ironsides.*

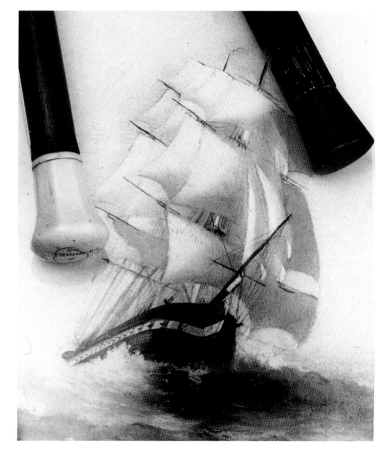

▲ 9/10 The attack on Tripoli on August 3, 1804, by the American Squadron under Commodore Edward Preble. The *Constitution* is visible in the foreground. The fleet forced peace on the Barbary Coast.
Courtesy, Museum, Department of the Navy, Annapolis.

▲ 9/12 Three Drum-Majors' Batons.
Courtesy, collection Kurt Stein.

▲ 9/11 In 1811, William Henry Harrison won the battle of Tippecanoe against the Indians. This battle showed that Canada was not to be easily conquered. This cane was cut on the grounds of the battlefield and presented to General Harrison in September 1840, the year he would run for President.
Courtesy, The Chicago Historical Society.

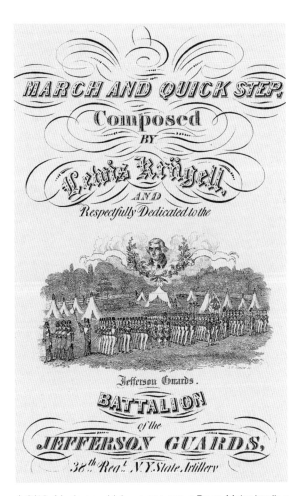

▲ 9/13 Music on which we can see a Drum-Major leading the band.
Courtesy, Kurt Stein archives.

The War of 1812

This second war with Great Britain began in 1812. The elections of 1810-1811 brought the War hawks to Congress, and this was considered the right moment to attack Canada. The United States Navy was in comparatively good fighting condition, but the Army was virtually non existent.

In 1813, Captain Oliver Hazard Perry, aged 28, arrived on the shores of Lake Erie. It took all his efforts to secure the launching of two 20-gun brigs and three gunboats. Eventually, he commanded a mini fleet of ten ships, including the *Lawrence* and her sister-ship, the *Niagara*. The battle with the British was fierce, but Perry triumphed at last, sending General Harrison the message: *"We have met the enemy and they are ours"*. This young Captain who refused to acknowledge the possibility of defeat secured for America what was then the Northwest Frontier: Ohio, Indiana, Illinois, Michigan, Minnesota, and Wisconsin.

The Army continued the battle on land. In 1814 Britain sent reinforcements in the form of more men and ships, and scored an initial victory by capturing the city of Washington, which they partially burned. Baltimore held fast, however, and Andrew Jackson won the Battle of New Orleans. The war was brought to an end by the Treaty of Ghent in February, 1815.

Perry's ship the *Lawrence* was sunk by order of the Government in 1815. Some of her timbers were first removed, which provided a pleasant windfall for the local population around Lake Erie who made and sold dozens of canes. In 1836, she was raised, only to be sunk again. In 1876 she was raised yet again, cut in two, and exhibited at the Philadelphia Centennial Exhibition. The *Niagara* was raised in 1913, a hundred years after its sinking.

▲ 9/14 Gold knob with an inscription on its top: *Old Ironsides a chip of the old block. August 19th, 1850*. It was presented to Enoch Louwe by the Democracy of Baltimore, Md. On the four sides, are the carved words:

Captured Guerrière, 19th August 1812, in 25 minutes. Comed by Isaac Hall.
Captured British Frigate Java, 29 Dec. 1812, in one hour and 55 minutes. Comed by Capt. Bambridge.
Captured Cyare and Levant, 28 Feby in 10 minutes. Comed by Capt. Stewart.
During her cruise destroyed 2 Eng. Brigs and recaptured the Adeline.
Courtesy, Museum, Department of the Navy, Annapolis.

▼ 9/15 Cane presented to President Madison which bears on its side etched drawings of the *Constitution, Java* and *Guerrière*, and the *Constitution, Cyare* and *Levant*. Written in full is: *Battle of Tripoli*.
Courtesy, collection Smithsonian Institution.

▲ 9/16 Two canes made of timber from the *Lawrence*, the flagship of Com. O. H. Perry. One top is ivory, the other gold.
Courtesy, Museum, Department of the Navy, Annapolis.

▲ 9/17 The famous words of Perry, *We have met the enemy, they are ours,* can be found on a plaque affixed to the shaft. Because the ship was raised so often, one finds in museums as many canes made from the *Lawrence* as those made from the *Constitution*.
Courtesy, collection Francis H. Monek.

▼ 9/18 Simple shaft on which is carved in high relief: *Cut from Perrey's flag Ship in 1839 by John Evill St. Louis Mo 1840.*
Courtesy, collection L.G.

Mexican War
1846 - 1848

1815 marked a turning point in relations between the United States and Great Britain. The Battle of Waterloo followed Napoleon's escape from Elba in February 1815. After Britain's decisive victory, peace was established on all fronts. Relations with America became friendly. In 1817 war broke out against Florida's Seminole Indians. Andrew Jackson took Pensacola and returned a hero.

John Quincy Adams had offered to buy Texas from the Mexicans in 1824, and Andrew Jackson renewed the offer when he was elected to the Presidency in 1828. By 1836 Mexico considered there to be too many Americans in Texas, and acted to limit immigration to the territory. In response Texas declared itself independent. General Antonio Lopez de Santa Anna attacked the Alamo and was then cut down by the Texas Cavalry with Sam Houston at the head. President Polk ordered General Zachary Taylor to limit military advancement to the Rio Grande. In May 1846, Polk declared war on Mexico.

Despite being greatly outnumbered by the Mexicans, U.S. Forces under General Taylor and General Winfield Scott went into the attack. A series of battles took place bringing fame to such names as Matamoros, Palo Alto, Resaca de la Palma, Monterey, Buena Vista, Vera Cruz, the Fort at San Juan de Ulua, Cerro Gordo, Chapultepec and Mexico City. Winfield Scott led an impressive fighting march and added 1,200,000 square miles to the United States by taking the Mexican capital. The war ended in 1847. This war resulted in an Army with several well-trained and battle-experienced generals, soon to be divided by the next tragic conflict.

▲ 9/21 A carved sword stick, with much carving below the eagle head: *Hope seemed to bid / the American arms farewell / and liberty wept / when gallant Lincoln fell / Buena Vista /*. On top of the blade, lengthwise: *My country right or wrong and Those are my jewels*. The names of seven officers follow.

On the shaft is a large eagle with an anchor, a dove and below it: *Make haste*. An open bible has the words: *Trust in God*. Then comes *Names of the brave officers who fell at Palo Alto Texas,* followed by eight names. Under the notation *wounded* there are 21 names. Behind these lists are the words *Resaca de la Palma*. Below is a poem:

To the memory of Mjr Samuel Ringgold
Where is the chief who defended the shore
The sod is upon him he will lead you no more
The Mexican has fallen Metamoras is low
And in their death now reposes the arm of their foe
Sleep soldier of merit your battles are oer
Metamoras has fallen the Mexican no more
But whilst the cypress is green or the wind rolls a wave
The tear of the soldier will hallow thy grave.

Finally, in smaller characters *Hennick*, no doubt the name of the carver.
Courtesy, collection Smithsonian Institution.

▲ 9/19 Two canes from the Mexican war. The one on the left belonged to General Bliss, who served under General Scott. On the gold head one can read: *From the fields of Resaca-de-la-Palma*. The cane on the right was made by Adam MacLean while he was recuperating from the battle of Chapultepec. The cane is decorated with numerous bones and brass inlay supposedly from the buttons of American soldiers.
Courtesy, West Point Museum.

▲ 9/22 Cane which belonged to Colonel Jefferson Davis, marked *Buena Vista* on top. The future President of the Confederate States of America received another cane after the same battle which is today in The Old Court House Museum in Vicksburg, Mississippi. Inscribed *Col. Jefferson Davis*, it was presented to him by his troops after he was wounded in the foot.
Courtesy, Chicago Historical Society.

◄ 9/20 An ivory top on a shaft made from the flagstaff of the *Castle of Chapultepec*. The inscribed collar records that it was given to *Lieut. Peter Valentine Hagner by his men in the City of Mexico, September 1847.*
Courtesy, Museum, Department of the Navy, Annapolis.

The Civil War
1861 - 1865

A large number of canes have associations with the Civil War. Where and by whom were they made? No one can say. Given the extensive movement of both armies, it is hard to imagine a soldier carving a cane and then keeping it by his side during months or years of action. Some were made in prisoner-of-war camps, but it seems likely that most were made after the war, when soldiers would make a sentimental return to a battlefield and there pick up a branch. Others were made by old soldiers in Veterans Homes who would carve a variety of souvenirs, sticks among them. The subsequent examples are listed chronologically by date of the battle or campaign commemorated rather than by date of manufacture.

1861

▲ 9/23 The bombardment of Fort Sumter in April 1861 saw the first shots fired in the Civil War. This cane is made from the Yankee flagstaff, and bears on its silver knob *Genl. Beauregard to F. H. Hatch*. Confederate General Pierre G. T. Beauregard directed the attack on Fort Sumter. The Smithsonian Institution has a cane made of the palmetto log used in the defence of Fort Sumter.
Courtesy, collection Smithsonian Institution.

1862

▲ 9/24 *U.S.S. Cumberland* being sunk by *C.S.S. Virginia* on March 8, 1862. The shaft of the cane is made out of wood from the *Virginia*. The *C.S.S. Virginia* was the first ironclad ship, built on the hull of the former *U.S.S. Merrimac*, which was burnt to the water line when the U.S Navy evacuated its Norfolk, Virginia base. The *C.S.S. Virginia* also sank the *U.S.S. Congress*. Shafts made from the wood of the *Virginia-Merrimac* are encountered very often. Many are found in historical societies; the Chicago Historical Society has one which was presented to Abraham Lincoln. They were often given to leading citizens.
Courtesy, Museum, Department of the Navy, Annapolis.

▲ 9/25 A shaft made from the timber of the *Monitor* and the *Merrimac*, with the date *March 9, 62*.
Courtesy, collection Smithsonian Institution.

▲ 9/26 Cane carved in prison with this message running along the top section: *The Liberty of Speach and of the Press cannot bee surprest by a Tyrant / Camp Chase, Ohio - Nov. 11, 1862. J. Sweeney, age 33 y.*
Courtesy, collection George H. Meyer.

1863

▲ 9/27 Stick marked with ink: *Cut in the center of 7 Pines Battlefield where 15,000 soldiers were killed May 31st - June 1st, 1862. Battle fought by Lee and McClellan. Battlefield guide L. E. Syme.*
Courtesy, collection Paul Weisberg.

▶ 9/28 Cane with a bullet imbedded in its handle. The ring bears the inscription: *C. H. Flick / 2nd Lieut. Co. B / 80th Ill's Infy / This cane cut from Missionary Ridge, Tenn. Battlefield, Feb. 1863.*
Courtesy, collection Paul Weisberg.

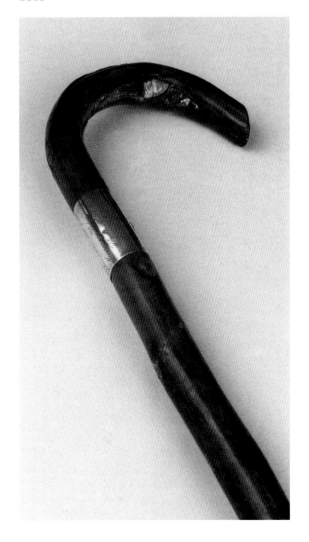

The Smithsonian Institute has a gold headed cane the wood of which was taken from the Shiloh Church (Pittsburgh Landing). This was the first major battle of the War and the site of much bloodshed. This cane was given to General Grant in recognition of his humane treatment of the sick and wounded, April 6-7, 1862.

▲ 9/29 Carved by *H. Templer, Fecit Dec. 1863* this cane was presented to *Brigadier General J.D. MacPherson / He who steals what isn't his / When he's caught will go to prison.*
Courtesy, collection Paul Wesiberg.

▲ 9/30 Wood from the *Mississippi burnt off Port Hudson Mch. 15, 1863.*The presentation of this cane to Commander George Dewey by his friend R. A. Melancton Smith makes it interesting.
Courtesy, Chicago Historical Society.

In the Kansas State Historical Society there is a cane with a handle made out of a fragment of marble taken from the mantel of the country house of Jefferson Davis, near Vicksburg, Mississippi. Union troops undoubtedly are responsible for this souvenir. Davis was President of the thirteen Confederate States of America.

▲ 9/31 The Missouri Historical Society has a cane inscribed: *From Jefferson Davis, Feb. 24, 1863 / Richmond, Va.* This 1880 picture of Jefferson Davis holding his cane was taken on the steps of *Beauvoir.*
Courtesy, Beauvoir, The Last Historic Home of Jefferson Davis.

The New Hampshire Historical Society has two magnolia canes. One is marked *Chancellorville, behind Pleasanton's guns where General Hiram G. Berry was killed. Not far, in front, General Stonewall Jackson was killed. (May 1 - 4 1863).* The other cane commemorates the battle which followed on May 7. Its label reads *Wilderness near where Gen. Wadsworth was killed.* Then follows the date *Sept. 5, 1894* when the branch was cut.

Large numbers of canes connected with Gettysburg can be found in museums. One of the more note-worthy examples can be found at the Hayes Presidential Center where there is a cane of wood from the *High Water Mark*. It was presented to President Hayes. (*The High Water Mark* was a position reached by Union soldiers during the Gettysburg battle).

The Museum of West Point has a shaft made from the flagstaff of the Confederate flag which fell in the third day of fighting at the battle of Gettysburg. The knob is made from a captured gun stick and is engraved on a silver band below the knob: *Gen. Alex S. Webb. Flagstaff of Va. Regt. Pickett and Evans Regt.*

▲ 9/32 Cane with a plaque placed around an imbedded bullet with the inscription *Gettysburg, July 4th, 63 / Stick to a friend Jas. P. Howatt to his friend Col. F. D. Grant.* (Son of General U. S. Grant).
Courtesy, collection Smithsonian Institution.

▲ 9/33 Cane taken from wood near Stonewall Jackson's tomb and inscribed with his numerous battles: *Hainesville / Manasas / 1st Kernstown / Mo. Dowell / Front Royal / Winchester / Port Republic / Gaines Mills / Cold Harbor / Malvern Hill / Cedar Run / Manassas / 2nd Harper's Ferry / Sharpsburg / Fredericksburg / Chancellorsville / Polonia Imperalis / from his grave, Lexington, Va.* The Chicago Historical Society has an affidavit concerning this cane, which was cut in 1894.
Courtesy, Chicago Historical Society.

▲ 9/34 A series of sun burnt canes sold by battlefield guides.The first cane has the name of *Gettysburg* burnt in. *Round Top* was near the southern end of the Gettysburg battle line. The *Gulp's Hill* was the northern point of the Union Forces.
Courtesy, collection Paul Weisberg.

▲ 9/37 A scrimshaw cane (see chapter Ten) with encrusted mother-of-pearl painted with the words *Chickamauga* (a battle fought on September 19 - 20, 1863) and *Mission Ridge* (Missionary Ridge, a battle fought on November 25, 1863.) The names *P. J. Hardman* and *Jones Boro* complete the handle which also features two inlays, one of the Corps Badge of the Federal Army and the other, the year *1863*.
Courtesy, collection Norman Flayderman.

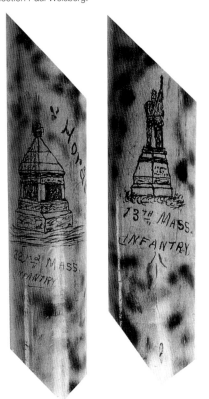

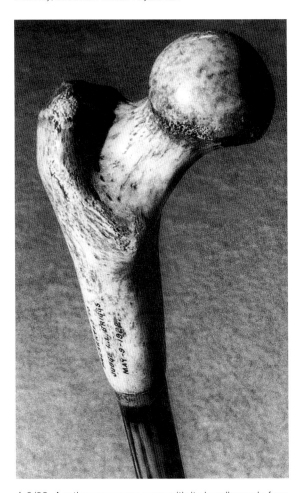

▲ 9/35 Canes inscribed with the monuments erected in memory of the two *Massachusetts Infantry Regiments, the 13th and the 22nd.* The signature reads *Horace A. Parker,* possibly a battlefield guide or the name of the owner who added the identification after purchasing the cane.
Courtesy, collection Paul Weisberg.

◄ 9/36 Because of its importance, the battlefield of *Gettysburg* is cited on numerous canes.
Courtesy, collection Paul Weisberg.

▲ 9/38 A rather gruesome cane with its handle made from the hip bone (femur) of a soldier. The shaft has brown vertical stripes with a printed legend: *Gettysburg July 1 - 2 - 3 1863 / Wood from Round Top*. It was presented to *Judge L. L. Briggs on May 9, 1922.*
Courtesy, collection Francis H. Monek.

▲ 9/39 A presentation cane made from wood of the Grant Pemberton Oak, given by *Colonel Eli C. Kingsley and Major Charles J. McCarthy to John Albion Andrew*, who was governor of Massachusetts during the Civil War. All three names are engraved on the top, together with the words *Grant and Pemberton Oak Vicksburg, Miss. July 4, 1863*.
Courtesy, Massachusetts Historical Society.

1864

▼ 9/40 Gold knob inscribed Major *Thomas T. Eckhert, Jan.1, 1864, Asst. Supt. U.S.M.T.* On the side reads the inscription: *Presented by / the employees / of the War Dept./ Telegraph office.* Next to the text are the figures of Liberty and a soldier. The particular ship featured is the most interesting aspect of the cane — she is the British steamship *Great Western*, which laid the first telegraphic cable across the ocean.
Courtesy, Harry S. Truman Library.

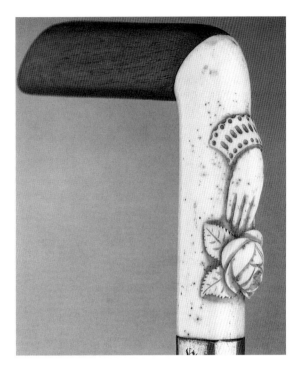

▲ 9/41 Shaft made of wood from the *Vanderbilt*. This 4000 ton ship with 15 guns, built in 1862-3, was offered to the Union Government by Mr Vanderbilt. It was later sold by the Navy in Feb. 1873.
Courtesy, Chicago Historical Society.

▲ 9/42 Shaft made of timber from *U.S.S. Kearsage*, which sank the *C.S.S. Alabama*.
Courtesy, Museum, Department of the Navy, Annapolis.

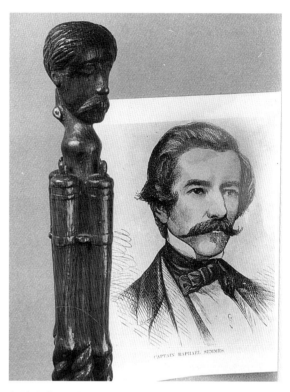

▼ 9/43 The French "L'Illustration" gives its interpretation to the sinking of the *Alabama*. People came from Paris by special trains to watch the battle. The Impressionist painter, Edouard Manet painted the scene which hangs today in the Philadelphia Museum of Art.
Courtesy, archives Catherine Dike.

▲ 9/44 Carved wood made from an oar of *C.S.S. Alabama*. Given to *Captain Evan Parry Jones*, Commander of the *Yacht Deerground*, which rescued survivors of the *C.S.S. Alabama* when she was sunk off Cherbourg, France, on June 19, 1864. The head represents Captain Raphael Semmes of *C.S.S. Alabama*.
Courtesy, Museum, Department of the Navy, Annapolis.

The Hayes Presidential Center has a cane with a handle resembling a bird's head, marked *Winchester 19 Sept. Red Bud Slough.*

The Museum of the Confederacy has a cane with a shaft made from the *Gunboat C.S.S. Florida* which was captured in the port of Bahia, Brazil, a neutral harbor, on October 7, 1864. The Union Navy towed her to Chesapeake Bay where she was sunk.

► 9/45 Silver knob on marked: *Dam' the Torpedoes GO AHEAD,* the famous words of Admiral Farragut spoken at the Battle of Mobil Bay, August 5, 1864. The shaft is made of timber from his flagship, *U.S.S. Hartford.* What Farragut referred to as torpedoes would today be called mines.
Courtesy, The Connecticut Historical Society.

1865

The Museum of the Confederacy has two canes linked with the *Battle of Spotsylvania.* One is marked in ink *Spotsylvania C.H. (Court House)* and the dates *May 12, 1864* and *October 23, 1892,* the first being the date of the battle and the second the day the battlefield was visited by the owner of the cane. The second stick has the inscription *Cut near spot where B.J. Julius Daniel was killed* and the name *Spotsylvania.*

The New Hampshire Historical Society has three canes cut by H. W. Harmon on August 31, 1894 in the *Crater of Petersburg, Va.,* on *Fort McGiley* and *on Fort Hell.* These battles took place between June 1864 and April 1865.

The Wisconsin Historical Society has a cane marked: *From site of Gen. S. E. Johnston surrender to General W. T. Sherman in Greensboro, N.C., May 3rd, 1865.* The Chicago Historical Society has a stick purportedly made from the tree under which Lee surrendered to Grant. As the formal surrender took place indoors, the stick obviously traces its origins to the well-known painting showing the ceremony conducted beneath a tree! In any case most of these sticks plainly were made of materials taken from battlefield sites years after the actual battles had taken place.

▲ 9/46 Civil War tin-type of a soldier. This is certainly a personalized stick, as the owner obviously knew the person represented.
Courtesy, collection Bruce I. Thalberg.

Souvenirs of the Civil War

▼ 9/47 A carved cane which bears the maker's or proprietor's name: *H. Keller*, then a soldier holding an American flag and a mounted soldier. Below the latter, can be read: *U.S. from 1862 to 1865 / 2B4OV* (Second Battalion Ohio, 4th Ohio Voluntary Cavalry). Some of the words which fill the rest of the cane appear to be either encoded or phonetically spelt to the point of absurdity: *Boyenk / Nashvi / (Nashville?) / Lanayy / Cheryn / Mongom / Masey / Macon / Averyp / Morish / Fridom*. The lapel of the uniform is not very military, but considering the spelling of the carver, any style is possible!
Courtesy, collection George H. Meyer.

▲ 9/48 Libbey Prison, in Richmond, Virginia, 1865. Hundreds, if not thousands, of pieces of wood were cut from the floors, window sills, and other parts of this prison. Carving these pieces often took place later. Most of these cuttings were taken from the prison when the building was moved to the Columbian Exposition in Chicago in 1893. Collector Watkins bought his two canes there.
Courtesy, The Museum of the Confederacy.

▲ *9/49 This cane was taken from Libbey's prison in 1878 and presented in 1894 to Comrade D. R. Wilson.*
Courtesy, collection Smithsonian Institution.

▶ 9/50 A cane carved with lizards, snakes, turtles and marked *Johnson's Island, Ohio*.
Courtesy, Minnesota Historical Society.

▲ 9/51 A carved four-sided cane with the inscription *Camp /*
Chase / Prison, Ohio. Camp Chase was first a military train-
ing camp for Union soldiers, and later became a prison, just
outside of Columbus, Ohio. The Hayes Presidential Center
has a similar cane, marked on its four facets *Camp Chase /*
1863 / Ohio Mar / G.B.Johnson. The carver gave it to a
friend in Richmond who presented it to General Hayes in
1877.
Courtesy, collection George H. Meyer.

▲ 9/52 The top part of this cane is four sided, each bearing
an inscription: *Johnsons / Island / J H. McKenzie / W.*
Sherman. Johnson's Island was a Union Prison on Lake
Erie, one mile from the coast.
Courtesy, Museum of the Confederacy.

▲ 9/53 A German inspired cane, with a cavalryman below
the American Eagle. On the rear of the carved handle is the
portrait of a General, perhaps U.S.A. C. P. Porter.
Courtesy, collection Eric Vaule.

▶ a) Many canes were made by this artist, whose signature in ink reads: *Trade Mark / R. M. Foster.* As opposed to the canes he made for fellow veterans, this one was for himself, since his name is followed by his address: *Sparta, Mo. R.M.* *Foster, Co C...8 Regt Wilcox Brig / Con. Vols.* and then by the phrase: *Accept this cane, tis all I have, carved by a rebel's hand, who gave his health, his wealth, his all for Dixie's sunny South land.*   Courtesy, collection L.G.

▲ b)   Various canes related to the Civil War. Top to bottom: This cane is different and interesting as the owner is known: *S.W. Wright - Boston* is found on the copper cap. He had received the Congressional Medal of Honor for heroism at the Battle of Antietam. At the end of the War, he formed one of the finest collections of Civil War relics. Can one imagine that this cane was made from a piece of wood of the picket-line he defended?

Below a cane made in Andersonville, Georgia with the words: *J.F. Brown / Where Liberty / Dwells / There is / My Home / April 24th - 1862.* The shape is very similar to other prison canes. One wonders whether they were made by the same hand.

Center, a cane-type often to be found. Carved with the Corp badges, there is *Liberty / In God we Trust / We will* *stand by the Flag.* The name of the receiver has been added: *Capt. James J. Butler, 81st Regt. N.Y. Vol's.*

Below, the inscription reads a *Peace relic of the War / Cut at the Antietam Battle fought September 17th, 1862 / Genl. Lee - Genl.Johnson - Genl. Burnside - Genl. Hooker - Genl. Jackson / Officers of the Battle / Carved by SF Hebb Ju.. / Presented by Joseph A. Jackson to Fr....* which proves that canes were carved after the War and were made as commemorative presents to former soldiers and officers.

The bottom cane was carved by a Confederate prisoner at Johnson Island. The cane was presented to General William Seward Perigo, U.S.A. in charge of the prison at that time.

Courtesy, collection Norman Flayderman.

◄ a) A more elaborate handle undoubtedly made for a
G.A.R. reunion, with the badge carved on the top of the
shaft. It represents an infantry man from New York, as written on his pack is: *F. 125 N.Y. Vol.*
Courtesy, George H. Meyer, *American Folk Art Canes,* 1992.

▲ b) A soldier's cane representing the
headdress of an Indian Chief and bearing
the word *Bisons*. It could have been carved
by an Afro-American who served in Europe
during World War I, their mascot being the
buffalo. It is signed by *M. Perrey*.
Courtesy, collection Catherine Dike.

▲► c) The handle depicts a hand grenade surmounting the
initial *U.S.A.*, two cannons, a turtle and the date *November
14, 1917*. The name *B.B.Wilmoth* is carved on the other
side, along with a rattlesnake. Wilmoth was from West
Virginia and served in France during World War I.
Courtesy, George H. Meyer, *American Folk Art Canes,* 1992.

▲ d) Many canes can be found like the one above left
signed *C. W. Teale, Bath.* The shaft is always painted black,
and the various military and patriotic emblems painted in
colored ink. An assortment of badges run down the shaft,
along with an eagle holding three arrows, a pen-knife and
the G.A.R. medal. C.W. Teale retired to the New York State
Soldiers Home and was buried in the Veterans
Administration National Cemetery in Bath, New York.

The middle cane is known to collectors as the
Jefferson cane, carved in large quantities by Thomas
Jefferson Craddock. This one was presented to *Col. Jos. H.
Sinex / 2611 Washington Ave. / Phila. PA. / Presented by
Wm. Skates of Culpepper / Va.*

Above right is another interpretation of the Flag cane
with a soldier bearing the flag. Again, badges run along the
shaft.
Courtesy, The Civil War Library, Philadelphia.

▲ 9/54 Presentation cane with a gold knob, marked *F. M. Hereford, M. D.* On the other side are the words: *Chief Surgeon / Gen. D.Peugglis Division/ C. S. A. /* Doctor Francis M. Hereford came from Louisiana. In 1862 he went to Montgomery, Alabama to oversee a Confederate Military Hospital.
Courtesy, collection Alex Peck.

▲ 9/55 A gilded cane handle presented to General Philip H. Sheridan.
Courtesy, collection Smithsonian Institution.

(Back)

(Front)

▲▶ 9/56 A very elaborate cane claimed to have been presented to General Philip H. Sheridan. The whole shaft is carved. The top is formed by the American Eagle; below it, the Statue of Liberty. On the back is all the paraphernalia of a soldier. Further down the shaft are portraits of Lincoln, Grant and Seward, and below them another woman standing on a bundle of wheat and a horn of plenty which is touched by the American flag.
Courtesy, collection Smithsonian Institution.

▲ 9/57 A carved cane by Robert M. Foster, who was commissioned by *The Sons and Daughters of the Confederacy* to present it to *Our Noble Leader and Chieftain General C.B. Gordon*. The shaft is carved with the usual animals and objects found on other canes carved by Foster.
Courtesy, Missouri Historical Society.

▲ 9/58 A silver handle with the words *Never Forget*, and the name *Enoch*, together with a Rebel flag staff, a cannon and a pile of cannon balls that turned to the right activates the tune Dixie. Turned to the left it stops the music. A gold key is installed to wind the box.
Courtesy, Beeman collection.

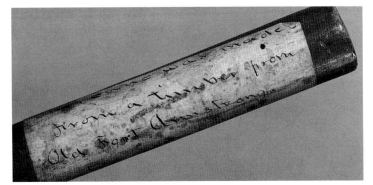

▲ 9/59 A tag mentions that: *This cane was made from the timber from Old Fort Armstrong*. The Fort was located on Rock Island in the Mississippi River, between the cities of Rock Island, Illinois and Davenport, Ohio.
Courtesy, Chicago Historical Society.

▲ 9/60 A cane representing Anna Elizabeth Dickinson, who aroused the greatest enthusiasm wherever she spoke during the Civil War. After the War, she turned to drama.
Courtesy, collection Francis H. Monek.

The Spanish-American War
1898

The United States was spoiling for War with Spain several months before hostilities officially began. The *Maine*, under the command of Captain Sigsbee, sailed to Havana ostensibly to protect U.S. citizens, and there she was blown up on February 15, 1898 with the death of 260 men. War was declared two months later. All ships on the U. S. Eastern seaboard sailed south to Key West searching for the Spanish Squadron. Commodore Schley found the squadron in the Cuban harbor of Santiago, and sank the collier (coal-carrying) *Merrimac* in the narrowest part of the channel. Rear Admiral W. P. Sampson, commanding the Atlantic Fleet, sailed to Guantanamo Bay where he based his vessels. On July 3 the Spanish Squadron was defeated.

The war in the Pacific, centered around the Philippine Islands, saw more action than the conflict in the Atlantic. The Navy and the Marine Corps took Guam. A protocol of peace was declared in August, with the official signing taking place on December 10, 1898. Spain ceded Puerto Rico, Guam, and the Philippines to the United States and gave up their sovereignty over Cuba.

Several museums have canes which were made from various ships of this period. The War Memorial Museum in Newport News, Virginia, has a cane made from a table on the *Brooklyn*, which was the Flag Cruiser of Commodore Winfield Scott Schley. The Museum of Annapolis has a cane made from timber of the Spanish battleship *Reina Christina*. A cane marked *Rena Mercedes* is with the New Hampshire Historical Society. The Carnegie Museum in Pittsburgh has a cane engraved: *Cuerpo De. E.M. Del Ejerciyo* around a five star wreath and crown. The copper ring is inscribed: *Cut from the mast of the Merrimac at Santiago De Couby July 25th 1898 by Geo. S. Gallupe Jr.* The Connecticut Historical Society has a cane inscribed: *Don Antonia de Ulloa*, a Spanish ship sunk by Dewey. Another Historical Society has a cane with a shaft made from wood of the blockhouse on *San Juan Hill*. The knob is made from wooden remains of the Maine.

▲ 9/61 The remains of the *Maine* rested in the harbor of Havana for fourteen years. In 1912 the wreck was towed out to sea and sunk.
Courtesy, Library of Congress.

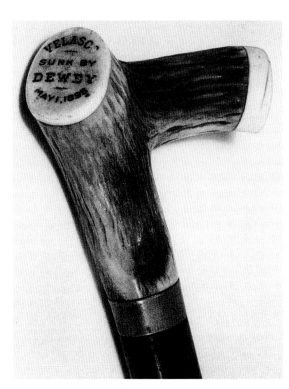

▲ 9/62 A cane with the inscription: *Velasco / Sunk by Dewey / May 1, 1898*.
Courtesy, San Francisco Maritime National Historical Park.

▲ 9/64 Two canes made from timber of Spanish warships, one marked: *May 1, 1898, Battle of Cavite*. the other with the inscription: *Battle of Manilla Bay, Castillo*;
Courtesy, collection L.G.

▲ 9/65 A gold-handled cane with its shaft encased in tortoiseshell. The knob is engraved with the initials *L.W.* for General Leonard Wood, a hero of the Spanish-American War.
Courtesy, collection Smithsonian Institution.

◄ 9/63 The shaft of this stick was carved from part of the Maine, which is pictured in Havana harbor.
Courtesy, Museum, Department of the Navy, Annapolis.

▲ 9/66 Cane carved in *Camp Alger, Virginia*, signed *Alden Brown, 1st Division Hospital*. On the top of the cane is written *H. G. H. 1898*. The cane has the dates of the Spanish War. Near the bottom, the inscriptions: *Uncle Sam to Spain: The boys in blue are too hot for you*. The carver presented this cane to Horam G. Haynes, North Bend, PA, 2nd Army Corps.

Courtesy, collection Smithsonian Institution.

World War I
1917 - 1918 (U. S. A)

World War I officially began for the United States in 1917, although volunteers had enlisted before this date. Canes can be found which were carved at battlefields where the Americans were active: the Meuse-Argonne in Lorraine and Meurthe-et-Moselle among them.

▲ 9/67 Two American canes made by a soldier and left in France (where they were found). The first has an opossum as a handle. This animal being unknown in Europe, it must have intrigued the finder. Near the bottom of the shaft is an arresting face with an American eagle above it. At the very bottom is a fish and a standing woman. This cane bears several military insignia. The second cane, carved in the same style, has a face positioned in the same location as the first. On the shaft is a decoration with six pointed stars representing the 8th Corps, and below the latter are the initials *L. G.*

Courtesy, collection G. & M. Segas.

World War II
1941 - 1945 (U. S. A.)

By the early 1940s, soldiers were not as skillful with their jack-knives as their forefathers, a statement which applies to both American and European troops. Fewer canes are found dating from this war than from the 1914 - 1918 conflict, when long hours spent in trenches allowed plenty of time to carve sticks. The only general who wore a cane was General MacArthur. In his Memorial are several canes carved by soldiers. Some read: *General D. MacArthur Liberator World War II./ Remembrance L.G.A.F. Lapham Grllas 103rd Infantry, Regt. Col V.C. Luluquisin Over-Ass Comd.* Another has the markings: *To General MacArthur from the fighting 57th, by Fermin Asence, Sgt. Major,* interesting since this soldier did not fight under his command.

▲ 9/68 A head *Cut and Carved by W.A. Willard, June 13th 1920 at Reunion of Veterans of Spanish War, Mexican Border and World War.* What is visible on the beard reads: *B.L. Burke, joined the Co.K. 1902, 3 wounds in World War, Battle of Verdun, Bellau Woods, Chateau Thierry, 1919.* Courtesy, private collection, Boston.

▲ 9/69 A picture of General MacArthur taken at Corregidor in 1942. He was advised to cease wearing a cane, as the era was approaching when a stick betokened an elderly man.
Courtesy, MacArthur Memorial, Norfolk, Va.

▲ 9/70 Three canes worn by General MacArthur. In the foreground is a stick carved with General MacArthur and a pentagon of five pointed stars. The remainder of the shaft is carved with flowers. At left is a crook handle with a double-headed arrow wrapped around the shaft. The third cane, on top, had belonged to the General's grandfather, Richard Beard. The knob is engraved: R. Beard D.D. from the senior Class of 1868. It is not known which college Richard Beard attended.
Courtesy, MacArthur Memorial, Norfolk, Va.

▲ 9/71 Two canes which had belonged to the Japanese. The snake had belonged to Okomoto Motokichi who gave it to General MacArthur in November 1945. The other was the cane of General Yamashita, who was tried as a war criminal, found guilty and sentenced to death by hanging. Colonel William P. Moore supervised the execution and took possession of Yamashita's cane. He donated it to the MacArthur Memorial in 1986.
Courtesy, MacArthur Memorial, Norfolk, Va.

▶ 9/72 If only one cane could be shown to represent all the European battlefields, this would be perfect. *Major General Paul W. Baade, Commander General of the 35th Division*, had his name and all his battles from July 1944 to V. E. Day burned into the cane. The cross indicates where he was injured. It is said that an aide picked up the branch on Omaha Beach, and gave it to the General who wore it all during the war. The woodburning of the shaft was done by a French woman in Nancy, who marked American dates.

Le Meauffe

7/13	Villiers-Fossard 122
7/16	Emilie-Hill
7/17	St. Lo
7/18	Torigny
7/31	Vire/River
8/3	Mortain-Hill 317
8/12	Châteaudun
8/16	Orleans
8/16	Montargis
8/23	Joigny
8/25	Nancy
9/15	Moselle-Meurthe-la Sânon Rivers, Canals de l'Est and Marne au Rhin
9/12 to 17	Fôret de Champeroux
9/22	Gremercy
10/1 X	Jallaucourt
11/8	Château Salins Woods
11/12	Morhange
11/15	Puttelange
12/4	Sarremines
12/5	Sarre-Blies Rivers
12/8 to12	Habkirghen, Germany

From bottom, reading up:

12/12 to 1/18	Lower Vosges
1/25 to 1/30	Roer River (Hilfart)
2/26	Venlo
3/1	Geldern
3/3	Reimberg
3/5	Rhine (Wesel)
3/11	The Ruhr Pocket
3/26 to 4/13	The Elbe (Tangedhutte)
4/15 to 2	Hannover
5/9	V. E. DAY

Courtesy, Harry Truman Library.

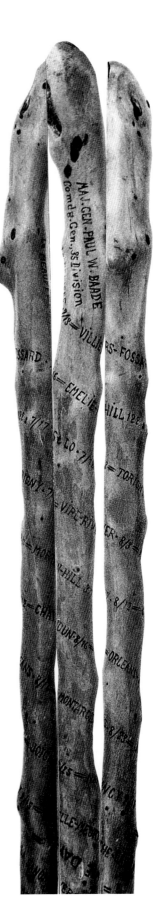

▲ 10/1   Sailors landing after numerous months at sea. One has a cane ready to exchange it against a glass of whisky!
Courtesy, Edward Wilson.

Scrimshaw Canes

Introduction

No one knows the exact origin of the word scrimshaw, which is used to describe handcraft work done on board whaling ships. Although used occasionally by English authors, the word is found primarily in American writings. Different authorities mention Dutch, Danish, Eskimo, or even American Indian roots. Scrimshaw objects were made by whalemen of all countries, but the major production was American. United States captains imposed less discipline aboard than did their British counterparts. On foreign whalers, scrimshawing was tolerated, but was not the main pastime. Between 1810 and the Civil War the whaling trade developed tremendously; over 700 vessels carrying up to 150,000 men between them were engaged in voyages lasting three to four years, mainly in the Pacific Ocean. This period (1810-1865) is considered the golden age of scrimshaw.

The making of a scrimshaw cane was an uncomplicated task which became more sophisticated over time as artistic decorations were added to the simple format. One could begin with a simple knob of marine ivory on a wooden shaft. Later one might cut a shaft from the jawbone of a whale (whose consistency is more like hardwood than elephant ivory) turn it on a lathe (if one existed aboard), polish, and eventually etch it. Later examples featured the intricate work of fashioning spirals, cross-hatching, rope carvings, and so forth. These folk artists developed their art under primitive conditions, although they had the benefit of a tremendous amount of raw material at hand.

Baleen, commonly called "whalebone" and found in the mouth of bowhead whales, was used not only in the manufacture of entire canes, but also to decorate shafts made from the jawbone. Ranging in color from dark brown to dark greenish-yellow, it is often mistaken for horn. Other materials used for decoration include mother-of-pearl, tortoiseshell, vegetable ivory, coconut shell, and the pine or cedar wood commonly found on board ship, mixed with scraps of metal, occasionally, but rarely, silver. Precious woods from the South Pacific islands could be used for the shafts as well.

▲ 10/2 A whale man working on various scrimshaw material. In the foreground are whale teeth. The long jaw bone will be used to make the shaft of canes.
Courtesy, collection Norman Flayderman.

Numerous logbooks mention the scrimshaw work done by whalemen, captains as well as sailors.

On board "Minerva" (New Bedford,1860): *Everybody scrimpshonting az the term goes / hear that iz making caines and corzet boards.*

On Bark "Messenger" (New Bedford,1863): *Done sundry jobs here and there, the Capt. is making canes and it always takes 3 or 4 to help him when he is doing anything.*

On Ship "Mary Frazer" (San Francisco, 1865): *All hands employed in making canes.*

On Bark "Globe", (off the Coast of Africa, 1871): *Sold a cane to the mate of an English Brig. The end of 1871 is fast approaching, also is eternity.....Scrimshawing....*

On Bark "Horatio" (San Francisco, 1898): *Everybody making canes....*

On Bark "Avola" (New Bedford, 1873): *I am making a cane. ...Finished my cane today.*

▲ 10/3 The tools used by a scrimshander. Top left, a square shaft, to the right a rounded piece. A design made of dots is punched by a needle, perhaps over a picture. The dots are then joined together with the punch or a knife. A small tooth of a sperm whale forms the handle of this cane. The dark cane is a good example of a combination of precious wood, baleen disks and sea ivory.
Courtesy, Mystic Seaport Museum, Inc.

▲ 10/5 The shaft of the middle cane has the peculiarity of being wrapped with bands of baleen. A hand holding a snake is a common representation, often found in other materials, but the hand holding a small whale is not often encountered.
Courtesy, the Barbara Johnson Folk Art collection.

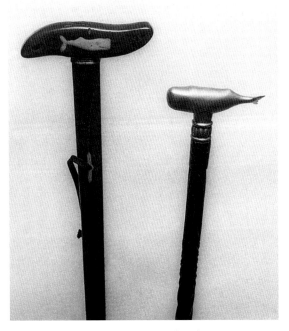

▲ 10/4 Two whales form these two handles.
Courtesy, the Barbara Johnson Folk Art collection.

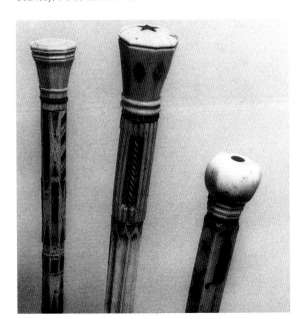

▲ 10/6 Three intricate scrimshaw canes, inlaid with numerous pieces of baleen.
Courtesy, the Barbara Johnson Folk Art collection.

▲ 10/7 Marked on this shaft is a travelling log of the "U.S.S. Constitution" during the years 1839-1841. *William S. Somerby*, a sail maker, carved the following: *U.S. Constitution. Captain Daniel Turner / Bearing the broad pennant of Commodore Alex./ Claxton / Norfolk March 1, 1839 / New York April 2 / Veracruz May 18 / Havanna July 4 Rio Janiero Sept 1 / Valparaiso Nov.2 Callao Jan 1. 1840 / Talcuhuana March 2 / Payta May 11 / Puna Sept 20 / Juan Fernandez. July 24. 1841. William S. Somerby*
Courtesy, Mystic Seaport Museum, Inc.

▲ 10/8 Abe Warner's Cobweb Palace Saloon in San Francisco where whale-men would often exchange a scrimshaw cane for a glass of whisky.
Courtesy, San Fransisco Maritime National Historic Park.

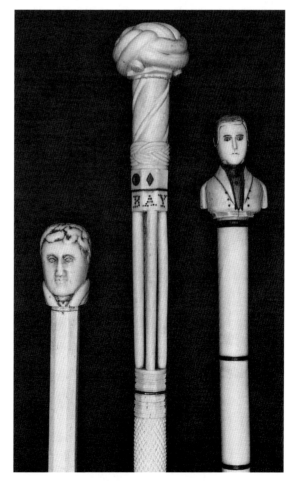

▲ 10/9 Two figurative knobs, one of a head, the other of a bust. The most commonly encountered sailor's knot, the Turk's head, decorates the middle cane which bears the letters C. Bayley in small nails .
Courtesy, Mystic Seaport Museum, Inc.

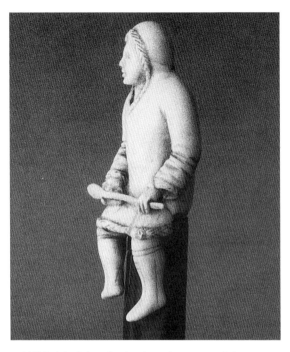

▲ 10/10 A Inuit handle showing a harpooner sitting on top
of the shaft.
Courtesy, collection Neils MacKenna.

▼ 10/11 A group of "new" scrimshaw canes which have
their handles etched and painted with maritime scenes.
Courtesy, collection Frank Monek.

▲ 10/12 An selection of authentic scrimshaw canes which
can still be found in the late 20th century.
Courtesy, collection Paul Weisberg.

When a whaleman retired, he continued to "scrimshaw" at home, using more sophisticated tools. It was a good way to pass the time and earn a little money. Later, others took over the work, copying the old techniques, making it difficult if not impossible to date any particular cane. The whaling industry collapsed at the turn of the century. Some experts date "old" scrimshaw as prior to World War I; others allow the period up to 1924, when the last American whaler, the "Wanderer", sank.

Close and careful examination must always be given when faced with a scrimshaw cane. "New" scrimshaw, including canes, exists in great quantities. These "new" handles are always an interesting addition to a collection. Intricate and beautifully carved shafts can even be molded in plastic, as examination of a plastic narwhal tusk shows. When used as presentation items, handles or knobs can bear names, initials, or dates. However, one firm guideline is that handles of "old" canes are never etched and colored with nautical scenes. The moisture of the hand and the wear of usage could erase the etching and ink upon the knob. This can be observed in examples among the hundreds of walking sticks in the East Coast whaling museums, in the Barbara Johnson and Norman Flayderman collections, and in the numerous books on scrimshaw.

Seaman's Craft

The carving of ivory dates back to early civilizations. Availability of ivory provided by sea mammals depended upon the fishing skills of men. In Alaska, whale hunting settlements date back to 100 or 200 A.D. Alaskan scrimshaw canes have a local style; they are more often carved rather than being etched or decorated. Offshore whaling was prevalent along the European coasts during the ninth century A.D. On the New Continent, as early as 1668, the first settlers were aided in their offshore hunting expeditions by a tribe of Algonquin Indians living in the area of the Ottawa River in Canada.

In addition to sea ivory, many other materials were found by fishermen and sailors. Seamen aboard commercial sailing ships and United States naval vessels executed typical scrimshaw work, using what raw materials they could find or buy. The most common materials were those found on board, usually wood. These canes could easily have been the work of whalemen, but one tries to differentiate between scrimshaw and "seaman's craft".

▼ 10/13 Two sawfish extremities, making more of a souvenir than a real cane. The middle one is made from the appendix of the flying swordfish.
Courtesy, collection Frank Monek.

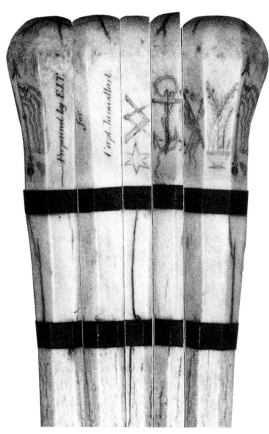

The "sea" cane most frequently encountered is the one made of shark vertebrae strung over a metal rod. These were not only made on shipboard; craftsmen ashore were given the materials by fishermen. In the same manner, walrus spines were used by whalemen and sailors to make shafts, these animals being hunted for their oil. The spines of other sea mammals or fish found their way onto metal rods to form intriguing staffs. One often encounters the stingers of the manta ray mounted on a metal rod. The "sword" of the swordfish made an unusual shaft.

Sharkskin could be wrapped around a metal or wooden rod. This latter work was performed in workshops on land, principally in France, where it took the name "galuchat", and which necessitated a great deal of work with acids.

▲ 10/14 A cane made for the captain and marked: *Prepared by F. J. T. / for / Capt. James Hart.* The sides have a masonic triangle, an anchor and what seems like flowers.
Courtesy, collection Norman Flayderman.

◀ 10/15 The vertebra of an unknown animal. Shark verterbrae have so called holes in each sections, that of walrus, have different holes. (Color picture).
Courtesy, collection Richard W. Carlson.

▲ 10/16 Modern canes made out of the jawbone of the whale can be found in various shapes.
Courtesy, collection W. Hentchel.

▲ 10/17 A manta ray's stinger mounted on a metal rod. The silver knob indicates that it was made on land, no doubt in a silversmith's shop.
Courtesy, collection Catherine Dike.

The list of animals which provided carving material to sailors and whalemen would not be complete without the noblest of all, the small Arctic whale known as the narwhal. The spiral tusk, formed by one of its two upper teeth (the other being atrophied) was greatly sought after throughout the centuries to make regal canes. All the legends of the unicorn are also attached to this tusk. It remains in great demand today, smaller tusks being used to manufacture canes and larger ones (some extending over two meters) mounted on pedestals. As very little carving, or scrimshaw, work is entailed, the narwhal tusk cane forms a category of its own, primarily as a splendid material for a shaft. The handles and knobs of such canes were often made by silversmiths. (Color picture).

Walking-sticks made of coral and from dried and twisted kelp are mere curiosities, but they deserve mention. Another material from a sea animal, tortoiseshell, is also of interest. Although sometimes used as decoration by whalemen, most canes found using this material were manufactured ashore in specialized workshops which made a variety of objects from tortoiseshell. Sea turtles being classified today as an endangered species, objects made from tortoiseshell are presently banned from entry into the United States.

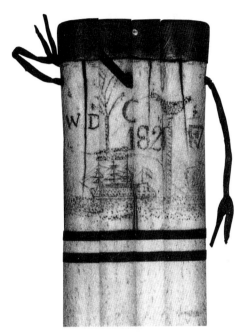

▲ 10/19 A 1827 scrimshaw cane depicting a Man-of-War. Was it made on board, or did a whaleman see such a ship and carved it on his stick?
Courtesy, collection Norman Flayderman.

▶ 10/20 Another unknown verterbrae with its apertures on the side of the shaft.
Courtesy, collection Mark Neider.

▼ 10/21 An X-ray of two shark vertebrae mounted on an iron rod.
Courtesy, collection L.G.

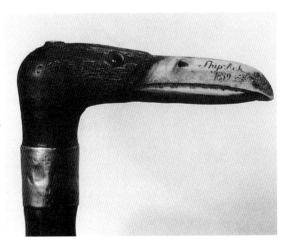

▲ 10/18 A sea bird, mounted as the handle of this cane. The beak bears the name of the ship: *Ship Auk / 1859*. It must have been a small ship, as the *Lloyd's Register* does not mention it during that time.
Courtesy, collection Albert Brown.

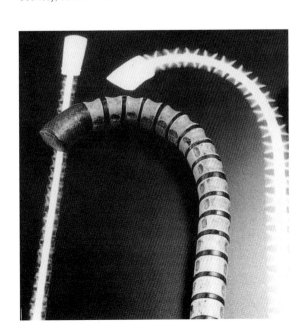

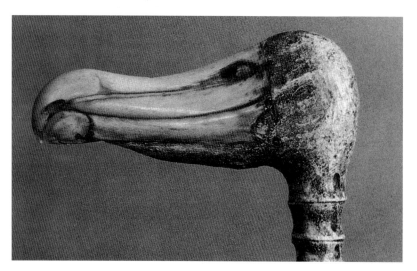

▲ 10/22 Albatross heads were used to make handles. This famous bird of ill-omen, known to every schoolchild from Coleridge's poem "Rime of the Ancient Mariner," was hated by sailors because they attacked and tried to crack the skull of any man who was overboard. At one time these birds were exterminated in great numbers.

God save thee, ancient Mariner !
From Fiends, that plague thee thus !
Why look'st thou so ? With my cross-bow
I shot the Albatross.
Courtesy, collection G. and M. Segas.

River Folk Art

Two final groups of sailors' work conclude this topic. Canes made by river sailors are catalogued as folk art, which they certainly are, without specific mention of "river art." A close examination of all the details carved on the shaft or handle is necessary to identify these specific productions. A few bear carved names which enable the origins to be pinpointed. A thorough knowledge of the history of the large American rivers will help identify such items. Secondly, it is most probable that canes were carved by sailors taken prisoner by the British during the American Revolutionary War and interned on the infamous prison ships. No such canes have yet been discovered, postponing debate on whether they might be classified as scrimshaw or prisoners' art.

▲ 10/23 A piece of dried kelp wrapped around a wooden shaft.
Courtesy, collection L.G.

◀ 10/24 A black coral stick twisted into a shaft.
Courtesy, collection G. and M. Segas.

▲ 10/25 Part of the *New Orleans,* a side-wheeler steamboat which was the first to sail the Mississippi in 1812. The ship was grounded in 1814 near Baton Rouge, Louisiana. Oak from the ship makes the shaft, the spike going through the top could be a nail. It is marked: *Ship New Orleans 1812 / Lewis W. Day / from C. E. E. / 1885.*
Courtesy, collection Neila MacKenna.

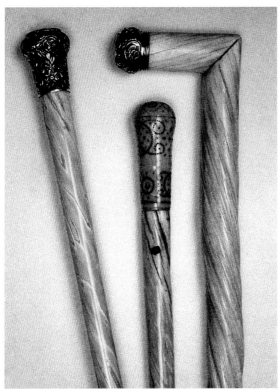

◄ a) Narwhal tusks are usually capped by silver work, with the unadorned ivory forming the shaft. In the examples shown here, the ridges of the tusk have been shaved and sanded down, creating a marbled effect. The center stick is English.
Courtesy, collection Catherine Dike.

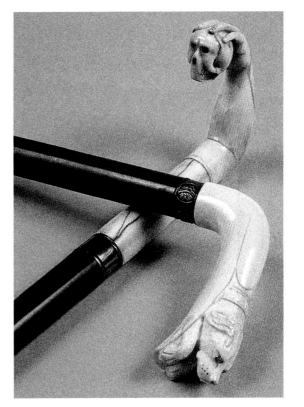

▲ c) Two handles made in walrus teeth. The shafts are in gutta percha.
Courtesy, collection Catherine Dike.

▲ b) Three scrimshaw canes, two of them made of wood. One often forgets how many wooden canes were made on board, as materials from sea animals form the basis for the majority of scrimshaw objects. These pieces were most likely made by sailors on ships other than whalers.
Courtesy, collection Norman Flayderman.

▶ d) The spine of a sea beast, perhaps a young whale, engraved on the side with the word: *Friendship*.
Courtesy, collection Mark Neider.

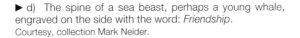

◀ a) A captain leans forward, allowing a good grip on the handle carved from a whale tooth. A similar cane exists in a whaling museum.
Courtesy, collection Mark Neider.

▶ c) Inuit canes are typically carved rather than decorated. Here a brooding head is carved as an integral part of the shaft.
Courtesy, collection Catherine Dike.

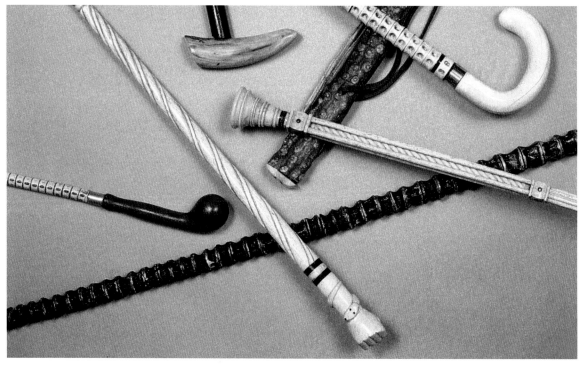

▲ b) A selection of scrimshaw canes. At left bottom, a cane made from the spine of a walrus; a shaft formed from the spine of a shark above it. Next is a cane made from twisted whale bone surmounted by a hand carved from a walrus tooth. Top, a handle made from an large tooth, possibly from a hippopotamus; a carved shaft embedded with baleen. A fine crook handle adorns a shark spine, undoubtedly fashioned in a workshop on land (crook handles are rare on scrimshaw canes), below it, small shells adorn a shaft made from the tail of a ray.
Courtesy, collection Catherine Dike.

▲ a) A group of scrimshaw canes. The center one is covered with strips of baleen one inch and 1/4 (3,2 cm) wide.
The handle in the shape of a bird is a rarity. Most of the
canes shown are examples of the often simple but genuinely
artistic work done aboard whaling ships.
Courtesy, the Barbara Johnson Folk Art collection.

▲ c) Two scrimshaw canes, the smaller one with the date
1827.
Courtesy, collection Norman Flayderman.

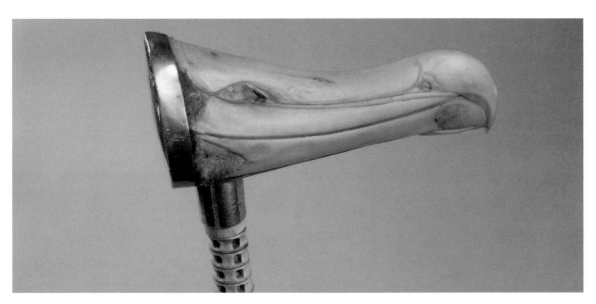

▲ b) Albatross head forming the handle of this cane. The silver decoration proves no doubt that the cane was mounted by a
silversmith.
Courtesy, private collection.

▲ a) Five snakes make up the shaft and handle of this heavy cane.
Courtesy, collection Richard W. Carlson.

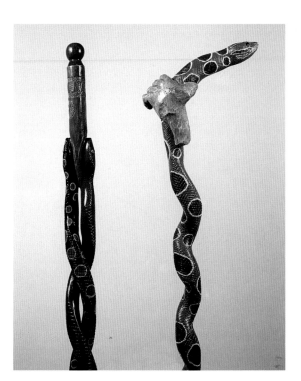

▲ c) Bill Pollard, born in 1928, carved these two canes in his later years. As a child he moved from North Carolina to Virginia.
Courtesy, Blue Ridge Institute, Ferrum, Va

▲ b) A dog's head carved by Mike Hammer.
Courtesy, collection Richard W. Carlson.

▲ d) Two animated canes made by Ross Rutherford of Wise County, Virginia, in 1970. In the cane to the left, when the hat is pushed, the man's arms and legs fly up, his mouth drops open and his eyes roll up. The monkey to the right licks his left hand which flies up to his mouth while his legs and tail move up.
Courtesy, Blue Ridge Institute, Ferrum, Va.

▲ 10/26 A heavy cane, roughly carved with the implements used on a river boat.
Courtesy, private collection.

▲ 10/28 A cane carved on a river boat, bearing a bale, a cask and an anchor.
Courtesy, collection Paul Weisberg.

▲ 10/27 A cylindrical wooden cane with the names of those who manned the *S.B. Phill.Allen. U.S. Mail and Bend Packet,* which was a side wheel packet with a wooden hull, built in Memphis in 1871. Bend refers to a point on the Mississippi River between Memphis and Arkansas City prior to the changing of the course of the river by the government. The cane belonged to Captain Samuel Stacker Lee, whose name one finds carved on the shaft, together with those of the Clerk, the Steward, one First Class Officer and two Second Class officers.
Courtesy, Mississippi River Museum.

▲ 11/1 The Vermont artist Rick Hearn carving one of his many sticks.
Courtesy, collection Rick Hearn.

Modern Folk Art Canes

When does "Modern" folk art begin? With walking sticks, the simplest definition would be the time when canes ceased to be worn as an article of dress, or roughly the period between the two World Wars. The cane at that point became an artistic expression of the carver. Subcategories include those 20th century canes produced by Native Americans and those made for tourists.

As opposed to 19th century canes, modern sticks are very often signed, especially after the middle of the 20th century. The list of modern cane carvers is long, and it is naturally impossible to show all their work. Finally, this chapter could also be written by a modern art scholar as the influences and movements are clear.

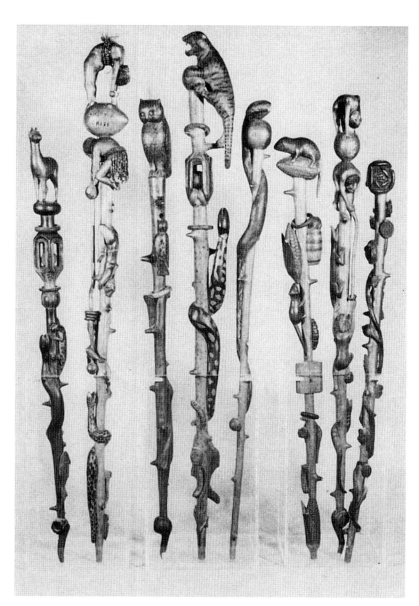

▲ 11/3 A group of sticks thought to have been made by the Chippewa Indians of the Saginaw Valley. They could be more Pow-Wow sticks than regular canes, because of the dimensions of the shafts and the soft wood used. The third from the right is signed: *March 2 11- 1930, made by Milton E. Boshaw, Chipwa, Pungee - Bo - Nishnobia., Flint, Mich. of America.* These canes were auctioned in 1991.
Courtesy, Frank H. Boss Gallery.

▲ 11/2 Three *Guard Sticks* carved in 1939 by José Inez Trujillo for Remington Schuyler. Canes of this type were used to guard fields, gardens or possessions. No one ever violated what was guarded. They were not supposed to be made for sale. It is interesting to note that one finds exactly the same carved animals on Indian canes made in Central America. In more recent days, these guard sticks are called *Flower Sticks.*
Courtesy, University of Missouri, Columbia.

▲ 11/4 A black face, signed *Blake Brewster* (1975).
Courtesy, collection Herbert Waide Hemphill Jr.

▲ 11/7 A picture of José Inez Trujillo who carved the sticks illustrated on the previous page.
Courtesy, University of Missouri, Columbia.

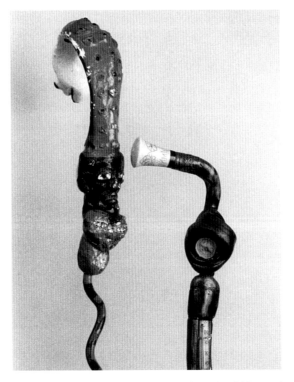

▲ 11/5 Two canes made by Afro-Americans in which metal and metal objects are used to decorate the shafts. (Color picture).
Courtesy, collection Francis H. Monek.

◀ 11/6 A cane presented to Franklin D. Roosevelt, representing an Indian Chief.
Courtesy, Little White House, Warm Springs, Ga.

▲ 11/8 The carving of a Native American together with animal figures readily appealed to tourists
Courtesy, collection L.G.

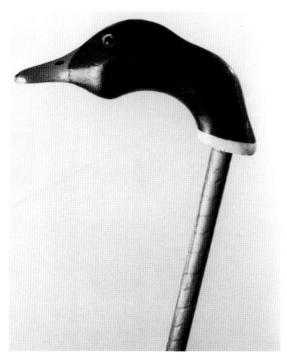

▲ 11/9 A duck decoy head serves as the handle of this cane. Made by *Miles Smith*. (1978, Lake St. Clair, Michigan).
Courtesy, collection Herbert Waide Hemphill Jr.

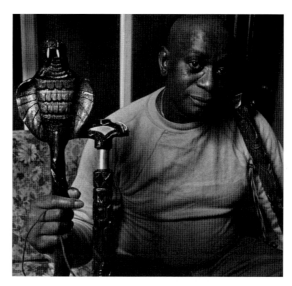

▲ 11/11 Milton Oliver Jews lives and carves his canes in Pennsylvania.
Courtesy, collection Milton O. Jews.

▲ 11/10 Together with the cane in 11/12, these two canes were influenced by the African canes made after World War II. The one on the right is signed *79*.
Courtesy, collection L.G.

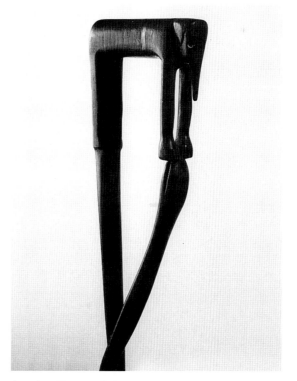

▲ 11/12 Emperor Bokasa used similar canes. The handle forms an enclosed space.
Courtesy, collection B. Grossman.

▶ 11/13 A carved snake, with the bark remaining on the shaft, signed by *Robert Lipe, Rogersville, Tenn.*
Courtesy, collection Herbert Waide Hemphill Jr.

◀ 11/14 A woman's hand throttling a snake, signed *H.A. Brown* and *Lagrange, Ga.* (1983).
Courtesy, collection Herbert Waide Hemphill Jr.

▲ 11/15 A horse carved by Ira Winkelman.
Courtesy, collection Ira Winkelman.

▲ 11/17 A fish forms the handle of this cane carved by Rick Hearn.
Courtesy, collection Rick Hearn.

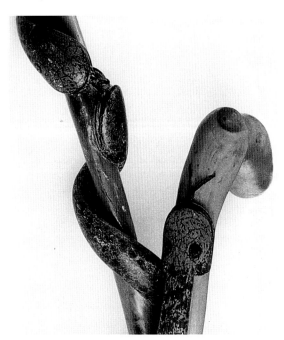

▲ 11/16 Two Ben Miller canes on which the painting is recognizable.
Courtesy, collection Richard W. Carlson.

▲ 11/18 Cane carved by Denzil Goodpaster representing Dolly Parton.
Courtesy, collection Herbert Waide Hemphill Jr.

▶ 11/21 A double profile carved on this stick.
Courtesy, collection Herbert Waide Hemphill Jr.

▲ 11/19 Walter Weinheimer began to carve sticks when he retired. He uses any piece of wood to be found, and decorates them with horn provided by his butcher.
Courtesy, collection Walter Weinheimer.

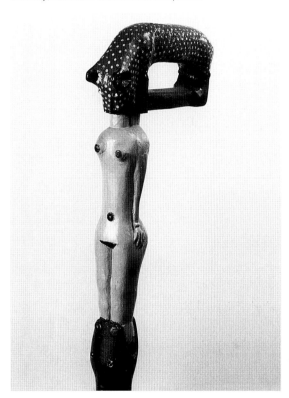

▲ 11/22 *Twice Eaten Lady* (by a snake and a leopard), carved by Denzil Goodpaster.
Courtesy, collection Herbert Waide Hemphill Jr.

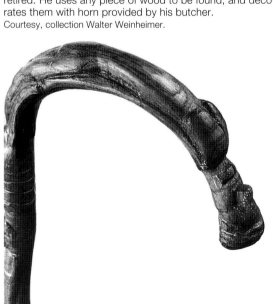

▲ 11/20 A reclining figure of a woman which could be Afro-American.
Courtesy, collection Herbert Waide Hemphill Jr.

▲ 11/20 Ralph Buckwalter carved this bikini-clad beauty.
Courtesy, collection Herbert Waide Hemphill Jr.

▲ 12/1 Two glass blowers ready for the 1912 Labor Day Parade.
They belonged to the Local Union 81.
Courtesy, American Flint Glass Workers Union.

▲ c) Ben Miller of Kentucky carved in 1982 this distinctive cane showing a salamander biting a snake.
Courtesy, collection Herbert Waide Hemphill Jr.

▶ d) Robert Davies of Richmond, Virginia, made this cane along with many others for patients at the Chippenham Hospital. Born in 1926, he was known as the *Stick Man*.
Courtesy, Blue Ridge Institute, Ferrum, Va.

▲ a) Two canes made by the same hand, with the heads carved from the root itself. The cane to the right retains its bark. Found in Alleghany County, Virginia.
Courtesy, Blue Ridge Institute, Ferrum, Va.

▼ b) Five canes made in 1988 by Denzil Goodpaster of Kentucky.
Courtesy, collection Anne and John Miller, Lousville, Ky.

◄ a) Carved in 1988 by Leon Zirkle, who brings humor and social aspects to all his canes. Two of his brothers are also carvers of canes.
Courtesy, Blue Ridge Institute, Ferrum, Va.

▲ b) A fish carved by Herbert Simpson, with the date *7.4. 1950* followed by the name of *Ketchikan* (Alaska).
Courtesy, collection Francis H. Monek.

▲ d) A bizarre looking woman; certainly a talking piece, but perhaps not the best companion for a walk!
Courtesy, collection Richard W. Carlson.

▲ c) Three animals carved by Kentucky artists. The cobra left, is by Larry Oliver, the orange tiger by Junior Lewis is quite long, (48" / 123 cm). The last cane, an alligator is by Gary Argus (41" and 1/4 / 105 cm).
Courtesy, collection Anne and John Miller, Louisville, Ky.

▼ a) This cane was found in an African-American home; the maker is unknown. Twenty-three separate pieces of wood make up the shaft. The pig tops a metal tube which holds the cane together.
Courtesy, Blue Ridge Institute, Ferrum, Va

▶ e) Right, an all-metal cane made by an Afro-American. The handle represents the head of a snake, with a watch dial below it. The shaft is a twisted metal rod, which makes the stick quite heavy. This is a good example of a cane fashioned as an artistic expression, not intended to be worn or used.
Courtesy, collection Francis H. Monek.

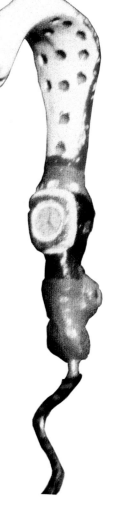

▶ b) Owner and maker of this *Morning Star* cane, Reverend Carl Thomas in Fayetteville, North Carolina, is an Afro-American inspired by biblical interpretation and religious revelations.
Courtesy, Blue Ridge Institute, Ferrum, Va.

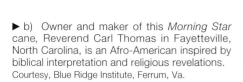

▲▶ c) Right, the top of a cane showing a snake biting a frog and a carved skull. The very top of the shaft has a hole which could have held a horizontal handle, or perhaps a candle. It is carved in high relief *GA* (Georgia) followed by the name *Lenard Megarr* and *Keep Me*.
Courtesy, collection Herbert Waide Hemphill Jr.

▶ d) A dark colored cane attributed to an Afro-American carver. A group of four heads adorns the top part of the shaft.
Courtesy, collection George H. Meyer,
          acquired from Herbert Waide Hemphill Jr..

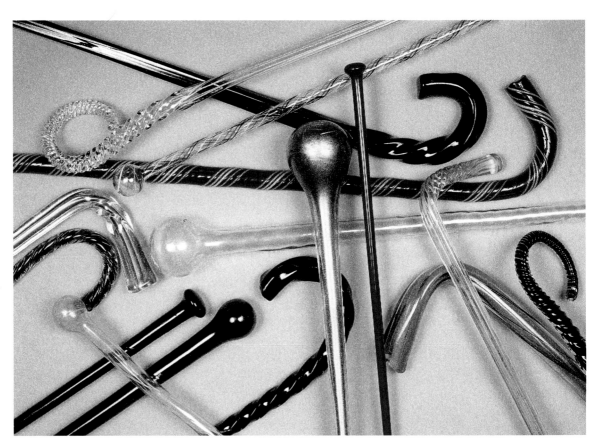

◄▲ a) A group of glass canes showing the great variety of colors used.   Courtesy, collection L.G.

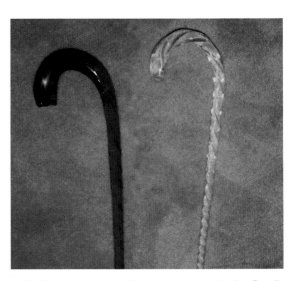

▲ b) Modern pressed glass canes made by the *Boyd's Crystal Art,* in Cambridge, Ohio.
Courtesy, collection Mr. Boyd.

Glass Canes

In Europe glass factories produced these canes by the thousand. They can present an amusing thumbnail sketch of national differences. In England, hollow canes were filled with barley sugar or comfits (small hard candies) in various colors; while in France the interiors were filled by wine or cognac! Legend has it that, on entering military school, conscripts broke their glass canes on the outside walls, or alternatively filled them with wine or cognac to be drunk on their return from military service. Glass canes were also made in Italy and Belgium. Only Germany seems not to have produced a large number, judging by the scarcity of examples in museums and collections.

Several glass manufacturers date back to the early Colonial period, but only during the first part of the 18th century did a truly American style became apparent. In 1739 Caspar Wistar set up a glass factory in Salem County, New Jersey. He imported from Europe numerous workers who brought with them the tradition of "whimsies." The making of these was regarded as an experiment, testing the skill and aesthetic taste of the glass blower in the production of a variety of useless objects. Each workman found a personal artistic outlet in the creation of these whimsies, and they would remain his property to be given to friends and family or as wedding presents. Glass workers would parade, carrying the canes, on Labor Day, or at the services on Glass Workers Memorial Day (2nd Sunday of May), visiting the cemeteries to honor their deceased brothers, wearing their Flint Workers ribbons turned onto the black side. These ribbons were reversible, red for celebratory parades on one side and black for mourning on the other. All these customs were dropped when mechanisation took over in 1920.

As no records were kept of these whimsies, there is no official association between glass canes and any particular factory. One can only say that all 19th century American glass workers produced canes and other whimsies during their lunch hour or at the end of the day, using the remaining molten glass.

One of the few mentions of cane making is reported by the diary of Warren Gay, a school-teacher, who visited the Suncook glasshouse, near Pembroke in 1840: *For the first time in my life, I saw them go through with the process of making glass. They blowed several ladles, small globes, canes and similar baubles for the Ladies and Gents who visited them in the course of the evening.*

Mr and Mrs Leonard S. Blake interviewed Eph Rountree, who was a glass blower in New Jersey at the Gayner Glass Co. As a supervisor, he had plenty of time in which to make whimsies. He died in 1981. Asked how he made glass canes, he answered: *Well, I would use what we called a cutting-off plate, which was nothing but an angle — a three - or four - inch angle — and I would go in with a punty and gather a piece of glass in the furnace. It would came out and I would "marvel" it, cool it down a little bit, and then start marveling more of it on this angle by working lengthwise to the angle. In other words, I stretched this piece of glass out to where I wanted it. Now, it would always work so that I worked the bulk of the glass on the far end; that is where I would put the handle. And that would make it a little bit bigger on that end. But, I have made them the same size. The idea, once you got it out there, we would swing it. I could swing it and stretch it a little more once it cooled down a little bit. You could square them or you could make them round. If you kept turning it, you kept it round. (....).It would be straight. Then you reheat it, not to the point of being molten, but to make it soft and start shaping it out where you wanted it. Now I made a lot of them, like I say, with a handle like this, and I have made a lot of them with a curved handle in which I used a piece of wind pipe. Get about five or six inches of it (glass cane) hot, keep turning it and lay it on that wind pipe. And it would drape down right where you wanted it.*

Interviewing another glass worker in a window glass plant where he worked as a "gatherer" during the period 1895-1920, Mrs Blake writes in her book *Glasshouse Whimsies* that Mr Smith told her that he and other workers made numerous whimsies between shifts and during lunch hours as people always wanted to buy them. It was difficult to make colors until the early 1900s. Mrs Blake writes: *One worker*

▲ 12/2 A group of workers ready for the Labor Day Parade. They are dressed all in white, each wearing a bright tie and carrying a cane. The members of Local Union 81 also wore white trousers.
Courtesy Antique & Historic Glass Foundation.

gathered a small amount of glass on a rod. At the same time, the color chips to be applied were heated to a comparable temperature. They were then put on the gathered glass and another small amount of glass gathered over the colors - all on the same rod.

Another worker with another pipe obtained glass of a larger amount. This was stuck to the original glob of glass containing the colors.

Then one worker would blow on the original pipe while the other one pulled, twisted and drew it out to the length desired. This process made a candy striped cane.

The Boyd's Crystal Art in Cambridge, Ohio, made various colored glass canes in 1983. The "presser" makes these by forming a rectangular block of glass on the end of his punty. The end of the block is held to the floor by a pipe, and the glass is pulled out while turning the punty. The smallest or thinner end is disconnected by applying water. The thicker end is then broken off and reheated to form the handle. The entire cane is then tempered in a lehr (a separate annealing furnace).

The Fairfield Historical Society has a coiled glass cane which was produced for the 1893 Chicago World Fair.

In the book on *American Glass* by George and Helen McKearin, the authors acquired a deep green glass cane with a bust of General Grant imbedded in the flat knob. It was made when Grant lived near Saratoga, during his last illness.

Following is an incomplete index of Glass Works, which are listed by the color used in their glass canes:

▲ 12/3 Photo taken in 1968 at the Libbey Glass factory, to celebrate the 150th anniversary of the company.
Courtesy, American Flint Glass Workers Union.

Aquamarine	Rensselaer Glass Works, Sand Lake, Rensselaer County, South Jersey, and New York State.
Amber	Libbey Glass Company, Ellenville Glass Works, Ulster County, Amber, light, Connecticut and Keene Pitkins Glass Works. Amber, reddish, Stoddard, New Hampshire Glass Houses.
Blue	Adolphus Bush Glass Works, Main & Dorcas, made by A.E. Lippets with white spiral on outside (Missouri Historical Society).
Brown	Produced with mercury.
Clear glass	With red, white and blue stripes, Modes Glass Co, (Frankfurt Kentucky Historical Society).
Gold ruby	Steuben Glass Works.

Olive	Olive-amber, Ellensville Glass Works; Ulster County; Pitkin Glass Works. Olive-green, Congressville Works (Saratoga); Ellensville Glass Works. Dark-olive, with a slight bluish or yellow tone, Congressville Works; Willington Glass Works, West Willington, Conn.
Opaque glass	With colors ranging from white, yellow, blue, green, brick red to black, Stiegel & Co., Mannheim, Pa.
Satin glass	Empty glass cane in which a coating of transparent color has been blown, Phoenix Glass Co.
Spangled glass	Hobbs, Buchunio & Co.
White	Corning Museum of Glass, has several canes with red, white, blue stripes Libbey Glass Co. Dorflinger Glass Works, White Mills Pa. with blue, green and red stripes.

III Silver Handles

13 *Early Silver*

Rest Fenner Smith & Co.

Gorham & Co.

Tiffany & Co.

Other Silversmiths

Presentation Canes

▲ 13/1 Interior view of the Rest Fenner Smith & Co. salesroom situated at 701 Broadway, New York, taken from a catalog. Most likely between 1875 and 1890.
Courtesy, The Winterthur Library, Winterthur, Delaware.

Silver Handles

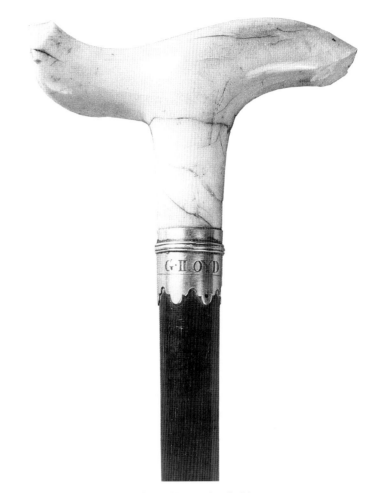

▲ 13/2 Cane which belonged to Grace Lloyd, who died in 1760. Although not marked, it is believed to have been made by her nephew, Joseph Richardson.
Courtesy, The State Museum of Pennsylvania.

Early Silver

As mass manufacturing of silverware in America did not begin until 1842, what pieces we find dating prior to that time are either imported from Europe or China or individually made to request. A client would place an order for a new cane with his silversmith, who also made knee buckles, rings, buttons, earrings, lockets, thimbles, canes, umbrellas and whip handles.

New York's leading silversmith, Jacob Boelen, made a silver topped cane in 1715 for John Underhill (1670-1728), whose name is engraved on the collar. Underhill was an important personality of the time. The cane remains in the family today.

Eighteenth century advertisements show canes offered for sale, both imported from Europe and made in the United States. A few examples:

The "Penna Journal", March 17, 1763, carries an advertisement from Philip Syng, of Philadelphia, mentioning: *Neat chased gold cane head.*

In the "South Carolina Gazette", October 12-19, 1765, John Paul Grimhe offers *Gold headed canes.* In the "Penna Packet" July 31, 1775, Nicolas Brooks (Second Street between Market and Chestnut Streets) *offers an assortment of gilt and other canes, with or without swords.* Others advertise that: *They make all kind of Jewelles and Goldsmith work as reasonable as they can be imported and can afford to sell them as cheap as they are generally imported from London or Birmingham.* ("South Carolina Gazette", April 3rd, 1775).

On December 20th, 1778, the "Royal Gazette" mentions that their Publisher, James Revington, *is going to open on this day a Glove Store.* In another paragraph is advertised: *The opening, also on this day, of The Cane and Walking Stick Warehouse, where the gallant, gay Lothario, or worthy Master Balance, the plain and respectable Citizen, may find an elegant and useful Variety of these Articles.*

Other silversmiths advertise that *they have received by the latest vessel from Europe a most brilliant assortment of the fashionable undermentioned articles.* ("Penna Journal", August 11, 1784).

On June 9, 1825, Samuel Bell advertised: *Whips, walking canes with or without spears.*

Joseph Richardson also made *heads for canes and whips.* There is a mention of his producing *gold headed cane or neat chased gold cane heads.*

Joseph Erwin is mentioned in a 1808 Baltimore Directory under Umbrella factory, which certainly produced umbrellas and most likely made cane handles as well. The same reference is made to Isaac Nicholas Toy.

In the "Nashville Union" of November 4, 1843 J. Campbell offers to *mount canes.*

In an 1860 Memphis City Directory, A.J.Warren & Co. advertises, among other objects, *watches, clocks, jewels and silver, pistols and canes.*

Most 19th century directories or newspapers would have carried similar advertisements.

▲ 13/3 This simple handle is marked *Brook Brothers, New York. Made in England*. Other examples do not indicate where they were made.
Courtesy, private collection.

▲ 13/4 A round silver handle with inlaid copper figures, bearing the *R.F.S. & Co.* signature.
Courtesy,collection Bruce I. Thalberg.

Rest Fenner Smith & Co.

It is difficult to trace the exact origins of this company. In 1868 this company had an address at 102 William Street; in 1870, at 534 Broadway; and in 1875, at 701 Broadway, where the company was incorporated in 1890. They continued to move, going to 140 Sullivan Street (1893), 43 Downing Street (1905) and finally to 35 Bleecker Street (1906). By 1908, they were no longer listed in New York Directories.

The factory was at 20-22 Pell Street, New York City, with a branch office at 206 Kearny Street, San Francisco.

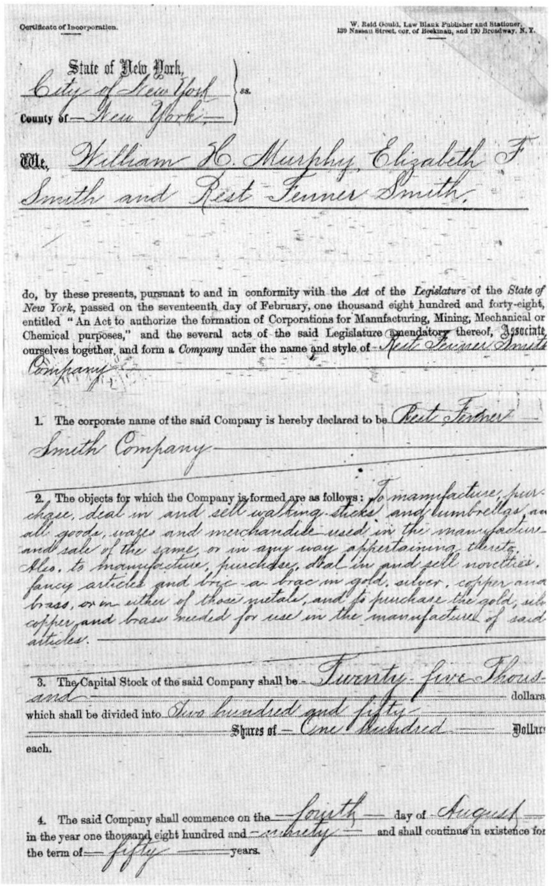

Certificate of Incorporation.

W. Reid Gould, Law Blank Publisher and Stationer, 139 Nassau Street, cor. of Beekman, and 130 Broadway, N. Y.

State of New York,
City of New York } ss.
County of New York

We, William H. Murphy, Elizabeth F Smith and Rest Fenner Smith,

do, by these presents, pursuant to and in conformity with the *Act* of the *Legislature* of the *State of New York*, passed on the seventeenth day of February, one thousand eight hundred and forty-eight, entitled "An Act to authorize the formation of Corporations for Manufacturing, Mining, Mechanical or Chemical purposes," and the several acts of the said Legislature amendatory thereof, Associate ourselves together, and form a *Company* under the name and style of Rest Fenner Smith Company

1. The corporate name of the said Company is hereby declared to be Rest Fenner Smith Company

2. The objects for which the Company is formed are as follows: To manufacture, purchase, deal in and sell walking sticks and umbrellas, and all goods, wares and merchandise used in the manufacture and sale of the same, or in any way appertaining thereto. Also, to manufacture, purchase, deal in and sell novelties, fancy articles and bric-a-brac in gold, silver, copper and brass, or in either of those metals, and to purchase the gold, silver, copper and brass needed for use in the manufacture of said articles.

3. The Capital Stock of the said Company shall be Twenty-five Thousand dollars, which shall be divided into Two hundred and fifty Shares of One Hundred Dollars each.

4. The said Company shall commence on the fourth day of August in the year one thousand eight hundred and ninety and shall continue in existence for the term of fifty years.

▲ 13/5 In 1890 William H. Murphy, Elizabeth F. Smith and Rest Fenner Smith formed a company under the name of *Rest Fenner Smith & Co.* which was to *manufacture, purchase, deal in and sell walking sticks and umbrellas*. Although it is mentioned that they can also deal in other *novelties*, it is assumed that they manufactured only canes and umbrella handles.
Courtesy, County Record Office, New York City.

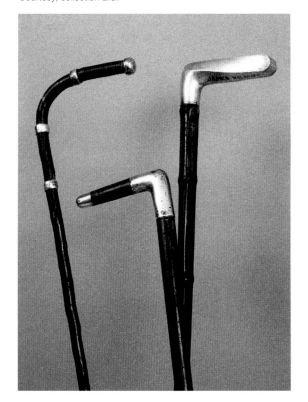

▼ a) Three handles marked with the seal of Gorham.
Courtesy, collection L.G.

▶ c) A gilded handle marked R.F.S. on the collar.
Courtesy, collection Eleanor Zelin, Mantiques Ltd.

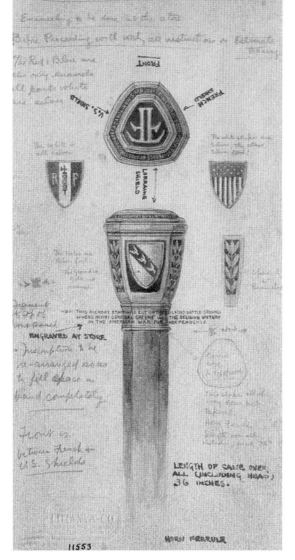

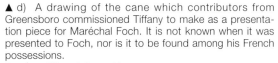

▲ d) A drawing of the cane which contributors from Greensboro commissioned Tiffany to make as a presentation piece for Maréchal Foch. It is not known when it was presented to Foch, nor is it to be found among his French possessions.
Courtesy, Tiffany & Co. archives.

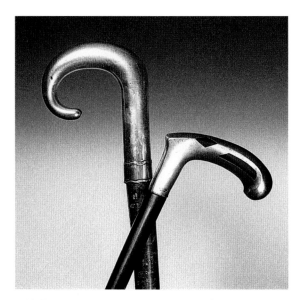

▲ b) Two handles marked with the same Gorham seal.
Courtesy, collection Catherine Dike.

▶ e) An early imported French handle bearing the words *Tiffany. Paris.*
Courtesy, collection Mark Neider.

◄ a) A drawing of three mice which was to become a handle.
Courtesy, Tiffany & Co. archives.

▲ b) Two eagle heads. The larger is one of the most commonly found pieces among collectors, and must have been made in quantity.
Courtesy, collection Catherine Dike.

▲ d) A group of Tiffany canes.
Courtesy, collection Catherine Dike.

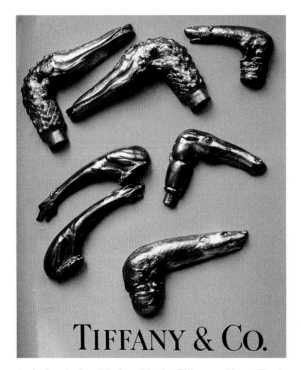

▲ c) A set of molds found in the Tiffany archives. Rarely does one find the handles themselves.
Courtesy, Tiffany & Co. archives.

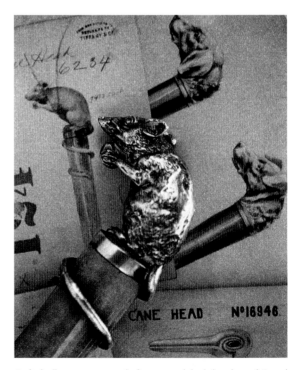

▲ e) A silver mouse made from an original drawing, pictured with other sketches.
Courtesy, collection Byron Evans.

Judging by the great number of canes found in various collections and museums, one can conclude that R.F.S. & Co issued thousand of handles. A selection of these, made either in silver or gold, appear in various chapters of this book. Two catalogs exist, one illustrated in this chapter, and another, also undated but specified as their fourth catalog, showing 110 various models. Some of these have ivory handles, with silver decorations. In the introduction, R.F.S. & Co. mentions: *As the manufacturing of walking sticks and canes is exclusively our business, and as we make it our study to combine utility with art, our customers may consider themselves safe in this respect.*

▲ 13/8 Copy of a European erotic knob which is often encountered in Europe. This American piece bears the *R.F.S. & Co.* signature.
Courtesy, Theodore T. Newbold.

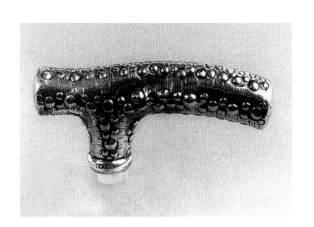

▲ 13/6 A silver handle marked *R.F.S. & Co.*
Courtesy, collection Catherine Dike.

▲ 13/7 Three identical silver handles marked *R.F.S. & Co.*, each having a different decoration.
Courttesy, collection Francis H. Monek.

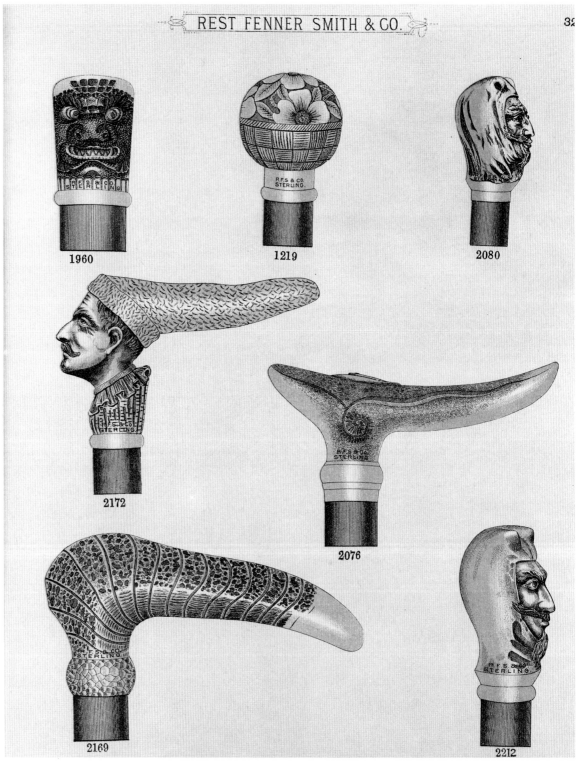

REST FENNER SMITH & CO.

1960

1219

2080

2172

2076

2169

2212

▲ 13/9   Page from a *R.F.S. & Co.* catalogue. The two middle examples bear their signature. To date, none of the canes on this page have been traced to private collections or museums.
Courtesy, Metropolitan Museum, New York.

Gorham & Co.

The Gorham & Company is the other of the three important silversmiths whose considerable influence on cane handles can be judged by the large quantity produced by the company. In 1898 all their non-figure handles made to date were photographed and numbered. Gorham has graciously supplied the author with many photocopies, beginning with Number 1 and concluding with Number 2362. Basically there were more than 300 shapes, among which many variations were made by using different dies and materials. This does not include the 90 dies representing animals such as dragons, snakes, dogs, tigers, monkeys, birds, frogs, butterflies etc., which are not included in the above-mentioned sequence of numbered designs and which do not appear in any ledger. Gorham also had dies of motifs for applied silver. Only photos of the dies exist, making it very difficult to date these handles.

Handles by Gorham are easily recognized, and are quite different from those by Tiffany or other companies. Camille Krantz, who directed the European newspapers at the time of the 1893 Chicago International Exhibition made the following comment: *The two big American silversmiths have quite different styles. Tiffany is the jeweller silversmith for whom silver is the support for jewels or enamel work. Gorham is the pure silversmith who produces large quantities for every day use, manufacturing daily hundreds of table services. Their equipment and mechanical operation enables them to satisfy their large clientele. At the same time, Gorham is capable of producing purely artistic and decorative works created by top quality craftsmanship.*

Until September 1904, the only maker of cane and umbrella heads was Christopher Webster.

The Gorham Archives are now part of the Brown University Library, Providence, Rhode Island.

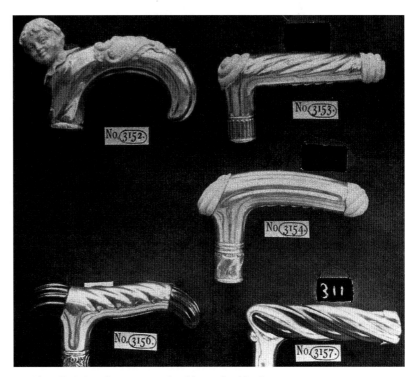

▲ 13/10 The basic handles on which various motifs were to be added. Here they are selected under the letter *U*, for umbrella.
Courtesy, Brown University Library.

▲ 13/11 Early handles were made of ivory. On this sheet, copied from a ledger, one can see the numbers.
Courtesy, Brown University Library.

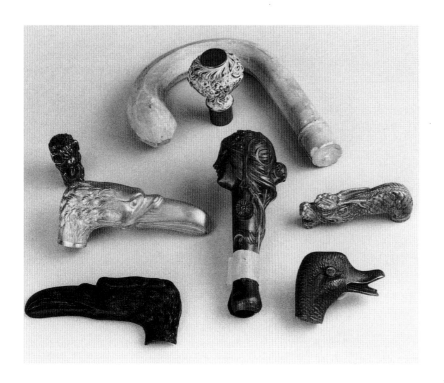

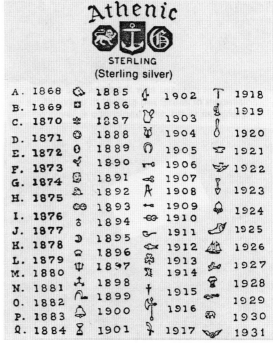

Athenic

STERLING
(Sterling silver)

A.	1868	1885		1902		1918	
B.	1869	1886				1919	
C.	1870	1887		1903			
D.	1871	1888		1904		1920	
E.	1872	1889		1905			
F.	1873	1890		1906		1922	
G.	1874	1891		1907			
H.	1875	1892		1908		1923	
		1893		1909			
I.	1876	1894		1910		1924	
J.	1877	1895		1911			
K.	1878	1896		1912		1925	
L.	1879	1897		1913		1926	
M.	1880	1898		1914		1927	
N.	1881	1899		1915		1928	
O.	1882	1900		1916		1929	
P.	1883	1901		1917		1930	
Q.	1884					1931	

▲ 13/13 The Hallmarks of Gorham up to 1931.

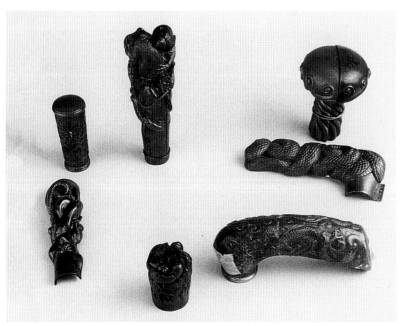

▲ 13/12 Various molds photographed at the Gorham factory in Providence. Only the Liberty mold bears a number 21,495.

On the lower group, the small fly sitting on top of the cap has no number / the dragon is No. 19,687 / the two snakes, No. 19,728 / the simple round handle is No. 28-1 / and the three mice on the top of the handle is No. 28-3. The half-mold is that of a snake attacking a monkey.
Courtesy, Gorham Inc., Providence, R.I.

▲ 13/14 A silver handle.
Courtesy, collection Paul Weisberg.

▼► 13/15 A variety of models taken from a scrap book at Brown University. They are not illustrated to scale.
Courtesy, Brown University Library.

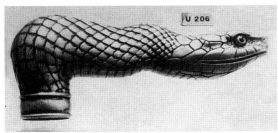

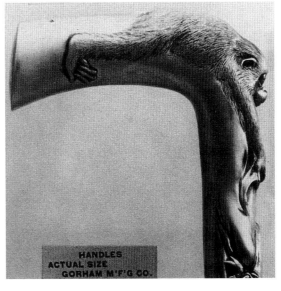

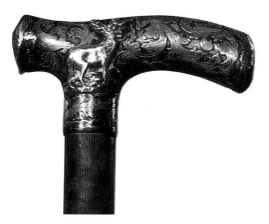

▲ 13/16 A straight handle ornated with a deer.
Courtesy, collection Albert Brown.

▲ 13/18 Gorham produced several Art Nouveau handles.
Courtesy, Brown University Library.

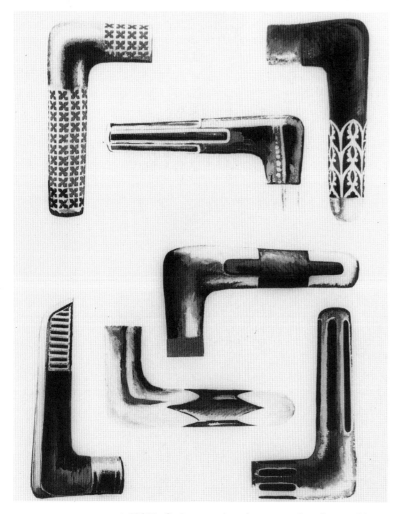

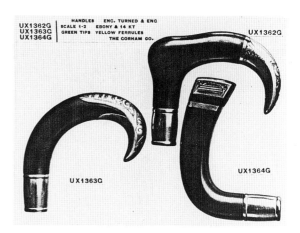

▲ 13/17 Gorham produced numerous handles combining mahogany and silver inlay.
Courtesy, Brown University Library.

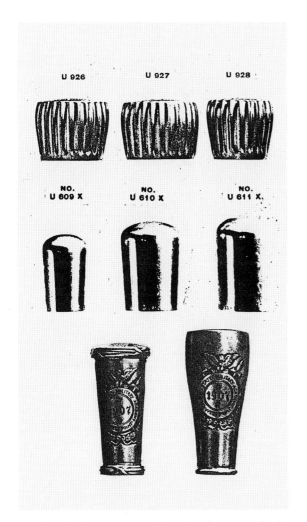

▲ 13/21 A Japanese influence was also to be found in some of the Gorham handles.
Courtesy, Brown University Library.

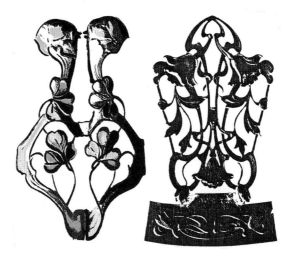

▲ 13/19 Gorham produced also the silver caps for the United States Army swagger sticks.
Courtesy, Brown University Library.

▲ 13/22 Drawing of a silver filagree which could be applied to wood, ivory or some other material.

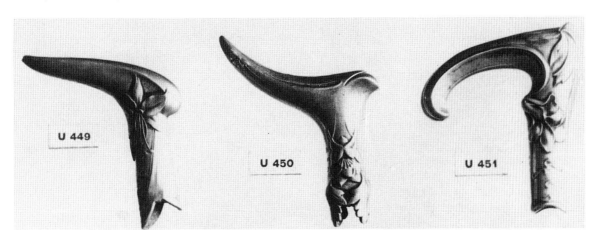

▲ 13/20 Three handles in the Art Nouveau style and which could have been made as parasol handles.
Courtesy, Brown University Library.

Tiffany& Co.

Today, a Tiffany silver or gold handle is the centerpiece of any American cane collection. This distinction is given to these coveted items not only because they bear the distinguished Tiffany name, but also because the collector believes that he possesses a rarity. Several East Coast collections contain perhaps half-a-dozen Tiffany pieces, and this is thought to be an impressive assortment. However, visiting the Tiffany archives and perusing the several hundred original drawings, one is astonished at the breadth and variety of styles of handles that the Tiffany designers produced in the latter part of the nineteenth century. Each drawing is numbered chronologically which enables the historian to follow the Tiffany styles and influences beginning as early as the 1850s.

When Tiffany and Young opened their Stationery and Dry Goods Store at 259 Broadway in 1837, umbrellas and canes were offered among the articles for sale. These, like many of the other articles, may have been imported from China, but since business records from this time have not survived, there is no documentary evidence. In 1841 Tiffany's business partner, John C. Young, traveled to Europe, returning with canes and umbrellas which were advertised in the firm's catalog in 1845 (the first of its kind in the United States.) The following is a listing from this catalog:

> *Walking canes, from low priced
>   to the richest, and most costly descrip-
>   tion made.
> Novelties in French cane mountings.
> A choice collection of Malaccas and other
> sticks for mounting.
> Canes mounted to order in any style.*

A high protective tariff was placed on all imported silver in 1844, forcing Tiffany's to turn to American-made silver. In 1851 Charles Tiffany made an agreement with John C. Moore, who supplied the top jewelry stores in New York, to work exclusively with Tiffany's. Upon his retirement, his son, Edward C. Moore, took over the reins of the silverware department. As Edward

C. Moore developed a style which became characteristic for Tiffany's, this new influence can be seen in canes and umbrella handles. The first recorded listing, number 1520, dating back to 1854, describes a cane head in the shape of the head of a greyhound.

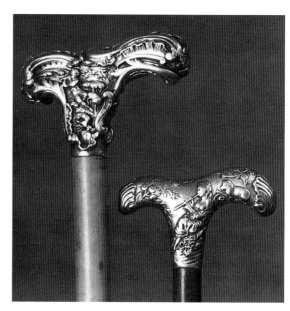

▲ 13/23 Left, a pure Louis XV Rocaille style silver handle marked *Tiffany & Co.* The subject and workmanship are so French that it simulates an imported item. Without any French hallmarks, it is hard to date a cane handle. Right, similar in style is an authenticated French handle.
Courtesy, collection Catherine Dike.

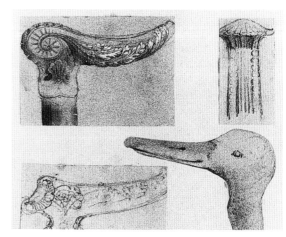

▲ 13/24 An early undated drawing from the scrapbooks found in the archives of Tiffany & Co. The drawings are probably mid -19th century.
Courtesy, Tiffany & Co. Archives.

In the early 1870s a dozen models are listed in the Tiffany silver pattern books. Between 1878 and 1882, a series of twenty different handles were created and embellished with over 150 decorations, either chased, pearled, etched, hammered, or applied with decorations in other metals. Numerous handles are executed in the Japanese style, decorated with floral or animal motifs. The vine pattern incorporates applied insects, also seen on other pieces of hollowware. The Japanese style continued to be utilized on cane and umbrella handles until Moore's death in 1891.

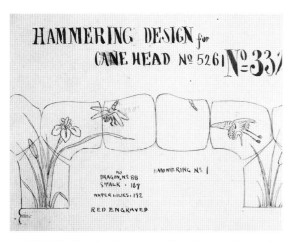

▲ 13/25 Working drawing of cane No. 5261 (1878) showing both floral and animal decorations. Dragonfly no. 88, Stalk no. 167, Waterlilies no. 192.
Courtesy, Tiffany & Co. Archives.

▲ 13/27 A French cane marked *Tiffany*, also bearing the inscription *Paris.* It could be allegorical, the man and woman representing France and England, holding the hand of what could be America.
Courtesy, collection Mark Neider.

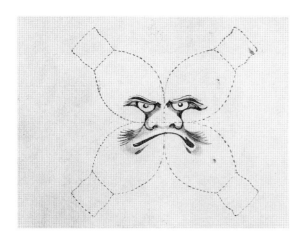

▲ 13/26 Handle No. 6974. Japanese visage on a round cane head, inspired by Noh theatre faces. (1882).
Courtesy, Tiffany & Co. Archives.

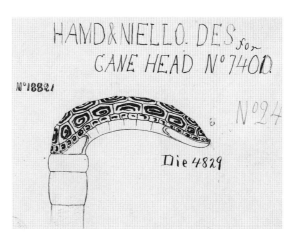

▲ 13/28 A niello decoration enhances this handle. (1883).
Courtesy, Tiffany & Co. Archives.

The patterns of the American Indian inspired Charles Grosjean, another talented designer. He incorporated the designs first into hollow-ware. Cane handles followed bearing simple decorative elements of Native American art and presaging the style which eventually became known as Art Deco.

Towards the end of the 19th century the Art Nouveau style became prevalent. Tiffany's produced very few pieces in this style (see Carpenter, p. 44), and only a few cane handles follow this trend, somewhat more restrained than the French versions. Their representation of animal forms assumes fantastic shapes.

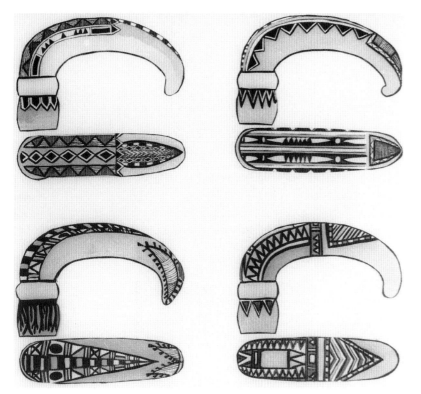

▲ 13/29 A group of various drawings representing the same handle with different interpretations. The handle is No. 6443 and dates from 1881.
Courtesy, Tiffany & Co. Archives.

▼ 13/30 A straight handle on which motifs of a table spoon have been applied. The center piece had a genuine carved head. The drawing dates from 1883.
Courtesy, Tiffany & Co. Archives.

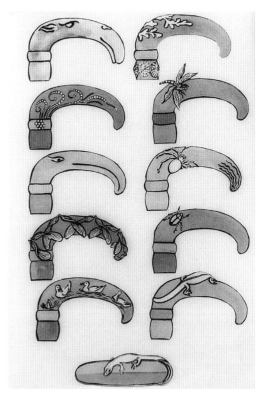

▲ 13/31 Various interpretations of a simple handle where the form is changed by the use of different methods, the piece either being chased, pearled, puckered, hammered or electroplated. (1879 and 1881).
Courtesy, Tiffany & Co. Archives.

▼▶ 13/32 A group of eleven drawings beginning with number 7337 (1883) to end with number 15,754 (1903).
Courtesy, Tiffany & Co. Archives.

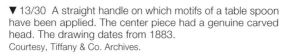

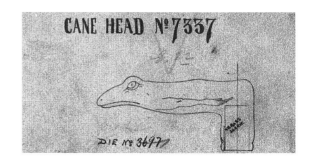

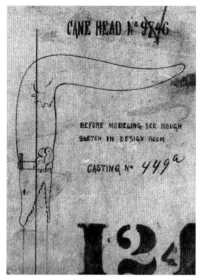

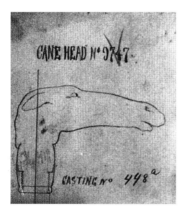

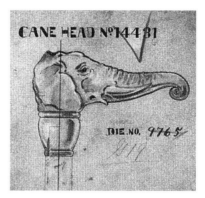

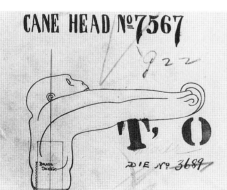

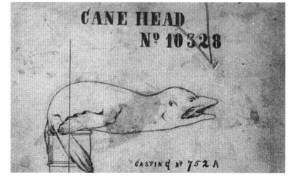

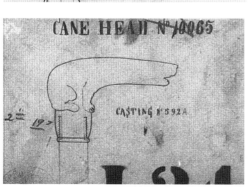

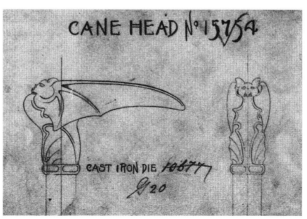

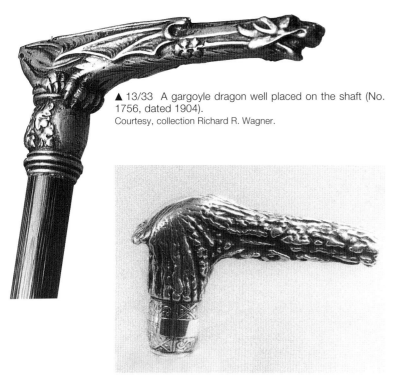

▲ 13/33 A gargoyle dragon well placed on the shaft (No. 1756, dated 1904).
Courtesy, collection Richard R. Wagner.

▲ 13/34   A Tiffany silver stag horn, bearing the number 7099 (1892). This motif was produced by numerous silversmiths, as well as Gorham .
Courtesy, collection Mannie Banner.

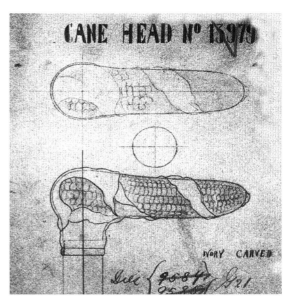

▲ 13/36   Ivory corncob surrounded by silver leaves.
Courtesy, Tiffany & Co. Archives.

The combination of silver and ivory is distinctively American. It is rarely found on European handles except when faces are made out of ivory (chryselephantine). Tiffany's produced such handles in both simple and elaborate styles. The elephant head and the corncob show impressive creativity of design.

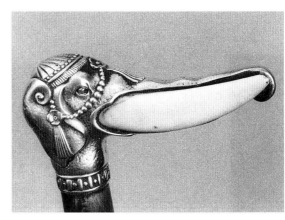

▲ 13/37   An elephant head with ivory tusks.
Courtesy, collection Julius Tarshis.

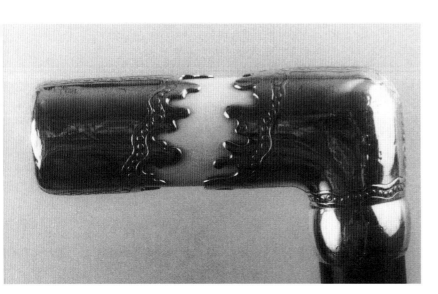

▲ 13/35   Cane number 14,371 (1900) combining ivory and silver.
Courtesy, collection Dr. J.H.

In an 1880 Tiffany's Blue Book catalog, are the following sticks: *Under Presents for Gentlemen, are listed Canes .... (of) Malacca and other woods, with ivory, tortoise-shell, silver, and gold handles, $2 to $75. Some of the new crutch-handles of hammered silver with enrichments of colored alloys and other metals, $15 to $45. These are exclusively made by Tiffany & Co.*

The great skill of the Tiffany silversmiths continued into the twentieth century, with an Art Deco style reflecting the trends which continued into the 1930s. Silver or gold decorations were incised directly into the wood at the tip of the crutch. Cane heads gradually became more sober and practical.

Bands were used to decorate the shaft, inscribed with the owner's initials or personalized with a simple design. Since men in the 19th century

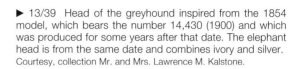

▶ 13/39 Head of the greyhound inspired from the 1854 model, which bears the number 14,430 (1900) and which was produced for some years after that date. The elephant head is from the same date and combines ivory and silver. Courtesy, collection Mr. and Mrs. Lawrence M. Kalstone.

accessorized their wardrobe with different canes depending upon their occupation or worn for the occasion, the wearer often possessed several examples.

Tiffany's produced very few gadget sticks, with the exception of watches and flashlights. Other specialty items were ordered to individual specification. In the archives over two hundred drawings exist which were designed for special orders. Examples include a regular handle on which a specific or personal decoration was applied. As the customers order lists were destroyed, one cannot trace for whom these canes were made.

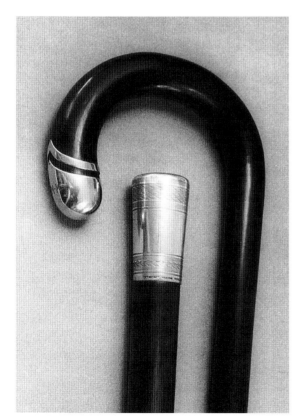

▲ 13/38 Two simple canes, the straight one bearing the letters W.M.K. and the crook one with the letters E.G.H. next to the signatures of Tiffany & Co. These initials are those of the Director of Tiffany. Courtesy, collection Mark Neider.

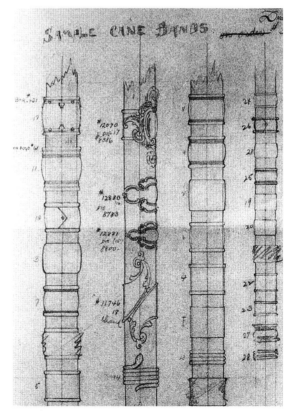

▲ 13/40 Drawings of cane bands produced byTiffany. Courtesy, Tiffany & Co. Archives.

▲ 13/41 Drawings of various Tiffany Art Deco handles.
Courtesy, Tiffany & Co. Archives.

They gave the work to be done by Tiffany who charged $ 300.00. It was to be presented to the Marshal as a Christmas gift (although the War was over on November 11). No trace of this cane has been found among the belongings of the French Marshal. (Color picture).

In conclusion, one particular cane handle and shaft illustrates the entrepreneurial spirit with which the founder, Charles Lewis Tiffany, imbued his firm in 1850s. Tiffany purchased from the engineer-inventor, Cyrus W. Field, twenty miles of the transatlantic telegraph cable which had been retrieved from the ocean floor. Cutting it into various lengths, he offered for sale numerous souvenirs such as watch charms, seals, paper weights, and umbrella handles, as well as canes.

In 1918, the citizens of Greensboro collected funds to present a cane to Marshal Foch who *had saved the World from ruin*. He was the Commander in Chief of the allied troops in Europe. The contributors were listed in the local newspaper, using the formula mentioned below.

They had provided a shaft made in wood from the Guilford Battleground, which was an important event in the fight for Independance.

▼ 13/42 Advertisement from the *Frank Leslie's Weekly, September 11, 1858* announcing the sale of various objects made from the Atlantic Telegraph submarine cable. The tip of the cane shows the copper cable surrounded by protective cables. The advertisement mentions that sections of the cable were to be sold in their original condition, without cleaning!

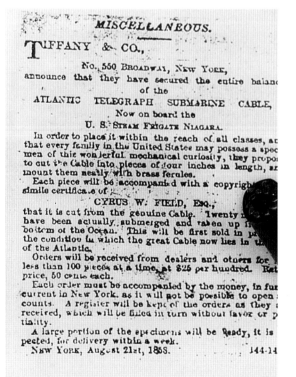

Silver Marks

The silver marks (*) can be found in Dorothy T. Rainwater's *Encyclopedia of American Silver Manufacturers*; those with (+) are mentioned in the chapter on silver-headed canes in K. Morrison McClinton's *Collecting American Nineteenth Century Silver*. Where the cane was found is also given, whether in a book, catalog, or the cane itself. It is difficult to know whether the companies were silversmiths, manufacturers or retailers. Some might merely be cane dealers (see chapter on the subject).

On January 5, 1886, the Alvin Company patented a new device to deposit pure silver on a non-metallic base. The first items used for this experiment were cane and umbrella handles. Handles made with this technique were purely American.

Benjamin Allen & Company
Retailers
"Busiest House in America".
(Catalog).
Chicago, 1888

Alvin Corporation *
Manufacturers
Providence, Rhode Island.
Established in 1886

Bailey, Banks & Biddle Co.*
Retailers
Philadelphia, Pennsylvania.
Established 1832
(Cane)

W.J.B. & Co.   W.J. Braitsch & Co.
Manufacturers
Providence, Rhode Island.
Established 1895
(Cane)

Jacob Boelen
Silversmith
1754
(Cane)

Samuel Bell
Silversmith
"Knoxville Register".
1825

A.G.B.
(Cane)

B.S. (Bristol Silver Company?)
(Cane)

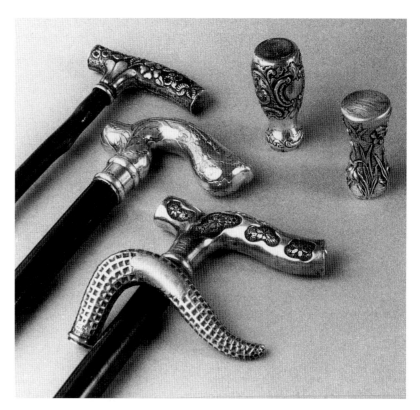

▲ 13/43 A group of identified cane handles, top left: *Hammersmith & Field / F.G.S. & Co. /* two handles together: *Lyon Maker /* the two small ones on the top right: *Mermod & Jaccard* and *J.E.C. & Co.* (for J.E. Caldwell & Co.).
Courtesy, private collection.

▼ 13/44 On this group is found: *Left to right : J.H.* (standing for John Hasselbring) / *K. & M. 28 / W. D. C.* in a triangle and *K. H.* (Kreis & Hubbard).
Courtesy, collection Francis H. Monek.

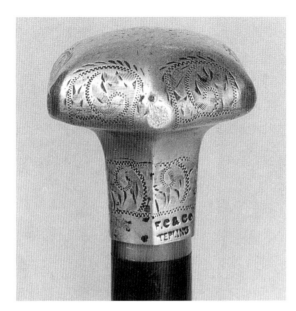

▲ 13/45   The marks of *F. Curtis & Co.*
Courtesy, collection Francis H. Monek.

▲ 13/46   The interwoven signature for *S. Cottle & Co.*
Courtesy, collection Bruce I. Thalberg.

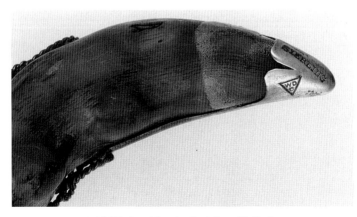

▲ 13/47   In a triangle, the letters *W. D. C.*
Courtesy, collection L.G.

W.G.B. & Co.
825/1000
(Cane)

H.C.B. Sterling
(Cane)

J.E.C. & Co.   **J.E.Caldwell & Co.***
Retailers
Philadelphia, Pennsylvania.
Established 1839
(Cane)

E.C.   E. Chittenden
(Cane)

C. S.C.   **Colonial Silver Co. Inc**
 Manufacturers
Portland, Maine
(Cane)

S. Cottle & Co.*
Manufacturers
New York, N. Y.
Established in 1865
(Cane)

L.A. Cuppia +

F.C. & Co.   **F. Curtis & Co. ***
Manufacturers
Connecticut.
Established 1848
(Cane)

W.D.C. Co. in a triangle
(Cane)

Durand & Co.
Manufacturers
Newark, New Jersey.
Established 1838/1919

Charles Downs, +

John Dold
Silversmith
Philadelphia, 1863
(Cane)

Erie Solid Silver Sterling
(Cane)

John Erwin
Silversmith
Baltimore, Maryland
Working 1804-1820
(Book)

▶ c) Amelia Earhart one of the first women aviators, and the first to fly the Atlantic, waves good-bye before take-off.
Courtesy, collection Catherine Dike.

▲ a) Two canes with overlapping ivory and silver.
Courtesy, collection L.G.

▲ d) A group of three American canes.
Courtesy, collection L.G.

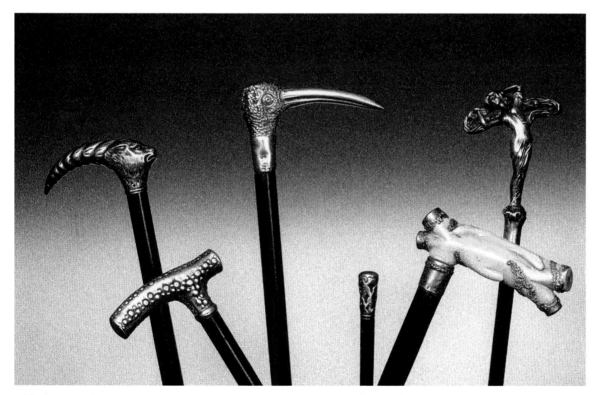

▲ b) A group of canes marked or signed as follows, from left to right: *Sterling / R.F.S. & Co. / Lyon Maker / Sterling / H. Shumann, N.Y. Maker / Sterling* and the letters *A.P.*
Courtesy, collection Catherine Dike.

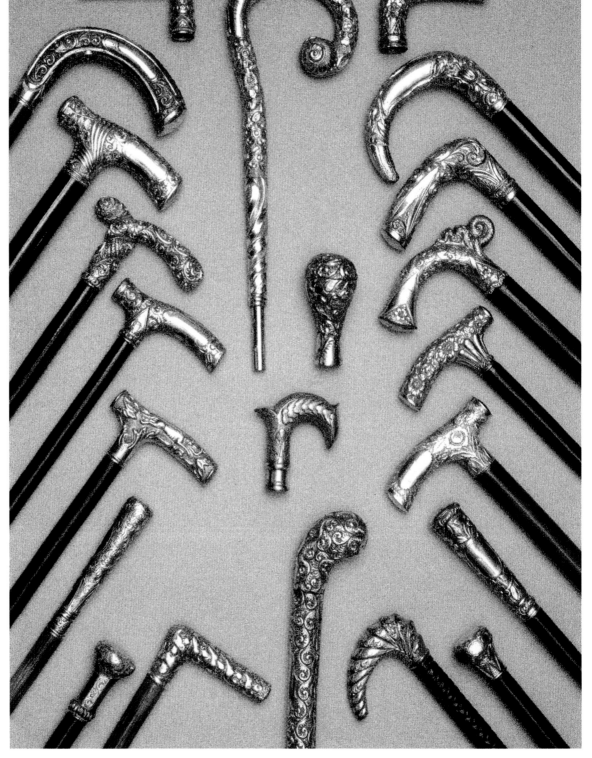

▲ a) A selection of gilded canes, parasol or umbrella handles. The two insets at left show how the handles were roll pressed rather than solid gold.
Courtesy, private collection.

J.F. Fradley & Co. *
Silversmith and manufacturers
New York, New York
Established 1870
(Cane)

A. Frankfield Co.
(Cane)

Albert J. Gannon *
Silversmith
Philadelphia, Pennsylvania
Established 1905-1914
(Cane)

Ger'sil,
German Silver.
(Cane)

Gorham Corporation *
Manufacturers
Providence, Rhode Island
Established 1831
(Cane)

Gowdey & Peabody
Offered walking sticks in 1845
(Book)

Hammersmith & Field *
Manufacturers
San Francisco, California.
Established 1889
(Cane)

W.W. Harrison Co.
353 Fifth Avenue
New York, N.Y.

J.H.   John Hasselbring *
Brooklyn, N. Y.
Established 1890
(Cane)

S. Heyman
189, 208 to 212, Springfield Ave.
Newark, New Jersey.
(Catalog)

William R. Hodge
Silversmith
1807/1879
Columbia, Tennessee
(Book)

Phillip Hubert Jr.
(Book)

W. Huntley Co.
Chicago, Illinois
(1913 Catalog)

Jacobi & Jenkins *
Manufacturers
Baltimore, Maryland
Established 1894
(Cane)

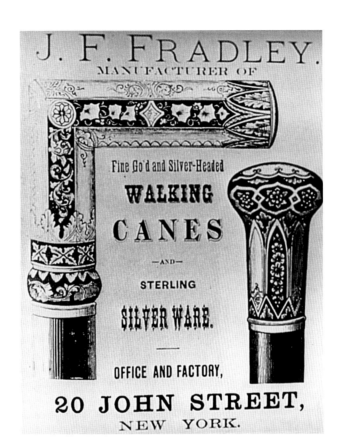

▲ 13/48 *J.F. Fradley* can be recognized by a Swastika
cross on its handles.
Courtesy, Catherine Dike archives.

▼ 13/49 The advertisement for *W.W. Harrison.*
Courtesy, Catherine Dike archives.

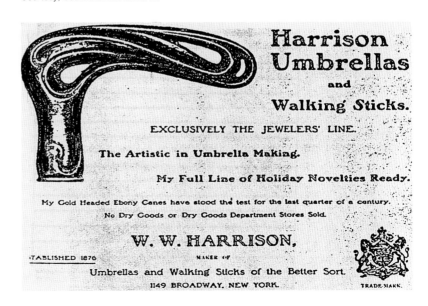

◀ 13/50 A silver handle representing a fox and signed on the collar by *Jacobi & Jenkins.*
Courtesy, collection Mark Neider.

▶ 13/51 A silver political cane marked on the back *M. R. U. Sterling.* It was quite unusual to have such canes made of silver.
Courtesy, collection Donald J. Grunder.

▼ 13/52 Two canes marked *Lyon Maker, Sterling.*
Courtesy, collection Catherine Dike and Mannie Banner.

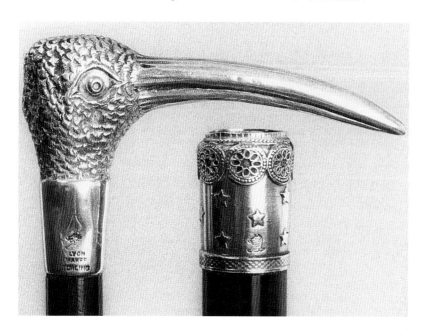

Kerr &Co.
(Cane)

Ketcham & McDougal *
Manufacturers
New York, N. Y.

Kirk Co. *
Manufacturers
Established in 1815.
To merge with the Stieff Co.
(Cane)

K. & H   Kreis & Hubbard
Franklin Street & Jackson Blvd
Chicago, Illinois
(Cane)

F.J.K
(Cane)

Lancaster Silver Plate Co. *
Lancaster, Pennsylvania
Destroyed by fire in 1893
(Cane)

P.H. Locklin & Sons *
Manufacturers
New York, N. Y.
Established 1920-1930

Lukenburg & Hassel +

Lyon Maker
(Cane)

Mermod, Jaccard & King Jewelry Co. *
Retailers
Saint Louis, Missouri
(Cane)

Miller Maker
(Cane)

M.R.U. Sterling
(Cane)

O.T. Sterling
(Cane)

Parker & Thomas
Wholesale
(Catalogue, 65 various items)

Peckham
Columbia, South Carolina
(Cane)

A.P.
(Cane)

Reed & Barton Co.
Manufacturers
New York, N. Y.
Established 1824
(Cane)

Otto Reichhardt Co. * +
Manufacturers
New York, N. Y.
Established 1925

R.F.S. & Co.   Rest Fenner Smith & Co.
New York, N. Y.
(Cane)

Joseph Richardson
Silversmith
Philadelphia, Pennsylvania
1750
(Cane)

George Collier Robbins
Silversmith
Portland, Oregon
1858
(Cane)

E. V. Rodin & Co.
Jewelry, Watches, Silverware
(1895 Catalog)

S.C.&Co.   Sandland, Capron & Co.
North Attleboro, Massachusetts
(Cane)

S.C. & I. Co.
(Cane)

A.G. Schultz & Co. *
Manufacturers
Baltimore, Maryland
Established 1898
(Cane)

The Schofield Co. *
Manufacturers
Baltimore, Maryland
Established 1903
(Cane)

H. Schumann, N.Y. Maker
New York, N. Y.
(Cane)

A. L.Silberstein *
Manufacturers
New York, N. Y.
(Cane)

Simons' Bro. & Co.*
Manufacturers
Philadelphia, Pennsylavania
(Cane)

Max Steinschneider
Manufacturers and importers
102 Fulton Street, New York, N.Y.

▶ 13/53 One of the rare handles representing a woman signed *A.P.*
Courtesy, collection Catherine Dike.

▲ 13/54 A slender cane bearing the signature of *H. Schumann, N.Y. Maker.*
Courtesy, collection Catherine Dike.

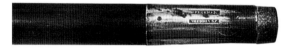

▲ 13/55 On this cane, the signature is on the ferrule: *Peckham, Columbia, S.C.*
Courtesy, collection Norman Flayderman.

▼ 13/56 *Max Steinschneider* advertised his *Largest Cane Department in the City of New York.*
Courtesy, Catherine Dike archives.

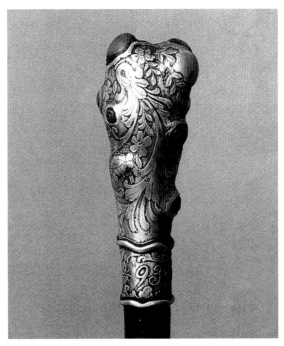

▲ 13/57 A graduation handle bearing the year '93 and the marks *S.Y.*
Courtesy, collection Stuart H. White.

▼ 13/58 *Simons' Bro. & Co.* offered Fine Jewelry together with Canes.
Courtesy, Catherine Dike archives.

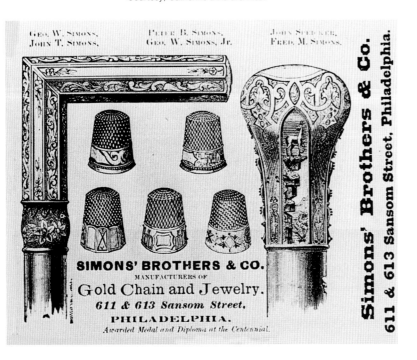

The Sterling Company of Providence +
Manufacturers
Providence, Rhode Island

The Stieff Company,*
Manufacturers
Baltimore, Maryland
(Cane)

Phillip Syng
Silversmith
Philadelphia, Pennsylvania
1703-1789
(Penna Journal)

Tiffany & Co. Inc. *
Manufacturers
New York, N, Y.
(Cane)

Isaac N. Toy
Silversmith
Baltimore, Maryland
(Book)

Unger Brothers *
Manufacturers
1872-1949
Newark, New Jersey
(Cane)

Waite, Thresher Co.
Manufacturers
1862
Providence, Rhode Island
(Cane)

A.J. Warren &Co.
Memphis City
1860
(Directory)

W.D.   Whiting & Davis Co.Inc. *
Manufacturers
Plainville, Massachusetts
Established 1876
(Cane)

Wallace International *
Manufacturers
Wallingford, Connecticut
1834
(Catalog)

C.W.W. Co. in a clover leaf
(Cane)

S.Y.
(Cane)

Otto Young & Co.*
Retailers
Chicago, Illinois
1886
(1900 catalog, 118 articles)

▲ 13/59 *C. W. W. Co* in a clover leaf.
Courtesy, collection John H. Sterne.

▶ 13/60 *Waite, Thresher Co.* used an intriguing layout for their publicity.
Courtesy, Catherine Dike archives.

▼ 13/61 A handle for a parasol or a cane, signed *Unger Brothers.*
Courtesy, collection Mr. and Mrs. Lawrence M. Kalstone.

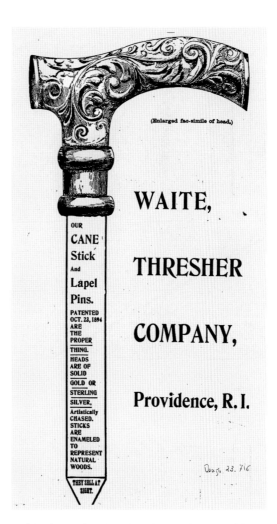

(Enlarged fac-simile of head.)

WAITE,

THRESHER

COMPANY,

Providence, R. I.

OUR
CANE
Stick
And
Lapel
Pins.
PATENTED
OCT. 23, 1894
ARE
THE
PROPER
THING.
HEADS
ARE OF
SOLID
GOLD OR
STERLING
SILVER,
Artistically
CHASED.
STICKS
ARE
ENAMELED
TO
REPRESENT
NATURAL
WOODS.

THEY SELL AT
SIGHT.

▼ 13/62 A catalog showing the production of *Unger Brothers.*
Courtesy, Catherine Dike archives.

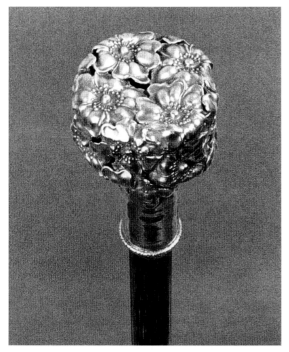

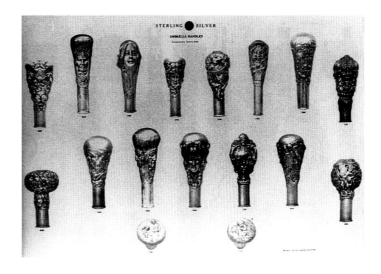

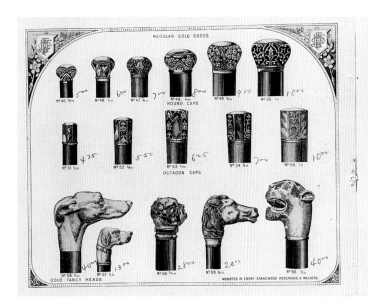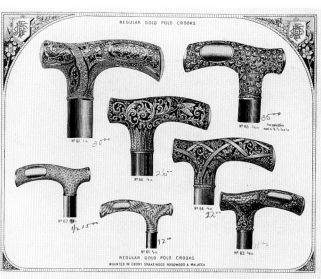

▲ 13/63 Two pages from a 40-page catalog of *Fradley & Co.* which presents 280 various models. Some are of the first quality, others of lesser workmanship.
Courtesy, Metropolitan Museum, New York.

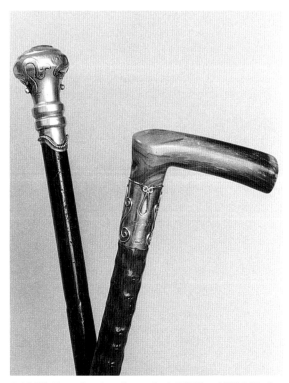

▲ 13/64 A silver hand holding a trumpet. The base is marked *Mason* who was the United States Consulate in Cuba.
Courtesy, collection Smithsonian Insitution.

▲ 13/65 Two silver handles maked *825 Fine / 1000 Sterling*
Courtesy, collection Francis H. Monek.

Gilded Presentation Canes

A typically American cane is the gilded presentation model which was produced by many manufacturers in tremendous quantities. Neither Gorham nor Tiffany, however, issued these mass-market gilded knobs or handles.

The description found in the "Boston Post" provides a good idea on how these canes were made: *The gold in the heads of the cane is of 14-karat fineness. It is rolled into sheets, cut to the desired size and soldered in a conical tube, then placed in a sectional steel chuck or form, which admits of its being drawn into the exact shape of the finished head. The tops are first cut into discs, and then soldered to the cane after it has been shaped. They are then filled with a hard composition and "chased", or ornamented, by hand, after which this composition filling is removed and they are sent to the polishing room for final finishing.*

There is always a cartouche on the top of the knob or on the side of the handle for a carver to indicate by whom and to whom it was given, and usually the date as well.

▲ 13/67 Although silver presentation canes were made in similar quatities as the gilded canes, it is rare to find them today among collections.
Courtesy, collection L.G.

▼ 13/66 Montgomery Ward catalog with various handles.
Courtesy, collection Leonore Zelin, Mantiques Ltd.

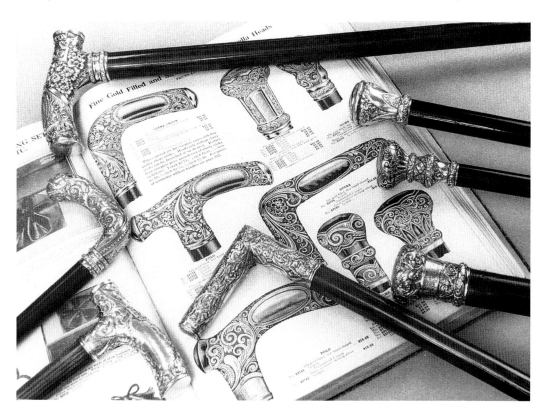

STERLING SILVER, ROLLED GOLD PLATED AND SILVER PLATED CANE
AND UMBRELLA HANDLES.
The Plated goods are well made and give satisfaction, but are not warranted.
The above (except sterling silver) are usually sold as solid gold, but are heavy gold filled.

▲ 13/68 The catalog of *Young Otto & Cie. (Chicago 1900) mentions that the cane are usually sold as solid gold, but they are heavy gold filled. The tops, ends and name plates are Solid Gold or corresponding quality.* Florence Alabame, in her book published by the "House of Collectibles" mentions that *American gentlemen carried silver or gilt-headed canes.*
Courtesy, Catherine Dike archives.

▲ 13/69 Four handles showing the metal interior. A visible seam shows lesser workmanship, as in the handle on the left.   Courtesy, collection Francis H. Monek.

▲ 13/71 Number and seal of a gilded cane. Often one finds such numbers on the various handles but rarely are they signed.   Courtesy, collection Mannie Banner.

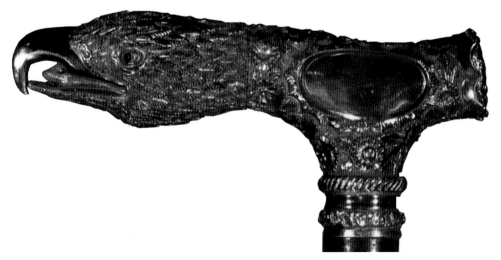

▲ 13/70 One of the very few gilded canes representing the U.S. eagle's head. The New Hampshire Historical Society has a similar cane to which a long collar was added with the names of eight Deputies who had presented it to the Sheriff of Carroll County.   Courtesy, private collection.

▲ 13/72 Another knob rarely seen, with a top opening upon a hinge to reveal waves of hair beneath a piece of glass. A picture could also be inserted.
Courtesy, collection Mannie Banner.

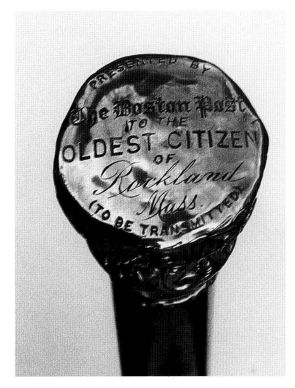

▲ 13/73 Well-worn handle to a cane presented by the Boston Post to the oldest citizen of the city of Rockland, Mass.
Courtesy, private collection.

Although not a silver or gold filled presentation cane, one walking stick continues to be given to the oldest citizen of Osterville. It took the name of the *Blount Cane*. William Davis Blount jumped ship as the *Old Ironsides* sailed into Boston in 1812. He settled in Osterville and left this whale-bone cane to be given to the oldest citizens of the town who had received him.

Known today as *The Boston Post Cane*, the name springs from a newspaper promotion. In 1909 the Boston Post was seeking new subscribers, despite having the largest circulation of any newspaper in the United States at the time. The publisher presented a stick to the oldest citizen of 700 New England towns. In 1983, 400 of these canes could still be accounted for.

The canes had been purchased at J.F. Fradley & Co in New York. Possibly the publisher picked them up at an auction. This is a plausible story as J.F. Fradley & Co. went out of business about that time.

As no list is available of the towns where these canes were distributed, one cannot trace the recipients with exactitude. The towns were scattered among the New England States of Massachusetts, Maine, New Hampshire, Rhode Island, and Vermont. Apparently, and oddly, no town in Connecticut received a cane.

The other presentation cane represented an award begun in 1919 by the American Association of Pathologists and given to a physician *who represents the highest ideal in pathology and medicine*. The cane is a symbolic replica of a cane used from 1689 to 1823 by five British royal physicians, whose story is told by the cane itself in the book "The Gold-Headed Cane."

By 1990, it had been presented to 22 awardees. In contrast with the five British doctor recipients of the "story" cane, each awardee was a teacher devoted to research in advancing knowledge of his science. Two won Nobel prizes.

IV Assorted Materials and Woods

THE CERAMIC ART CO. 🦎 🦎 🦎
Makers and Decorators of Exclusive 🦎
Productions in Artistic China and Porcelains

Stamps on Ware

Walter S. Lenox
President and Treasurer

BELLEEK
White

LENOX
Decorated

H. H. Brown
Secretary

Pottery and Salesroom, Trenton, N. J.

▲ 14/1 The front page of *The Ceramic Art Co.* which was apparently the only porcelain factory to have made handles.
Courtesy, New Jersey State Library, Trenton.

Assorted Materials and Woods

Ivory Handles

Ivory handles appear in many chapters of this book, so popular was this material in days when thought was seldom given to the notion of endangered species. It is difficult to differentiate between European and American handles, and even some handles of Asian origin can be hard to identify if they treat their subject in an occidental manner.

The combination of silver and ivory is practically never found in Europe, although in parts of Slovakia in the 19th century wooden dog heads were made with ears or muzzle covered in silver. This combination is particularly American. The silver may be inlaid, or may simply adjoin the ivory. Often the silver has American hallmarks.

There are distinct differences between the elephant ivories found in Africa. The ivory of the West Coast is more transparent and elegant than that of the East Coast. Green ivory, even more transparent, comes from Gabon. The finest ivory is that of Guinea, which is hard and fine-grained; with age, it becomes more white, as opposed to other ivories which tend to take on a yellowish tint. Ivory from the middle of the Continent has less value, the climate being too arid.

▲ 14/3 Three horse heads with silver harness, give the hand a good grip.
Courtesy, collection Bruce I. Thalberg.

Other ivories come from the teeth of the sperm whale, the walrus and the narwhal. These were used in profusion by Scrimshawers, and are described in that chapter. The teeth of the hippopotamus, although small, provided another source. Ivory and bone may appear very similar, but an experienced eye can usually see the difference. In the chapter on Plastic Handles, a brief description will be given of the fake ivory made from celluloid or rubber.

Several patents were filed in connection with the use of silver on ivory. In January 1886, the Alvin Company filed a new device to deposit pure silver on a non-metallic base.

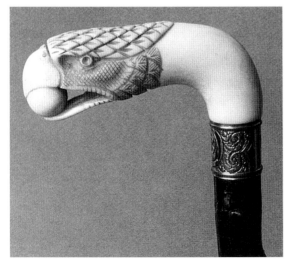

▲ 14/2 An American eagle holding a ball. The metal band has an American mark.
Courtesy, collection Stuart H. White.

▲ 14/4 A simple ivory knob, marked with the name of the owner and *Charlestown, July 4th, 1836.*
Courtesy, collection Norman Flayderman.

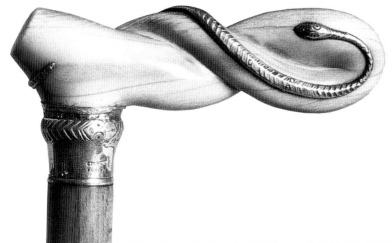

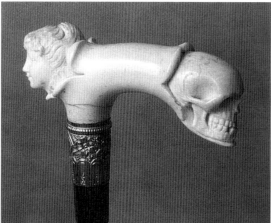

▲ 14/6 A handle which may have been imported and mounted in the United States. The gilded band is typically American.
Courtesy, collection Stuart H. White.

◀ 14/5 The silver mark F.C. & Co. (F. Curtis & Co.) appears on several handles combining silver and ivory. In this one the silver curves onto the ivory handle.
Courtesy, private collection

▲ 14/8 Two American canes, the lion stands on a silver platform.
Courtesy, collection Eleanor Zelin, Mantiques Ltd.

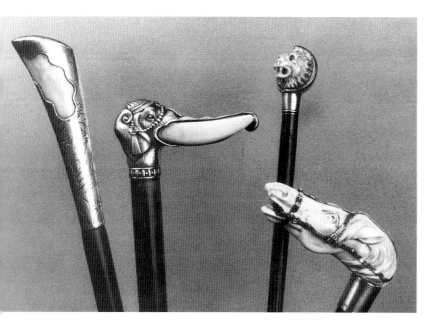

◀ 14/7 Four handles featuring the combination of silver and ivory. The elephant was made by Tiffany.
Courtesy, collection Julius Tarshis.

▶ 14/10 The ivory section is completely covered by the silver design.
Courtesy, collection Mannie Banner.

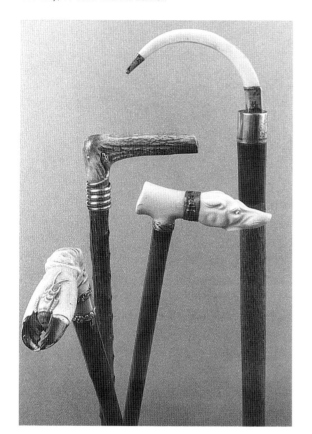

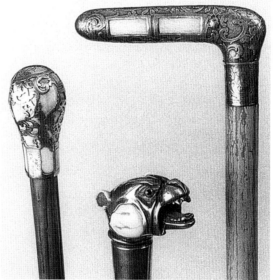

▲ 14/9 Four cane handles featuring the combination of silver and ivory. The crab claw at left has an American mark, and the gold snake mounting the horn handle bears the mark *R.F.S. & Co.*
Courtesy, collection Paul Weisberg.

▲ 14/11 Three different applications of silver. The dog is marked *Solid Silver,* the other two have the mark *Sterling Fine 900/1000.*
Courtesy, collection Bruce I. Thalberg.

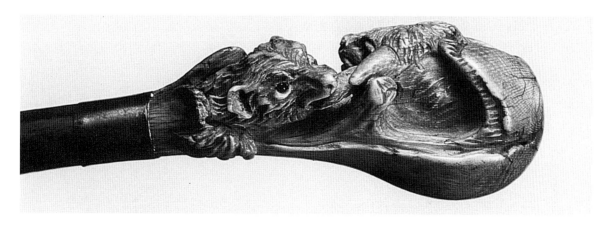

▲ 14/12 A bone handle depicting a bear biting the ear of a bull, for the Wall Street dandy!
Courtesy, collection Catherine Dike.

◄14/13 Gorham also made the ivory-silver combination, such as this ell-shape handle.
Courtesy, collection Paul Weisberg.

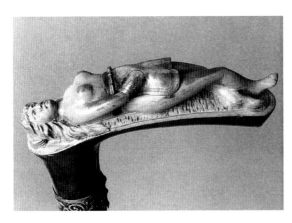

▲▼ 14/14 An early 20th century "risqué" handle. A silver apron covers the recumbent lady, but it can be lifted!
Courtesy, collection Stuart H.White.

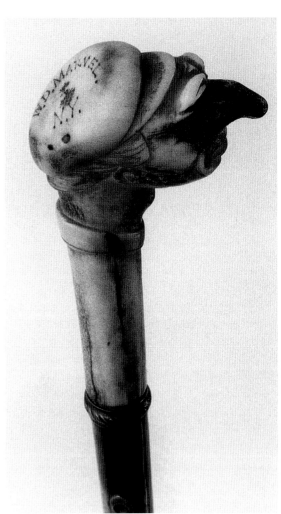

▲ 14/15 A bone handle marked atop the cap: *W.D. Marvel - N.Y.* It could be a College cane, as the cap resembles those of university students.
Courtesy, collection Richard W. Carlson.

▲ a) A handle undoubtedly belonging to some Wall Street financier. The Bear bites the ear of the Bull.
Courtesy, collection Catherine Dike,

◀ b) A frightened man looking down at a snake. Although found in the United States, this cane could be European.
Courtesy, collection Catherine Dike.

▲ c) A handle featuring the combination of silver and ivory.
Courtesy, Catherine Dike.

▲ a) An ivory handle which fits the hand very comfortably.
Courtesy, collection Catherine Dike.

▶ c)   Effigy of Buffalo Bill. Supposedly two copies of this
cane were made in Paris, one to be presented to Buffalo Bill
on his visit to that city, the other to be kept by the
carver.
Courtesy, collection G. and M. Segas, Paris.

▼ b) A rather erotic handle (for the time), whose shapes
would be concealed by the grasping hand. The lady is rather
plump!
Courtesy, collection Eleanor Zelin, Mantiques Ltd.

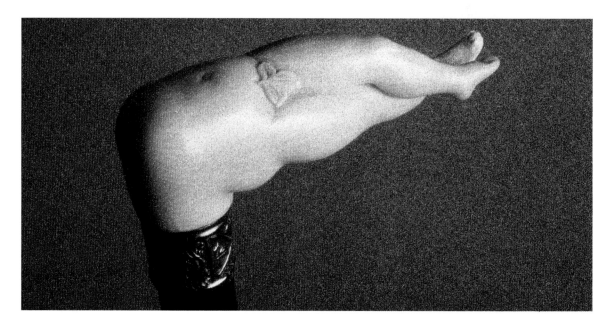

▲ c) A handle made in the same style as the one pictured
on the opposite page.
Courtesy, collection Stuart Howard White.

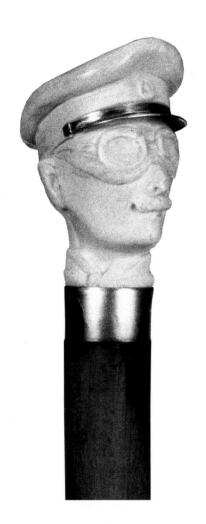

◀ a) A very dignified motorist with a silver rim to his cap.
Courtesy, collection Catherine Dike.

▼ b) A gold and ivory handle marked: *From the noiseless
friends*, a presentation cane from deaf mutes to *E.L. Clark*.
The gold is marked with the Lyon sign, the number 4820
and 14 K, which is a low alloy number but invariably present
on any real gold handle.
Courtesy, collection Mark Neider.

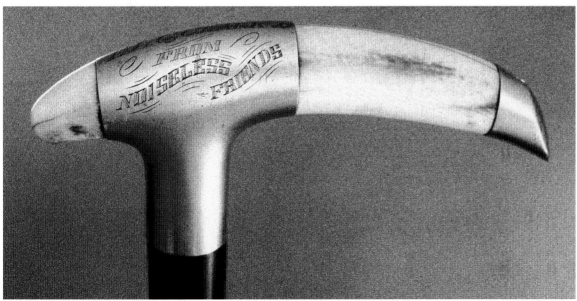

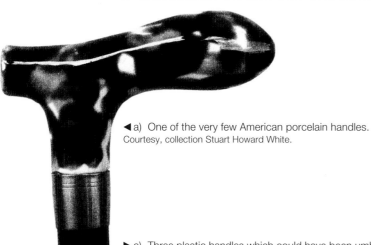

◄ a) One of the very few American porcelain handles.
Courtesy, collection Stuart Howard White.

► c) Three plastic handles which could have been umbrella handles.
Courtesy, collection Mark Neider.

▼ b) A group of porcelain handles sold at fairs or given as prizes.
Courtesy, collection Bruce I. Thalberg.

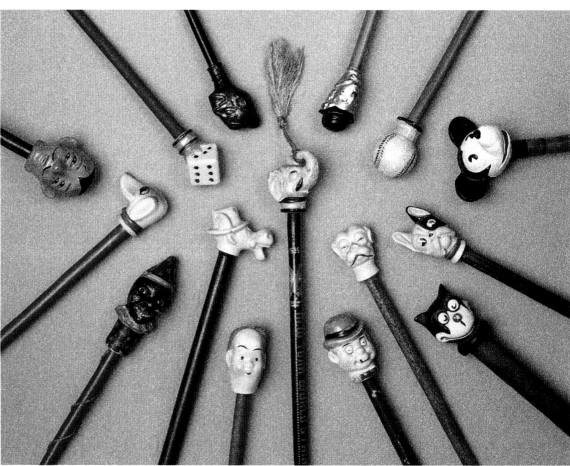

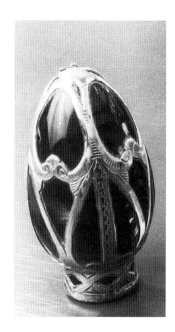

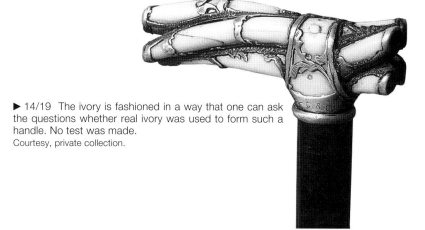

► 14/19 The ivory is fashioned in a way that one can ask the questions whether real ivory was used to form such a handle. No test was made.
Courtesy, private collection.

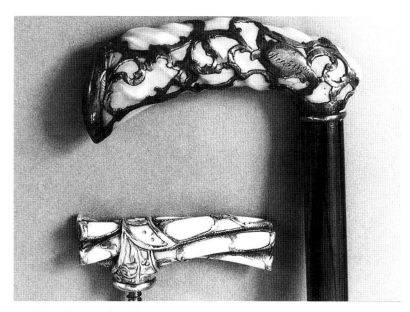

▲ 14/20 Two handles. The lower one resembles that in photo 14/19., both bear the mark *F.C & Co.*
Courtesy, collection Stuart H. White.

▲ 14/16 Two examples of cut glass and silver together. Three patents were filed for a method to brush a flux composed of silver and other chemicals onto a chosen base. The object was then put in an electrochemical bath through which passed a steady flow of current.
Courtesy, collection John H. Sterne.

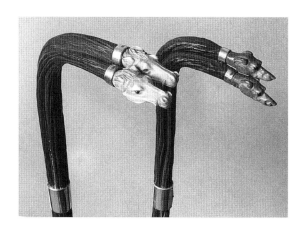

▲ 14/21 Two handles treated the same way.
Courtesy, collection Stuart H. White.

Porcelain Handles

The Ceramic Art Co. seems to have been the only factory to have made china cane or umbrella handles in the United States. The author made extensive inquiries among porcelain collectors and museums specialising in the subject, and always received a categorical *no* in reply. The following pictures were taken from a catalog.

▼ 14/22 Roughly fifteen assorted handles. Some of them were undoubtedly painted.
Courtesy, New Jersey State Library, Trenton.

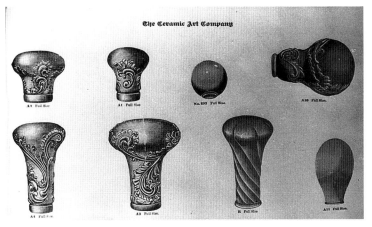

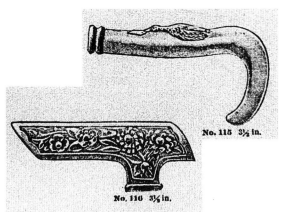

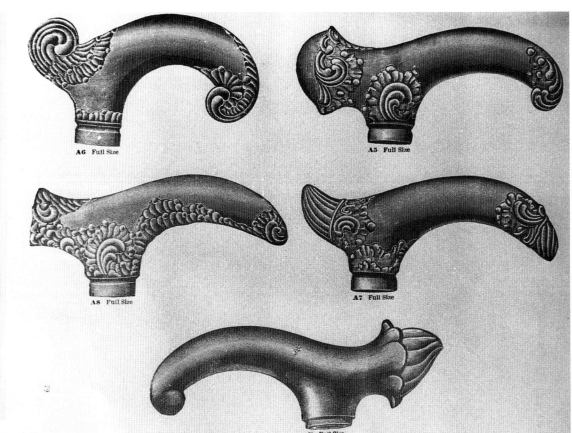

Tortoiseshell Handles

Plastic Handles

Natural Plastic

Natural plastics are derived from rubber, gutta percha, milk, and shellac, among others, while artificial plastics, such as Celluloid, spring from the chemical laboratory.

Corozo nuts, grown in South America, formed the basis of a material used to imitate ivory. Other tropical nuts could also be used. Pressed milk could be processed into a material as hard as ivory which could be used to make knive handles, combs and cane handles. The lowliest of vegetables could literally be pressed into service. Similar objects were formed from a substance derived from potatoes, and carrots were used to imitate coral!

Unfortunately cane handles made of these substances have not survived. The materials may originally have been as hard as ivory, but they disentegrated with time. One handle is pictured - although not American - to illustrate the material.

▲ 14/23 We will see later in this chapter how easy it is for plastic to imitate tortoiseshell. These two canes have a silver ornament covering what appears to be tortoiseshell. The test was not applied.
Courtesy, collection Bruce I. Thalberg.

▶ 14/24 These heads are carved in corazo nuts to resemble ivory.
Courtesy, collection Bruce I.Thalberg.

Beginning in the 1820s, scientist/inventors were at work on rubber as a raw material. In 1839 Charles Goodyear filed a patent on a process which combined rubber and sulphur under heat to form a material which kept its shape. Hard rubber (also named vulcanite or ebonite) became the most important of the natural plastics. Goodyear had a stand at the 1851 London Exhibition where he presented canes among a host of objects made with the new material.

By 1855 Goodyear referred to over a hundred varied articles made from what he called "caoutchouc whalebone" or "caoutchouc ivory". He sold the right to produced hard rubber canes and handles to Heinrich Christian Meyer, of Hamburg, Germany. Towards the last quarter of the 19th century, Meyer was the world's leading cane manufacturer. He was also prominant in the United States.

Gutta percha, gum from another species of tree, differs chemically from rubber by containing oxygen. It cannot be vulcanized. It resisted not only the action of sulphur, but that of any corrosive or caustic substance. It was mainly used for the insulation of telegraph cables, and took a back seat with the development of synthetic resins in the 1920s. E. Remington & Sons, of Ilion, N.Y., used gutta percha to cover their numerous gun canes. It is rarely found on shafts in Europe.

Papier-Maché

Papier-mâché was another natural plastic which was very much in vogue during the 19th century. It is made with moistened paper reduced to a paste, to which is added plaster and pitch. Papier-mâché was developed in Europe during the 18th century. Although no chemical reaction took place, the material could be shaped, molded and hardened to great durability. Tables and chairs were made in papier-mâché! The author believes that cane handles and even shafts were made in that material.

Shellac-based Material

One of the most important of the composition plastics, which was invented in 1854 by Samuel Peck of New Haven, Connecticut. Daguerreotype cases were his main production. Gelatin and wood flour or blood could be added for color. The combination of shellac-limestone-carbon black composition was used for phonograph records. Many cane handles can be found made from shellac combined with one material or another for dye.

▲ 14/25 How celluloid was manufactured.
Courtesy, *Arts et Métiers Illustrés*, 1893.

▲ 14/26 The handle on which one can see the irregularities of the material used. It could be potatoes or milk substitute.
Courtesy, collection Catherine Dike.

Artificial Plastic

Celluloid is obtained by plastifying nitrocellulose with camphor. It was first produced in England in 1865, but in 1869 the Hyatt brothers of Albany, New York, were responsible for the industrial manufacture of what they called *celluloid*.

Celluloid was used to imitate horn, ivory, meerschaum, amber, coral, pearl and wood for handles of umbrellas and sticks.

Blowing a cane handle. A celluloid tube is placed on a two-sided mold of the desired shape. The mold is then placed on a hydraulic press. The resulting two pieces are welded by acetone, trimmed by a scraper, and finally polished and decorated. If an ivory imitation is desired, the handles are filed with fine plaster.

Molding a cane handle. Handles can also be molded from solid celluloid. This method is used mainly for massive handles, curved or shaped at right angles. It was the preferred manner for the imitation of finely veined ivory, since the blowing method distends and distorts the veins of the celluloid.

Celluloid can be used to imitate porcelain, producing handles far less fragile than the real thing. Placing a sheet of paper or steel between two transparent celluloid sheets produces an imitation of enamel.

Celluloid enables a wooden cane to be covered with a closely-fitting sheath imitating wood, horn, ivory, tortoise-shell, and countless other natural materials. If a cane is encountered which appears to have a shaft covered in tortoise-shell, this could only be a celluloid covering. Let the buyer beware!

There is only one way to ascertain with certainty if a material is plastic or the "real thing". Heat a needle to glowing red and point it into the ivory, amber, tortoise-shell, or whatever material is suspect. If the needle does not penetrate, nor is there a characteristic smell, it is real!

Bakelite

The name Bakelite is derived from that of its inventor, Baekland, who invented it in 1906. It is a synthetic resin which is obtained by heating phenol with formol and a catalyst. Bakelite could be used as a covering for delicate objects, and was strong enough to enable entire shafts to be made in this material.

The introduction of Bakelite was the spur which inspired chemists in the direction of the multitude of plastics we find today. At the end of the 20th century many cane shafts are still made in artificial plastic, mainly for lights and for invalid usage.

The Truman Library has a clear plastic cane with a crook handle. Its hollow shaft is filled from top to bottom with silk flowers in shades of blue. Is it in celluloid or in bakelite?

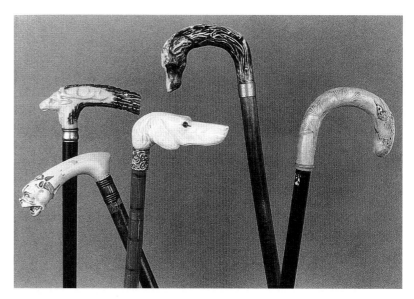

▲ 14/27 Five handles in celluloid, each representing a dog or other animal. It is impossible to say with absolute certainty that they are all American, but such handles were made in large quantities in the United States.
Courtesy, collection L.G.

Other Materials

Almost as diverse as the types of wood used for shafts is the variety of other materials used to make canes or their handles. Several note-worthy examples have been seen in preceeding chapters and among the color pictures.

The Historical, Memorial and Art Department of Iowa has a cane made in buffalo hide. Great numbers of these were made and sold. Theodore Roosevelt brought back some hippopotamus hide to have a cane made.

Apart from the various snake skins used, there was a multitude of horns worked either in the whole length, for the handle or made by segments of horn placed on a metal rod. President Cleveland received such a cane with the horns of all American bovine strung on a shaft.

The bull's penis was dried and hung in barns before making.a shaft. Polished it would take a honey colored tint.

Many canes have as handles the supposed first nugget found in California, so many, in fact, it is small wonder the Gold Rush resulted! (Color picture).

▲ 14/29 An unknown material was used for this cane and its handle. Animal, vegetable or mineral?
Courtesy, collection Francis H. Monek.

◀ 14/28 A group of handles made from the hooves of deer. Today one would not dare be seen wearing such a cane, but as it was once fashionable to display the heads of ani-mals killed upon one's walls, so it must have been elegant to sport such canes.
Courtesy, collection L.G.

▲ 14/30 A group of canes made in various rattan, bamboo and other light materials.
Courtesy, collection L.G.

▲ 14/31 A great variety of snake skins can be found on wooden shafts.
Courtesy, collection L.G.

Varieties of Woods

In this book the type of wood used for the shaft of a particular cane is seldom given, primarily because of the enormous range of woods used. The Rudolph Block Collection, now at the Smithsonian, (but stored in boxes, alas) illustrates the huge variety which can be found.

Rudolph Block collected woods, not walking sticks, but he chose to present the fourteen hundred specimens in his collection in the shape of canes. On woods too hard to be bent into a crook he placed a knob of some natural material. These knobs also encompass a wide range; turquoise, jasper, marble and tiger-eye being some examples of semi-precious minerals, while the animal kingdom provided knobs fashioned from the horns of rams, bison, stags and rhinoceros.

The color of the woods ranges from the white of holly to the jet black of ebony. Red, yellow, brown and olive shades mix with striped and interwoven patterns. Truly exotic are sticks fashioned from the pink guayatil colorado of Panama and the blue mahoe from Cuba. There is even a purple cane, made of nazareno or amaranth.

Most of the woods come from sub-tropical countries. Only a hundred originated in the United States, which seems very few considering the vastness of the nation. Perhaps Block saw no mystique in what could be found in his own back yard. There are also very few woods from European forests.

Modern conservationists would find Block a sympathetic figure. He sought an interview with Harvey S. Firestone, who had acquired vast tracts of land in Liberia for planting rubber. This meant the destruction of one million acres of forest. Block induced Firestone to pay a scientist to explore the forest. Six hitherto unknown species were discovered. The first was named Cassipourea Firestoniana!

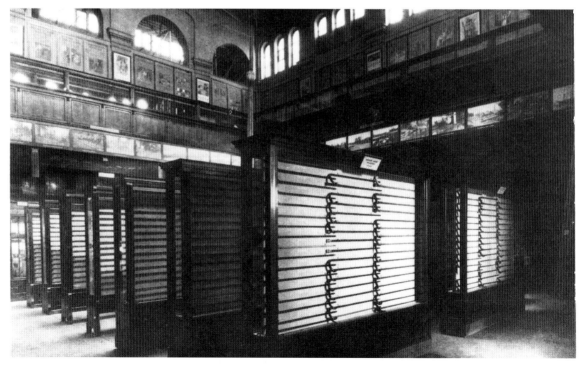

▲ 15/1 The Rudolph Block collection of walking sticks presently at the Smithsonian. Between 1929 and 1931 it was on loan to the New York Botanical Garden. This amazing collection was thought so noteworthy that it was considered for exhibition at the 1939 New York World's Fair.
Courtesy, collection Smithsonian Institution.

It would be impossible to list all the types of wood used in making cane shafts or handles. Any attempt would result in a book in itself!

The Smithsonian also has sixty-six canes made of assorted woods, collected between 1880 and 1906, given by John R. Gilpin.

Canes made from many kinds of wood were popular in America. A cane featured at the Philadelphia Exhibition was fashioned from forty varieties. Another had 350 separate piecesof wood deriving from twenty different types of tree assembled to form the cane. The Minnesota Historical Society had a cane made of 60 pieces of wood; and F. D. R. was presented with a cane made of several colored pieces of the original railroad ties from the Panama railroad built by the French.

▲ 15/2 Five canes carved with the names of the tropical woods they represent. Each is listed in Block's catalog.
Courtesy, Tradewinds Auctions, H. Taron, Manager.

▶ 15/4 Fifty-seven distinct woods are present on this cane, each stemming from a tree grown in Nebraska. The cane was finished with valspar varnish and lists the following trees:

1.	Apple	29.	Jasmine
2.	Red Elm	30.	Inn
3.	Water elm	31.	Tame Grape
4.	Horse Chestnut	32.	Chinese Elm
5.	Ash	33.	Black Locust
6.	Oak	34.	Osage Orange
7.	Diamond Willow	35.	Birch
8.	Box Elder	36.	Maple
9.	Red Willow	37.	White Elm
10.	Pussy Willow	38.	Bird's Eye Maple
11.	Crab Apple	39.	Currant
12.	Iron Wood	40.	Rose Wood
13.	Catalpa	41.	Red Cedar
14.	Honey Suckle	42.	Bridle Wreath
15.	Mulberry	43.	Linden
16.	Lilac Purple	44.	Yellow Pine
17.	Compas Cherry	45.	Honey Locust
18.	Red Haw	46.	Peach
19.	Water Willow	47.	Wild Plum
20.	Wild Grape	48.	Norway Spruce
21.	Silver Maple	49.	Dog Wood
22.	White Lilac	50.	Tame Plum
23.	Elder Berry	51.	Shumac
24.	Poplar	52.	Red Root
25.	White Willow	55.	Walnut Black
26.	Wild Cherry	56.	White Pine
27.	Cherry	57.	Hackberry.
28.	Walnut		

▲ 15/3 Twenty different woods, each one and one-half inches (4 cm) in length, together form this cane. It was presented to F.D.R., one of several similar models he was given.
Courtesy, Franklin D. Roosevelt Library.

Courtesy, collection Catherine Dike

▲ 15/5 The hand of nature helped by the hands of men. Left to itself, a vine will always grow in the same way, as illustrated by the stick lying atop the others. Human intervention is needed to train the tendrils in opposite directions. Center, the circular loop hold has obviously received some help in achieving its final form.
Courtesy, collection L.G.

▲ 15/6 Here the root of the sapling has been cleaned and carved slightly to give an impression of fantastic animals.
Courtesy, collection L.G.

▼ 15/7 Two more modern shafts made with various pieces of wood.
Courtesy, private collection.

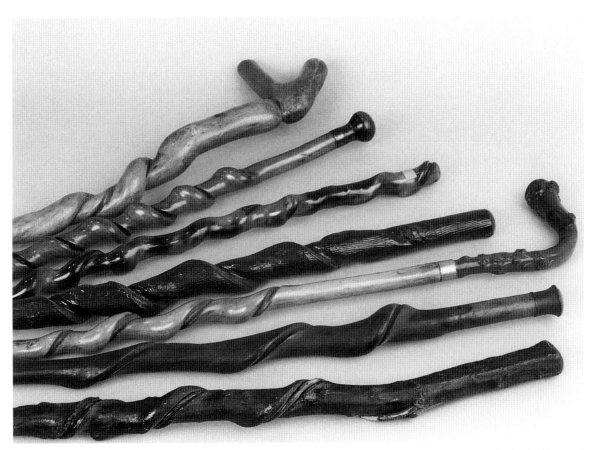

▲ 15/8 A group of naturally twisted woods. By planting a vine at the foot of a young sapling, which would twine itself around the wood as it grew, a twisted shaft would result. On the example in the foreground, a small twig still remains on the shaft.
Courtesy, collection L.G.

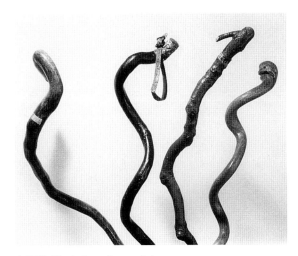

▲ 15/9 Roots form these sticks.
Courtesy, collection L.G.

▲ 15/10 Corn cobs make up the entire cane. The stick at the top is made from the corn stalk. Three such canes were presented to F.D.R. (Warm Springs), and another is in the Carnegie Musuem in Pittsburgh.
Courtesy, collection L.G.

Diamond Willow

Diamond willow was the popular name given to *Salix cordata* or *Salix missouriensis,* which includes the cottony headed willow and erio-cephala. It ranges from North and South Dakota south to Indiana, Nebraska, Missouri and Kentucky, with certain specimens found in Alaska. The trees grow along the banks of rivers and because of the dense foliages, are hard to get at.

Although these trees may be as much as 100 years old and can reach a height of 50 feet (16 m) with a diameter of 18 inches (45 cm), most measure 15 to 25 feet (4,5 m -7,5 m) with a diameter of 6 to 8 inches (15-20 cm). In 1958, botanists assigned different names to various types of diamond willow, generally the Latin salix followed by the name of the scientist who identified it.

In the Observations on Diamond Willow by H.J. Lutz, he writes: *The term "diamond wil-low" seems to have first been applied in the mid-dle and upper Missouri River valley to willows that showed peculiar diamond-shaped depres-sions on their stems. When the stems were carved or otherwise finished, a striking pattern resulted from the curious diamond-shaped cavities and the contrast between the white or cream sapwood and reddish-brown heartwood. Unusual and very attractive canes were fashioned from this wood. The wood of the "diamond-willow" was also regarded as very durable, and was said to be equal to red cedar in this respect. Post, stakes and rails of "diamond-willow" were used in fences by early settlers.*

Willows with diamond-shaped depressions on their stems were probably known in the Missouri River valley around the middle of the nineteenth century, or earlier. Burgess (1877) was convinced that the so-called "diamond-willow" and "red-willow" were new species rather than "Salix cor-data" with a variety. It would appear that he was rather impatient when he wrote: *How long shall we wait for names to be assigned by the Masters? Or, shall we who alone have the tree, alive, or in lumber, to study with all due care, call them "Salix rhomboidea" and "Salix Rhomboi-indentata"? For both species are noted for their diamond-shaped depressions in root and trunk, from which our most unique canes are made.*

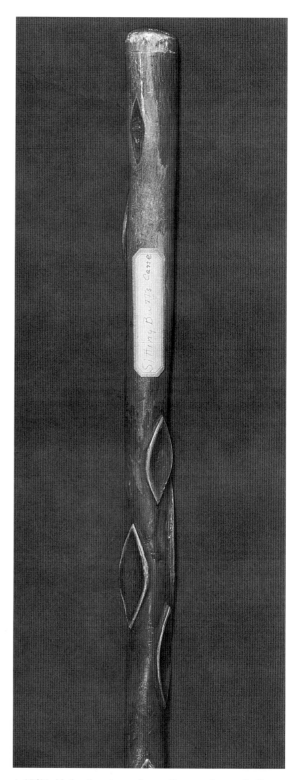

▲ 15/11 Native Americans "carved" many diamond willows. The example shown was made by *Sitting Bull.*
Courtesy, South Dakota State Historical Society, Pierre.

Robert W. Farnas, one-time governor of the state of Nebraska and later an agent in the U.S. Department of Agriculture, wrote in 1884: *Experience demonstrates it to be as durable almost for underground uses, post, etc., as red cedar. The Indians seem to have known of its valuable characteristics. They call it "twat", which interpreted, signifies "durable".*

The characteristic diamond-shaped depressions are caused by the fungus *Valsa Sordida*, which is responsible for damaging a variety of willows. This fungus attacks the shoots and branches and enters the trunk where it destroys the living bark, thus creating the depression. In the foreground of the color picture is a stump of a willow "not cleaned".

The branches should be dried for at least one year before carving. Using a large pocket knife, the diamond is outlined and the bark removed from the depression. After all the diamonds have been thus worked, the bark between the lozenges is removed. No two diamond sticks are identical. The New York Historical Society has a diamond willow cane marked in ink on the side *To Sourdough Bill Sulzer/ From the Sourdoughs of Gulkana, Alaska.*

Burning, Pyrography, Coloring, Jeweling

At the end of the 19th century it was fashion to "work" on wood, producing perhaps a jewel box, a frame or a cane. Particular examples of burning work on canes can be found in the chapters on Canes carved by Soldiers.

One could buy complete sets with points to carve, colors to tint and this work of pyrography can be found in the chapter on the Canes worn by U.S. Presidents and Patriotic Canes. In some examples practically the entire shaft is covered with pyrography and colored.

A decoration used in Folk Art is the "jeweling" of canes, in which the "Flemish Sparkling Jewels" were imbedded into the shaft. These "jewels" came in assorted sizes, representing diamonds, rubies, emeralds, sapphires etc.. They were sold making them more brillant than any ever showm for pyrography purposes. (Color picture).

▼ 15/12 A shaft made of cactus wood is another American wood often found. (Color picture).
Courtesy, Esbola collection.

V Miscellany

▲ 21/1 A poor reproduction from a 1926 newspaper showing the executioner Captain M. C. Patterson who had led 45 men and one woman to the electric chair. He holds a cane on which a "lifer" carved the name of each of Patterson's subjects, including Leon Czolgosz, who had shot President McKinley.
Courtesy, archives Francis H. Monek.

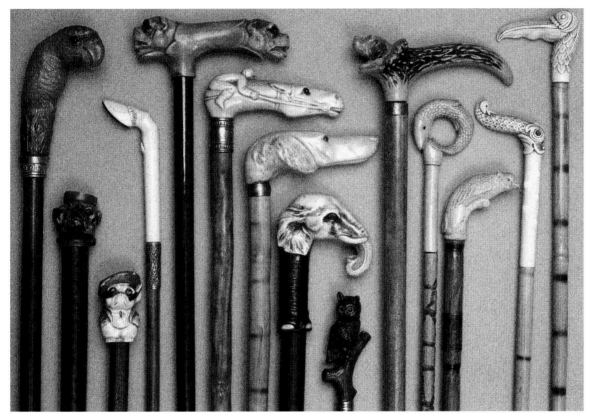

▲ a) A selection of plastic handles made in the United States. There is a wide range of colors.
Courtesy, collection Bruce I. Thalberg.

▶ b) Fifty-seven various woods growing in Nebraska form this cane. Each segment of wood is numbered.
Courtesy, collection Catherine Dike.

▲ c) A selection of marsh woods grown in Florida, one of which is marked *Waa. Nerwin, Winter Haven, Fla.*
Courtesy, collection L.G.

◀ b) An apprentice's cane, demonstrating all the techniques learned. Every piece is inlaid, and the date 1888 appears on the front. It could be European.
Courtesy, collection Mark Neider.

▲ a) A selection of *Diamond Willows* showing the great variety of injuries this fungus can bring to a simple branch. In the foreground is a piece of a branch which has not yet been affected.
Courtesy, collection L.G.

▲ c) Distinctively American, a group of cactus shafts.   Courtesy, collection L.G.

▲ a) A bull's penis can be polished lightly or heavily. The cane at top was more intensively treated than the other two. Courtesy, collection L.G.

▲ c) A gold nugget forms the head of this cane. The collar is marked *Ezekiel Jones Esq. Capt. U.S. Revenue Marine from his nephew in California*
Courtesy, collection Norman Flayderman.

▲ b) The cane in the foreground was made of porcupine quills cut into lengths and woven onto a shaft. Behind right, a cane made in a broom factory, where employees, like glassworkers, could use the left-over material to make objects for themselves.
Courtesy, collection Catherine Dike.

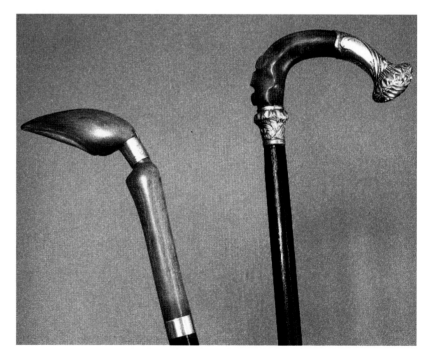

▲ d) Horn was often used to make handles or even complete shafts. The chapter on Canes Worn by U.S. Presidents instances a cane given to President Cleveland made of pieces of horn found in the United States.
Courtesy, collection Mark Neider.

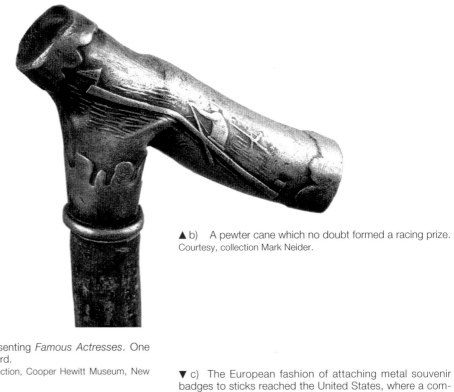

▲ b)   A pewter cane which no doubt formed a racing prize.
Courtesy, collection Mark Neider.

◄ a)   Etched cane representing *Famous Actresses*. One
can recognize Mary Pickford.
Courtesy, Walter Scholz collection, Cooper Hewitt Museum, New
York.

▼ c)   The European fashion of attaching metal souvenir
badges to sticks reached the United States, where a company issued a whole series of these colorful tags.
Courtesy, Hike America.

Miscellany

Children's Canes

In the earliest daguerreotype pictures, a child is often seen holding a small cane. For the purposes of the photographer, the cane served to keep the small hands steady. Nevertheless, children did wear canes in those days when dressing formally on Sundays was the fashion.

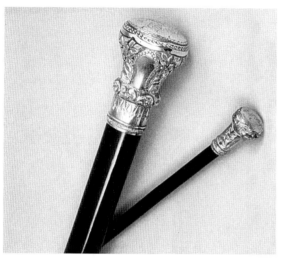

▲ 16/1 A silver presentation cane next to a child's cane. Longer versions of such slender canes could be made for women.
Courtesy, collection L.G.

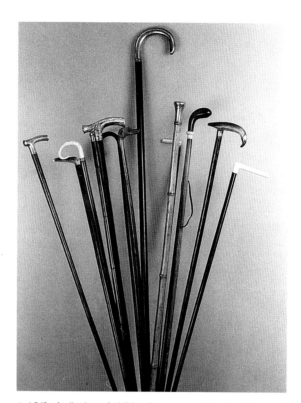

▲ 16/3 A display of children's canes, pictured with one of normal size to show the difference in scale. The handles were made just as finely as those for grown-ups.
Courtesy, collection Eleanor Zellin, Mantiques, Ltd.

▲ 16/2 Norman S. Dike Sr. in 1865, a cane in his hand.
Courtesy, collection Anthony R. Dike.

▲ 16/4 A child holding a small cane. In other pictures children can be seen holding adult canes!
Courtesy, archives Catherine Dike.

Art and Entertainment

In the sphere of musical films, the mention of a cane summons up the image of the ever elegant Fred Astaire with his top hat, white tie and tail coat and the cane which he so often used as an integral part of his choreography. Many music hall dancers wore canes in their routines, giving them an elegant prop to hold which could also mark the rhythm of the music.

Many artists and entertainers wore and/or collected canes. It is not the purpose of this book to list them, but the few cited or pictured will surely entice collectors to search for more.

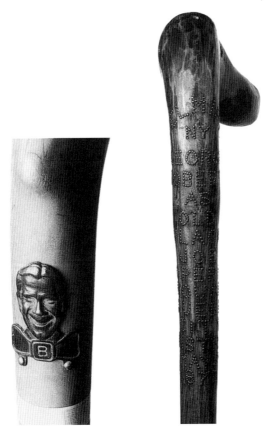

▲ 17/1 A cane picturing *Joe E. Brown.*
Courtesy, collection Bruce E. Thalberg.

▲▶ 17/2 A heavy stick (1 3/4 " 45 mm) with the following words nailed into the wood: *Elmira / N.Y. / George / Robert / as /old / Black / Joe / Opera / House / Queen / City / Minister / May 3rd / 1878.*
Courtesy, collection Paul Weisberg.

▲ 17/3 Like those made for political candidates, a cane was made for Anton Dvorjak who spent three years in New York from 1892 to 1895. In 1898 the Emperor of Austria presented him with the Medal of Honor for the Arts. One surmises that the year 1898 written across a lyre in front of the bust could refer to that event. On either side of the bust are the American flag and what appears to be the Austrian flag, with the characteristic three horizontal stripes but without the imperial eagle.

The bust does look like Dvorjak, although the beard is longer than his pictures show. There was speculation that it might be of John Philip Sousa, but Sousa would have worn a uniform and he did not conduct at the Trans-Mississippi Expositions in 1898.
Courtesy, collection L.G.

▲ 17/4 Harpo Marx holding his rubber horn. As he was always mute in his films, it was this cane which he tooted to attract the attention of his brothers.
Courtesy, archives Catherine Dike.

▲ 17/5 An ivory handle which belonged to *Caruso*. The height of the cane (30 1/4 ", 77 cm) underlines his short stature.
Courtesy, Esbola collection.

▲ 17/6 An etched cane representing *Famous Actresses*. *Mary Pickford* has the place of honor at top, followed by *M.M. Minter, C. Young,* and *B. Daniels*. This is the first etched cane which is signed: *Made by Fred Brown*. Another cane, unsigned, is in a private collection and bears the effigies of Mary Pickford, Pola Negri, Clara Young, B.B. Daniels and E.P. Mares.
Courtesy, the Walter Scholz collection, Cooper-Hewitt Museum, New York.

Souvenirs

Towards the end of the 19th century, souvenir sticks were often purchased at the site of tourist attractions, in the manner in which today one might buy a T-shirt. This was especially true in Europe where one attached a metal badge from the various resorts visited to one's stick. The habit seems to have also reached the United States where one can find many colorful badges to put on one's canes. (Color picture).

A few walking sticks bear Stanhope views of tourist resorts such as Niagara Falls or San Diego. Undoubtedly many more existed than have survived to the present day; sadly for collectors, such ephemera are often thrown away.

Visitors to Florida prompted the production of a large number of souvenirs featuring the alligator. Usually the animal is carved on a piece of wood which is then attached to the shaft, easier than an integral carving to mass-produce.

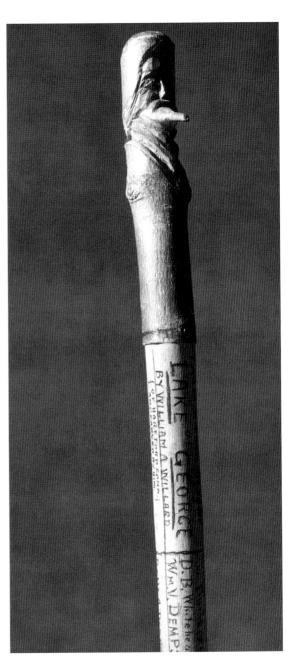

▲ 18/2 William A. Willard carved many canes that he would cover with ink inscriptions. One is mentioned in the chapter on World War I. This one was *Cut from a tree on shore of Lake George by William A. Willard of Hartford Conn. and carved by him in 1926.* Further down one can read *Returning from a three days tournament of American Lawn Bowler Association at Buffalo N.Y. Aug. 10-12, 1926.*
  Another cane by Willard is in the Henry Ford Museum. He had cut a branch on the ground of Mark Twain's home in Hartford and covered it with inscriptions relating to the life of the writer and also describing Henry Ford, Edsel Ford and Thomas Edison. It is dated 8/20/1928.
Courtesy, private collection, Boston.

▲ 18/1 Alligators carved in various positions.
Courtesy, collection Paul Weisberg.

▲ 18/3 An assortment of alligators. Some are carved on the shaft.
Courtesy, collection Bruce I. Thalberg.

▲ 18/4 More elaborate alligators make up this group. They could have been made by a professional carver.
Courtesy, collection Mark Neider.

▶ 18/5 Unique souvenir of a stay at *Glengae,* a guest house on Lake Sunapee in New London, N.H. Fifty guests each put forward his name to be written in ink on this branch of a cherry tree. The bark was left on, except where wide strips spiral down the stick.
Courtesy, New Hampshire Historical Society.

Sports

In the world of sports, it is in the area of boxing that one finds the most intricate canes. Such sticks are usually etched. One such is inscribed: *This stick is of the material used in erecting the amphitheater at Dallas Texas for accommodation of Corbett and Fitz Simmons in the contest for the championship of the world, seating capacity 52,000. Oct. 31st. 1895.*

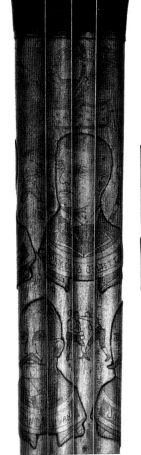

▲ 19/1 Three canes related to boxing. The one to the left celebrates the match between Fitzsimmons (the winner) and Corbett. The tiger refers to the animal which Fitzsimmons kept as a pet.
     The cane to the right shows a boxer in front of a boy. An alligator ascends the shaft. Below the two canes is the cane represented to the right.
Courtesy, collection George H. Meyer.

▶ 19/2 *Champion of the World* is written on a band on the top of the cane. Below are portraits of *James J. Corbett* and of *John L. Sullivan*. Still lower, a third head represents *Charley Mitchell*. The championship match, in which boxing gloves were used for the first time, took place on September 7, 1892. Corbett won in three rounds; thus the words *Third Round* above a triumphant Corbett after many scenes of fisticuffs.
Courtesy, collection George H. Meyer.

▲ 19/4 A baseball bat with the inscription *House of David,* a religious sect established in Michigan in 1903. Initially all the players were drawn from members of the sect, whose trade mark was long hair and beards.
Courtesy, Eleanor Zellin, Mantiques Ltd.

▲ 19/5 Part of the team of the House of David.
Courtesy, archives W. Gladstone.

▲ 19/3 *Noted Pugilist of the World* is inscribed at the top of this cane, followed by the portraits of *Bob Fitzsimmons, J. Corbett, John Sullivan, Chas Mitchell* and *Peter Jackson,* all boxing champions. The handle, a boxing glove, was added to the shaft later, as certain encounters would have been fought with bare knuckles.
Courtesy, collection Catherine Dike.

▲ 19/6 A presentation cane given to the baseball hero *George Gibbon from a few London Baseball Friends, Oct. 08.*
Courtesy, collection Eleanor Zelin, Mantiques Ltd.

▲ 19/7 Oars on a pewter handle celebrating an unknown rowing race. (Color picture).
Courtesy, collection Mark Neider.

▲ 19/8 A modern knob celebrating the golfer Ben Hogan.
Courtesy, Eleanor Zellin, Mantiques Ltd.

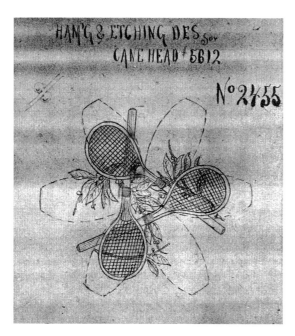

▲ 19/9 Tiffany drawing for a knob displaying tennis racquets. Tiffany also made handles featuring golf clubs and horse-shoes.
Courtesy, Tiffany & Co. Archives.

▶ 19/11 Bowling pins topple! Made by Gorham, doubtless as a competition prize.
Courtesy, Brown University Library.

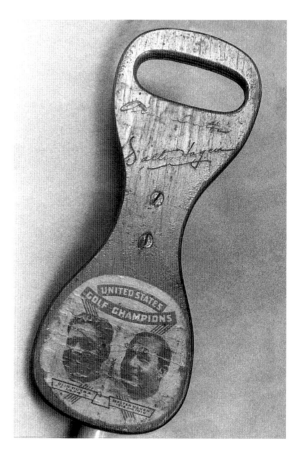

▲ 19/10 A golfing seat picturing *United States Golf Champions Olin Dutra* with the date *1934* and *Walter Hagen* with the dates *1914* and *1919*. Facsimile of their signatures are near the handle.
Courtesy, private collection.

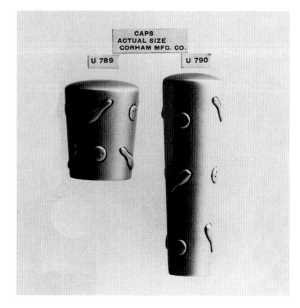

▲ 19/15 A Gorham handle illustrated with two open cars.
Courtesy, Brown University Library.

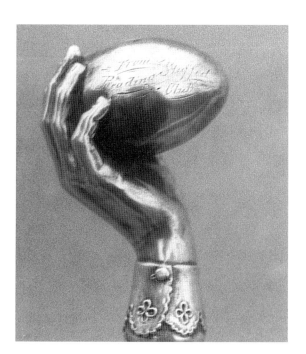

▲ 19/12 A silver football marked *From Prading Stuffed Club*.
Courtesy, collection Eleanor Zelin, Mantiques Ltd.

▲ 19/13 Modern versions of what accompanies the sports-man on a stroll — tongue firmly in cheek, one hopes!
Courtesy, collection Francis H. Monek.

▲ 19/14 A souvenir of the *Kentucky Derby*.
Courtesy, private collection.

▲ 19/16 An etched cane picturing trotting horses. At top is a driver in a sulky, with *Nancy Hanks* (the name of the horse) and the time *2.04.* below. Six other horses and their times follow, along with many other animals. The handle and the lower part of the cane are exactly similar to those of etched canes seen in former chapters.
Courtesy, collection George H. Meyer.

Advertising

Today advertising logos appear on ball-point pens, lapel pins, T-shirts, or anything which can catch the eye. At the beginning of this century it was often customary to hand out canes which were so marked. The most common are walking sticks which have the advertisement stamped on all four sides of a square shaft. At both the Hayes Presidential Center and the Benjamin Harrison Home there are canes marked *Aultman, Miller & Co. / Akron Ohio / Buckeye Harvesting Machine.* It is likely that this go-getting company sent one of their advertising sticks to each new President.

There exists a large number of these advertising canes, spanning more than a century. To cite a few among thousands: one bears the legend *Furlock Live Stock Auction / New Orleans Stock Yards., Inc. / The Oldest Central Market in Deep South.* Another has *Sun-Glow Industries, Inc. / Mansfield, Ohio* marked on one side. The Henry Ford Museum has a cane carved by L.B. Huntoon to celebrate the millionth Ford in 1931. Production of these novelties continues, as shown by the stick which bears the message *N.Y.A.B. / New York Air Brake / A Unit of General Signal / Starbuck Avenue / Watertown / N.Y. 13801.* Because of the serial code, this cane must be quite recent.

▲ 20/2 *Sun-Glow Industries Inc.* is marked on the shaft.
Courtesy, collection Francis H. Monek.

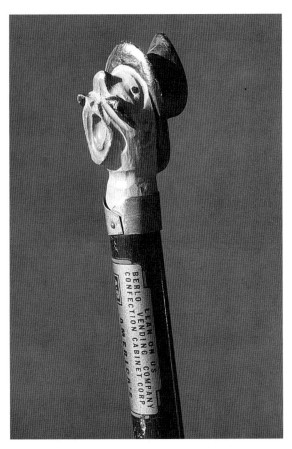

▲ 20/3 The message is simple: *Lean on Us / Berlo Vending Company / Confection Cabinet Corp. / America's Best Candy / The Prop for Profit.*
Courtesy, private collection, Boston.

▲ 20/1 Insurance companies also had their advertisements: *Dorchester Mutual Fire Insurance Co.*
Courtesy, collection A. Brown.

▲ 20/4 Here a metal band gives a message: *Farm & Home / Orange Judd / Weeklies / Dakota Farms / The National Farm Power.*
Courtesy, collection L.G.

▲ 20/5 Such seats often received advertisements. Here *Schenley's Red Label* offers *Right because its Light.*
Courtesy, collection Francis H. Monek.

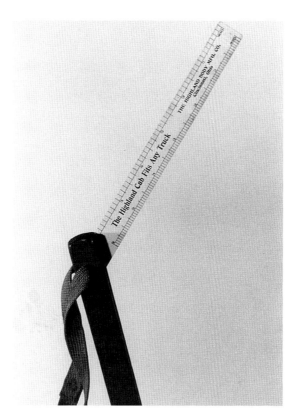

▲ 20/6 A good way to hail a cab. (Color picture).
Courtesy, collection A. Brown.

▲ 20/7 *Heywood Wakefield Co.* used the Chicago slogan: *More than a Century of Progress - 1826 to 1933.*
Courtesy, collection Francis H. Monek.

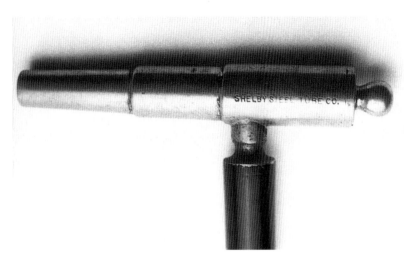

▲ 20/8 A small cannon which resembles a Cheroot gun (see chapter on weapons) and is marked on the side *Shelby Steel Fire Co.*
Courtesy, collection Henri Cayre.

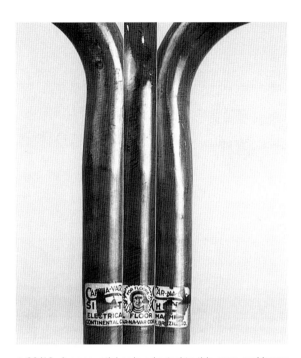

▲ 20/10 A paper sticker is adapted to this cane and bears the inscription: *Car-na-var / Sl....T Electrical Continental / For Floors* above an Indian / *Floor / Car-na-var / Car-na-var Ch..../ Machine / Corp. Brazil ID.*
Courtesy, collection H.S.

▲ 20/9 A rubber cane marked *Kelly Springfield Tire Co.* The Smithsonian Institution has a similar cane marked *Goodyear.* The cane at right has *Ross Valve Co.* marked on its valve!
Courtesy, collection Paul Weisberg.

▲ 20/11 Could an advertisement bear a patent number on the back of the head? The front of the handle has the words *W.E US & Co.* Such puzzles are endlessly fascinating. (Color picture).
Courtesy, collection L.G.

▲ 20/12 Makers of barbed wire distributed canes made in this material to their good customers with the words: *Compliments of J. Haish / "S" Barb / Steel Fence Wire / Kekalb, Ill.*
Courtesy, collection Francis H. Monek.

▲ 20/14 Five tubular flasks can fit inside this shaft. The handle advertises *Pinch Whisky,* (probably the premium brand of scotch made by Haig and so named for United State sales. In the United Kingdom, the brand is called Dimple Haig).
Courtesy, collection Jack Gulick.

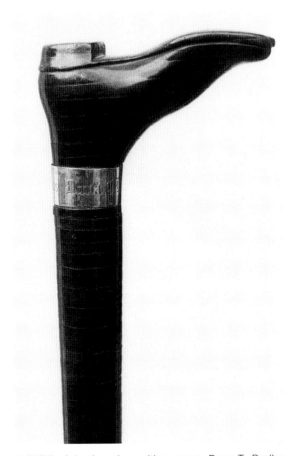

▲ 20/13 A leather shoe with a name, *Dana T. Dudley, Haverhill, Mass.* marked on the sole. It could be a gift to a long-time employee on the occasion of his retirement.
Courtesy, collection Theodore T. Newbold.

▲ 20/15 A set of brass canes made by *Scovil Mfg. Co.*
Courtesy, collection Bruce I. Thalberg.

Prisoners

The long empty hours which make up a prisoner's life have always enticed inmates of jails, prisons or concentration camps to do something with their hands. A large collection can be made up exclusively of canes made by prisoners of war from a multitude of campaigns.

Today's concepts of human rights and basic decency are of very recent origin. During the last part of the 19th century, death of prisoners by hanging took place all over the country. Less well known is the fact that the bodies were often skinned, and the hide used for making razor strops and walking canes. Several of these sticks exist, museums describing them as "leather" canes. One is at the Kentucky Historical Society under the description *Leather cane made at the old prison for Clark Overton, Flemingsburg, Ky.* Sing-Sing prison also "provided" such canes, one of which was given to a minister. The custom stopped in 1936.

The Wisconsin Historical Society has heavy canes used to separate fighting prisoners given them by a former guard at the Waupun State Prison. The museum of San Quentin likewise displays canes used by their guards.

◀ 21/2 One of the "leather" canes made in the 1880s by a medical student at the University of Cincinnati.
Courtesy, private collection.

These were canes of repression, but there were also the numerous canes made to pass the time. The Fairfield Historical Society has canes which were made in horsehair by the prisoners of the Colorado Prison. In *Romance Behind Walking Sticks,* the author William J. Burscher mentions that a Dr. Hill received a stick made by an inmate of the Virginia Penitentiary which was formed by 400 different pieces of wood. Two of the etched canes seen in former chapters are known to have been made by prisoners. It is the author's feeling that these canes could have been made in penitentiaries.

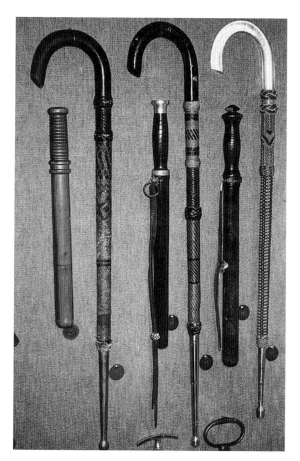

▲ 21/4 Three heavy canes on display at the San Quentin Museum. They were made by inmates in hardwood and covered with woven leather and fabrics. The one at right has a bakelite handle. It was an unwritten policy for the guards to carry such canes, and by tapping the floor (the tips of the cane are loaded), order the convicts to rise, sit, return to their cells, and so forth. The sticks obviously also served as defensive weapons, and were later replaced by the batons also pictured.
Courtesy, collection San Quentin Museum.

▲ 21/3 A carved cane from a prisoner serving a life sentence, who tells us of his life: *Since man to man is so unjust / I hardly know which one trust / I have trusted / and to my sorrow / I'll trust tomorrow.* A snake forms the handle.
Courtesy, collection Francis H. Monek.

Cane Dealers

Looking through the many lists found in business directories, one is amazed at the great number of manufacturers involved in cane making.

First were the importers, who were numerous during the early 19th century. W.A. Drown & Co. in Philadelphia imported canes from Samuel Fox & Co. Ltd. in England; Nathaniel Ellis in Boston imported *fancy walking sticks* and Wurmser & Grun imported from Vienna, Austria.

In 1842, Congress passed the first of a series of restrictive tariffs on imported goods. The tax on canes was 30% in 1842 and 35% in 1862, whether the canes were finished or not. Even the whalebone from foreign fishing was taxed.

Consequently, more and more companies produced their own handles and shafts and mounted them together. Some also manufactured umbrellas and whips. A distinction must be made between those who *manufactured* canes and those who *mounted* canes.

They were also *turners* in hard wood and ivory. In 1878, there were 53 turners in New York, among which was J. F. Remmey, who tells us that the company was established in 1783 and was located at 92 Fulton Street.

In 1880 there was one notable dealer, Otto Partisch of 18 Vesey Street, New York City, who advertised *The Hard Rubber & Cane Co., importer and manufacturer of all kinds of walking sticks, whip, stock mounting, etc..* Goodrich of the rubber company fame had sold part of his patent to Heinrich Christian Meyer, the largest cane manufacturer in Hamburg, Germany. Could Partisch have been Meyer's representative in the United States? Many canes were made in rubber, but the only surviving example is the bust of Grover Cleveland, found in the chapter on Political Canes. Rubber disintegrates over time, and canes from that period are unlikely to have survived to the present day.

Among manufacturers working with less common materials one finds *Tortoiseshell Work* in Providence, R.I., *the oldest Manufactured Tortoiseshell Goods in the United States.* They produced shafts and handles. The *Celluloid Novelty Co.* made handles.

At least one cane manufacturer was in uninterrupted business for over fifty years. First known in 1846 under the name of Abraham Cox, in 1884 the company became Cox & Sons of 25 Maiden Lane, New York. Their advertisement reads *Manufacturer and Importer of Gold, Silver, Ivory, etc. Mounted Canes.* They were still listed in 1906. It is particularly curious that no canes appear to have survived bearing their manufacturing mark, when one considers the very large quantities they must have sold during those years.

Between 1841 and 1902 20 dealers were listed in New York alone. The names would come and go over the years, with the exception of the long-time established manufacturers exemplified by A. Cox & Son, J. F. Fradley & Co and Rest Fenner Smith & Co.. Gorham and Tiffany were never listed, handles not being their primary item of manufacture.

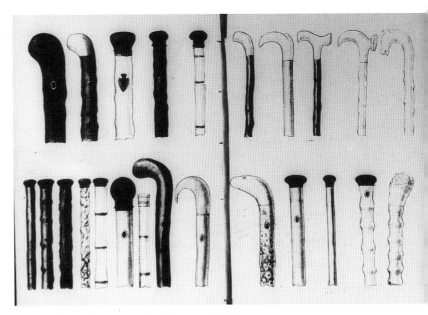

▲ 22/1 One of the earliest catalogues offering walking canes issued by *Hardware Toys* between 1800 and 1809. The wood and the handles are very simple.
Courtesy, archives Catherine Dike.

▲ 22/2 An advertisement from *A. Cox & Sons.*
Courtesy, archives Catherine Dike.

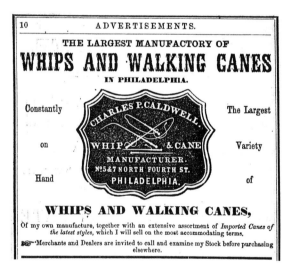

▲ 22/3 In 1862, Charles P. Caldwell mentions that he has *The Largest Manufactory of Whips and Walking Canes.*
Courtesy, archives Kurt Stein.

▲ 22/4 One of the many *Turners in Hardwood and Ivory* who advertised *Walking Canes.* (1874).
Courtesy, archives Catherine Dike.

◄22/5 A Philadelphia advertisement offering *Plain or Sword Canes.* It is interesting to note that John Ashton offered hippopotamus teeth for sale. (From the *New Hampshire Statesman and Concord Register, November 3, 1827.*)
Courtesy, archives Kurt Stein.

▲ 22/6 The billhead of the firm of John McAllister & Son, Philadelphia, who offered *Whips, Canes and Spectacles.* Arriving in Philadelphia in 1785, he manufactured whips and canes. In 1842 his son joined him as partner.
Courtesy, archives Kurt Stein.

▼ 22/7   In the 1890 *Sieger & Guernsey's Cyclopedia of the Manufacturers and Products of the United States,* are the following dealers:

Under *Canes* are listed:

A Cox's Sons, 25 Maiden Lane, New York.
Wm. Demuth & Co., 507 Broadway, New York.
J. Fox & Son, 167 Main St., Cincinnati, O.
J.F. Fradley & Co.,23 John St., New York.
Wm. Harvey & Co., 392 Broadway, New York.
Hearn & Braitsch, Providence, R.I.
F.J. Kaldenburg, 213 E. 33d St., New York.
C. Lingemann & Co. Detroit, Mich.
F.P. Locklin & Bro., 209 Canal St., New York.
Rest Fenner Smith & Co., 701 Broadway, New York.
A.G. Schwab & Bro., 53 W. 5th St., Cincinnati, O.
Simons, Bro. & Co., 615 Chestnut St., Philadelphia, Pa.
Isaac Smith's Son & Co., 928 Broadway, New York.
L. Winkler, 142 Fulton St., New York.
Wright Bros. & Co., 450 Broadway, New York.

Under *Cane Mountings*:

Simons, Bro. & Co., 618 Chestnut St., Philadelphia, Pa.
A.T. Wall & Co., Providence, R.I.
L. Winkler, 142 Fulton St., New York.
Wright Bros. & Co., 322 Market St., Philadelphia, Pa.

Under *Cane Heads*:

J. Briggs & Sons, 65 Clifford St., Providence, R.I.
Celluloid Novelty Co., 313 Broadway, New York.
R.F. Smith & Co., 701 Broadway, New York.
Emil Fox, 133 Crosby St., New York.
F. Grote & Co., 114 E. 14th St., New York.
Hearn & Braitsch, Providence, R.I.
E.J. Kaldenberg Co., 213, E. 33d St., New York.
F.P. Locklin & Bro., 208 Canal St., New York.
Simons, Bro. & Co., 618 Chestnut St., Philadelphia, Pa.
William Tietze, 4 Liberty Pl., New York.
L. Winkler, 142 Fulton St., New York.

▲ a) An intriguing handle with the words *We Us & Co.* written on the eye patch. At the back of the head is a patent number which is illegible, perhaps part of the advertising pitch and intentionally so!
Courtesy, collection L.G.

▲ c) An advertisement for a cab company.
Courtesy, collection Albert Brown.

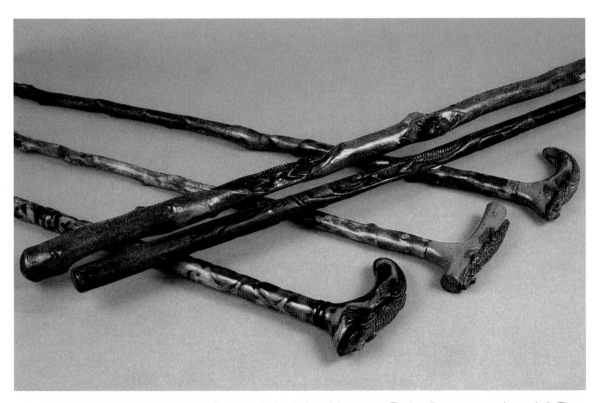

▲ b) A selection of souvenir canes made in Florida at the beginning of the century. The handles are mounted on a shaft. Those laid on top could have been made by local artists.
Courtesy, collection L.G.

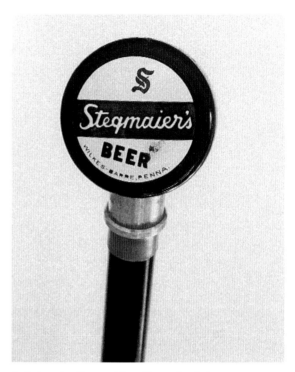

▲ a) An advertisement more creative in concept than practical in execution. One must grasp both the cane and the
end of the cloth, as the latter is on a tight spring.
Courtesy, collection Catherine Dike.

▲ c) An advertisement for a Pennsylvania beer.
Courtesy, collection Mark Neider.

▲ b) A group of advertising canes. At bottom, left to right, messages from the following companies: *Carl Savage, Inc. (Frozen
eggs and Packs of Dressed Poultry); First State Bank & Trust (Rio Grande City, TX.); Fretz-Moon Tube Co. (Steel Pipes); and C.
Aultman & Co. (Threshers and Engines)*. Lying across them, bottom to top, are a cane from *Farm & Home (Dakota Farmers)*;
Citgo (Dealerama, 1967); and finally a cane with the marking *Car-na-var* advertising an Electrical Floor Machine from Brazil, ID.
Courtesy, collections L.G. and H.S.

Cane Cabinets

It was an American custom to keep one's canes in a showcase or cabinet, and many manufacturers would provide their clients with such pieces of furniture. Dealers, of course, also used such showcases. Among many examples can be cited: *Abraham Harris*, Maker of Umbrellas in Baltimore, *A. N. Russell and Sons,* in Ilion, N.Y., *Simons Brothers & Co,* in Philadelphia, and *Oscar Onken Co.* in Cincinnati, Ohio.

A look at the display of showcases in the picture by Rest Fenner Smith & Co. (page 236) makes one realize how great a number of such cases must have been destroyed.

▲ 22/8 In 1916, Gorham offered these cane stands on casters, undoubtedly for dealers.
Courtesy, Brown University Library.

▲ 22/10 This case allowed one to remove a cane from either the side or the top.
Courtesy, collection Walter Scholz.

▲ 22/11 A triangular case which takes up less space.
Courtesy, collection Walter Scholz.

▶ 22/12 It is possible to exhibit two rows of canes should one choose to do without the protection of glass.
Courtesy, collection L.G.

◀ 22/9 A walnut and glass case which opens and can hold 120 canes. It is marked *Exhibition Showcase Company, pats. May 8th '77 and Nov. 14th '82, Erie, Pennsylvania.*
Courtesy, Tradewinds Auctions, H. Taron, Manager.

VI Gadget Canes

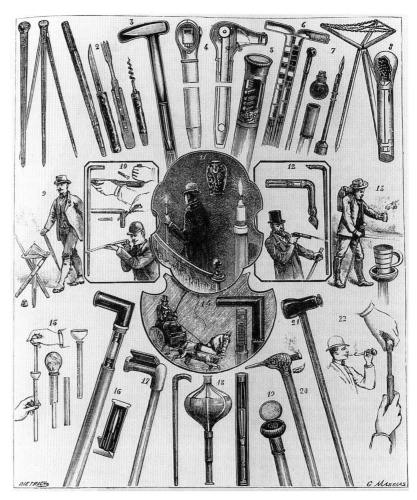

▲ 23/1 The Scientific American Supplement, No. 882, dated November 26, 1892,
gives a good example of Cane contrivances in which it described a series of French
drawings.
Courtesy, Catherine Dike archives

Gadget Canes

Introduction

In the English of today, a cane that deviates from a utilitarian walking stick, particularly if it conceals an object, is referred to as a *gadget cane*. In France the translation is *canne à système;* in Italy it is *baston con anima* (literally, animated stick); and in Germany it is *Stöke mit Seele,* or stick with soul. All these terms were coined in this century to describe this category of canes.

In previous times, the cane was an essential part of fashionable dress, but that did not mean it could not also have utilitarian uses. It was as common to have a watch, a snuffbox, or a sword hidden in one's cane as it is for a lady of today to carry a lipstick in her handbag.

The range covered by what we call gadget canes is so huge that distinctions are made within it. Broadly speaking, these canes divide into those which conceal something and those which serve a dual purpose. The dual-purpose canes are further subdivided into two types. One type is purely functional; for example, the cane can be converted into a seat, a music stand, or a hammer. The second variety is associated with a profession or rank.

Gadget canes are also grouped in four main categories. Sticks used:
- for energetic outdoor walking
- for urban use, and therefore more elegant
- professionally, and
- as weapons.

The weapon cane forms an important category of its own. Great ingenuity was required to conceal the variety of weapons which can be found in canes. While they were primarily meant for hunting, these weapons could also be used defensively.

Toward the middle of the 19th century, the development of the mechanical industries made these types of walking sticks quite popular. A series of novelty gadget canes were made as souvenirs for exhibitions, fairs and political parades. These fragile canes, meant to last but a day, were often broken, thrown away or tossed into a lumber room and forgotten. Grandfather's old canes with their ivory or silver knobs may still remain in the family umbrella stand, but the gadget cane was rarely attractive enough to be so displayed. If it survived at all, it would often be found in the attic, used by the children as a plaything on rainy days. The small objects contained in many multiple-compartment canes are rarely found in their original condition, and the assortment is often incomplete. So it is that despite having been produced in large quantities, these canes are quite rare today, and thus can become an important part of a collection.

Patents

No chapter on gadget canes could be complete without mention of the hundreds of United States patents filed for this type of stick. Indeed, most American gadget canes have the word *patent* and the date marked either upon the collar or on the shaft. Not all of these canes are home-grown, so to speak; from time to time European inventors as well patented their designs in the United States. Some inventors would mark their cane *Patent pdg.*, meaning Patent Pending, but never complete the often arduous process of filing a patent. Undoubtedly a certain percentage of patented designs never see the light of day in a fully-realized execution, but prior to 1940, a good number of these patented canes were made. The patents tend to fall into two groups, one covering the gadget device itself, and the second filed to cover the design, perhaps the shape of a knob or the carving on a shaft. A very general listing is given at the end of this chapter. After 1940 patents for canes continued to be filed, but most were for sticks which function as an aid to invalids or the handicapped, a thing unheard of during the 19th century.

This chapter is in no way a catalog of all the gadget canes known to exist. Sadly, patent drawings are found more often than the canes themselves. It is rather odd to note that no model was required to be submitted when patents were applied for.

Outdoor Activities

A stick is a natural adjunct for any hiker. Even on a simple neighborhood stroll, the feel of a stick in one's hand, whether it be a finely wrought cane or a mere tree branch, is a pleasurable sensation. We will see in this chapter the range of sports which had canes designed to accompany their devotees. Patents were filed for sticks containing billiard cues; those which counted the number of steps the hiker took; those which imitated the call of a bird. A cane existed to accompany any outdoor activity one could conjure up, from taking the dog for a walk (Color picture) to the cane with three flasks nestled in its shaft, a welcome companion at a long and chilly football game (Color picture).

▲ 23/3 A similar cup was patented in 1888. Many others were to follow.
Courtesy, U.S. Patent Office.

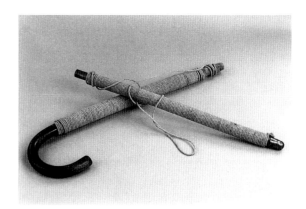

▲ 23/4 This cane could save one's life when mountain climbing. In the event of a fall, the cane was to be thrown, with the hope of its catching and securing a hold. Perhaps a trifle optimistic!
Courtesy, collection Francis H. Monek.

▼ 23/2 A butterfly net made of cotton fabric. Two metal loops attached to a telescoping stick hold the net open. When not in use, the loops lie alongside the shaft, and the net is wrapped around the stick. Inside the shaft under the handle is a brass tube with two compartments, one glass-lined for carrying ether, and the other for holding tweezers, lancet, a small sharp-pointed utensil, and other instruments needed by the butterfly collector. The cane is marked *Harrimac,* and the net *Richardson, Chicago.*
Courtesy, collection Dr. J. H.

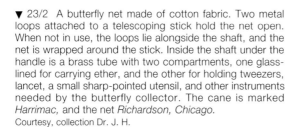

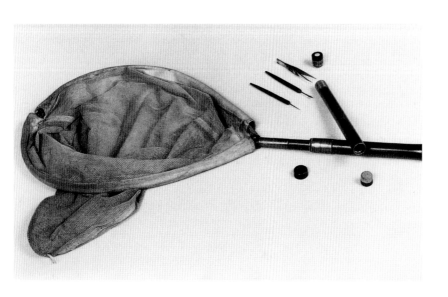

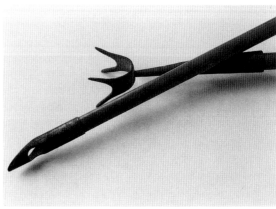

▲ 23/5 Two garden tools which adorn the end of a cane. Their exact function is somewhat hazy! One can also find small trowels on the end of canes.
Courtesy, collection Francis H. Monek.

▲ 23/6 This modern cane includes everything a jogger might wish for.
Courtesy, collection Catherine Dike.

▲ 23/8 Many patents have been issued for canes with fishing rods hidden in the shaft in one fashion or another.
Courtesy, archives Catherine Dike.

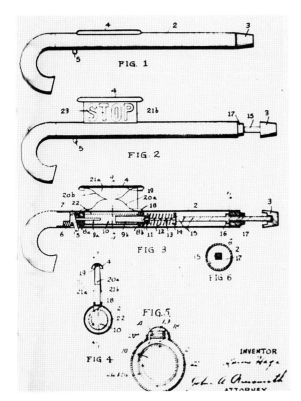

▲ 23/7 Before pedestrian crossings existed, this patent allowed one to brandish a *Stop* sign while crossing the street.(1933).
Courtesy, U.S. Patent Office.

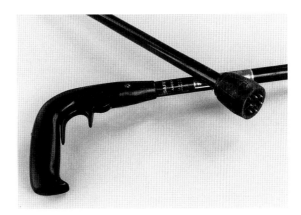

▲ 23/9 A cane to be used for walking on icy surfaces. The prongs emerge when the handle is activated. Patents are still filed for this type of cane.
Courtesy, collection Francis H. Monek.

Seats

When seat canes first appeared, they were intended to be primarily for hunting use, which gave rise to their common name of *shooting sticks*. Originally there were two types of seats; a comfortable, three-legged model, and the classic one-legged shooting stick which gave support for a semi-seated position and allowed some mobility when shooting. For the latter type, a disk is added to the end of the cane to keep it from sinking into the ground, and it is the disk which offered the possibilities for a great variety of patents.

The United States Patent Office has an unbelievable quantity of designs for various seats, with one, two or three legs. A varied collection could be formed comprising only seat sticks. The group shown in the color pictures gives a good idea of the great variety of American canes of this type.

◀ 23/10 Shooting stick marked *Kan O Seat Pat. 1935. Stafford Johnson S402.504 pteating Corp. Iona Mich.*
Courtesy, collection Francis H. Monek

▲ 23/12 A virtually identical cane to that shown above, called the fisherman's seat, was given a U.S. patent on February 16, 1875. When in use as a seat, the stick is placed upside down. The fishing rod fits into the protuding ferrule, thus leaving the hands free to work the tackle or unhook a fish. The cloth is carried separately.
Courtesy, collection Catherine Dike.

▲ 23/11 A Folk Art model featuring a seat which is wide and stable when assembled.
Courtesy, private collection, Easton, CT.

▲ 23/13 Stick with four metal rods which emerge from the handle. Either the purpose is to serve as a footstool, or a piece of cloth is missing, as sitting on the contraption as shown would certainly be torture!
Courtesy, collection Francis H. Monek.

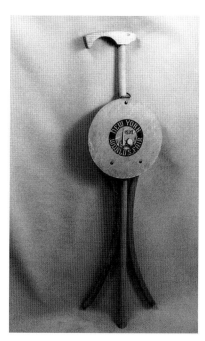

▲ 23/14 Three-legged seat for the 1939 New York World's Fair, where attendances were large and lines were long. The round disc forms the seat, and the handle serves as a back rest. Seats like this are still offered for sale.
Courtesy, private collection, Easton, CT.

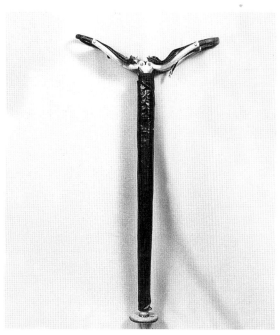

▲ 23/16 A shooting stick combined with an umbrella, inscribed *The perfect Pat*.
Courtesy, collection Francis H. Monek.

▶ 23/17 A modern cane with a mirror in a type of periscope design which allows one to scan the action while at the back of the crowd. Marked *Fair Seat - Trans American Specialities Inc. New York City*.
Courtesy, collection Francis H. Monek.

▲ 23/15 The lid of the handle is dated 1893 and the inside is marked *Benoit cane stool - Chicago*. A look is enough to make one wince - a more uncomfortable bottom-pincher can hardly be imagined!
Courtesy, collection Francis H. Monek.

▲ 23/18 This stick disassembles into two sections, a top piece containing the cloth for the seat, and a lower piece which splits lengthwise to form a base. The long rod attached to the handle goes through all three pieces and holds them together. The cloth bears the inscription *Patd. Dec. 8 1863 C.P. Pascomb*.
Courtesy, collection Francis H. Monek.

Tobacco

In comparison with European canes, few American handles are found covering the wide range of tobacco usage: chewing, snuffing, smoking of pipes, cigars, and cigarettes, and matchboxes to initiate the process. Chewing tobacco was in vogue during the 19th century, as witnessed by the large spittoons in every public place.

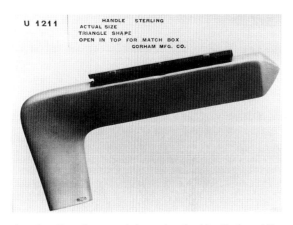

▲ 23/19 The silver match box advertised by Gorham Mfg. Co.
Courtesy, Brown University Library.

▲ 23/21 A silver cigarette case in the shape of a golf club. It bears the word *Sterling* and the swastika cross, emblem of Albert J. Gannon.
Courtesy, collection Julius Tarshis.

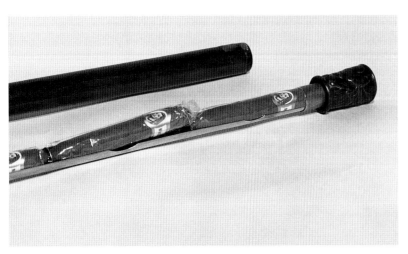

▲ 23/20 Cigar case. The cigars are placed one on top of another in the open tube 34 inches long (86 cm). The tube was then slid into a hollow cane. (Patent 1887). A cigar-cutter was often found in the handle of such canes.
Courtesy, collection Francis H. Monek.

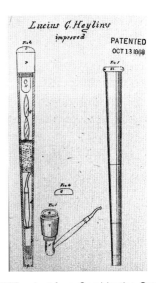

▲ 23/22 A 1868 patent for a *Combination Cane* which provides cigars, a cigar-cutter, a pipe, tobacco and matches near the ferrule.
Courtesy, U.S. Patent Office

▲ 23/23 Cigarette case formed to the same design as the cigar container, and covered by the same patent. (1887).
Courtesy, collection Walter Scholz.

▲ 23/24 A tinder wick lighter. The top of the handle holds the striker which has the wick embedded in it. It is marked *The Norlipp Co. Pat. Chicago Ill. Pend.*
Courtesy, collection Richard W. Carlson.

▲ 23/26 A simple top slips over a butane gas lighter.
Courtesy, collection Stuart Howard White.

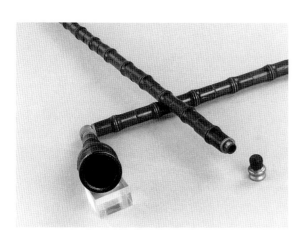

▲ 23/25 Two modern opium pipes, with the shaft forming the stem of the pipe.
Courtesy, collection Francis H. Monek.

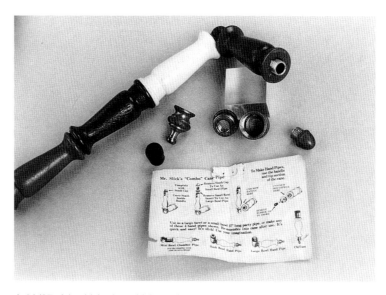

▲ 23/27 A hashish pipe which can be assembled in several fashions. It was sold as a "novelty" by *The Stick Manufacturing, Cleve, Ohio.*
Courtesy, collection Francis H. Monek.

Photography

"Spy cameras" were quite common toward the end of the19th century. Should the user happen to be a detective, or, even more exciting, a genuine spy, they served as a working tool, but for most people, of course, they were merely a novelty item which allowed one to take photographs discreetly. Cameras could be hidden in a multitude of objects — books, hats, ties, coat lapels, watches, and naturally, a fashionable walking stick.

Tripods were often patented. Modern cameras need only straight single-legged supports, but the three-legged tripod was revived for the first video cameras.

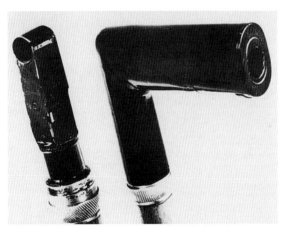

▲ 23/28 Uniquely constructed camera specially made for reporters of the *New York Daily News.* It uses 16 mm film. Left, the handle has been removed.
Courtesy, *Cane Curiosa.*

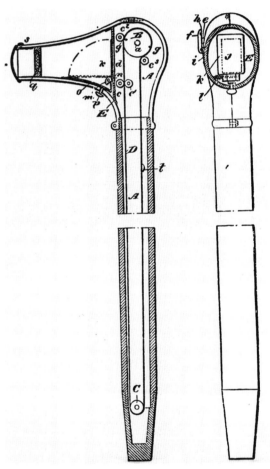

▲ 23/30 Drawing of a camera seen in the November 1892 issue of *Scientific American,* making a reasonable case for it being of American invention. The film negative descends into the shaft and is moved by turning a knob (*f*) on the side of the handle. No indication was made for pictures taken. It is not known whether this model was ever manufactured.
Courtesy, US. Patent Office.

PARSELL'S PORTABLE PHOTOGRAPHIC CAMERA AND TRIPOD.

◀ 23/29 An American tripod cane of 1885 which was part of the *Detective* camera outfit of H.V. Parsell & Sons.
Courtesy, *Cane Curiosa.*

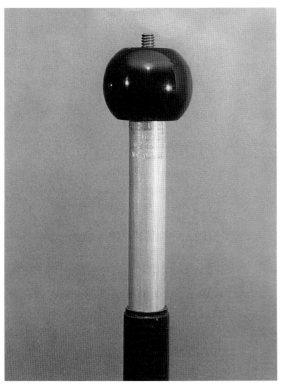

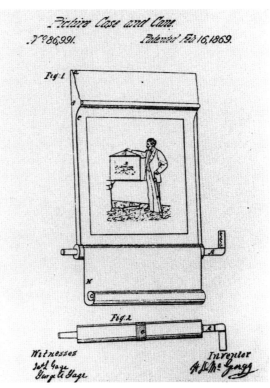

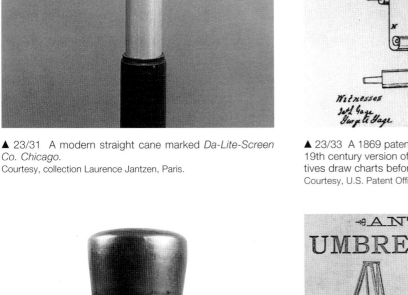

▲ 23/31 A modern straight cane marked *Da-Lite-Screen Co. Chicago.*
Courtesy, collection Laurence Jantzen, Paris.

▲ 23/33 A 1869 patent for a picture drawn out of a shaft. A 19th century version of the boards on which today's executives draw charts before the assembled shareholders!
Courtesy, U.S. Patent Office.

▲ 23/32 A Stanhope opening on the side of a shaft allowed one to peep at a small picture. The opening went through the shaft, so the image was a type of transparency. Stanhope views were patented in the 1870s and used on a wide diversity of objects, including the 1876 centennial canes.
Courtesy, collection Catherine Dike.

▲ 23/34 An umbrella tripod offered for sale by *Anthony & Co.* It is not clear from the sketch where the umbrella section comes in!
Courtesy, collection Catherine Dike.

Optical Instruments

Theatre and opera-goers depended on binoculars to see the performance and (often a more fascinating spectacle) the other members of the audience. Some opera glasses could be mounted on a shaft in the fashion of a spyglass. These were especially popular with birdwatchers. Because of their high quality and fine workmanship, optical instrument canes are especially sought-after by collectors.

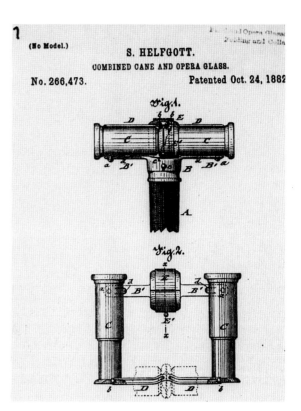

▲ 23/36 Opera glasses patented in 1882.
Courtesy, U.S. Patent Office.

▲ 23/35 In 1860, W.H. Baker filed a patent for securing lenses in a shaft to be attached to firearms. This cane was made as a walking stick and bears the inscription below the handle. The piece at the bottom pulls out to adjust the focus.
Courtesy, collection Donald J. Grunder.

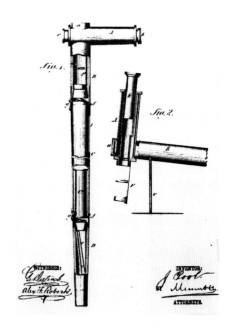

▲ 23/37 A 1877 Patent filed for a microscope. Its accessories, including the feet that support it in a vertical position, are stored in several compartments in the shaft.
Courtesy, U.S. Patent Office.

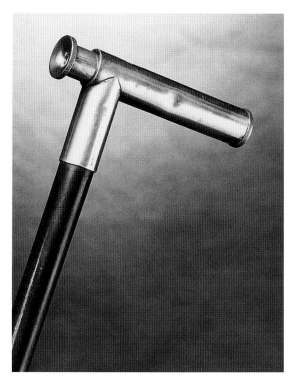

▲ 23/38 A spyglass cane marked *Pat'd Jan 20 ?80 by W&C.*
Courtesy, Tradewinds Auction, H. Taron, Manager.

Musical Instruments and Whistles

Before the existence of the portable radio, the only way to have music on a walk or excursion was to take an instrument along. In Europe one finds all manner of flutes, violins and wind instruments tucked away in walking sticks. The U.S. Patent Office has relatively few designs for instrumental canes, but several for music stands.

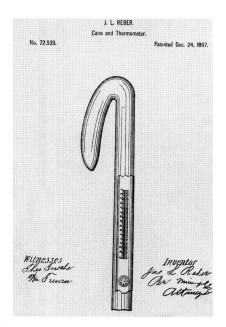

▲ 23/39 A thermometer placed along the shaft of a cane. (1867). These thermometers had to be embedded into the wood.
Courtesy, U.S. Pattent Office.

▲ 23/40 In 1866 Jacob David filed a patent for the eponymous music stand shown in the advertisement. The back of the pamphlet mentions that the stick was used by band leaders.
Courtesy, collection Catherine Dike.

In reference to the engravings, No. 1 represents the Stand folded into the Walking Cane shape; No. 2, in use as a Music Stand.

Your attention is also called to the following recommendation from many of the leading professional musicians of this city:

"Having used DAVID'S PATENT EXCELSIOR STAND, we cheerfully recommend it to the profession and amateurs."

C. S. GRAFULLA,	.	.	.	7th Reg't Band.	U. HILL,	.	.	Vice-Pres't Philharmonic, N. Y.
T. J. DODWORTH,	.	.	.	Dodworth's Band.	GEO. CONNERS,	.	.	. 14th Reg't, Brooklyn,
H. B. DODWORTH,	.	.	.		THOS. BAKER,	.	.	Leader Wallack's Theatre.
D. L. DOWNING,	.	.	.	71st Reg't Band.				
THOMAS KINGSLAND,	.	.	Dodworth's Band.		FRANK PETERSCHEN,			
GEO. WALLACE,	.	.	.	Wallace's Band.				Leader Park Theatre, Brooklyn.
Prof. R. O. DOREMUS,	.	Pres't Philharmonic, N. Y.		JOSEPH NOSHER,	.	.	.	Music Composer.

To Musical Societies and Bands ordering them by the dozen a liberal discount will be allowed.

PLEASE SHOW THIS TO LEADER OF BAND.

▲ 23/40 *Please show this to Leader of Band* can be read on the back part of the Jacob David advertisement. Courtesy, collection Catherine Dike.

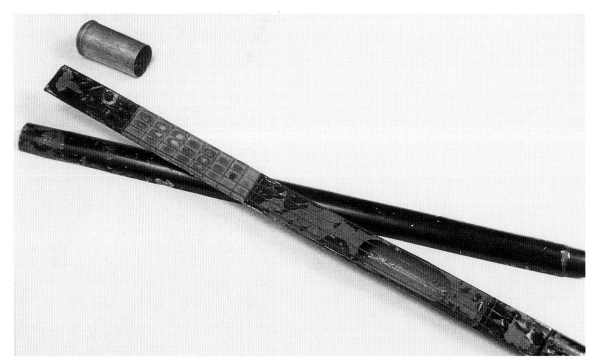

▲ 23/41 Tin guitar patented in 1926. Sold no doubt at fairs, it was easily damaged because of its light and weak construction. Courtesy, collection Francis H. Monek.

▲ a) A tiny selection of the huge number of seat sticks that were manufactured in the United States. From left to right: (1) *Seatscope,* with the periscope visible below the handle, made by *Maco Corporation, Huntington, Indiana.* (2) A simple bar acts as seat, made by the *Chair Cane Co. Pa.* (3) Collapsible *Swagger Seat,* made in Willsboro, N.Y. (4) In front, missing the cloth seat, metal bars patented on Aug. 14. 1877. (5) The oval seat (with its shaft stuck in the foliage) takes the name of *Yankee Snap Seat,* made by the *New England Box Co.*, in Greenfield, Mass. (6) What appears as only a handle bears the name *Fischer-Lang,* Chicago. (7) Straight shaft, opening at the top, made by the *Estix Co.,* Hollywood. (8) The metal seat is marked Pat. 2,629,429, *Precision Seat Co.* L.A. (9) In front, the round seat was patented by *Kan-O-Seat* in May 1935, and made by *Seating Corp.,* in Ionia, Michigan. The four examples at right are (10) marked *Seat Cane,* U.S.A. (11) *The New York Worlds Fair,* name engraved into the metal. (12) *Wilson Turf rider,* made by Wilson Sporting Goods. The height can be altered. (13) *Scott Seat Co.* Phoenix, Arizona.

As this assortment illustrates, American gadget canes carry the markings of the manufacturer, and in most cases a patent number as well.   Courtesy, collection Francis H. Monek.

▲ b) The spittoon cane, pictured against its 1881 patent.
Courtesy, collection Catherine Dike.

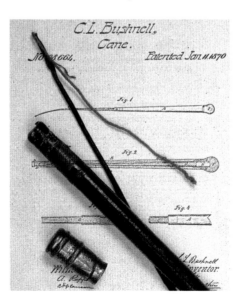

▲ c) This buggy whip was first patented in 1870. Many other patents followed.   Courtesy, collection Catherine Dike.

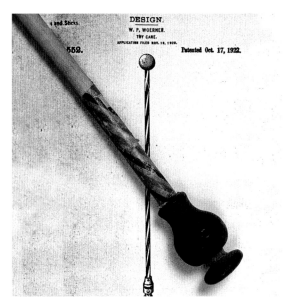

▲ a) Firecrackers were frequently patented, as can be seen in the chapter on *Political Canes*. This is rather a late model, dated 1922.
Courtesy, collection Catherine Dike.

▲ c) A lumberman's cane which measured the number of planks a tree could yield.
Courtesy, collection Catherine Dike.

▲ b) Aluminum money-box bearing the initials of Franklin D. Roosevelt. It contained $63 in dimes for *The March of Dimes,* a charitable organization founded to combat infantile paralysis and launched by Roosevelt. The cane was given to FDR for his 63rd birthday by a New York hardware company. The dimes could be removed by unscrewing the ferrule.
Courtesy, Franklin D. Roosevelt Library, Hyde Park.

▲ d) An oil or gasoline lamp with a flame-protecting metal hood which also serves as a reflector, the front part is covered by a thin mica window. The vent holes control the ventilation. It has its patented mark.
Courtesy, collection L.G.

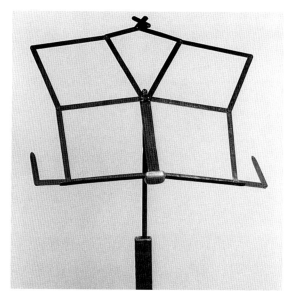

▲ 23/42 A metal music stand patented in 1893. The frame folds and slides into the shaft.
Courtesy, collection Francis H. Monek.

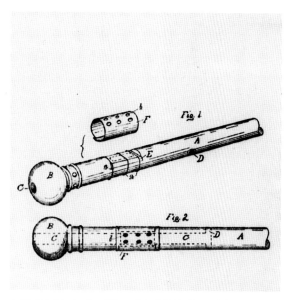

▲ 23/44 Musical walking stick (1887). Part of the hollowed stick is removed and a membrane placed across the opening (E). A thin protective, metallic band around the membrane allows the sound volume to be controlled by the six finger holes.
Courtesy, U.S. Patent Office.

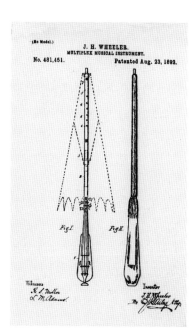

▲ 23/43 Little orchestra in an umbrella cane which contains a violin and two harmonicas of different registers. These are placed so that they can be played at the same time by two players standing side by side. A transverse flute at the very end becomes a straight flute when a mouthpiece is fitted and the mouth hole covered. Its inventor described it as a *multiplex musical instrument* and certified that *in the hand of capable musicians it is capable of producing novel and genuine musical effects, as well as being an unfailing and irresistable source of merriment.*
Courtesy, U.S. Patent Office.

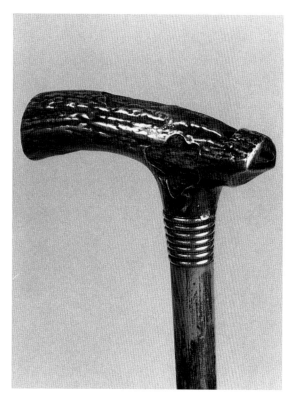

▲ 23/45 A whistle made of horn and silver.
Courtesy, collection Francis H. Monek.

Lights

Streets were obviously dark in the days before gas or electric street lighting, and wise pedestrians took along a lantern or torch when venturing out at night. Candles, by their shape, were well-suited for canes. A spring was normally used to adjust the height of the candle so that the flame did not sink into the hollow of the cane.

Lamps in canes used various fuels - generally the most freely available - including oil, alcohol, kerosene, acetylene, gasoline and compressed gas. When batteries first came into existence, early models were large, making flashlights too heavy and bulky for a pocket. A cane made an ideal carrying place.

Light canes are still used today by the blind to render them visible at night to drivers and other pedestrians.

▲ 23/46 A variety of the benzine or oil burner seen in the color pictures. There are no ventilation holes to assist the flame.
Courtesy, collection Francis H. Monek.

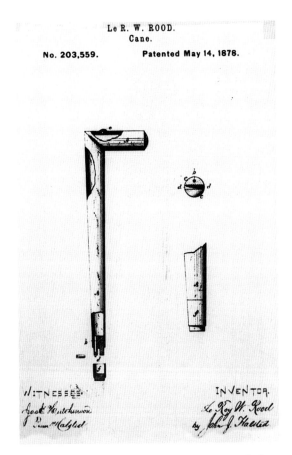

▲ 23/48 An 1878 patent for a light using liquefied gas. The burner is at the ferrule, which acts as cover. In another patent (1898), the gas burner is on the handle.
Courtesy, U.S. Patent Office.

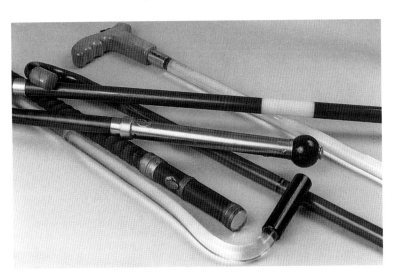

◄ 23/47 A series of flashlights. The plastic one at bottom is marked *The Guiding Light*. Above it is an old flashlight marked *Pat. Jan. 10.1899.* Across the latter is a cane that flashes light with each press of the button on top of the knob. The cane in the middle is lit at the end of the crook handle, while the two at the top light in the shaft.
Courtesy, collection Francis H. Monek.

▲ 23/49 The candle pushes up and is held in position by a taper on the side of the handle. It is marked *US patent, 1897.*
Courtesy, collection Walter Scholz.

▲ 23/50 A candle held in position by the same principle of a lever on the side. Patented in 1887, the back of the handle opens on a match safe.
Courtesy, collection Francis H. Monek.

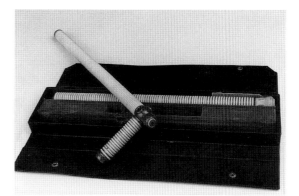

▲ 23/51 A gift to FDR. The tubular bulb forms a four-sided shaft which is covered with plastic coils. It was presented in a velvet-lined box.
Courtesy, Franklin D. Roosevelt Library.

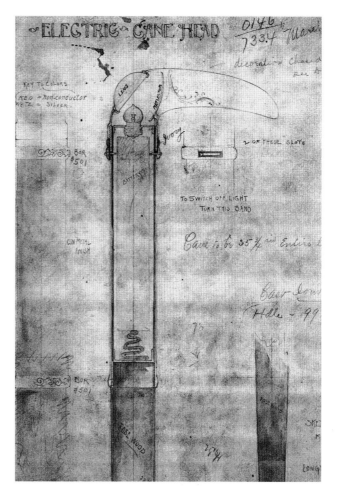

▲ 23/52 One of the few gadget canes made by Tiffany. This was a special order, as is seen from this drawing.
Courtesy, Tiffany archives.

Ladies' Canes

American canes for ladies lack the frivolity
of their European counterparts. Only a few
ladies' handles were produced by Tiffany and
Gorham, in contrast to the smelling salts, per-
fume-scented handles, atomizers, parasols or
fan models which adorned Continental beau-
ties, particularly the ever-elegant *Parisiennes*.

▲ 23/54 A silver pill box with European hallmarks, but
marked *Tiffany & Co.* on the side.
Courtesy, Esbola collection.

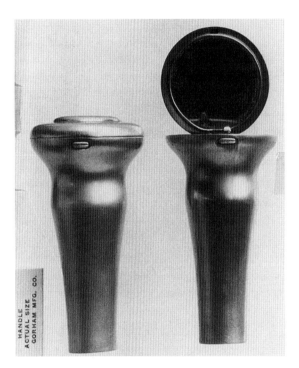

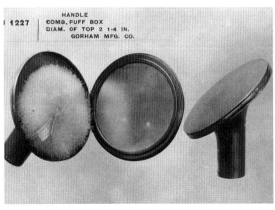

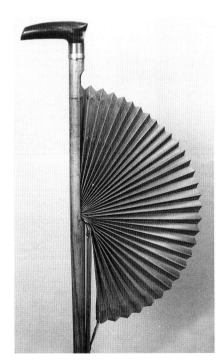

▲ 23/53 Two powder-puff boxes created by Gorham Mfg.
Co. The one on the top dates from 1905, and the model
below from 1910.
Courtesy, Brown University Library.

▲ 23/55 A fan which was patented in 1882. When folded, it
disappears entirely into the shaft.
Courtesy, collection Catherine Dike.

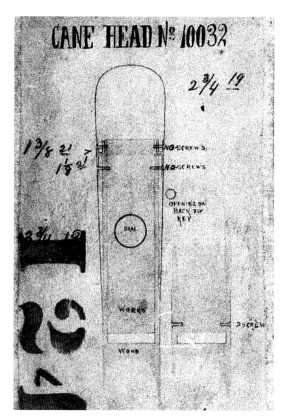

▲ 23/56 A Tiffany lady's watch cane with the watch movement in the shaft. The Viennese L. Holuska patented this design in 1885. This drawing is dated 1888. Another 1888 watch of this type is marked *Tiffany & Co., Maker* on the side.
Courtesy, Tiffany archives.

Gentlemen's Canes

This chapter covers canes which formed part of the wardrobe of a well-dressed gentlemen and cannot easily be assigned to other categories. Many more patents were filed for men's canes than for women's.

Practical vanity cases have been found in the handles and shafts of walking sticks. No doubt they accompanied their owners on secret amorous rendezvous and allowed the lover to straighten up before returning home. The contents could include a mustache brush and comb, but not a shaving brush and razor, as the gentleman would have shaved before going out.

Some canes concealed brushes, for clothes or shoes or both, which allowed the dandy to remove any dust before entering the drawing room. Other sticks carried coins in the handle for discreet tips.

▲ 23/57 Coin counter combined with a match safe that slips into one side of the handle. When the handle is turned the coins, which are stored in the shaft, come out one at a time. Marked *Pat. Dec. 11 1888*.
Courtesy, collection Francis H. Monek.

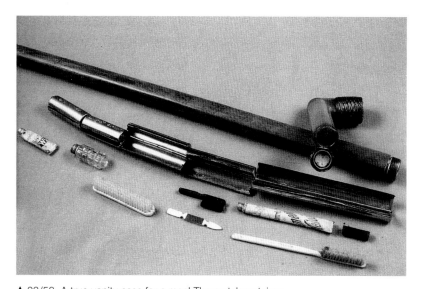

▲ 23/58 A true vanity case for a man! The metal container, which slips into the shaft, is marked *P. Kampfe's Patent Toilet Walking-Cane Sublime - Patented in America and all European States.* From left to right: a tube of mustache wax, perfume bottle, ivory brush, nail cleaner and file, mustache brush, toothbrush, a tube of Koldonit and a piece of black mustache wax. All the objects are marked *Kampfe's Sublime,* which means that this cane was manufactured in large numbers. It is rarely found complete today. (1892).
Courtesy, private collection, London.

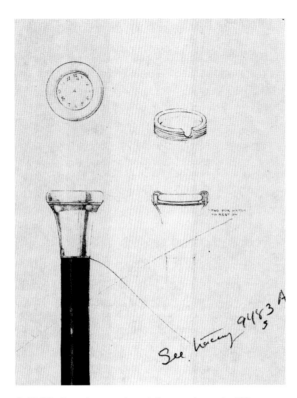

▲ 23/59 A custom made watch cane drawn by Tiffany.
Courtesy, Tiffany archives.

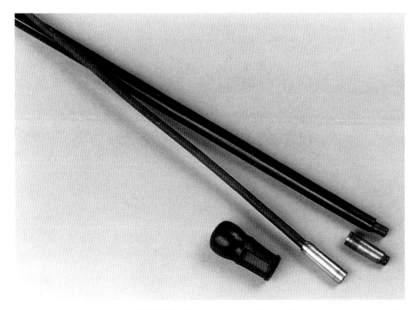

▲ 23/60 A buggy whip differing from the one patented by
Bushnell in 1870. (Color picture). Several patents were filed
for such whips.
Courtesy, collection Francis H. Monek.

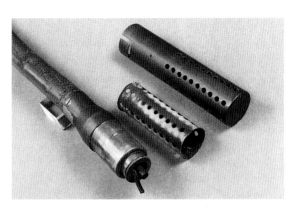

▲ 23/61 Hand warmer that burns a liquid contained in the
shaft. Other models exist which use the slower-burning
charcoal.
Courtesy, collection Francis H. Monek.

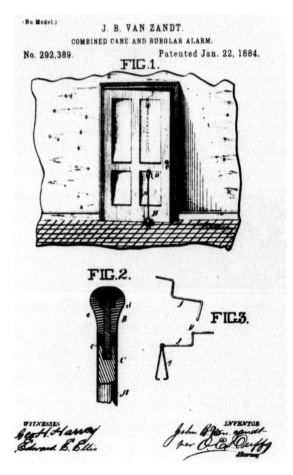

▲ 23/62 In the 1880s hotel doors did not have locks, so
this patent was applied for a burglar alarm which attaches to
the door with a hook that traverses the ferrule. When the
door is pushed, the stick falls, and the explosive which is
placed in the handle is set off. (1884).
Courtesy, U.S. Patent Office.

▲ 23/63 A cane to hold one's newspaper. It has a gilded collar marked *G.A.* The newspaper is not contemporary!
Courtesy, collection Julius Tarshis.

784 Open

784

Cane Flask

▲ 23/64 Gorham offered a combination of a flask and a set of dice to be put in a cane. Canes bearing a flask and a small glass were imported from Germany and Austria in great quantities during the Prohibition years.
Courtesy, archives Gorham Inc.

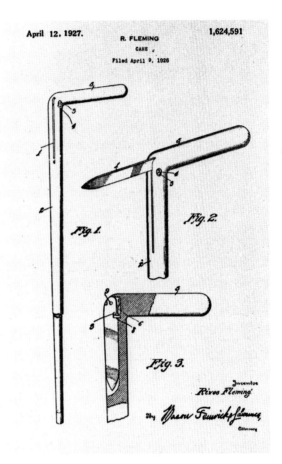

April 12, 1927.   R. FLEMING   1,624,591
                                        CANE
                                 Filed April 9, 1926

Fig. 1.   Fig. 2.

Fig. 3.

Inventor
Rivos Fleming
By

Attorney

▲ 23/65 A carving knife was hidden in the shaft of this stick. (1926).
Courtesy, U.S. Patent Office.

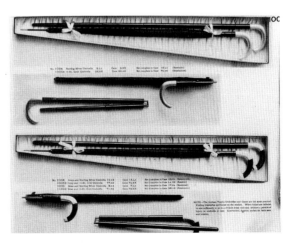

▲ 23/66 A walking stick and umbrella set offered by Gorham in their 1911 catalog. Also illustrated are the folding canes that one could pack in a suitcase.
Courtesy, Brown University Library.

Medical Canes and Invalids

The association of the stick with medicine is legendary and dates back to antiquity. Notable examples are the sticks associated with Aesculapius, the Roman god of medicine, and Mercury, the Roman herald/messenger and god of trade. (Asklepius and Hermes in the corresponding Greek pantheon). According to mythology, while Aesculapius was attending a patient, a snake entered his tent, coiled around his staff and bestowed upon him the art of healing. Thus Aesculapius is always represented by a knotty staff twined about with a snake.

Apollo used a thin wand to part two fighting snakes, and this became a symbol of peace. When given to Mercury, the stick was topped with wings to represent his speed as a messenger. Much controversy is centered on how, why and when the caduceus of Mercury became the emblem of the medical profession.

Many patents were applied for various devices to assist in carrying parcels or pieces of luggage. Along with those designed for the handicapped, these patents form the bulk of those applied for after 1940. One patent (1949) had a spring which allowed one to climb or descend stairs.

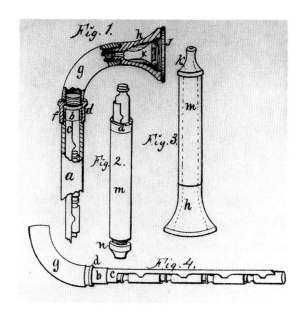

▲ 23/68 An 1874 patent for a stethoscope placed at the bottom part, the shaft hiding various bottles. The cane mentioned above was no doubt done on this model. Courtesy, U.S.Patent Office.

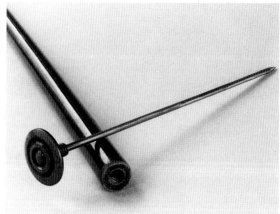

▲ 23/69 A veterinarian's cane which hides a sharp point used to puncture the side of a bloated cow. The shaft contains cotton soaked in ether to disinfect the point. Courtesy, collection Francis H. Monek.

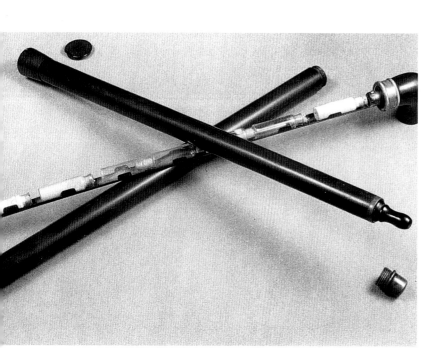

◄ 23/67 Stethoscope formed by the lower part of the shaft. The ear piece fits in the ferrule, with the other end fitting in the handle. A system of side clamps in the half tube holds the 15 vials in place. Although the inventor lived in Des Moines, Iowa, he must have applied for a British patent, as the cane was produced in that country with the inscription *English Patent Nov. 8 1874,*. Courtesy, collection Francis H. Monek.

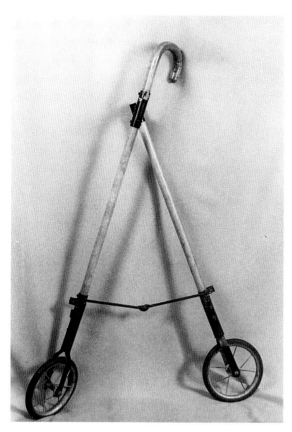

▲ 23/70 A pair of wheels to help carry a parcel or a suitcase. It has a U.S. Patent number.
Courtesy, private collection, Easton, Ct.

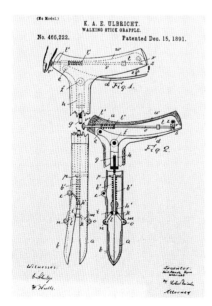

▲ 23/71 For invalids, pick-up tools were very often patented.
Courtesy, U.S. Patent Office.

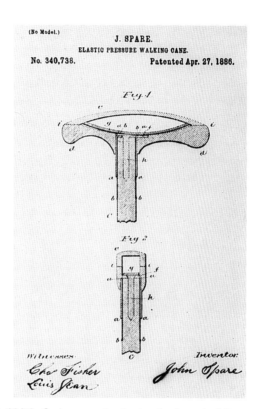

▲ 23/72 Spring cane to deaden the impact of the cane striking the ground. The handle has a rubber cushion and the shaft a long spring - a principle found in the numerous patents filed for the same purpose. (1886).
Courtesy, U.S. Patent Office.

▶ 23/73 In 1860 E. T. Trowbridge applied for a patent for a cane with a set of bottles held in the shaft.
Courtesy, collection Catherine Dike.

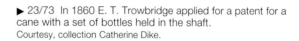

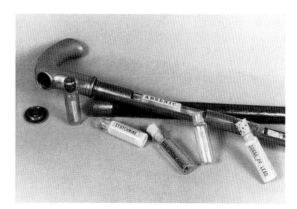

▲ 23/74 A similar idea was adapted in 1886 to produce this medical cane with the inscription: *Patented 1886 LaBette Kansas, W. Conners.* The patent was filed in Kansas before the Territory became part of the United States. The contents of the handle are missing.
Courtesy, collection Francis H. Monek.

NO MORE DEAFNESS!

Thanks to the invention of the ACOUSTIC CANE, which permits hard hearing persons to hear distinctly at a distance without exposing their infirmity. This Cane is tastefully gotten up, and by putting it to the ear it acts so powerfully on the drum that the most refractory case is overcome, and the organ regains its functions immediately. Also the little Ear Cornets of different sizes, which are placed in the ear so as not to be seen, enabling the afflicted to hear distinctly any conversation held.

H. WALDSTEIN, Optician,
INVENTOR AND MANUFACTURER
41 UNION SQUARE, NEW YORK.

EYES FITTED WITH PROPER GLASSES.
H. WALDSTEIN,
Expert Optician,

▲ 23/75 An advertisement for an *Acoustic Cane*, which appeared in the *Ridley's Fashion Magazine*, Winter of 1884.
Courtesy, collection Kurt Stein.

◄ 23/76 Ear trumpet which uses an electric battery to amplify sounds. It was patented and manufactured in the United States in 1886.
Courtesy, collection Francis H. Monek.

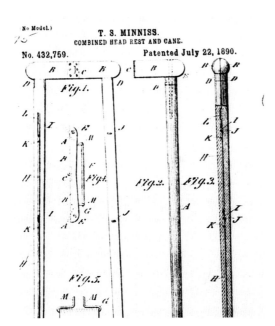

▲ 23/77 A head-rest formed by opening the cane. One wonders how well it functioned once a head was laid on top!
Courtesy, U.S. Patent Office.

Trades

The chapter on advertising featured many canes related to trades, but not specifically gadget sticks. Here we will see canes containing the impedimentia of certain professions.

Several patents were applied for canes which would collapse, part of the magician's stock-in-trade. An interesting sidelight is the fact that one never seems to find any type of measuring stick. Apart from the lumberjack's cane (Color picture), one rarely comes across a cane to be used by a geometer or a land surveyor, or a stick used to measure anything at all, whether horses or beer casks.

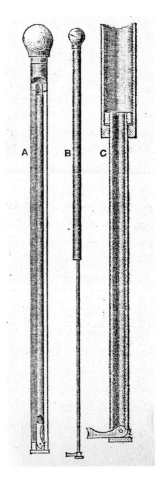

▲ 23/78 Telescopic undertaker's cane with a hook to close the lid of the casket once it was lowered into the grave. This allowed the mourners to gaze at the deceased until the very last moments when earth was thrown in.
Courtesy, *Scientific American*, 1886.

▲ 23/79 Oil-can held inside the knob, marked *Cushman and Denison, N.Y. Pat. 4-89.* The purpose of the small brass pipe at the ferrule has not been determined.   Courtesy, collection Catherine Dike.

Toys

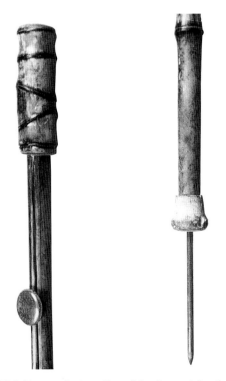

▲ 23/80 Paper collector with a sliding tip, enabling the user to detach the picked-up piece via a lever near the handle. Marked *Knob Lars*. The Truman Library has an identical cane.   Courtesy, collection Francis H. Monek.

▲ 23/81 Two toys which eject plastic pellets from their mouths. (1968).
Courtesy, collection Francis H. Monek.

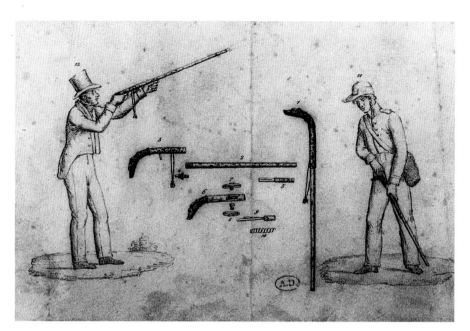

▲ 24/1 Sketch of a nineteenth century gentleman aiming a gun cane.
Courtesy, Musée des Arts Décoratifs, Paris.

Weapons

Sword Sticks

It is very rare to find an American blade mounted as a sword stick. Most of the canes found in the United States have blades marked *Toledo, Solingen* or even *Paris*. Possibly it was not the custom for American manufacturers to sign their blades as was the norm in Europe, but it is more likely that these sticks are made up of an American shaft and an imported blade.

▲ 24/3 It is difficult to know whether this blade is English or American. It bears the motto: *Defense not Defiance*.
Courtesy, collection Walter Scholz.

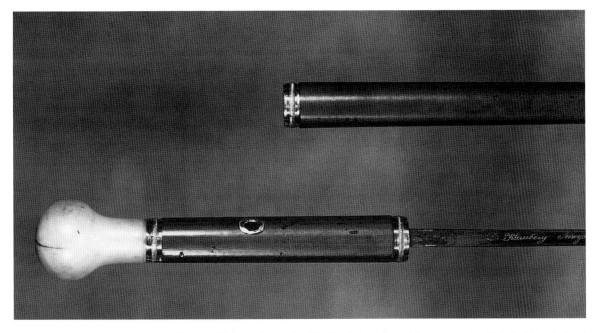

▲ 24/2 An early 19th century sword cane, which can be easily dated by its handle and the manner in which the blade is freed - a straight pull. The steel is triangular and blued a third of its length. It is engraved *D. Klauberg, Newyork (sic)*. In 1820, D. Klauberg was a steel polisher and cutler.
Courtesy, collection Howard H. Miller. Jr.

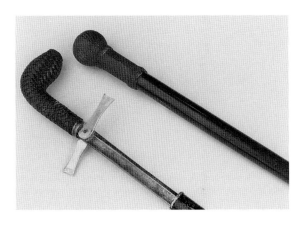

◀ 24/4 Two weapons which could be American, Gutta Percha being commonly used in the United States during the 19th century. The blade could have been imported.
Courtesy, private collection.

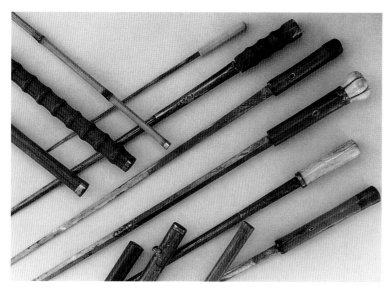

▲ 24/5 The straight pull of the blade, together with the style, make these canes a 19th century group. Are they American? The collector to whom they belong has a good eye for American weapons!
Courtesy, collection Kurt Stein.

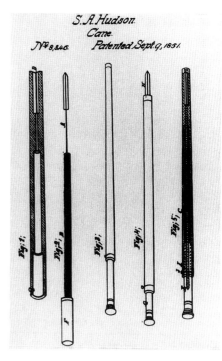

▲▼ 24/7 Two patents filed in 1851 and in 1886 in which the blades are ejected at the point of the cane.

A 1926 patent was filed for a blade which was hidden along the shaft, mounted on a spring. When the release button is pressed, the blade springs into action and the cane can be used *as a tomahawk* (!), or so said the inventor.
Courtesy, U.S. Patent Office.

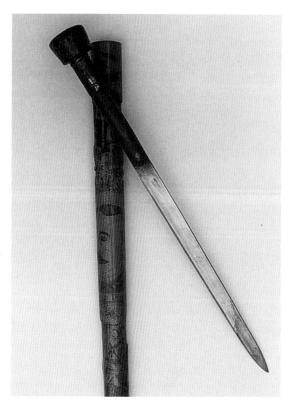

▲ 24/6 An unsigned blade was mounted on this American cane.
Courtesy, collection George H. Meyer.

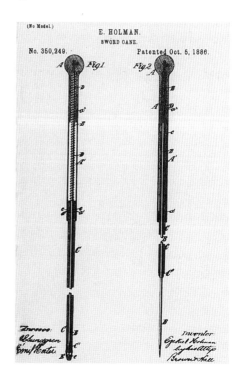

▲ 24/8 A short blade appears when the cane is pushed against someone. It bears the patent date mentioned before: *St. 8, 1851*. To the right, a short blade is expelled when one gives a sharp trust to the handle. The ornaments of the cane have American markings.

Courtesy, collections Francis H. Monek and Paul Weisberg.

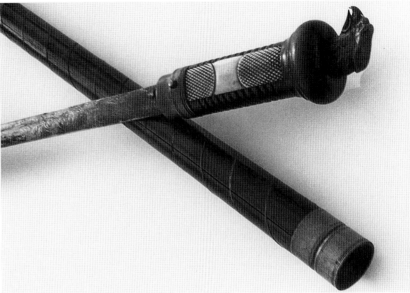

▲▼▶ 24/10 The only definitively American sword stick the author has encountered, bearing the head of an eagle which usually adorns the American military swords. The blade has the American eagle holding the shield, looking up to the bearer. The shaft is covered with baleen.

Courtesy, private collection, Boston.

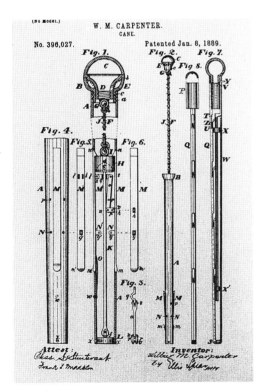

▲ 24/9 Patent for a clobbering stick which looks horribly lethal. One can grasp the cane and swing the ball, or vice versa.

Courtesy, U.S. Patent Office.

Firearms

In the United States, fifty patents were applied for various firearms and gas-driven cane rifles. A few of these were European patents that were also filed in America. These patents will be cited chronologically and pictures of the canes given when obtainable. Patents numbers 527 and 10,910 are missing. There are obviously many more illustrations of patents than pictures of canes. It can be interesting to note the name that inventors gave to these canes: cane gun, gun cane, walking stick rifle, fire-arms, with or without a hyphen. These types of sticks are more likely to be found in the possession of weapon collectors than cane collectors. With two exceptions, few cane collectors amass many gun canes.

The name of the inventor is followed by the year he filed a patent or issued a cane gun.

Joseph Saxton
1824

In Philadelphia, at the begining of the 19th century, Saxton was an associate of Isaiah Lukens (see end of this chapter). For the July 1968 Gun Report, Jerald T. Teesdale wrote the following interesting article on Saxton's Cane Gun: *For sev-*

eral years, Saxton kept a notebook of his work and experiments and a sketch therein dated 1824 shows a breech-loading cane gun which used a percussion-primed, completly self-contained metallic cartridge. Apparently the gun was never patented. Close examination of the sketch reveals a gun carefully thought out, thoroughly workable and practical, and beautifully un-complicated. It is also very much up-to-the-minute, if not downright advanced for its time.

How many of these cane guns and cartridges were made and are any of them still to be found? In 1935, The Franklin Institute in Philadelphia had an exhibition of some personal effects of Joseph Saxton loaned by a descendant. Included are the following items:
One stock for cane gun, 8" long, with ivory handle.
One stock for cane gun, 6" long, with walnut handle.
One gun barrel covered with tape and black varnish, 33 3/4 long.
One gun barrel covered with tape and black varnish, 28 1/2 long.

It seems likely that these four items comprise components of the two gun canes made by Saxton. Where these pieces are today, and whether any others are to be found, remains a mystery.

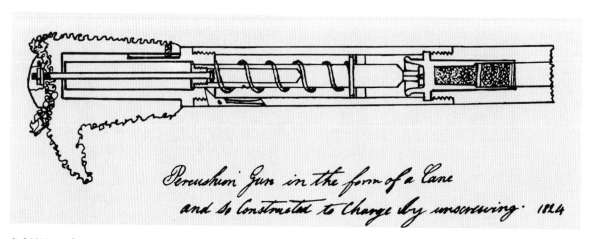

▲ 24/11 In Saxton's handwriting: *Percushion Gun in the form of a Cane and so constructed to charge by unscrewing.*
1824.
Courtesy, Archives of the Smithsonian Institution.

▲ a) The leash cane allowed one to take a walk without having to secure one's dog.
Courtesy, collection Catherine Dike.

▲▶ b) *The Cherrot* cane mounted on a simple staff.
Courtesy, collection Catherine Dike.

▼ b) Two silver handles, one with a match striker on the point of the handle, the other with a match box.
Courtesy, collection L.G.

▼ d) Abercrombie and Fitch sold this cane in the 1970s for football games. Three flasks allowed for a good provision of liquor. Alternatively, they could hold cigars, and there is a lighter in the top part of the handle.
Courtesy, collection L.G.

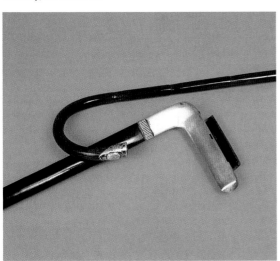

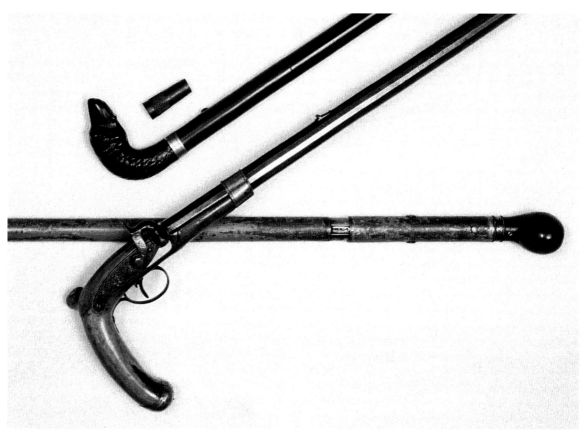

▲ a) Three American cane guns: The bottom one is signed
Deringer, Philadelphia; the well-known *Remington* is at top,
and lying under the Deringer is the hard-to-find, *Daigle
"machine gun"*.
Courtesy, collection Catherine Dike.

▼ b) A folk art cane copying a sword, to be used by a post-
man to ward off dogs. Made completely of wood, the
"blade" slides neatly into the wooden sheath.
Courtesy, collection Mr. and Mrs. Lawrence M. Kalstone.

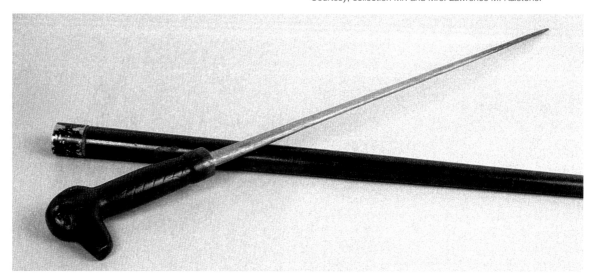

Alvin Duncan Cushing
1831

Alvin Duncan Cushing was born in Vermont in 1800. He worked in Lansingburgh and Troy, where he was a well-known gunsmith, and no doubt worked with John M. Caswell who trained many of the gunsmiths in the area. He died in 1856 and was buried in New Mountain Ida Cemetery in Troy. He trained numerous apprentices and even had a journeyman in the shop. One of these apprentices, C. E. Medbery, began working for Cushing in 1828. A rifle exists which bears the signature of Cushing on the barrel and *C. E. Medbery* on the wood behind the trigger guard, indicating that Medbery made the stock.

Research, H.J. Swinney.

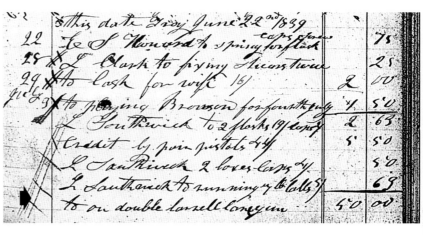

▲ 24/13 An account book of A.D. Cushing dated July 30, 1839. The last entry is: *A double barrel cane gun.* Price: *$50.00* (a very steep price at that time).
Courtesy, Rensselaer County Historical Society, Troy, N.Y.
Research H.J. Swinney.

▲ 24/12 In 1831, A. D. Cushing received a patent for a walking stick gun and produced this .30 caliber cane. Between 1830 and 1850 Cushing sold 35 cane guns and repaired 8. His classifications can be confusing; he alternates between the words *cane gun*, *cane rifle* or *rifle cane*. After 1842, the terminology becomes even more difficult, as his entries were written in pencil and have become illegible over time. This also casts some doubt on the accuracy of the figure of 35 cane guns.
Courtesy, The Henry Ford Museum.
Research H.J. Swinney.

▲ 24/14 Another identical signed cane by A. D. Cushing with .38 caliber percussion. It has an under-hammer action mounted on an engraved German silver frame. It is signed: *A. D. Cushing, Maker, Troy, N.Y.*
Courtesy, The Henry Ford Museum,

▶ 24/15 Another page of an October 20, 1842, account book, where the last line mentions a double-barrel cane gun at a price of $36.00. The regular cane guns sold for an average of $18.00, a fair price for the time.
Courtesy, Rensselaer County Historical Society, Troy, N.Y.
Research, H.J. Swinney.

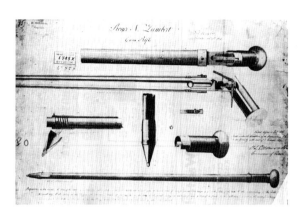

▲ 24/16 Silver medal inscribed *Knowledge is Power / awarded to / A.D. Cushing / For a / Rifle walking Cane / of Ingenious Construction / October 1835.* The other side has the inscription: *Mechanics Institute / New York / Furst.F.*
Courtesy, Rensselaer County Historical Society, Troy, N.Y.

▲ 24/17 The Lambert Patent dated Feb. 27. 1832 which was salvaged after the Patent Office fire in 1836. The original document is in poor condition, but one can still decipher reference to these *articles are for sale at N.W. Sandford's, No. 212, Pearl Street, New York.*
Courtesy, National Archives.

Roger N. Lambert
1832

In 1832, Doctor Roger N. Lambert applied for a patent describing a cane rifle that apparently was first made by Ethan Allen, the famous gun-smith. Dr. Lambert continued to make these canes at his home in Lyme, New Hampshire, and his son continued the practice. These canes vary greatly in quality.

▼ 24/18 The band on the shaft must be turned one-eight of an inch to the right. By pulling back the handle and pressing downwards, the cap on the ferrule and the trigger is released, a unique feature of cane guns. The slit in the cock serves as a guideline in aiming the rifle, while the screw on the ferrule serves as a sight.
Courtesy, Esbola collection.

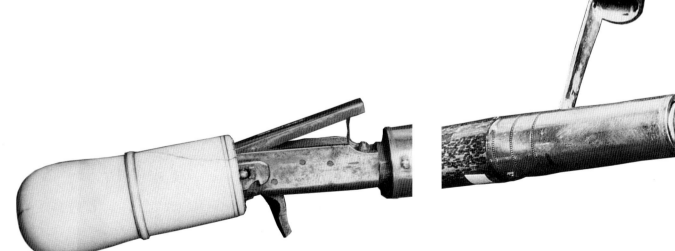

Willard, Case & Co.

▲ 24/19 No patent was filed by Case Willard who signed this cane *Case Willard New Hartford Conn.*
Courtesy, Winchester Museum.

▲ 24/20 The same gun cane comes with a shoulder rest which is seldom found on American canes.
Courtesy, private collection, Boston.

Moses Babcock

▲ 24/20 Moses Babcock was another who did not apply for a patent. He produced a fine gun cane with an extension stock and signed the hammer *M. Babcock - Charlestown - Mass*. Several identical models are known to exist.
Courtesy, private collection, Boston.

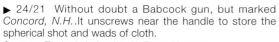

▶ 24/21 Without doubt a Babcock gun, but marked *Concord, N.H.*.It unscrews near the handle to store the spherical shot and wads of cloth.
Courtesy, Tradewinds Auction, H. Taron, Manager.

Alonzo D. Perry
1850

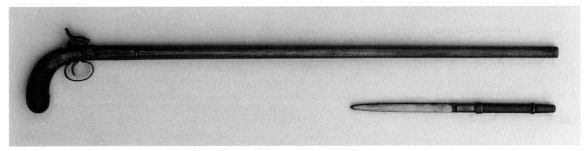

▲ 24/22 *The Perry Cane Gun* is marked *Perry Patent Arms Co., Newark N.J.* No individual patent was filed for the gun cane; the patent for the Perry pistol served for both firearms. The ferrule has a dagger, added no doubt at a later date.
Courtesy, collection Michael Harrison.

Henry Deringer Jr.
1850

A.O.H.P. Schorn
1855

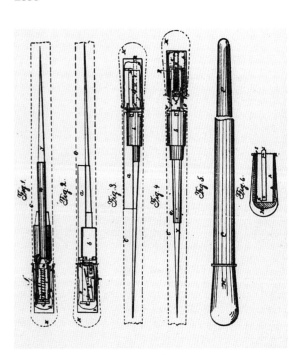

▲ 24/23 Signed behind the hammer *Deringer - Philadelphia,* this stick has a barrel with 16 facets. The gun has a front and rear sight and a compartment for percussion caps in the grip handle.
Courtesy, collection Catherine Dike.

▲ 24/24 *Revolver* combined with a dagger, January 30, 1855 (12,328). There is no way of knowing whether such a weapon was manufactured. It was a precursor to the French and Belgian inventors who applied for patents in 1869-1891.
Courtesy, U.S. Patent Office.

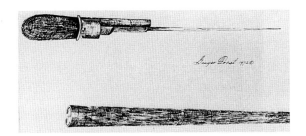

▲ 24/25 A sketch made of Schorn's new combination.
Courtesy, *Blades and Barrels.*

Ira Buckman
1857

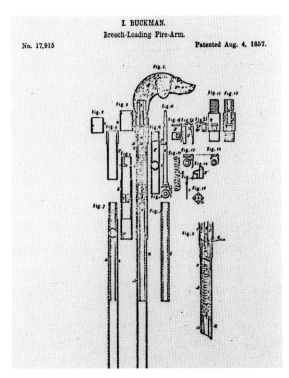

▲ 24/27 *Breech-Loading Fire-Arm,* August 1857 (17,915).
The author has found no examples, despite extensive viewing of many collections. We know that Ira Buckman made
cane guns, as witnessed by a medal given him in 1857.
Courtesy, U.S. Patent Office.

John Tilton & Floyd
1857

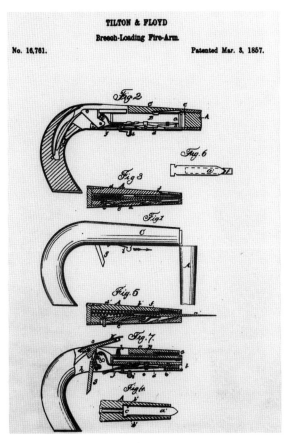

▲ 24/26 *Breech-Loading Fire-Arm,* March 3, 1857 (16,761)

▲ 24/28 A medal given by the *American Institute* in *New
York* which it *Awarded to Ira Buckman Jr. / For the best /
Cane Gun / 1857.*
Courtesy, private collection, Boston.

Samuel Remington
1858 - 1872

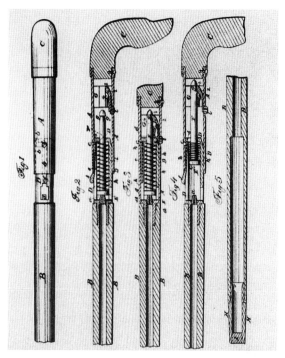

▲ 24/29 In February 1858 John F. Thomas, of Ilion, New York, filed a patent (19,328) for a cane gun on behalf of Samuel Remington and himself. The patent could apply to either percussion or cartridge cane guns, and was extended in 1872.

This would be the most important cane rifle manufactured in the United States. It began as a percussion muzzle-loader (.31 and .44 caliber) from 1858 to 1866, then developed into a cartridge breech-loader from 1866 to about 1888 (.32 rim fire), and finally evolved into model No. 2 (.22 rim fire) from about 1869 to 1888. In that year *E. Remington & Sons* went bankrupt and the company changed its name to the *Remington Arms Company.* Cane guns were no longer manufactured, but the remaining stock continued to be sold until well into the new century.

All these canes have a well-concealed trigger below the handle. Thomas covered the cane rifles with gutta-percha instead of wood, which will often split. He also had the good idea of inserting a piece of cork in the lower end of the open ferrule to prevent an accidental discharge and any danger of bursting the barrel. But there exist various ferrules.

The cane rifles are usually signed by the maker with either the year of the first patent (February 9, 1858) or the second (February 9, 1872). Each one bears a manufacturer's serial number. Indications are that at least 500 percussion models were made, along with nearly 1,800 metal cartridges.

During the 1876 Centennial International Exposition in Philadelphia, E. Remington & Sons offered for sale rifle canes in different colors, black, brown, coral, and white, purporting to be ivory.

The Remington cane guns have been re-classified as *Antiques* and are not subject to the *Gun Control Act of 1968.*

Following is a list of the serial numbers of these canes which have been located in public or private collections. The majority were identified courtesy of the list drawn up by Paul Berg (*The Bulletin of the American Society of Arms Collectors, No. 49*). He mentions serial numbers found on the ferrules and on the barrels.

Percussion Models		Cartridge Models		-	505
				539	539
				558	
Ferrule	Barrel	Ferrule	Barrel	34	584
9	9	18	-	630	-
10	-	20	-	742	742
13	13	-	23	-	790
17	-	-	38	10	791
42	-	-	38	-	863
52	-	32	-	884	884
59	-	39	-	890	890
62	-	53	-	941	941
64	-	55	-	958	-
69	-	58	-	-	1108
70	-	-	62	1218	-
76	-	62	-	1267	1267
112	-	-	66	1290	1290
133	-	80	72	-	1306
257	-	84	84	-	1310
278	-	8	92	1362	1362
		99	-	-	1506
		145	145	1531	1531
		-	157	1558	1558
		248	248	1567	-
		269	--	1580	-
		276	-	1597	1597
		326	-	1663	1663
		26	374	1743	1748
		21	454		
		10	467		

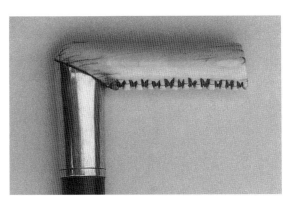

▲ 24/30 Some gun canes had ivory handles.
Courtesy, collection Jeffrey Rhoades.

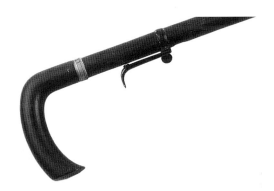

▲ 24/31 A device added to a Remington cane to make for an easier trigger release. The Smithsonian assigns to it the curious calibre of .25 rim fire, and also refers to the maker's stamp on the breech, an unusual location: *Remington & Sons, Ilion, N.Y. Pat'd Feb. 9th, 1872, S.N. 1506.*
Courtesy, Smithsonian collection.

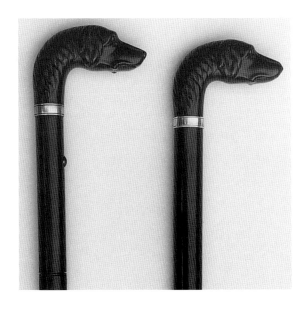

▲ 24/33 A large display of Remington cane rifles.
Courtesy, collection Francis H. Monek.

◄ 24/32 The cane at left is a Remington gun cane, while the visually identical one at right is a simple walking stick. Both are covered with gutta percha. The simple stick was possibly made by Remington, or alternatively, an unknown hand may have adapted a Remington dog head. Another fascinating question!
Courtesy, collection Michael Harrison.

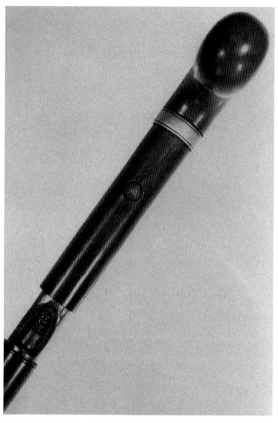

▲ 24/34 A .44 caliber percussion model, pictured uncocked.
Courtesy, collection Francis H. Monek.

▲ 24/36 Ferrules can have a front sight either directly on the barrel or on a ring. Both types may allow for the insertion of a sliver of cork to insure against dirt entering the barrel.
Courtesy, collection Catherine Dike.

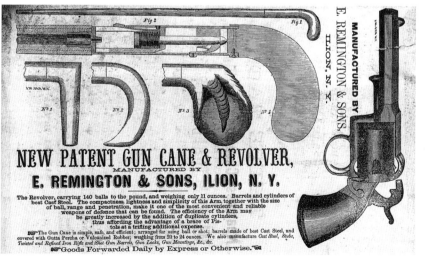

▲ 24/35 An advertisement from the George W. Hawes Ohio State Gazetteer and Business Directory for 1859 and 1860, showing the muzzle-loading percussion cane guns and the variety of handles available.
Courtesy, The New York Historical Society.

▲ 24/37 An advertisement (approximately 1880) picturing a choice of cartridges for the Remington Rifle Cane, and mentioning that it can be used with Shot as well as Ball Cartridges.
Courtesy, Remington Gun Museum.

R.R. Beckwith
1858

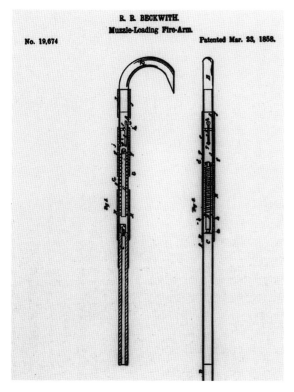

▲ 24/38 *Muzzle-Loading Fire-Arm*, March 23, 1858 (19,674).
Courtesy, U.S. Patent Office.

A. Crow
1860

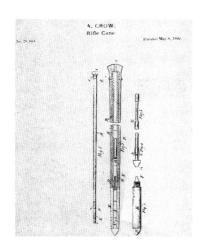

▲ 24/39 *Rifle Cane*, May 8, 1860 (28,160), used as a blow-gun.
Courtesy, U.S. Patent Office.

T. Restell
1867

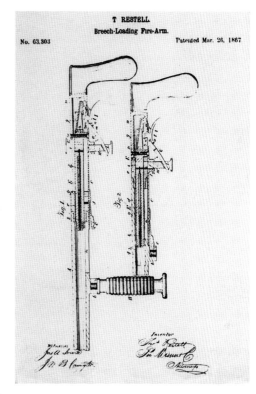

▲ 24/40 *Breech-Loading Fire-Arm*, March 26, 1867 (63,303).
Courtesy, U.S. Patent Office.

▲ 24/41 The under-hammer cane gun made to the model of the patent.
Courtesy, collection Francis H. Monek.

W.H. Werner
1870

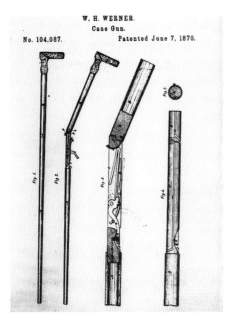

▲ 24/42 *Cane Gun,* June 1870 (104,087).
Courtesy, U.S. Patent Office.

A. Karutz
1872 - 1874

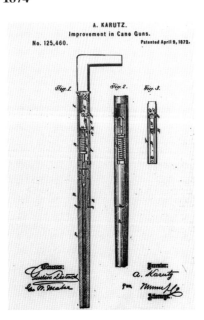

▲ 24/44 *Improvement in Cane Guns*, April 9, 1872
(125,460). He filed another patent on July 14, 1874 for a
Breech-Loading Fire-Arms (152,998).
Courtesy, U.S. Patent Office.

C. Melaye
1875

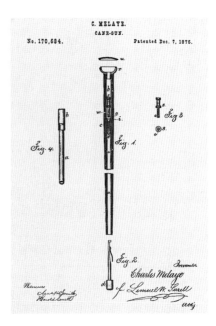

▲ 24/45 *Cane Gun*, December 7, 1875 (170,684), to be
used as a blowgun.
Courtesy, U.S. Patent Office.

Marcelin Daigle
1877

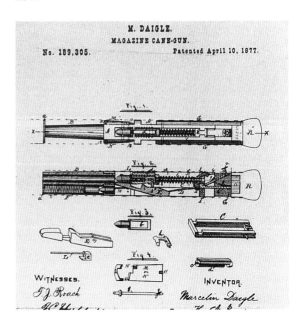

▲ 24/45 *Improvement in Magazine Cane-Guns,* April 10,
1877 (189,305).
Courtesy, U.S. Patent Office.

▲ 24/46 A magazine cane gun which features housing for fifteen .22 caliber cartridges in a tube lying alongside the barrel in the shaft of the cane. A push-button disengages the handle slightly so that it can be drawn back in order to press the cartridges into the tube or magazine. When the handle is pressed forward, the gun can fire; when pulled back, the empty shell is ejected and a new cartridge presents itself. The name of the inventor appears on the collar of the handle. This gun cane was previously in the collection of Dr. W. R. Funderburg.
Courtesy, collection Catherine Dike.

E.D. Bean
1885

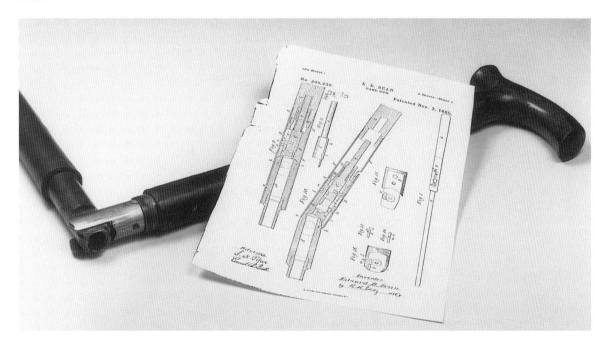

▲ 24/47 *Cane Gun,* November 3, 1885 (329,430). *A Cane Gun Barrel* was filed on April 10, 1888 (380,975).The cane breaks into two sections to allow the cartridge to be placed in the lower part. The top part is pulled backwards, which cocks the firing pin. A small push trigger appears. This gun is covered in leather which was added at a later date. The cane was previously in the Dr. W. R. Funderburg collection.
Courtesy, collection Catherine Dike.

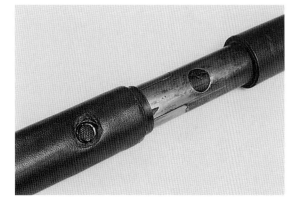

▶ 24/47 Once straightened, the push trigger appears. After firing, the leather is slipped back into position.
Courtesy, collection Catherine Dike.

F.A. Wardwell
1886

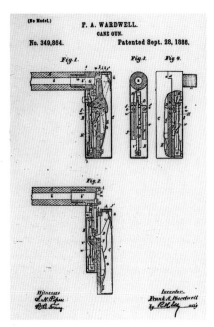

▲ 24/48 *Cane Gun,* September 28, 1886 (349,864).
Courtesy, U.S. Patent Office.

D.A. Draper & A. Tonks
1889

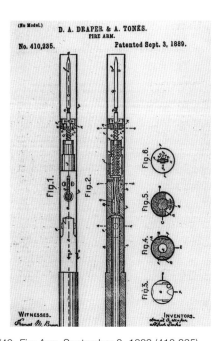

▲ 24/49 *Fire Arm*, September 3, 1889 (410,235).
Courtesy, U.S. Patent Office.

J. Frick
1890

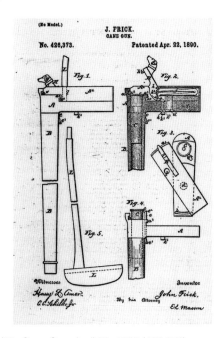

▲ 24/50 *Cane Gun,* April 22, 1890 (426,373).
Courtesy, U.S. Patent Office.

R.F. Cook
1894

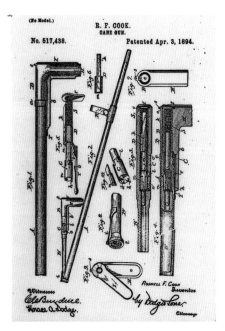

▲ 24/51 *Cane Gun,* April 3, 1894 (517,438).
Courtesy, U.S. Patent Office.

O. Janke
1894

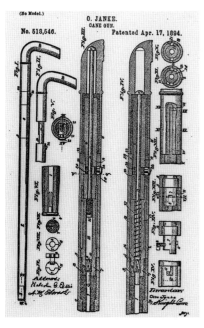

▲ 24/52 *Cane Gun*, April 17, 1894 (518,546).
Courtesy, U.S. Patent Office.

A. Balensiefer
1894

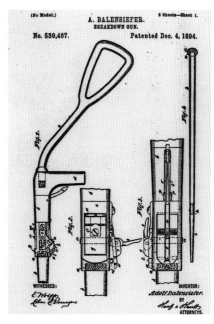

▲ 24/54 *Breakdown Gun,* December 4, 1894 (530,467).
Courtesy, U.S. Patent Office.

E.E. Dyball
1894

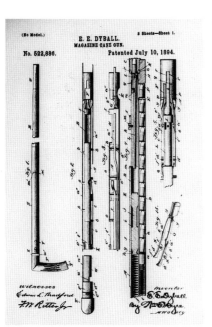

▲ 24/53 *Magazine Cane Gun*, July 10, 1894 (522,886).
Courtesy, U.S. Patent Office.

N.G. Hanson
1895

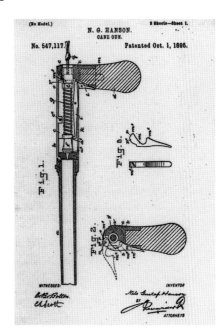

▲ 24/55 *Cane Gun*, October 1, 1895 (547,117).
Courtesy, U.S. Patent Office.

J.H. Hammer
1897

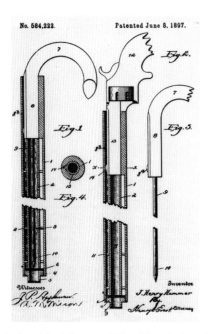

▲ 24/56 *Combined Cane and Pistol Barrel,* June 8, 1897
(584,222).
Courtesy, U.S. Patent Office.

E.H. Ericson
1898 & 1899

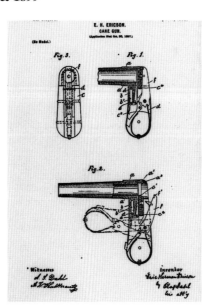

▲ 24/57 *Cane Gun,* September 13, 1898 (610,675). An
improvement was filed on July 4, 1899 (628,142).
Courtesy, U.S. Patent Office.

G. Tresenreuter
1902

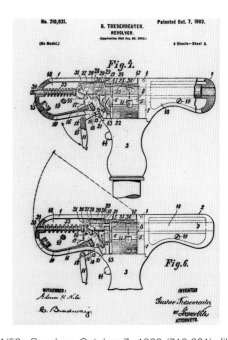

▲ 24/58 *Revolver,* October 7, 1902 (710,821), filed in
numerous countries.
Courtesy, U.S. Patent Office.

G.S. Webber
1905

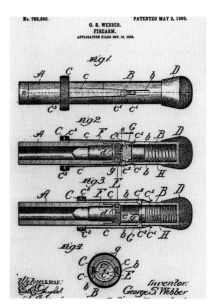

▲ 24/59 *Firearm,* May 2, 1905 (788,866).
Courtesy, U.S. Patent Office.

H. Tarvadian
1910

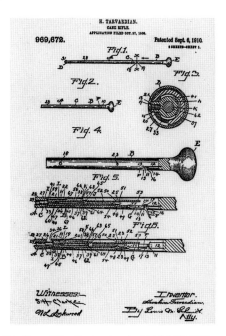

▲ 24/60 *Cane Rifle,* September 6, 1910 (969,672). Courtesy, U.S. Patent Office.

I. Brzostowski & V. Krakowski
1918

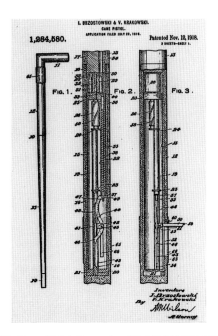

▲ 24/62 *Cane Pistol,* November 12, 1918 (1,284,580). Courtesy, U.S. Patent Office.

F. Yung
1918

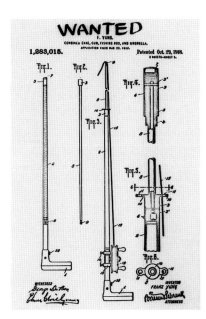

▲ 24/61 *Combined Cane, Gun, Fishing Rod, and Umbrella,* October 29, 1918 (1,283,015). Courtesy, U.S. Patent Office.

S. and F. Pelc
1919

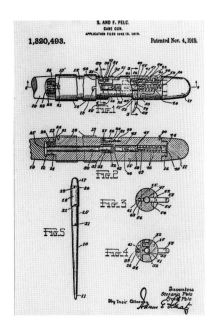

▲ 24/63 *Cane Gun,* November 4, 1919 (1,320,493). Courtesy, U.S. Patent Office.

H. Renard
1923

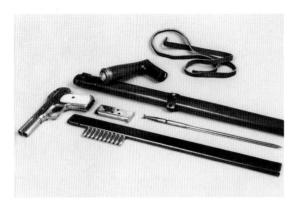

▲ 24/64 Hubert Renard was a Belgian citizen who filed a U. S. patent for what he called a *Walking-Stick Machine Gun* on November 13, 1923 (1,474,292). It is not known whether this cane was manufactured in the United States. Shown here is the Belgian model which was manufactured by the *Fabrique Nationale de Herstal S.A.* (Belgium).

The shaft conceals a charger capable of holding 42 center-fire cartridges. The Browning automatic pistol was carried separately and mounted on the shaft when necessary. It bears Belgian and Chinese proof marks. The wooden handle holds a flashlight for Morse code signals, and the ferrule, when turned around, is a sharp bayonet. The wooden shaft, which is styled in the manner of military rifles, has black metal rings bearing *Serial Number 307, Breveté, H.R.*. A leather strap allows the cane to be slung over the shoulder.

Edie Rieder, an American weapon collector who owned a similar cane *(Serial number 171)*, discovered that the Chinese Government had ordered 500 of these canes in 1924 for use in fighting rebels. Only three models have been traced to private collections. The author would be interested to hear of any others which may exist.

Courtesy, collection Catherine Dike.

C. Joriot
1924

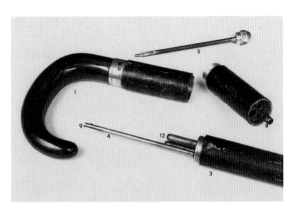

▲ 24/65 Another cane invented by a Frenchman. Again, it is not known whether any models were produced in the United States. The patent was filed in France in 1921 and in the U.S. in February 1924 (1,484,650), under the name of *Pistol and Mechanism which can be concealed in any portable object.*

It is a two-shot pistol using .22 caliber cartridges bearing the trademark *Magister* (6). Manufactured in aluminum, these weapons are often defective. Their main weakness is the spring of the shaft, which can snap when the pistol is remounted onto the stick.

Under the collar of the handle (1) is a flat trigger (2) that when pressed frees a long metal rod (4) which retracts to separate the shaft (3) from the handle (1). The pistol can be fired.

A metal rod on the ferrule (5) closes the security pin (6) that crosses the handle at the collar; the ferrule is also used to extract shells and to clean the rifled barrels. A cylindrical hook (8) is used to pull a small pivoting slot (9) bringing out the metal rod (4) from the shaft. This rod can cock the hammers through the hole (10) on the rear of the handle (1). The rod (4) then slips into the third hole (11) next to the two barrels (7), into which are inserted the two rounded brass pistons (12) in the shaft (3). Both elements are then assembled with a quarter-turn. It is at this final moment that the springs may snap, making it impossible to re-assemble the walking stick.

Courtesy, collection Catherine Dike.

◄ 24/64 The Browning automatic pistol with Belgian and Chinese proof marks.
Courtesy, collection Catherine Dike.

F.S. Bernabe
1926

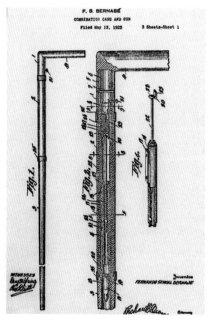

▲ 24/66 *Combination Cane and Gun*, January 12, 1926
(1,569,700).
Courtesy U.S. Patent Office.

B.B. Walker
1927

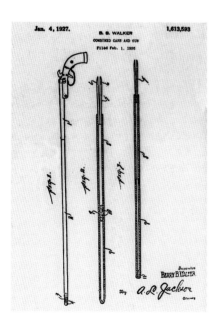

▲ 24/67 *Combined Cane and Gun,* January 4, 1927
(1,613,593).

V. Capolupo
1927

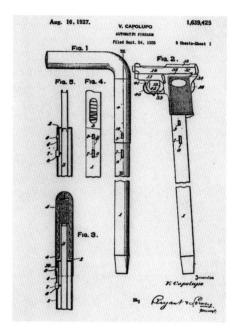

▲ 24/68 *Automatic Firearm,* August 16, 1927 (1,639,425).
Courtesy, U.S. Patent Office.

I.J. Tatum
1928

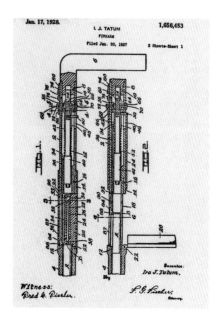

▲ 24/69 *Firearm*, January 17, 1928 (1,656,453).
Courtesy, U.S. Patent Office.

Cheroot Guns

So-called by cane collectors. A small, usually brass, cannon is mounted as the handle of a cane. It tilted to allow the introduction of the bullets. An opening at the top of the cannon gave access to the gunpowder, which could be lit by a burning cigar, providing this firearm with its name.

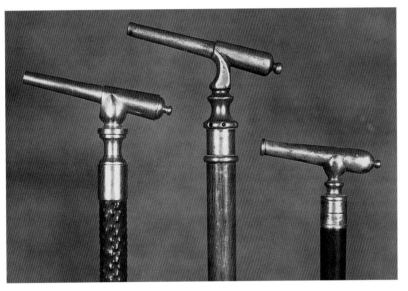

▲ 24/70 Small cannon handles. Their shapes vary widely.
Courtesy, collection Merton E. Price.

▲ 24/71 Top of a cannon showing the ignition hole.
Courtesy, collection Catherine Dike.

Air Guns

One cannot describe American air guns without reference to the excellent articles written by Henry M. Stewart, Jr.. Stewart was a paragon of a collector, who not only assembled an outstanding collection of weapons, but spent much time and effort in researching his acquisitions.

He was particularly intrigued by air guns, which first surfaced in Europe circa 1650 and reached their apex during the 19th century. Mr. Stewart researched those manufactured in the United States, and found much historical data concerning the *Lewis-and-Clark* air rifle He certainly encountered the cane air guns manufactured by Isaiah Lukens and Jacob Kunz.

Today his collection, including the following Air Gun Canes, belongs to the Virginia Military Institute.

Isaiah Lukens
1825

Isaiah Lukens was an early clock maker in Philadelphia. An inventive mechanical genius, he also dealt in air rifles and air canes. Henry M. Stewart, Jr. considers that Isaiah Lukens had Jacob Kuns make his air guns, given the great similarity between the guns signed by each of them. To quote Mr. Stewart: *The air cane reached its peak, as close as I can determine, in England, about 1870. The continental air cane should not be confused with the English as it really was only the use of the barrel as a cane with reservoir butt and receiver concealed beneath the greatcoat of c.1780-90. Lukens and Kunz followed Lukens' design apparently from 1825 on, with Lukens dying with an inventory of air canes in 1846. The English and American types are comparable.*

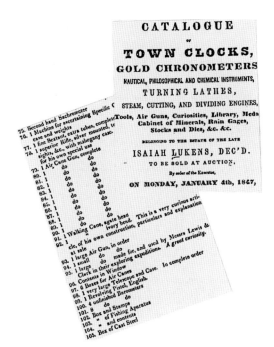

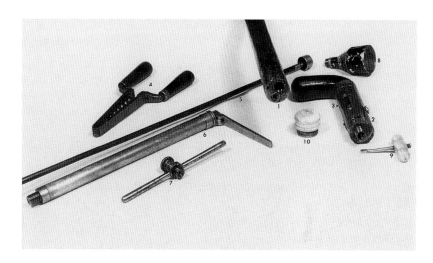

▲ 24/72 Part of the catalog issued after Isaiah Luken's death in which is noted the *12 Air Cane Guns* along with a few box cases.
Courtesy, the Franklin Institute of Philadelphia.

▲ 24/74 *Air Gun Cane* by Isaiah Lukens who in fact invented the first American air gun cane with a reservoir for compressed air distributed around the barrel (1). The firing mechanism is inside the handle (2), the trigger (3) visible on the outside. The box contains: a bullet mold (4), ramrod (5), pump (6), key to open the reservoir (7), funnel (8), key to cock the mechanism (9) and a more elegant interchangeable handle (10). The pump has a round steel washer instead of a leather one. The cane is muzzle-loading.
Courtesy, collection Henry M. Stewart, Jr..

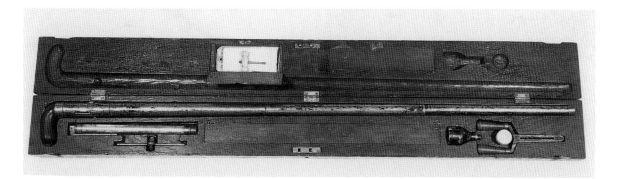

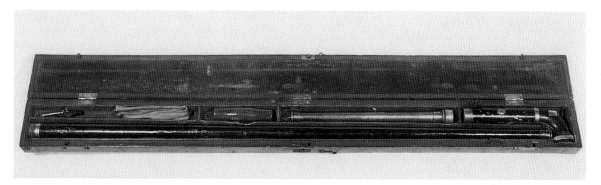

▲ 24/74 The two Air Gun Canes made by Lukens and Kunz, in their respective boxes.
Courtesy, collection Henry M. Stewart, Jr..

Jacob Kunz
1830

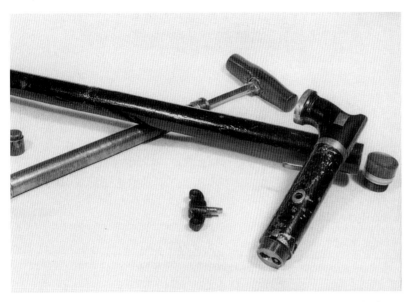

▲ 24/75 *Air Gun Cane* created by Jacob Kunz, who introduced numerous improvements to his weapons, one being the loading of the projectiles at the breech. The mechanism, cocked by a key, is in the top part of the cane. A round handle transforms the cane into a more elegant one.

    Illustrated in Eldon G. Wolff *Air Guns*, the air gun cane by Kunz has a cylindrical reservoir in the crook handle. A particular distinction is the brass ramrod put in a separate tube below the barrel, which is rifled. The lock is marked *J. Kunz philada.* The cane is cloth-covered.

Courtesy, collection Henry M. Stewart, Jr..

▲ 24/77 Portrait of Isaiah Lukens, painted in 1816 by Charles Wilson Peale.
Courtesy, The Franklin Institute of Philadelphia.

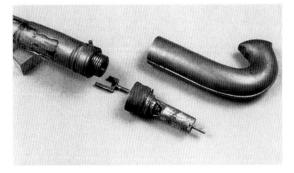

▲ 24/76 Although this cane has no markings, it is the same shape as the cane made by Kunz which is illustrated in Eldon G. Wolff's book. For the picture, the valve which holds the air in the handle as been taken out. Mr. Wolff also mentions in his volume a receipt book of *F. W. Harrold in Philadelphia: Rec. Nov. 7 1851 of Mr. John Krider 15 21/100 dollars in full for one air cane gun.* Was this a cane of his own manufacture, or was he selling one made by Kunz? Such questions provide the enthusiast with much happy speculation.
Courtesy, collection Francis H. Monek.

Paul Giffard
1873

    Paul Giffard of Paris (1837-1897) was the second inventor to have the idea of using CO2 as a propellant for guns, and the first to produce models which were used. Giffard was an prolific inventor, the father of the pneumatic telegraph, icebox, vacuum cleaner, universal pump and gas liquifier. He filed over 200 patents, including many for air and carbon dioxide weapons which are still in use today. One patent of his was for a cane using miniature carbon dioxide cartridges to expel the bullet. Somewhat confusingly, he always used the term air gun instead of gas gun for the carbon dioxide model for which he was famous.

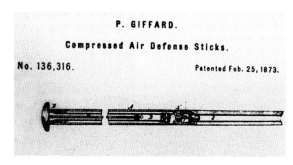

P. GIFFARD.

Compressed Air Defense Sticks.

No. 136,316.   Patented Feb. 25, 1873.

▲ 24/78 *Compressed Air Defense Sticks*, February 25, 1873 (136,316). Was this cane ever produced in the United States? L. Wesley, author of the book *Airguns and Air Pistols* says that Giffard's canes must have been made, although he never saw one.
Courtesy, U.S. Patent Office.

Stick-Fighting

Many books have been written on this branch of the martial arts. Most stem from the Orient. The staffs used are 6 feet long (180 cm), have a hand guard, and are covered with foam rubber at the point.

Patents

Over 700 United States patents for canes were filed between 1841 and 1970, a figure which does not include the great number of patents for ferrules, types of umbrella, and seats. Several of these patents were filed by foreigners. When canes were first patented in the nineteenth century, people were familiar with their use. The patents were filed under class 33/ + sub-class. In approximately 1920, canes were put under the class *Tents, Canopies, Umbrellas and Canes,* and are to be found in the following classes:

135/65	Canes, Sticks, Crutches and Walking Aids: 196 patents.
135/18	Imitation, artificial canes.
135/33	Umbrellas (but canes can be found in this group).
135/66	Combined and convertible models, 420 patents. Sword sticks, certain gadgets.

Under the entry *135/65*, there are numerous sub-entries, but most of these are for invalid aids. (*135/67-68-69-70-71-72-73-74-75-76-77-78-79-80-81-82-83-84-85-86) 135/910* are illuminated canes or umbrellas, and *135/911* are canes for the blind.

4/515	Walking cane combined.
42|52	Cane guns.
70/59	Locks for cane racks.
211/62	Receptacles for canes.
297/118	Convertible stand to canes (seats).
446/403	Detonating cane.

Designs

Primarily found under the class *D/3* + a sub entry, under the title of *Travel Goods, Personal Belongings, Umbrella or Parasol, Walking Support.* This last description defines the cane as it is known today, as a means of support.

The sub-entries are the same as those for the patents under *D3/5* to *D/18*. Most cover umbrellas, as designs for handles. Both umbrellas and canes shared a category. Of the 640 designs, fewer than 200 cover handles or shafts of canes. Some of these designs were shown in earlier chapters.

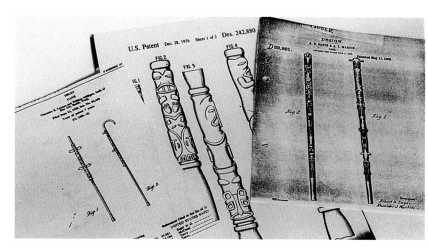

▲ 24/79 Three design patents from the middle of the 20th century.
Courtesy, U.S. Patent Office.

VII Fakes

25 Copies

Fakes

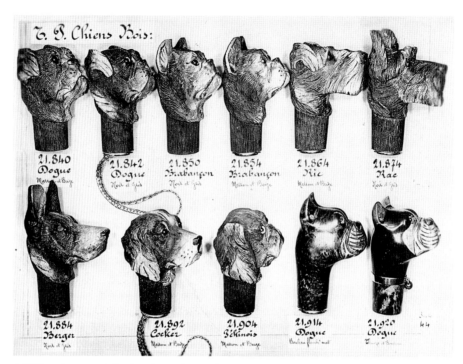

▲ 25/1   A group of dog heads used as umbrella handles.

Fakes

Introduction

Fakes abound in the world of antiques, and canes are no exception. Imitations fall into two categories; those sticks with modern copies of older handles, and the bogus gadget sticks. Some collectors do not mind owning fakes or copies. Perhaps they take the view that the object itself is the point of interest rather than its provenance, or perhaps they cannot believe that a fake could have slipped by their discerning eye. If the reader is such a collector, he is advised to skip the following chapter! Alas, the only way to learn is to be taken for a ride, as the author has ruefully acknowledged over the passage of years.

When examining any cane, always begin by taking it in hand in the manner in which a cane is held. The handle should fit the palm and should feel comfortable. Animal heads with pointed ears which could prick the palm were used for umbrellas or parasols, which obviously are held with the handle pointing down rather than up. Second, examine the shaft and look closely at the ferrule. Some old sticks have had their crook handles cut off and discarded, and a new handle substituted. The careful collector will check for the characteristic inclination to one side which a crook handled cane will show.

If the cane is old, then the ferrule should show signs of wear. Ferrules should always be made of metal. (A few sticks, mostly from the 18th century, will have a ferrule made from ivory or light horn to match the handle. Some old European canes even had silver or gold ferrules, but these are exceptions). Ferrules should be flat, with a iron base mounted on another metal, and not the pointed type usually put on umbrellas. When one has to replace a ferrule, one is usually forced to use a modern umbrella type, as old ferrules are very hard to find. The contrast between a modern pointed ferrule and a shaft of obvious age speaks for itself. But again, beware - wood can be chemically treated to take on the appearance of age. Today's fakes often have a ferrule made from dark horn which has been shaven down to match the modern shaft. Dark horn is always of modern origin.

The next piece of advice is to see as many collections as possible. Unfortunately, most museums do not have their collections on display, but if you manage to gain access to their storage, follow the same guidelines outlined above. It will be particularly noticeable that old handles were made to fit the hand.

At the turn of the century workmen took a particular pride in making beautiful and harmonious objects. They would never marry brass with shiny metals, a piece of silver with a brass ring, or a dark object with a shiny band. An ivory handle would have a silver ring rather than a brass one, and so forth.

With American Folk Art canes, the handle is always an integral part of the entire cane. Carved handles joined to shafts do exist, but these sticks will not be of United States origin. In Europe one can find roughly hewn animal heads which were originally made as umbrella handles and later set on a shaft. At the right price, they can be collectible.

▼ 25/2 A variety of ferrules. To the left, old ferrules, then a pointed umbrella ferrule, and at bottom right, a modern example of dark horn.

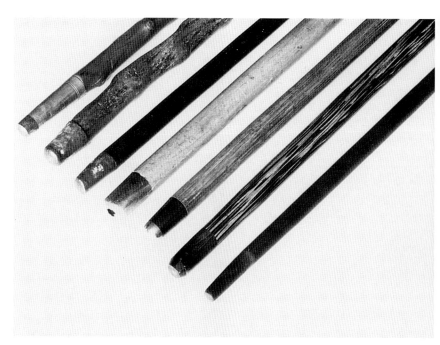

Ivory Handles

Size is one of the most obvious betrayals of the spurious. Often found nowadays are chunks of ivory which could be covered only by the hand of a giant. Plainly, it is easier for the forger to carve a large piece than a small one. These pieces will prove to have been produced in the last ten or twenty years. Genuine old ivory acquires a slight yellowish shade, but many of these imitation handles are either glaringly white or have been badly tinted. With time, ivory can crack and take a grayish tinge. One of the most commonly encountered handles is the scrimshawed globe-sun dial in ivory. Hundreds must have been made. The chapter on Scrimshaw explains why such handles could not be scrimshawed.

Much fascinating trivia surrounds the identification of fakes. As an example, during the late 19th century, the cat was not the popular pet he is today. In Europe, the French author Colette did much to popularize the feline as companion rather than barn rat-catcher. Thus, it is only in the past half century that one finds cats on handles.

Special attention should be paid to those sticks which fall into the category of erotica. These are often made of ivory. Modern imitations are often far too blatant. At the turn of the century, one usually had to look closely at a handle to discern that it was erotica, whereas what one finds today might better be classed as pornography. Pictures inserted in the lid often are not original.

▲ 25/3 A hat pin can make a nicely turned round knob.

Silver Handles

In Europe at the beginning of the 20th century, the cost of labor was cheaper than the price of silver. For the cane handles of the time, molds were used to produce two thin shells that the craftsman soldered together and filled with some variety of plaster. The handles remained light. Today, with labor costs more expensive than silver, the mold will be filled with solid silver, producing a heavy handle which is out of balance with the stick as a whole. Many such canes can be found on the market today, especially in Germany, England and the United States.

▲ 25/4 Metal busts of notables placed on a shaft make tempting finds for the unwary collector. This bust depicts Madame Tussaud, of the famous London wax museum, who began her career casting death masks during the French Revolution. Note the give-away shiny metal band attached with a modern glue.

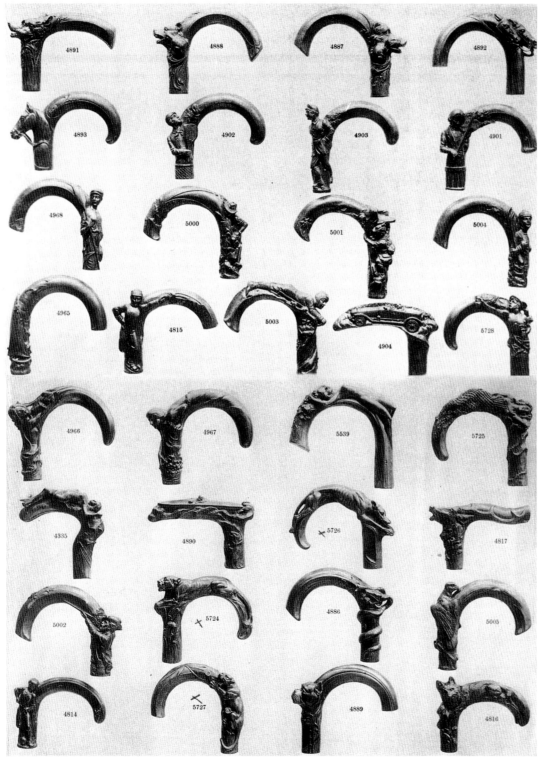

▲ 25/5 Two pages of models made by the German company B. Ott & Co., of Gmünd, now out of business. Modern silver is 950 alloy, as opposed to the 800 alloy used in the early 1900s. These handles are shamelessly marked *800*, despite being made of modern silver. Many can be found on today's market.

Gadget Canes

It is particularly in this area that so many fakes are found. An everyday object and a shaft are separately worth little, but when mounted together as a *Gadget Cane*, a very high price indeed can be commanded. Ask yourself questions. What makes a fake? Why would someone at the turn of the century need such an article hidden in his — or her — cane? For example, what would a lady do with a toothbrush in her cane? Where did she keep the toothpaste? (which did not come in the convenient tube in which it is found today!) It is easy to drill a hole in a shaft and thus secrete any number of small objects. Some useful guidelines: Sword sticks always fit snugly into the shaft and were made with a cloth wrapping around the blade. Never would a blade – or any other object – rattle inside the stick. The whole idea of hiding something in a cane would be betrayed by any noise

heard as the user strolled about. Beware of pocket objects which are simply slid into a recess of a shaft. If a metal container forms part of a genuine gadget stick, it must slot into a recess of the wood. It will never be simply glued onto a shaft.

The hinges should be delicately made and nearly invisible. The threading of a screw should also be given careful scrutiny.

Leather was never used to hide any seam between object and shaft. Telescopes are always of the same wood as the shaft, or they are an integral part of the stick.

Flashlights were patented to be part of the shaft and were never mounted on top. A particularly horrid piece, bogus in every regard, sports a brass cylinder flashlight used as a horizontal handle, with a shiny nickel-plated ring attaching it to the shaft!

Following is a series of examples, leaving scope for many more fakes!

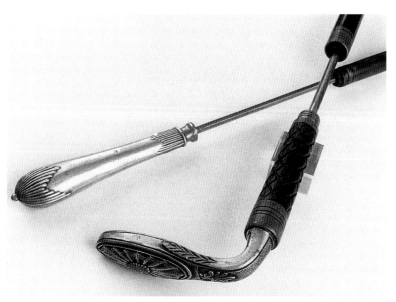

▲ 25/6 Unscrupulous dealers may think that any simple rod on a handle can pass as a sword-stick! Often fencing blades will be found masquerading as sword sticks. Others apparently feel that a knife handle or a door knob can pass scrutiny!

▲ 25/7 An example of rough and clumsy work on a handle.

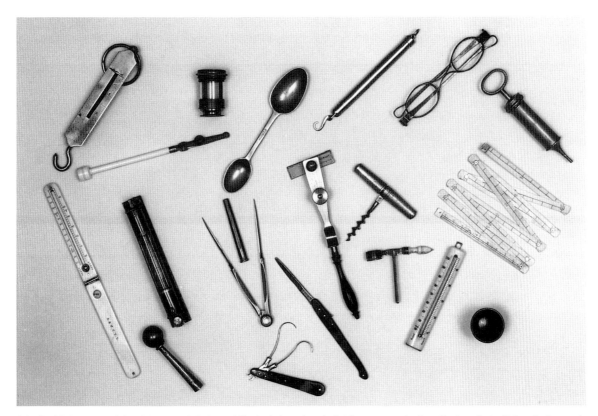

▲ 25/8 All the enterprising faker need do is to drill a hole into the shaft of a cane and adapt the handle to fit the shaft, usually by a screw thread. At that point, only his imagination limits the number of small objects he may choose to secrete. All the objects pictured have been found inside canes purporting to be genuine gadget sticks.
Courtesy, Scientific Antiquities, Geneva.

▲ 25/9 Totally far-fetched! A barrel tap has been mounted on a shaft. The hapless dealer hoped the illustration of the barrel would make it more convincing!

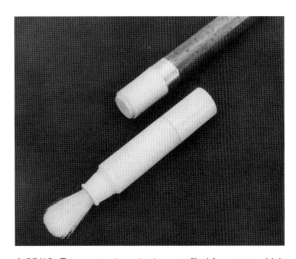

▲ 25/10 Two separate patents were filed for canes which held all the paraphernalia a gentleman might use to freshen up after a five o'clock rendez-vous! But even Kampfe's patent did not cater to a late-day shave. What would a 19th century gentleman do with a shaving brush missing the soap? Geniune gadget canes, while often ingenious, are never fanciful.

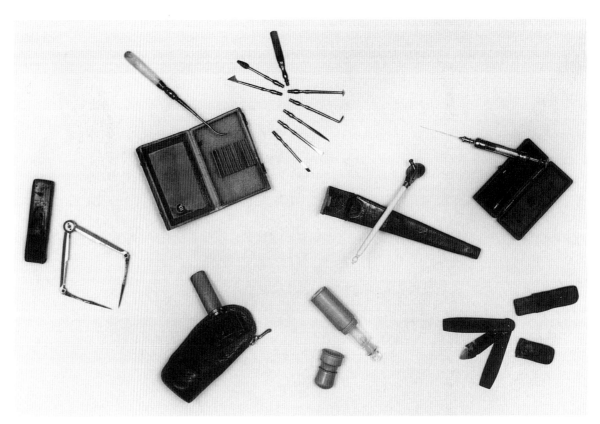

▲ 25/11 Typical miniature trinkets which can be found inside canes to form a fake gadget stick.
Courtesy, Scientific Antiquities, Geneva.

◀ 25/12 An assortment of fakes: (1) An adding machine that can easily become the top of a cane. (2) A compass can nestle into an ivory billiard ball, a ridiculous juxtaposition. (3) The shape of a spy-glass makes it an obvious candidate for mounting on a shaft, but this is never a genuine example of a gadget cane. The example at right has a recess which forms a sun-shade for the telescope. As for a pair of opera glasses, visualize them mounted alone! And can they unscrew? In addition, it should be remembered that in Europe, it was forbidden to take a cane into the auditorium of a theatre. (4) The small spy-glass is often put through an ivory billiard ball. (5) Any small camera can hope to pass as a *spy camera*. (6) An alcohol tester can fit into a handle.
Courtesy, Scientific Antiquities, Geneva.

▲ 25/13 This picture gives a good idea of the variety of fakes waiting to entice the inexperienced collector. Left to right: A borer screw mounted upon a sawn-off handle, the whole then replaced onto the shaft; a comb and a brush; a set of small playing cards; a shaving brush; and a knife and fork simply dropped into a hollow shaft, without any case.
Courtesy, Scientific Antiquities, Geneva.

▲ 25/14 An old flute is made in one piece and rarely has metal keys. In this case a piece of wood was added to top and bottom.

▲ 25/15 Similar canes were manufactured by the thousands in India in the 1970's.

◀ 25/16 A British patent was filed for this adding machine sized for the pocket. When an object was placed directly on a shaft, either glued to it or screwed into the wood, a band would often be used to hide the telltale join. With fake telescopes, a leather covering would take the place of the band.

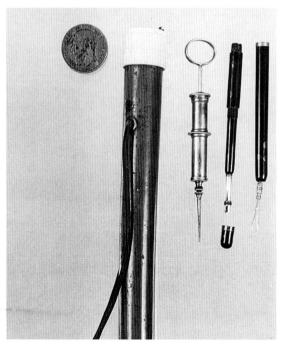

▲ 25/17 All these medical implements must rattle noisily in a shaft which lacks compartments for them.

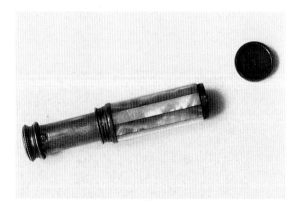

▲ 25/18 This perfume sprayer, marked *Kid, Bvte S.60, France,* can be simply screwed onto the wood of a shaft. Such a join is a dead give-away.

◀ 25/19 For several years an Italian company manufactured canes. The shafts of these canes bear a small plastic disc set into the wood which carries the date 1867. This date represents the year in which the factory was founded and not the date of manufacture of any individual cane.

▲ 25/20 A double magnifying glass, a common pocket trinket, simply glued onto a shaft. How it was to be used is the first puzzle.

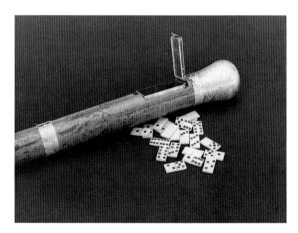

▲ 25/21 A variety of metals is characteristic of the clumsy fake. Here the knob and the ring are in silver and the domino container is in brass!

▲ 25/22 A nice pocket tool kit, marked *Pat. Nov. 28, 1893 Improved / Horace E. Britton / Stoughton. Mass. USA.* Alas, it needs a screw head fixed to attach it to the cane.

▲ 25/23 Genuine cork-screw canes must slot into a groove which fits the circular boring of the cork-screw, not just a hollow in the shaft. In addition, the metal portion of old cork-screws was round.

▲ 25/24 Small microscopes are often found inside shafts. But when they form part of the shaft, one may well wonder how they were to be used!

▲ 25/25 An ivory spinning die. To convert to a pocket object, the protruding pieces at top and bottom would be reversed to slot into the large cylindrical center. In this fake, however, the spike at bottom slots into the top hole. The shaft can then be adapted to the ivory piece. The grasping hand would have no protection from the spike at top. Genuine gadget canes were never so poorly designed.

▶ 25/26 The top part of this cane was made and covered with leather to conceal a pipe. The leather also disguises the join of two different woods. Most likely the top section was the original pipe holder.

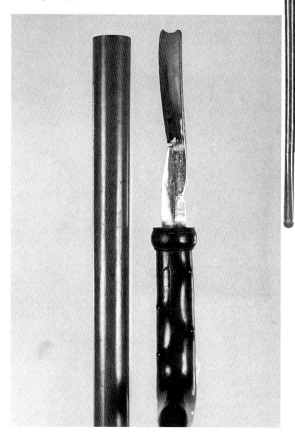

▲ 25/27 Although this appears a fake at first glance, it is possible that the owner adapted his stick in order to have, as a weapon, a razor blade handy. Still, it remains a doubtful piece.

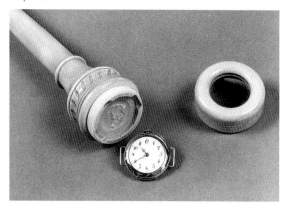

▲ 25/28 A wrist watch, minus its leather strap, placed in a recess which has been carved in an ivory container. Wrist watches did not exist at the turn of the century. The example here, a mid-20th century model, does not even attempt to pass itself off as an earlier style.

VIII Appendix

Bibliography

Index

Origin of Illustrations

Selection of Museums and Historical Societies

Collectors

Bibliography

Books often consulted

Dictionary of American Biography. Charles Scribner's Son, New York, 1936.

Encyclopedia of American History. Harper & Row.

Columbia Encyclopedia. Columbia University Press, New York & London, 1963.

Burtscher, William J.. *The Romance Behind Walking Canes.* Dorrance & Company, Philadelphia, 1945.

Stein, Kurt. *Canes & Walking Sticks.* Liberty Cap Books, York, Pa., 1974.

1. The Spanish Vara

Charles, Tom (Mrs). *New Mexico.* "Unraveling the Mystery of the Lincoln Canes", (12,13-46,47), April 1954.

Coffin, Charles Carleton. *Old Times in the Colonies.* Harper & Brothers, New York, 1881.

Faris, Chester E.. *Pueblos Governors' Canes.* Not published, 1952.

Iverson, Marion Day. *Antiques.* "Color in Pilgrim and Puritan Dress", March 1952.

Kubicek, Earl C.. *Mankind.* "The Cane that Lincoln Gave", 1968.

Sticks and Umbrella News. London, November 1892.

2. Canes worn by Presidents

Brooks, Noah. *Washington in Lincoln's Time.* New York Century Co., New York, 1896.

Collins, Herbert R.. *Wills of U.S. Presidents.* Communication Channels, Inc., New York, 1976.

Cordonnier, Henri. *Les 100.000 Curiosités d'hier et d'aujourd'hui.* (Chapitre 9). Paris, 1909.

James, Marquis. *The Raven.* "The Life Story of Sam Houston", Gordon City, New York, 1919.

Longstreet, Stephen. *We all went to Paris.* MacMillan, New York, 1993.

Lucas, Ann M.. *The World of Thomas Jefferson at Monticello.* Harry Abrams, New York, 1983.

McClellan, Elisabeth. *Historic Dress in America, 1607-1800.* Georges W. Jacobs & Co., Philadelphia, 1904.

Meriwether, Robert L.. *University of South Carolina.* " Preston S. Brooks on the Canning of Sumner", Waverly Press, Baltimore,

Ostendorf, Lloyd. *Lincoln Herald.* "Lincoln and the Hoblits", Spring 1975.

VeZolles, Virginia. *The Harrison Home Stateman.* "Canes", (Volume Six, Number Three). Indianapolis, March 1980.

3. Political Canes

Crew, Dr. Dan O.. *Communication.* Gastonia, N.C..

Gores, Stern. *Presidential and Campaign Memorablia.* Wallace-Homestead Books Co., Greensboro, N.C., 1988.

Lorant, Stefan. *The Glorius Burden.* Harper & Row, New York, 1968.

Melder, Keith. *Hail to the Candidate.* Smithsonian Institution Press, Washington, London, 1992.

Sullivan, Edmund G.. *Collecting Political Americana.* Crown Publishing, Inc, New York, 1980.

4. Canes worn in Colleges

Brown Alumni Magazine Company. 1909.

Class History. no date. (*Bucknell*).

Dartmouth Traditions. "The Cane Rush",The Darmouth University Press, Hanover, 1901.

The Dartmouth. "Senior Canes Go on Sale Today", May 5, 1960.

Detroit Free Press. May 12, 1935. (Michigan).

University Records. April 1954. (Michigan).

Franconia Aerea Heritage Council. "Saving the Great Stone Face", Canaan, N.H., 1984.

The University Magazine. (Vol. 4 No 1). 1878. (Pennsylvania).

The Red and Blue. Philadelphia, Nov. 1, 1889. (Pennsylvania).

The Pennsylvania News. May 20, 1954.

The Pennsylvanian. "The Cane Rush", (Vol VI, No. 19). Dec. 4, 1890.

Hey Day. 1967. (Pennsylvania).

Princeton Alumni Weekly. "The History of the Cane Spree", March 8, 1911.

The Nassau Sovereign. "The Cane Spree", Nov. 1941. (Princeton).

The Nassau Sovereign. "Cane Sprees", Sept. 1948. (Princeton).

New York Times . "M.B. Cary '72 New York Oldest Alumnus, Discusses Cane Sprees", April 3, 1938. (Princeton).

A Bicentennial History. Richard McCormick "The Transformation of the College". (Rutgers).

Daily Palo Alto. "Stanford University", May 9, 10, 29, 1895.

The Tuftonian. "The Locals", (Vol. 8, No 2). Nov. 1881.

Cynic. (III). Sept. 30, 1885. (Vermont).

Student Life at University of Virginia, 1825-1861. (Not published).

Mr. Jefferson's University. "The First Century".

Four Years at Yale. Charles C. Chatfield & Co., New Haven, 1871.

Out of Yale's Past. Privately printed, 1960.

5. Patriotic Canes

Edgerton, Jr., Samuel Y.. *Early American Life.* "The Murder of Jane McCrea", June 1977.

6. Secret Societies

Beeman, Linda. *The Cane Collector's Chronicle,* "Masonic Canes", Vol 5, No.2, April 1994

Stevens, Albert C.. *The Cyclopedia of Fraternities.* E.B. Treat and Co., New York, 1907.

Whalen, William J. *Handbook of Secret Organizations.* The Bruce Publishing Co., Milwaukee, 1966.

7. Fairs

Friz, Richard. *World's Fair Memorabilia.* House of Collectibles, New York, 1989.

8. Folk Art
11. Modern Folk Art

Folk Art Finder. Gallery Press, Essex, Ct., Vol. 13 No. 2, Apr-June 1992.

Davidson, Basil. *African Kingdoms.* Time-Life Books, New York, 1966.

Evans, David. *Mississippi Folklore Register.* "Afro-American Sculpture from Parchman Penitentiary", (p.141-152). 1972.

Grider, Sylvia. *Indiana University.* "Indiana Folklore", (Vol VII, No 1-2). The Indiana University Press, Bloomington, 1974.

Hackley, Harry. *Sticks: Historical and Contemporary Kentucky Canes.* Kentucky Art and Craft Foundation, Louisville, Ky, 1988.

Hall, Michael D.. *Elijah Pierce.* "Hands-on-Work", (26-36). University of Washington Press, Seattle & London, 1992.

Hartigan, Lynda Roscoe. *Made With Passion.* Smithsonian Institution, Washington D.C., 1990

Herrick, Virginia A.. *Bandywine River Museum.* "Antiques Show", 1986.

Higgins, W. Robert. *The Geographical Origins of Negro Slaves in Colonial South Carolina.* South Atlantic Quarterly, 1971.

Klein, Herbert S.. *The Middle Passage.* The Princeton University Press, Princeton, N.J., 1978.

Livingston, Jane. *Black Folk Art in America, 1930 - 1980.* University Press of Mississippi, 1982.

Machmer, Richard S. and Rosemarie. *Just For Nice.* The Historical Society of Berks County, Reading, Pa., 1991.

Meyer, Georges H.. *American Folk Art Canes. Personal Sculpture*, Sandrigham Press, Bloomfield Hills, Michigan, 1992.

Pope-Hennessy, James. *La Traite des Noirs dans l'Atlantique*. Fayard, Paris, 1969.

Vlach, John Michael. *The Afro-American Tradition in Decorative Arts*. The University of Georgia Press, Athens, Ga., 1978.

Willett, Frank. *African Art*. Oxford University Press, New York and Toronto, 1971.

9. Canes carved by Soldiers

Barnby, H.G.. *The Prisonners of Algier*. The University Press, Glasgow, 1966.

Callahan, E.W.. *List of Officers of the United States Navy and the Marine Corps, 1775-1900*. L.R. Hamersly & Co., New York, 1901.

Dyer, F.H.. *Compendium of War of Rebellion*. (Vol 2.). Thomas Yoseloff, New York, 1959.

Faust, Patricia. *Historical Times Illustrated Encyclopedia of the Civil War*. Harper & Row Publishers, New York, 1986.

Heitman, Francis B.. *Historical Register and Dictionary of the United States Army*. Washington Government Printing Office, Washington, 1903.

Hoehling, A.A.. *Naval Incidents of the Civil War*. Winston-Salem, N.C., 1989.

Lacour-Gayet, Robert. *Histoire des Etats-Unis*. Fayard, Paris, 1976.

Leckie, Robert. *The Wars of America*. Harper & Roe, New York, Evanston, London, 1968.

Long, E.B.. *The Civil War Day by Day*. Doubleday, New York, 1971.

Overton, Albert G.. *Ancestors I Wish Were Mine*. Micro-Records Publishing Co., St. Louis, Mo, 1977.

Pennsylvania Commission. *The Seventy-Fifth Anniversary of the Battle of Gettysburg*. "Volume IV", Gettysburg, Pa., 1939.

10. Scrimshaw Canes

Flayderman, E. Norman. *Scrimshaw and Scrimshanders*. Norman Flayderman, New Milford, Conn., 1972.

Lloyd's Register of British and Foreign Shipping, Cox & Wyman, Lincoln's Inn Fields, 1859.

Malley, Richard C.. *Graven by the Fishermen Themselves*. Mystic Seaport Museum,Inc., Mystic, Conn., 1983.

12. Glass Canes

Banzhaf, Dieter W.. *Kunst & Antiquitäten*. "Die gläsernen Glucksbringer", March 1981.

Beeman, Linda. *The Cane Collector's Chronicle*. "The Glass Cane", (Vol. 3, No. 4). October 1992.

Blake, Joyce E.. *Glasshouse Whimsies*. Joyce E. Blake, Elma, N.Y., 1984.

Fauster, Carl U.. *Libbey Glass Since 1818*. Len Beach Press, Toledo, Ohio.

McKearin, George S. & Helen. *American Glass*. Crown Publishers, New York, 1941.

13. Silver Handles

Antiques. "An Eighteenth-Century Cane", October, 1953.

Beales Jr., Ross W.. *The Bay State Historical League Bulletin*. "The Boston Post Gold Headed Canes, Origins of a Tradition", Vol. 8, No. 3 & 4 (1982-83).

Caldwell, Jr., Benjamin H.. *Tennessee Silversmiths*. MESDA, Winston-Salem, 1988.

Carpenter, Mary Grace and Charles H.. *Tiffany Silver*. Dodd, Mead & Company, New York, 1978.

Carpenter, Jr., Charles H.. *Gorham Silver*. Dodd, Mead & Company, New York, 1982.

Clark, Tim. *Yankee Magazines*, "Keepers of the Cane", March 1983.

Constantian, Harold M.. *Worcester Medical News*. " An Old Book and a Gold Headed Cane. January 1970.

Dike, Catherine. *Silver*. "Silver & Gold Cane Handles in the United States". July-August, September- October, November-December 1987.

Fales, Martha Gandy. *Philadelphia Silversmiths*. Waseleyan University Press, Middletown, Conn.,

Luckey, Caryl F.. *Silver - Silverplate*. House of Collectibles, Florence, Alabama, 1948.

McClinton, K. Morrison. *Collecting American 19th Century Silver*. Charles Scribner's Son, New York, 1968.

Phelps Stokes, I.N.. *The Iconography of Manhattan Island*. "Royal Gazette, 20 December 1778", Robert H. Dodd, New York, 1926.

Pleasants, H.. *Maryland Silversmiths 1715 - 1830*. Baltimore, 1930.

Prime, Alfred Coxe. *The Gleanings from Newspapers*. "The Arts and Crafts in Philadelphia, Maryland, South Carolina", The Walpole Society, 1929.

Rainwater, Dorothy T.. *Encyclopedia of American Silver Manufacturers*. Schiffer Publishing Ltd., West Chester, Pa., 1986.

The Osterville Historical Newsletter. *Society Presents Historic Blount Cane to Marie De Witt*. Vol. Two, No One. Spring 1991.

14. Ivory and Plastic Handles

Manuels-Roret, *Marqueteur de l'Ivoirier*. Leonce Laget, Paris, 1977.

Masselon, Roberts & Cillard. *Celluloid*. Charles Griffin & Co. Ltd., Philadelphia, 1912.

Philippovich, Eugen von. *Elfenbein*. Klinkhardt & Biermann, Munich, 1982.

14. Assorted Woods

Bingham, Karen. *Creative Crafts*. "Carving Diamond Willow Canes". June 1982.

Block, Rudolph. *Catalog of a Private Collection of Walking Sticks*. New York, 1928 .

Constantine, Jr., Albert. *Know your Woods*. Scribner & Sons, New York, 1959.

Lutz, H.J.. *Observations on "diamond willow", with Particular Reference to Its Occurence in Alaska*. Reprint from The American Midland Naturalist by University of Notre Dame Press, Notre Dame, Ind., Vol. 60 (1): 176-185. 1958.

Miller, Robert Cunningham. *California Historical Society Quarterly*. "The California Academy of Sciences and the Early History of Science in the West", California Historical Society, San Francisco, Vol. XXI, No. 4, December 1942.

Record, Samuel J.. *The Rudoloph Block Collection of Walking Sticks*. (32: 253-260). Journal of the New York Botanical Garden, New York, 1931.

17. Art and Entertainment

Thomson, David. *Who was Who on Screen*. William Morrow & Co., New York, 1981.

22. Dealers

Bishop, J. Leander. *A History of American Manufacturers from 1608 to 1860*. Philadelphia, 1864.

Sieger & Guernsey, *Cyclopedia of the Manufacturers and Products of the United States,* 1890.

23. Gadget Canes

Dike, Catherine. *Cane Curiosa, from Gun to Gadget*. Les Editions de l'Amateur, Paris & Catherine Dike, Geneva, 1983.

24. Weapons

Berg, Paul. *Bulletin of the American Society of Arms Collectors*. "Remington Cane Gun", (Bulletin 49, p.40 - 50).

Burnside, Graham. *The Gun Report*. "The Walking Stick Machine Gun", Aledo, Ill., April 1958.

Cole, Whiteford R.. *The Gun Report*. "The Remington Patented Rifle Cane", (14 - 22). September 1983.

Flayderman, Norman. *Guide to Antique American Firearms*. DBI Book Inc., Northbrook, Ill., 5th Edition, 1990.

Gardner, Col. Robert. *A Directory of Fabricators of Firearms*.

Logan, Herschel C.. *Underhammer Guns*. The Stackpole Co., Harrisburg, Pa.

Mouillesseaux, Harold R.. *The Gun Report*. "The Search for Doctor Lambert's Cane Rifle", (p. 17 -20), December 1973.

Mouillesseaux, Harold R.. *The Gun Report*. "Early Allen Firearms".

Smith, W.H.B.. *Gas, Air & Spring Guns of the World*. Castle Books, New York, 1957.

Stein, Kurt. *Man-at-Arms*. "Swordcanes", 42 47), 1980.

Stewart, Jr., Henry M.. *Monthly Bugle*. "The Air Gun in Antiquity", Pennsylvania Antique Gun Collectors Association, Philadelphia, 1985.

Stewart, Jr., Henry M.. *Monthly Bugle*. "The American Air Gun School of 1800", Pennsylvania Antique Gun Collectors Association, Philadelphia, February 1977.

Stewart, Jr., Henry M.. *Monthly Bugle*. "Lewis & Clark and the American Air Gun School of 1800", Pennsylvania Antique Gun Collectors Association, Philadelphia, 1985.

Teesdale, Jerald T.. *The Gun Report*. "Saxton's Cane Gun", (p. 25 - 27), July 1968.

Tegner, Bruce. *Stick Fighting*. Thor Publishing Co., Ventura, Colorado.

Weise, A.J.. *History of the City of Troy*. Troy, N.Y., 1876.

Winant, Lewis. *Firearms Curiosa*. Arco Publishers Ltd., London, 1956.

Wolff, Eldon G.. *Air Guns*. Milwaukee Public Museum, Milwaukee, Wisconsin, 1958.

Books published on Collecting Canes

In English:

Boothroyd, AlbertE. *Facinating Walking Sticks*. London, Salix Books, 1970, 1973.

Burtcher, William J.. *The Romance behind Walking Canes*. Dorrance and Company, Philadelphia, 1945.

Dike, Catherine. *Cane Curiosa, from Gun to Gadget*. Les Editions de l'Amateur, Paris and Catherine Dike, Geneva, 1983.

Dike, Catherine. *Walking Sticks*. Shire Publications Ltd.,Princes Risborough, GB. 1990, 1993.

Hackley, Harry. *Historical and Contemporary Kentucky Canes*. Kentucky Art and Craft Foundation, Louisville, 1988.

Meyer, George H.. *American Folk Art Canes. Personal Sculpture*. Sandringham Press, Bloomfield Hills, Michigan, 1992.

Real, Antoine. *The Story of the Stick in All Ages and Lands*. Translation François Fernand-Michel. J.W. Bouton, New York, 1875.

Snyder, Jeffrey B.. *Canes, from the Seventeenth to the Twentieth Century*. Schiffer Publishing Ltd., Atglen, Pa., 1993.

Stein, Kurt. *Canes and Walking Sticks*. Liberty Caps Books, York, Pa., 1974.

In French:

Dike, Catherine. *Les Cannes à Système, un Monde Fabuleux et Méconnu*. Les Editions de l'Amateur, Paris and Catherine Dike, Genève, 1982 and 1985.

Dike, Catherine, Bezzaz, G.. *La Canne Objet d'Art*. Les Editions de l'Amateur, Paris and Catherine Dike, Genève, 1988.

Faveton, Pierre. *Les Cannes*. Ch. Massin, Paris, 1988.

Girard, Sylvie. *Cannes et Parapluies et leurs Anecdotes*. MA Editions, Paris, 1986.

In German:

Hassan, A. *Stöcke und Stäbe im Pharaonischen Aegypten*.Münchner Aegyptologische Studien, number 33, Munich, 1976.

Klever, Ulrich. *Stöcke*. W. Heyne Verlag, Munich, 1980.

Klever, Ulrich. *Spazierstöcke*. Callwey, Munich, 1984.

In Italian:

Coradeschi, Sergio, and Lamberti, Alfredo. *Bastoni*. Mondadori, Milan, 1986.

In Slovak:

Polonec, Andrej. *Tvarované a Zdobené Palice*. Vydavateľstvo Osveta, Martin, Cs., 1977.

Index

Origin of Illustrations

Abby Rockefeller Folk Art Center, Williamsburg, Virginia (Colonial Williamsburg), 8/23

Albany Institute of Art, 6/25

American Flint Glass Workers Union, 12/1

Antique and Historic Glass Foundation, (Commercial Photographic Inc.), 12/2 - 12/3

Barbey, Roger, 21/4

Beauvoir, The Jefferson Davis Shrine, 9/31

Beeman, Joe and Linda, 9/58

Blue Ridge Institute, Ferrum, (David Fulton), Va., 5/23 - a/p.50 - c/p.218 d/p.218 - a/p.227 - d/p.227 - a/p.228 - a/p.229 - b/p.229

Boss, Frank H., 11/3

Boston Society, (Barney Burstein), 1/16

Bourne, Richard A., 2/35

Buffalo Historical Center, Cody, Wy.,1/32

Butterfield & Butterfield, 1/32

Bydgoszcz, Muzeum Okregowe, Poland, 5/15

Chicago Historical Society, 1/28 - 2/33 -3/24 - 9/2 - 9/11 - 9/21 - 9/30 - 9/33 9/41

Columbus Museum of Art, b/p.162

Connecticut Historical Society, (Arthur Kelly), 5/9 - 9/45

Cornell University, Department of Manuscripts and University Archives, 101 Olin Library, Ithaca, N.Y., 4/12

Dartmouth College Library, 4/1 -4/14 - 4/15

Essex Institute, Salem, Ma., 1/4

Etnier, Daniel, 5/18

Evans, Byron, e/p.240

Flayderman, Norman, 10/2

Fort Edward Historical Association, N.Y., 5/1

Fort Tigonderoga Museum, Tigonderoga, N.Y., 6/8

Franklin D. Roosevelt Library, Hyde Park, N.Y., 2/53 -2/54 - b/p.334

Gettysburg College, Musselman Library, 4/16 - 6/21

Gettysburg National Military Park, 9/1

Gifford, Jim, 3/12 - 3/21 - 3/25 - 3/27 - 3/32 - 3/39 - 3/42 - 3/47 - 3/48 -3/62 3/69 - 3/72 - 3/77 - 3/78 - 3/80 - 3/81 - 3/82 - 3/85

Grunder, Donald J., 3/53 - 3/59 - 23/35

Harrison, Michael, 24/22 - 24/32

Harry S. Truman Library, Independence, Mo.,(G. Plowman), 2/42 - 2/ 59 - 2/57 - (N. Georgieff), 2/58, (G. Plowman), 6/2 - 6/4 - 6/35 - 9/40 - 9/72

Henry Ford Museum & Greenfield Village, Dearborn, Mi. 3/19 - 3/46 3/64 - 24/12 - 24/14

Hike America, c/p.298

Institute of the Great Plains, Lawton, 8/2

Iowa State Historical Department, 6/38

James K.Polk Ancestral Home, Columbia, Tn., 3/10

James Monroe Museum, Fredericksburg, Va., 2/16

Jews, Milton, O., 11/11

Kaufman, Robert, c/p.315

Kentucky Historical Society, Frankfort, 3/8 - 5/16 - 8/6

Lafayette College, Special Collections and Archives, 2/1 - 4/20

Library of Congress, 9/61

Library of the University of Michigan, 4/24

Lincoln Memorial University, Harrogate, Tenn., 2/30 - 2/32

Little White House, Warm Springs, Ga., (Larry R. Buker), 2/6 - 2/45 - 2/56 - 3/75 - 6/36 - 8/66 - 11/6

Martin Van Buren National Historic Site, 2/20

Massachusetts Historical Society, 1/17 - c/p.49 - b/p.50 - c/p.50 - d/p.50 e/p.50 - d/p.102 - 9/39

McArthur Memorial, Norfolk, Va., 9/69 - 9/70 - 9/71

Metropolitan Museum, New York, The Elisha Whittelsey Collection, 13/9 - 13/63

Miller Jr., Howard H., 24/2

Minnesota Historical Society, 5/12 - 8/32 - 9/50

Mississippi River Museum, Mud Island, Memphis, Tn., 10/27

Monticello, Thomas Jefferson Memorial Foundation Inc., 2/14

Morrison, Steve, 8/43 - 15/2 - 23/38 - 24/21

Mount Vernon Ladies' Association, a/p.49

Murrill, Roy, 5/17 - 5/18 - 5/20

Musée Barbier-Mueller, Geneva, (P. A. Ferrazzini), 8/14 - 8/15 - 8/17

Museum of Early Decorative Arts, Winston-Salem, NC., a/p.158 - 8/40

Museum of New Mexico, (Frasher), 1/2 - (T. H. Parkhust), 2/31 - 8/7

Museum of the Confederacy, Eleanor S. Brockenbrough Library, 9/48 9/52

Mystic Seaport Museum, Inc., (Claire White Peterson), 10/3 - 10/7 - 10/9

Nairn, Charles B., d/p.49 - b/p.119 - c/p.119 - d/p.119 - b/p.140 - a/p.162 b/p.179 - d/p.179 - a/180 - a/p.198 - c/p.198

Nebraska State Historical Society, 2/3 - 3/35 -3/54 - 5/21

New Hampshire Historical Society, 1/6 - 2/24 - 3/7 - 18/5

New York Historical Society, New York, 1/12 - 24/35

New York Public Library, Portrait File, Miriam & Ira D. Wallach Dvision of Art, Prints & Photographs. Astor, Lenox and Tilden Foundations, 2/40 - 2/47

New York State Historical Association, Cooperstown, N.Y., 3/11

Ohio Historical Society, 3/4 - 3/5 -3/23 - 3/49 - 4/17 - 6/24

Oklahoma Museum of Higher Education, Oklahoma Historical Society, 4/28

Peabody Museum of Salem, 1/26

Peck, Alex, 9/54

Plymouth Notch Historic District, 2/51

President James A. Garfield National Historic Site, 2/39

President Benjamin Harrison Foundation, Inc., Indianapolis, 2/4 - 2/21 2/43 - 3/37

Price, Merton, 24/70

Princeton University, Seely G. Mudd Manuscript Library, 4/36 - 4/37

Randall, Alder, 8/57

Region of Peel Archives, Robertson Matthews Collection, Brampton, Ontario, 3/1

Remington Gun Musem, 24/37

Rensselaer County Historical Society, 24/13 - 24/15 - 24/16

Rhoades, Jeffrey, 24/30

Roanoke Museum of Fine Arts, a/p.160

Rutherford B. Hayes Presidential Center, Fremont, Ohio, 2/37 2/38 - 3/14

Rutkowski, James, 8/1

Sagamore Hill National Historic Site, N.Y., 2/46

Sam Houston Memorial, Huntsville, Tx., 1/15

San Diego Museum of Man, 8/35 - 8/37

San Fransisco National Historic Park, 9/62 - 10/8

Sherwood Forest Plantation, Va., (Carole Nix), 2/22

Smithsonian Institution, 1/21 - b/p.49 - c/p.68 - 15/1 - 24/11

SouthDakota State Historical Society, Pierre, 15/11

Selection of Museums and Historical Societies

Selection of Museums and Historial Societies with Cane Collections

Up to 15 - 20 canes, the mention is *small.*

Between 20 and 50, it is marked *medium.*

Between 50 and 100, *large* and over 100, *very large.*

No indication is given as to the interest of these collections.

Adams National Historic Site
135 Adams Street
P.O.Box 531
Quincy
Ma 02269
Canes collected: small

Albany Institute of History and Art
125 Washington Avenue
Albany
NY 12210
Canes collected: small

Beauvoir
2244 Beach Blvd
Biloxi
MS 39531
Canes collected: small

Buffalo Bill Historical Center
P.O.Box 1000
Cody
Wyoming 82414
Canes collected: large

Chester County Historical Society
225 North High Street
West Chester
PA 19380-2691
Canes collected: small

The Society of the Cincinnati
2118 Massachusetts
Avenue
Washington
DC 20008
Canes collected: small

Cincinnati Art Museum
Eden Park
Cincinnati
Ohio 45202-1596
Canes collected: small

The Civil War Library and Museum
1805 Pine Street
Philadelphia
PA 19103
Canes collected: medium

The Connecticut Historical Society
1 Elizabeth Street at
Asylum Avenue
Hartford
Conn. 06105
Canes collected: very large

Cooper-Hewitt Museum
2 East 91st Street
New York
NY. 10128
Canes collected: small

Daughters of the American Revolution
Museum
1776 D Street N.W.
Washington
DC 20006-5392
Canes collected: medium

Essex Institute
132 Essex Street
Salem
Mass. 01970
Canes collected: medium

Fairfield Historical Society
636 Old Post Road
Fairfield
CT 06430
Canes collected: very large

Henry Ford Museum & Greenfield Village
P.O.Box 1970
Dearborn
Michigan 48121-1970
Canes collected: very large

Forbes
Forbes Building
60 Fifth Avenue
New York
NY 10011
Canes collected: small
(Fabergé)

President James A. Garfield National
Historical Site
8095 Mentor Avenue
Mentor
Ohio 44060
Canes collected: small

President Benjamin Harrison Memorial Home
1230 North Delaware
Indianapolis
Indiana 46202
Canes collected: medium

Rutherford B. Hayes Presidential Center
Spiegel Grove
Fremont
Ohio 43420-2796
Canes collected: small

The John Woodman Higgins Armory
100 Barber Avenue
Worcester
Mass. 01606
Canes collected: small

State Historical Society of Iowa
Capitol Complex
Des Moines
Iowa 50319
Canes collected: large

Kansas State Historical Society
6425 S.W. Sixth
Topeka
KS 66615-1099
Canes collected: very large

The Kendall Whaling Museum
27 Everett Street
P.O.Box 297
Sharon
Mass. 02067
Canes collected: large

Kentucky Historical Society
Old State Capitol
P.O.Box H
Frankfort
KY 40602-2108
Canes collected: medium

Little White House
Route 1 Box 10
Warm Springs
Georgia 31830
Canes collected: very large

MacArthur Memorial
MacArthur Square
Norfolk
Va. 23510
Canes collected: medium

Maryland Historical Society
201 West Monument
Street
Baltimore
Maryland 21201
Canes collected: ?

Massachusetts Historical Society
1154 Boylston Street
Boston
Mass 02215
Canes collected: very large

The Metropolitan Museum of Art
Fifth Avenue & 82 nd St
New York
NY 10028
Canes collected: small

The University of Michigan
Baits Drive at Broadway
Ann Arbor
Michigan 48109
Canes collected: small

Milwaukee Public Museum
800 West Wells Street
Milwaukee
Wisconsin 53233
Canes collected: very large

Minnesota Historical Society
1500 Mississippi Street
St. Paul
Minnesota 55101
Canes collected: medium

Missouri Historical Society
PO Box 11940
St. Louis
Mo 63112-0940
Canes collected: large

The Mount Vernon Ladies' Association
Mount Vernon
Va 22121
Canes collected: small

Mystic Seaport Museum
Mystic
Conn. 06355-0990
Canes collected: large

Museum of our National Heritage
P.O.Box 519
Lexington
Mass 02173
Canes collected: small

Nebraska State Historical Society
P.O. Box 82554
Lincoln
Nebraska 68501
Canes collected: small

New Hampshire Historical Society
Thirty Park Street
Concord
N.H. 03301
Canes collected: large

Museum of New Mexico
Palace of the Governors
Santa Fe
N.M.87504-2087
Canes collected: small

The New York Historical Society
170 Central Park West
New York
NY-10024-5194
Canes collected: medium

New York State Historical Association
P.O. Box 800
Cooperstown
NY 13326
Canes collected: very large

The Newark Museum
P.O.Box 540
Newark
N.J. 07101-0540
Canes collected: small

Ohio Historical Society
1982 Velma Avenue
Columbus
Ohio 43211-2497
Canes collected: very large

From the collections of the Oklahoma Museum
of Higher Education
Oklahoma Historical
Society
2100 North Lincoln Blvd.
Oklahoma City
Oklahoma 73105
Canes collected: large

Whaling Museum Old Dartmouth Historical
Society
18 Johnny Cake Hill
New Bedford
Mass. 02740
Canes collected: small

Maritime Museum Peabody Museum
Salem
Mass. 01970
Canes collected: very large

The State Museum of Pennsylvania
Third and North Streets
P.O. Box 1026
Harrisburg
Pa 17108-1026
Canes collected: small

James Knox Polk Ancestral Home
301 West 7th Street
Columbia
Tennessee 38401
Canes collected: small

The Rhode Island Historical Society
121 Hope Street
Providence
R.I. 02906
Canes collected: large

The Abby Aldrich Rockefeller Folk Art Center
307 South England Street
P.O.Box C.
Williamsburg
Va.23185
Canes collected: small

Franklin D. Roosevelt Library
259 Albany Post Road
Hyde Park
NY. 12538
Canes collected: very large

The Saint Louis Art Museum
Forest Park
Saint Louis
Mo. 63110
Canes collected: small

National Museum of American History
Smithsonian Institution
Division of Agriculture
and Natural Resources
Washington
DC 20560
Canes collected: very large

National Museum of American History
Smithsonian Institution
Division of Costume
Washington
DC 20560
Canes collected: large

National Museum of American History
Smithsonian Institution
Division of Military
History
Washington
DC 20560
Canes collected: large

National Museum of American History
Smithsonian Institution
Division of Musical
Instruments
Washington
DC 20560
Canes collected: small

National Museum of American History
Smithsonian Institution
Division of Political
History
Washington
D.C. 20560
Canes collected: medium

National Museum of American History
Smithsonian Institution
National Museum of
American Art
Washington
DC 20560
Canes collected: medium

National Museum of the American Indian
Smithsonian Institution
155 Street and Broadway
New York City
NY 10032
Canes collected: very large
(Indians)

Strong Museum
One Manhattan Square
Rochester
NY 14607
Canes collected: very large

Library of the Supreme Council, 33°
1733 Sixteenth Street,
N.W.
Washington
D.C. 20009
Canes collected: small

United States Military Academy
West Point
NY 10996
Canes collected: small

United States Naval Academy, Museum
B.P. 5034
Annapolis
Maryland 21402
Canes collected: large

The Valley Forge Historical Society
Box 122
Valley Forge
Pa 19481-0122
Canes collected: small

Vicksburg and Warren County Historical
Society
Court Square
Vicksburg
Mississippi 39180
Canes collected: small

Virginia Musem of FineArts
Boulevard and Grove
Avenue
Richemond
Va 23221
Canes collected: small
(Fabergé)

The State Historical Society of Wisconsin
816 State Street
Madison
Wisconsin 53706-1488
Canes collected: very large

Woodland Cultural Centre
P.B. Box1506
Brantford
Ont. N3T 5V6
Canes collected: small

Woodrow Wilson House
2340 S Street N W
Washington
DC 2008
Canes collected: large

Collectors

Selected private collectors

The following list is of those collectors whose addresses are available. The name of the collector quoted below the illustrations, is that at the time of taking the photograph.

Mrs Linda Beeman
Cane Collector's Chronicle
99 Ludlam Crescent
Lower Hutt
New Zealand

Mrs Joyce E. Blake (Glass Canes)
1220 Stelle Road
Elma
N.Y. 140 59

Mr Dick Carlson
3051 N Street
Georgtown
D.C. 20007

Mr and Mrs Byron Evans
The Whaler's Belle
11 Salem Drive
Saratoga Springs
N.Y. 12866

Mr Norman Flayderman
P.O.Box 2446
Fort Lauderdale
Florida 33303

Mr Jim Gifford
P.O.Box 51
Bath
Ohio 44210

Mr Grunder
16 Niles Road
Binghamton
N.Y. 13901

Mr and Mrs Larry Kalstone
250 East 73rd Street
4 F
New York
N.Y. 10021

Mr Neils MacKenna
P.O.Box 5143
Beverly Farms
Ma. 01915

Mr and Mrs George H. Meyer
Sandringham Press
100 West Long Lake Road
Suite 100
Bloomfield Hills
Michigan 48304

Mr Francis H. Monek
950 East Westminster Road
Lake Forest
Il. 60045

Mr Ted Newbold
112 Cuthbert Street
Philadelphia
Pa. 19106

Mr Alex Peck
P.O.Box 710
Charleston
Il. 61920

Mr Eric Vaule
Wewaka Brook Road
Bridgewater
Ct. 06752

Mr Richard R. Wagner
1 Old Fitzwilliam Road
Jaffrey
N.H. 03452

Mr Paul Weisberg
The Quest
P.O.Box 581
Schoharie
N.Y. 12157

Mrs Eleanor Zelin
Man-tiques Ltd.
1050 Second Avenue
New York
N.Y. 10022

Disclaimer

The objective of this book is to present a broad history of American canes, not to give facts relating to specific historical, political or any other form of information. If there are mistakes, the Author cannot take responsibility for inaccuracies beyond her control.

If the reader does not accept the above conditions, the book may be returned to the publisher for a full refund.